Which One

BY David
Frankham
WITH Jim Hollifield

Was

David?

Published in the USA by:
BearManor Media
PO Box 1129
Duncan, Oklahoma 73534-1129
www.bearmanormedia.com

ISBN 978-1-59393-218-3

Printed in the United States of America.
Book design by Brian Pearce | Red Jacket Press.

Table of Contents

Foreword

To be identified as the voice of a much-loved Disney character is one of film-land's highest accolades and if David Frankham had done nothing else but speak for that heroic, frightfully British feline, Sergeant Tibbs (without whose aid the puppies in *101 Dalmatians* would have ended up as a coat for Cruella de Vil) he would — unquestionably and deservedly — be guaranteed of immortality.

Being a modest man, David will probably respond in Tibbs' words: "Fiddle faddle and rot, sir," but it is true: his richly comic vocal performance during the dogs' liberation from Hell Hall contributes, in no small measure, to one of the most exciting and hilarious escapades in any Disney classic.

However, as this engaging autobiography reveals, David's career has spanned many more than any cat's conventional nine lives.

As an only child with a father in the navy, David's early years were spent shuttling to and fro between the parental home in England and that of his mother's family in Scotland. As a result, he grew up with a sense of not belonging although, being intelligent and observant, he stored up many memories: of his Scottish shepherd grandfather; of the 'blitz' years of the Second World War; of falling under the spell of the movies and the film stars who, as a teenager, gave him the desire to act, and of being a reluctant student of architecture — his parents' attempt to derail his thespian ambitions — only to find himself taking to the stage as a reluctant and underweight Falstaff in *The Merry Wives of Windsor*.

As a rather solitary boy he endured rather than enjoyed his formative years but always showed a stoic talent for making the best of a bad job: alleviating the tedium of his army training, for example, with visits to the cinema where he lost his heart to a young actress who, though he did not know it then, would one day become a friend — Angela Lansbury.

A child of two countries, David's life-story became one of many continents as his military service took him to the hot and hostile atmosphere of pre independence India before going on to Malaya where he stumbled on the delights of broadcasting — a talent that, back in Britain resulted in his becoming a newsreader, announcer, producer and interviewer for the BBC. Audio encounters with a veritable Who's Who of British and American film, stage and singing talents reignited his aspirations to act, and with a list of starry contacts from Dirk Bogarde and a useful hint from Greer Garson to leave behind any suggestion of a 'bowler hat and umbrella' attitude, he was soon California-bound.

The rest is a unique Hollywood saga: giving a chillingly villainous turn in *Return of the Fly*, taking on Charles Bronson in *Master of the World*, dubbing voices for William Wyler (and Disney's Dalmatian-rescuing cat) as well as appearing in a host of legendary TV shows such as *77 Sunset Strip*, *The Outer Limits*, *Alfred Hitchcock Presents*, *The Beverly Hillbillies* and, in the third season of *Star Trek*, playing a character destroyed by his jealousy of an alien.

Away from the cameras, he found himself being given a tour of the MGM studio by Basil Rathbone (whose performance as the brutish Mr. Murdstone in *David Copperfield* had terrified him as child), taking tea with Boris Karloff, playing bridge with Rock Hudson, reading Japanese poetry with Marlon Brando and being taught to drive (and make marmalade) by Gladys Cooper.

The former star-struck kid found himself meeting many of his celluloid heroes and becoming friends with a galaxy of glamorous ladies, among them Greer Garson, Elizabeth Taylor, Doris Day, Rita Hayworth, Barbara Stanwyck and Rosemary Clooney, whom he would never have met had he not once pulled a poisonous snake —

But that is where David's book begins, so the most useful thing I can do is to let him get on with telling you his singularly intriguing story...

Brian Sibley
London
July 2012

Introduction

If I hadn't pulled a poisonous snake from a stream in Malaya, I never would have met Elizabeth Taylor. Before I get to that life-changing event, though, it's best to start at the beginning. When I was a student in an English architecture school toward the end of World War II, my first acting assignment came when an instructor forced our group to stage a weekend production of Shakespeare's *The Merry Wives of Windsor*. My only exposure to acting had been through the movies, so it's a miracle that I made it through the play.

I suppose our group performed as well as we could, considering we were studying to become architects, not actors. The audience seemed to respond to our production well enough, and my parents were among those watching my acting debut that evening.

As they traveled home, my father leaned over to my mother and said, "That was nice, but which one was David?" With my makeup and costume, I was unrecognizable to my father, who hadn't even bothered to look at the program!

"Which one was David?" is an appropriate title for this exploration of my life's work. As you will learn, it's still remarkable that a young boy who spent his time between England and Scotland would end up arriving in Hollywood at nearly age thirty. With just that one amateur stage credit under my belt, I ended up on live television during the medium's Golden Era. A thirty-year career in television and movies followed.

Acting on film was my primary obsession from the moment I saw two of my heroes on screen, Gladys Cooper and Laird Cregar. A seven-year, on-air stint with the BBC only confirmed that I would have been miserable if I had not pursued my acting ambitions. My goal was to become a jobbing, or working, actor, never a household name.

To that end, I was successful. But while I may not be as well-known as some of the names that you'll encounter throughout my story — Elizabeth Taylor, Sir Alec Guinness, Walt Disney, Greer Garson, Rock Hudson, Rosemary Clooney, Dirk Bogarde, Vincent Price, and many others — I nevertheless enjoyed the good fortune of working in a number of creative projects that still resonate with audiences.

In life, there's an element of luck, to a degree, but we really make our own luck by seeing to it that we're prepared to succeed at the right place at the right time. I've always believed that philosophy, no matter any temporary appearance to the contrary. In my case, I was at the right place at the right time to work on the kinds of projects still fondly remembered by fans today:

The voice of a classic Walt Disney animated character in *101 Dalmatians*.

The villain in Fox's 1959 sequel to *The Fly*.

Dubbing on *Ben-Hur, King of Kings, Grand Prix*, and other films.

A Federation engineer and designer of the *USS Enterprise* on *Star Trek*.

Numerous science fiction or fantasy-themed episodes of *The Outer Limits* and *Thriller*.

And so many more, including work with George Cukor, Vincente Minnelli, Jack Benny, Shirley Temple, Bob Hope, Ernie Kovacs, Troy Donahue, Suzanne Pleshette, Dorothy Provine, Boris Karloff, Richard Chamberlain, *The Beverly Hillbillies, Alfred Hitchcock Presents, Dr. Kildare, Gomer Pyle, Dobie Gillis,* Efrem Zimbalist, Jr., Andy Griffith, *Maverick, The Six Million Dollar Man,* Robert Duvall, Sean Connery, and even *The Bold and the Beautiful*.

A network of assistance is always a powerful help when one's starting a career. I had that from Rosemary Clooney, Dirk Bogarde, Elizabeth Taylor, Alec Guinness and other good people. You just never know where your good fortune is coming from, but you can be sure it's constantly on its way, provided you're doing your part, which is to be enthusiastic and ready for what comes. "Be Prepared" isn't just for Boy Scouts, I found.

Only in the movies would a young kid from a village in Scotland or England have the temerity to show up in Hollywood to be an actor. Early along the way, many times I thought that I would always be stuck in England, not realizing that it was all part of the professional mosaic. Although some pieces are smaller than others, they all have significance.

I suppose memory sort of edits and cuts out all the parts that I don't care to remember and retains the better parts. If you're hoping to find a paper trail detailing who slept with whom, I'm afraid you'll be disappointed. But if you're interested in learning more about what it was like to be a successful, working actor during those years following the collapse of the studio system, as well as television's early heyday, you're at the right place. I lived and breathed entertainment's evolving changes through the 1950s, 60s, 70s and 80s.

I feel that it's increasingly important to record for future generations all that can be known about that golden era. A few years ago, a nurse asked what I had done for a living. I told her that I was an actor.

"Oh, were you in Hollywood?" she asked.

"Yes," I told her.

"Did you know any stars?" she replied.

I told her that I knew Vincent Price, Barbara Stanwyck, Doris Day, and Rita Hayworth.

There was a pause, and she said, "I don't think I know those people."

I felt like a dinosaur! Apologizing, she told me, "I'm only twenty-five."

How fleeting is fame. Once you're gone, you're gone with the young people today. Appreciation of art, from any era, shouldn't be that way, though. Film is timeless. Mozart was born more than two hundred years ago and people still enjoy his handiwork. The same should be true for movies and television.

Actors are lucky in that regard; theatre performances are usually lost forever, unless they're in musicals successful enough to have cast albums recorded. But if you were in the movies or on television when I worked, from 1956 through 1988, there were enough jobs for any actor who could act and who was willing to work.

I was a jobbing actor for more than thirty years and never really stopped working. This was the era when television seasons offered viewers thirty-nine weeks' worth of episodes. If you could remember your lines, if you were professional, and if you could act, you could get work. Without the breaks, things might have been different. On any given day, ninety percent of the membership of the Screen Actors Guild is without work. That's a really terrifying prospect. Thanks to positive thinking, that never entered my mind, so I never had to confront that reality.

Opportunities are essential to any kind of continuity of career in acting. I was glad to work non-stop before the business sort of fragmented and became less satisfying for me. I picked and chose what I wanted to do and gradually drifted away.

Here am I today, mostly retired. I always look at the end of a book to see how it turns out. In 1938, I was twelve. I started reading *Gone with the Wind*, which was the big book just before the movie came out the following year. I waded through the beginning, and it was all about Scarlett and Rhett.

I thought, "Well, obviously they have a happy ending, but I'll confirm that," so I turned all the way to the end and saw, "Frankly, my dear, I don't give a damn."

It ruined the book for me! Yet I still can't help it. For biographies, I still like to look at the end to see how it went for whomever it happened to be. My ending has yet to be written, ironic for an actor who seemed to specialize in dying on screen. For years, I've meant to make a video collage of all the times I came to a violent end. I seemed to specialize in expiring. "Let's get Frankham," the casting agents would say. "He does good death!"

Life is for the living. As you'll also discover, it's never too late in life to rediscover all that you've enjoyed throughout earlier stages in your life. Before I finished this book, I found myself working on yet another movie starring an actor who appeared in *Avatar*, the movie world's highest-grossing feature to date. We also live in a remarkable age, where DVDs or the Internet allow us to rediscover people, places or projects that would have once been forgotten.

So, come along to the days when Deanna Durbin and Rita Hayworth inspired schoolboy swooning, when audiences flocked to the movies to escape World War II, when live television meant working without a safety net, and when the likes of Walt Disney, George Cukor and Alfred Hitchcock actively created classics still enjoyed today.

I'll mention and thank many more along the way, but before we begin, please indulge me and allow me to acknowledge those in my life who have made this endeavor possible: Jim Hollifield for assisting me with the writing and editing; Jonathan Dixon for assistance with recording interviews and scanning of photos; Todd Sawvelle for help with other photos; and to all my friends, in fact, my appreciation and love.

David Frankham
Santa Fe, NM
July 2012

David Frankham, January 2011.

CHAPTER ONE

An Artistic Son

I came from the county of Kent, about thirty miles south of London. I was born there February 16, 1926, of an English father, Alfred Edward, and a Scots mother, Elizabeth Gatherum Kellock, or Bess, as my father called her. Money was scarce, so my mother went to a village school in Scotland and left in her early teens to work in service to the local lord and lady of the manor. My father joined the Navy at age eighteen. When they met during World War I, my father was a sailor and my mother a ladies' maid to a local squire.

My parents were really opposites, but they both came from large families. My mother had three sisters, two brothers, and one who died just before I was born. His name was David, so that's how my parents named me. My father had two sisters and a brother and another little sister who died in infancy. My paternal grandfather was a quartermaster sergeant in the Army, which meant that he was in charge of uniforms. When soldiers were drafted and came to his window, he would hand their uniforms to them.

My mother got so bored with living in her little village in Scotland that when World War I broke out, she decided she would join the British Women's Royal Navy Service (WRNS), the American equivalent of the Women Accepted for Volunteer Emergency Service, or WAVES — ladies who joined the Navy.

She had to go down to England to join the Navy. I still have a card from my father to my mother inviting her to a dance in southern England when they were courting, as they would say in those old days. They both met in the Navy, and when my parents married, their goal was to have a large family. Then I put a stop to that.

I was born in England, in the Royal Naval Hospital in Gillingham, Kent, thirty miles south of London. I was christened David Alfred George, the Alfred for my father, and the George for my father's brother. When I was born, I started screaming. My parents told me that I was a noisy

ABOVE: *My Scottish grandparents and their children. My mother is standing behind her father.* BELOW: *My English grandparents and their children. The boy in the middle is my father.*

baby. Through the first six months of my life, I never cried; I was either asleep or screaming out my lungs. My father was fortunately home, one of his few times staying put in England because he was usually away on two-year tours of duty to Malta or other places.

My mother really had to cope with this fussy baby by herself. When my father saw her holding at arm's length this screaming child, it was

My mother the year I was born, 1926.

his decision, to which she agreed, that she should go back from Kent to her family up in Scotland. He felt that she needed help with this incessantly screaming baby.

Apparently I screamed all the way up on the train while the other passengers tried to sleep. They tried everything, looking to see if there was a safety pin in my diapers or what the cause might be, but nothing seemed to account for the fact that I screamed. When my poor mother arrived in Scotland, she was exhausted by this going on day and night. She handed me one day to her mother, who was a very ample, maternal, mother earth-type. I was told that the moment I was handed to her, I looked up at her smiling face and never screamed again. Nobody knew the cause or really why I stopped screaming when I was about six months old. From then on, I cried like normal children.

My father said to my mother, "Bess, I won't be around very much at a time, two years as you know, and I'm not going to see you through this again, so we're to have no more children. I don't want you to be on the verge of a nervous breakdown."

So that's why I was an only child, even though my parents originally intended to have a large family. My early penchant for screaming led some friends and relatives to predict that I would grow up to be a famous singer. In their estimation, singers probably screamed a lot when they were born. Well, they were close; I didn't turn out to be a singer, but I would become a professional broadcaster and performer who frequently had to use my voice to earn a living.

ABOVE: *Nine-week-old me in April 1926.* BELOW: *The only nude scene of my career!*

We would spend a few years in Scotland, followed by a few years in England. The Scottish way of life was very laid-back. I don't recall my mother ever raising her voice to me. She was a good disciplinarian; she wouldn't threaten. She just said, "I told you that once, David." That was like somebody shouting at me, because I knew that her word was law. My father was in the Navy and wasn't home very much, so my mother was determined that I was not going to be, as she put it, "tied to my apron strings," meaning, she was determined that I was not going to be a mother's boy.

In those days, nobody said, "I love you." Oddly enough, years later when I was in America, my mother would write three times a week and end with, "All my love — mum," but we never used the L-O-V-E word when I was growing up. No other child I knew did, either.

My mother used to call my father "highly strung." She used to say that of me: "David, you're highly strung like your father," meaning somebody who is practically on the edge of a nervous breakdown most of the time. Everything was a crisis to my father. Yet he was a good disciplinarian, too, with his Navy background. He started as a naval seaman and worked his way up to a warrant officer by the 1940s and ended up as an instructor to the WRNS, the ladies who joined the Navy. I'm sure he was a very good instructor.

It was hard to break through to him because he was a professionally disciplined man with his naval career. We were never really together long enough to bond in the way that I see American fathers and sons do. He was an edgy man, and my mother was quite the opposite, quiet and low-keyed.

My parents weren't very well off. My father was an able seaman, but his salary wasn't much. He sent money home all the time. We lived simply in small rental houses in England. When we were in Scotland, we stayed with family. My parents were truly products of the Victorian era. You couldn't tell with my mother how she felt because of her English reserve. I think they were happy, if you can be happy with seeing each other only for a few weeks every two years. My mother would get exasperated with my father because he had his disciplinarian ways from his professional work in the navy. He had to adjust to her rules of the house when he was there, and why not, because she took care of things non-stop while he was away.

Once when I was about eleven, we had Guy Fawkes Night and were burning bonfires. There was a field outside where we lived in England, and my dad had just left that day to be away on tour for two years. I enjoyed the fireworks and the blaze from the fire. When I went in, my mother was sitting by the fire. I heard her sniff. When I looked at her, she had tears in her eyes.

"What's wrong?" I asked. She said, "Nothing!" in her Scottish way. "Nothing's wrong! Well, your father just left." She missed him. I think they had a loving relationship, but it was hard to tell, because I don't really remember my father clearly until I was thirteen, around 1939.

When my father's schedule changed and he began spending more time at home, it was difficult for me. By then I was used to my mother's

In a garden owned by the squire who employed my mother, 1930.

low-keyed discipline. I was accustomed to listening to her. He began saying, "Don't do that." In fact, one time I was sent upstairs because he said, "Don't do that," and as I ran up the stairs, I told him, "You can't tell me what to do. My mother tells me what to do." That was an indication of our prickly relationship, which more or less was like that all the time we were together. Very rarely did he express pride in me.

As a child, my earliest memory is running away from home. We had a rental home, a rather simple house in Ipswich, in the county of Suffolk. My father was off in the Navy. I don't recall what propelled this at age four, but I opened the front gate to the garden and wandered away while my mother was in the house. I wasn't running away from anything, but I was running away to something, even at that early age, which I've always done. All my life, I've been interested in what's next or what the next big adventure will be. That day I didn't wander far, but I went to what we called a common, a moor of sorts with bushes. I just wandered around there by myself until two girls, thank God, came up to me and asked why I was there.

I told them that I had run away from home. One of these girls said, "Are you sure you want to do that? You know, there are monkeys here on the common." I didn't know what a monkey was, but it sounded scary to me.

LEFT: *Age five, at the beach at Felixtoe.* RIGHT: *My school portrait, May 1934.*

The girls said, "Come on, little boy, come with us. Show us where you live." I can still see it today, two teenage girls, one on each side of me, walking me back home to my astonished mother. That's my earliest memory because it's a vivid one, with a happy ending. Imagine how it could have ended had anyone but two innocent teenage girls found me!

When I was eight, my Scots grandmother died. We went up for the funeral. In fact, I remember her being lain out in the living room. In those days in Scotland, the end of the living room was a kind of boarded bed where we climbed into it like a bunk. There she was, sleeping peacefully, but in reality, she was dead. I was sent away with the neighbor kids to stay out of the way of the mourners. I watched as the funeral procession went by to the cemetery.

For some reason, presumably because my father was often overseas and it was cheaper to stay at home, my mother and I would stay in Scotland for two-year stretches in the county of Fifeshire on the east side of the country. I attended the village school in Rathillet. I still have a funny photo of me with a kind of crew cut, huge boots, and shorts; I looked like the village idiot!

The simple village school offered rather rudimentary teaching. One time the school put on a play. Whether I was told to do this or I imagined it myself, I decided to be Yankee Doodle Dandy. I had a scooter with a board, handle and wheels that I propelled around the room. Preparing for this play and wearing a green and yellow costume, I went around the room singing, "Yankee Doodle went to town, riding on a pony..." so I already must have had my sights set on becoming a Yankee in America.

I used to go rambling on my summer holidays with two dogs. One was called Tony, and the other was called Brigitte, a great big, tall, slender red setter. These were constants in an otherwise transient life, marked by a month or two with my father before he would be sent away on a two-year

My school portrait, May 1934.

tour of duty, and then another two years of life in Scotland.

Moving frequently between the two countries, I wasn't English, and I wasn't Scottish. Maybe because I was an only child or because I inherited my father's sensitivity, I always felt that I didn't belong. In Scotland I was called a Sassenach, the way the Scots talk disparagingly about the English. Around others my age, I was kind of dismissed as an odd man out because I was not Scots like other children.

The same thing happened in England. Other kids would say, "Oh, he's not English," or "he's half-English." I never felt that I belonged in England, because I never felt that I spent time enough in either country to feel roots.

The only other time I saw my mother cry was when I was eleven. At their insistence, I had applied to secondary school. Public school in those days meant that anybody could attend, but you could apply to a secondary school for additional education. I applied because we all did. It was a way for working class people to better themselves. I got home for lunch one day to find my mother smiling through tears in her eyes. She waved a piece of paper and said, "Look! You've passed the exam!"

It meant nothing to me, but my acceptance to school meant a great deal to my parents. I was to go to secondary school at age eleven. Attending secondary school, I started to learn French, German, and Latin, to play cricket and rugby, and to swim, all of which would have been forbidden to me had I stayed on in the regular public school. Secondary school was also the first time anyone ever mentioned art or music to me. I hadn't paid much attention to either at that age. Our instructors taught us the basics of Beethoven, Brahms, and Mozart. It meant that I heard that music for the first time in my life.

I had a great ability for learning French; I loved French. German wasn't too difficult because much of it sounds and looks like English. It came easily to me. Latin was a big bore, and I felt that if I was going to be a doctor, that ancient, defunct language would have been fine, but if it was a beautiful sunny day outside, it seemed pointless to conjugate Latin verbs. A dead language had no significance for me at all.

If Latin proved of little use to me, I really hated sports, team sports, to be specific. At that stage in life, I was beginning to find out about myself. I was not much of a "team player." I did like competition and striving to be first and best, so I excelled at sprinting or running. I was hopeless at football, rugby, and cricket. I hated cricket; that bat weighed a ton, and the leather cricket ball could kill you if some idiot smacked you in the head. We were required to play these sports, one in the afternoon every week.

When we got to sprinting, I turned out to be first, the best. For the first time in my life, I discovered a bit of ego rising in me as I thought, "Wow, I'm better than all these kids at this. I'm the first one at the tape to break it. I can jump over the hurdles."

That was the beginning of ambition and determination, which I had never had before in my young life. My success at sprinting was significant in that I found a sport at which I could excel, but not in my father's eyes. On the mantelpiece above the fire, he had on each side several silver cups that he won for football. I won a little cup for sprinting, but it was never allowed up on the mantelpiece near my father's cups.

Once when he was home on leave, he came up to watch a rugby game in which I played. In rugby, there's dribble, where you put the ball between your foot and kick it toward your opponent's goal. I had the ball between my feet, and I knew my dad was watching. I was dribbling away, but unfortunately, I was dribbling against my own team, and he never, ever let me forget that. "Big sissy!" he called me.

War broke out in September 1939, when I was visiting my aunt Liz in Suffolk. I was on vacation with her and my English grandparents, so my parents wrote to say that my school had closed down until everyone could see how the war unfolded. They instructed me to stay in Suffolk, where I remained for part of 1940. My parents later wrote that the local children would be sent to Cardiff to attend school. My home was only thirty miles from London, so the town decided to send the children away from the potential harm of bombers passing overhead.

My aunt packed me off on the train so I could arrive the day before school started. I was to be an evacuee off for Cardiff in Wales. On the train back home, I began scratching my face. When I arrived in London from Suffolk, I crossed over to the train taking me to my home thirty miles south. My mother took one look at me and said, "What's wrong with your face? It's all red!"

The doctor's office was right up the street. He took one look at me and said, "It's chicken pox. He can't travel." My classmates departed — without me — for Cardiff, where they spent a year in air raid shelters with virtually no teaching at all. Cardiff became one of the most heavily bombed cities that year in the United Kingdom. Chicken pox had spared me that trauma.

I went up to Scotland instead, where I received a marvelous education, miles ahead of my English instruction. When my poor war-torn buddies came back from Cardiff in 1941, I came back down from Scotland. I had become the smartest kid in class, yet I was a loner. I think it stemmed from being an only child. I would have friends over from school for tea, but always I felt that I was looking up at grown-ups. I really didn't have a close friend at all in school, because I was learning to make my own entertainment with my own imagination. Movies began to hold an attraction for me. I took note at the cinema, particularly the kinds of films where Mickey Rooney and Judy Garland put on a show. That seemed fun and glamorous compared to sports or Latin.

When I took long walks in solitude, I sang from *Strike Up the Band* and *Girl Crazy* and all the songs from musicals I heard during my formative years. Perfectly happy within myself, I created my own world of entertainment. In those dark years leading up to World War II, I suppose that there were many of us looking for happiness through entertainment wherever it was found.

I had always gone to the movies like anybody. We casually looked to see what was playing, such as Errol Flynn in *The Adventures of Robin Hood*, and not really paying attention or connecting it beyond the entertainment that it gave for two hours sitting in a theatre. I had no thoughts about my future as my teenage years began.

I eventually did develop a useful friendship with one chum at school, a fellow named Denis Brain. We were in the same class. One afternoon in 1941, we had our homework assignment, geography and history. I can't remember which of us was better at which, but we said to each other, "I'll do your homework and you do mine."

We stopped at my house first; his house was down the street from mine. With the outbreak of World War II, my mother had rejoined the Navy, so she was in the dockyard working as an assistant to an admiral. She wasn't home much then, so I was a latchkey kid. The key was under the mat, so Denis and I went inside. We were hungry, but I had not yet learned to cook.

That wouldn't do, so Denis said, "Okay, my mom's home, so we'll go down to my house and we'll do the work there." We sat down at his house to do our homework. Neither one of us really wanted to think about geography or history, so we put things off by having a glass of soda or putting on a record.

I didn't yet own a record player, but Denis did. One day he put on a record called "Elmer's Tune." I said to Denis, "Who's that?" I really liked the sound of this Glenn Miller and his orchestra. There was something so appealing and magical about the music, so I conned my mother into getting me a gramophone. I started collecting all the Glenn Miller records, but that actually was a loner thing to do, because then I didn't need anybody in the room except me and Glenn Miller and the orchestra. Poor Denis!

My newfound hobby was a fixation, I suppose. With my father frequently away for long periods, I needed a hero to worship. At school we were taught about classical music. At home, I discovered that I had not paid much attention to popular music, but suddenly this devotion to the Glenn Miller sound was happening. I found out all about Glenn Miller, how he was forty and joined the Army even though he didn't have to and how brave he was. I became a member of the Glenn Miller Society, again, nothing shared with any friends. Listening to Miller's music was all just me and going into my room after school. I thought, This is wonderful.

I have two or three hours to do my homework, and I'll listen to nothing but Glenn Miller."

While Glenn Miller's music and military service inspired people on both sides of the Atlantic, I spent much of World War II in Scotland because the German bombers flew right over our little town in Kent on their way to London and often dropped their loads on our town. Our neighbors were killed that way, but we came through unscathed. I survived the Battle of Britain and the London blitz of 1941.

Survival meant that much of our time was spent in air-raid shelters. A siren went off when the Nazi bombers crossed the English Channel. We were about ninety miles from Dover, so hearing the sirens meant a run down our garden path. Everyone's shelters were dug into gardens. Only the roof, made of corrugated iron, was visible above the ground. To get inside one, we had to step down into this tiny constructed thing. *Mrs. Miniver* got laughed at in England because it depicted Greer Garson living in a palatial shelter at the bottom of her garden when there really was no such thing.

All the bomb shelters were small. My family actually didn't have one of our own, but a neighbor had a shelter. During the day my mother and I ran down the path to their shelter, hearing thuds as bombs dropped not too far from the house. We would wait, and then the all clear would sound at dawn. Most of the time, we heard nothing.

The same scariness happened almost every night during two or three in the morning. If we stuck our heads out, we could see the glow of London on fire from thirty miles away. One night we ran down the path, and while we fled, we heard the awful swish of a bomb. There was a dull thud. A neighbor's house about five hundred yards up from ours disappeared. The next morning we went up and looked. There was just a crater where the house once stood. They were vaporized. There was nothing there.

Such were the horrors of war for English civilians, yet for many kids like me, there was a certain sort of excitement to it. Sometimes during the day, if the air-raid sirens hadn't gone off and there were just fighters going over, we could see Spitfires having a dog fight in the sky. Sometimes we saw a plane fall. We all cheered if it was a German plane.

One time my aunt Liz, a nurse and midwife, was called to the church-yard because a plane had crashed there. A German pilot was wounded. Aunt Liz marched down — she was very much a Margaret Dumont type — and looked inside the wreckage. There was the stunned pilot. She pulled him out, took his pistol from him, and asked if he spoke English. When she saw that he spoke a little English, Aunt Liz marched him down the street to her house. She sat him down and made sure he wasn't badly injured before calling the authorities. She had a firsthand confrontation with the war.

In Kent, the bombs were falling. I joined a fire brigade group as most people my age did. Big or small, everyone pitched in to help Churchill in what would be our nation's finest hour. One night a week I had to stay in a big school on fire patrol not too far from where we lived. I had a little hose and a bucket of sand to fight fire should one erupt. There was an older boy in charge of the operation.

This older boy and I went from classroom to classroom making sure an incendiary bomb hadn't dropped onto the school. The incendiary bombs were just made of light aluminum. When some didn't go off, you could pick them up and look at them. If they did go off as designed, it was like a fireworks display and then they were dead. If these devices went off in a house or building, though, they could immediately start a huge fire.

We never did see any fires, but I thought it was quite exciting to go from room to room with my little hose and bucket to see if anything was smoldering. In hindsight sixty-five years later, the war was simply terrible because so many people were dying, but that was my sense of adventure as a boy. That's how the time passed in our lives.

By 1944, there were bombings literally every night as the war reached a fever pitch. Sometimes the sirens went off and then the bombers changed in Dover to go back to France or Germany. There was no reason for the alarm to stay on, so we got the all clear at midnight. Imagine spending every night this way, waiting to see if you survived until morning!

Eventually my parents bought an indoor shelter made of steel, about the height of a piano. These shelters used steel wire all around. To protect ourselves from errant bombs, we lifted a flap and crawled in and waited. These shelters were so small that we couldn't even sit; we had to lie down and wait for the all clear. If the house was bombed, the steel shelter was designed to prevent occupants from being killed. Fortunately, ours was never put to the test. I suspected that if the whole house was falling or burning, the thing wouldn't have worked.

Many people turned to their faith until the proverbial bluebirds appeared over the White Cliffs of Dover. Everyone in my family was a member of either the Church of England or the Church of Scotland, so that meant Sunday school and church membership. My mother was very active in the social side of her Scottish church; my father believed only vaguely in God but loved to sing hymns, so he really only went to her church for that pleasure. As their only child, I went along dutifully enough with it.

When we were in Scotland, my mother and I lived with relatives. My grandfather was a chief shepherd in his village. He was a wonderful shepherd from my observation. I watched him working with his two collies. With just one or two words of command, his dogs controlled the movement of sheep walking around in front of them. He just said a word to these collies and they crouched. The moment he said a certain word, they started rounding up the sheep. The moment he said another word, they stopped.

The beautiful dogs were not allowed in the house, and I was not allowed to speak to them because they were working dogs. My grandfather didn't want them spoiled with another human's voice when they were used to his voice of command. When it snowed, my grandparents had a back porch closed to the elements. Then there was another door into the house, so his dogs were indoors there during the really bad weather, but even then, I was never allowed to talk to them.

While my grandfather actively spoke to his dogs, he never spoke to me! It wasn't that he didn't approve

My Scottish grandfather never spoke to the boys in the family.

of me, although I was only half Scot, and the Scots are very loyal to Scotland; it was simply that he was from the Victorian era, when "children should be seen and not heard." He would not acknowledge boys in the family. I had girl cousins, and he always talked or joked with them. I checked with a boy cousin, Forbes, and said, "Does he ignore you?" because he lived near my grandfather full time. He said, "Yeah, he never speaks to me, either."

Being a loner, I was hiking alone through a meadow one day when I passed my grandfather. He was coming toward me with his two collies on a narrow path through a meadow with no bushes for me to hide behind. I thought, "Should I say 'hello, granddad,' or something? How will he react to me?"

It was like *High Noon* with the two of us coming toward each other. I smiled and he nodded, but he never said a word as we passed each other. That was the only time in all my dealings with him that he actually acknowledged me. I was really quite thrilled with that. Even when we left for England, we weren't a hugging family, especially the Scottish side. My grandfather would say a few kind words to my mother, but he didn't take my hand or anything.

After my grandmother died, it was the girls' duty to take care of my grandfather. In the evening, when he trudged in after a hard night with the sheep in the snow, he would sit in an old horsehair chair. When he was gone, I tried sitting in it, but the horsehairs hurt my rear end. When my grandfather sat in his chair, he often visited with friends, all the while weaving baskets made from willows, called creels. He truly was gifted at his weaving. I could tell that he was highly respected and admired in the village, because friends frequently called on him. They would sit by the fire, laugh with him and call him "Auld Forbes."

While he sat and weaved, he spat tobacco in a spittoon. Just the sound of it made a racket that I can still hear. Poing! What an awful sight it was, yucky stuff building up in the spittoon. He wouldn't always hit his target. Sometimes his spit ended up on the floor. The ladies wouldn't say anything in the morning as they cleaned out the spittoon. That was the Victorian way. He was the patriarch, and I admired him. I wish I could have known this wonderfully interesting man, but I was a boy, so I never did.

I spent all of 1940 with my mother, grandfather, and my aunt. My grandfather owned a pretty house, but there were no lights. Everyone used oil lamps. In front of the house was a little court area with hens, chickens, and a pig.

One Sunday we went off to church in the wee village. Coming back, I joined some kids across the way. Agnes, Jimmy, and I were playfully singing and dancing by a mill near a stream. Instead of my grandfather coming out to tell us to be quiet, my mother came out and said, "No, no, no, you're not to sing on the Sabbath." That was the law with my grandfather. We all had to shut up.

Once at lunchtime, my grandfather was sitting where he always sat, at the head of the table. I sat farther down with my aunt and my mother next to me. Auld Forbes wanted the salt from my end of the table. So instead of saying, "David, pass the salt," he said, "Tell yon laddie to pass the salt." That was the only time he actually referred to me. He could not address me directly because of this firm conviction that children should be seen and not heard.

Auld Forbes had porridge every morning for breakfast. He ate lentil soup almost every day with boiled potatoes for dinner. We were not well-off people. I could tell that my relatives lived simply but healthfully on my grandfather's earnings as chief shepherd. Living the rural life meant that we churned our own butter. When my grandfather tended his sheep, I talked to his wonderful pig. When the time came for us to have ham or pork, my grandfather took the pig and killed him like Jack the Ripper. We would then have sausages and bacon all season long. The war may have been exciting for this wee lad in England, but in Scotland, I could really see some high drama!

I couldn't fault my grandfather for doing that to the pig, because I could see that he otherwise cared for animals. During the lambing season, inevitably there would be a sheep that gave birth and just walked away. My grandfather would bring the abandoned lamb inside. Holding it in his arms, Auld Forbes sat by the fire with that lamb, sometimes all night long, with a milk bottle to get it started in life. The pig aside, he loved animals. He really didn't have a bad side to him.

Life was simple in many ways in England, too. My aunt's cottage was illuminated only by oil lamps and candles, and there was no indoor plumbing. She had a copper pot in the kitchen which she filled with buckets of water. She would light wood underneath the copper to heat water for the Saturday evening tin bath, which hung outside the back door. That may sound like *Tobacco Road*, but she was actually a successful district nurse in a rural community in the county of Suffolk. That's how life was in many of the little villages in England during those times.

My parents were like most people in England, very mindful of a distinct class system. They looked up to upper class people and thought those people were better. We were all brainwashed in that there were posh people, and the rest of us weren't posh. All the acting in the movies or everyone on the radio meant that everyone we saw or heard was frightfully correct. We assumed that if we didn't talk like the posh people in the movies or on the radio, we were not posh.

My father's brother — Uncle George — was the black sheep of the family because he lived with a fan dancer. I thought he was very exciting, because I had never met anyone wicked before, especially not one who lived with a fan dancer! My father shunned him forever for "living in sin," but I loved him.

School was where somebody could step up and become semi-posh if you could get into a secondary school and learn cricket and a second language. These were all sophisticated things that my mother and father, coming from humble beginnings, would have never considered for themselves, but they did want that for me.

All the students wore purple blazers and ties, knee-high socks and short pants. The day came when the boys decided to buy long pants as we became teenagers. From my house up to school, the distance was about half a mile. A great breeze always blew along the walk to class. Some of my buddies were walking ahead of me and looked back and saw my first long pants fluttering in the breeze. They said, "Oh, here comes flutter britches!"

That just devastated me, because my father had already called me a sissy for not playing rugby the way he thought I should. Now my friends were ridiculing me. I could not get rid of the name because they stuck me with it. I was "Flutter Britches" from then on. "Flutter Britches" didn't sound tough or heroic to me.

Something was happening to "Flutter Britches" from spending two years in Scotland and a year in England. I was beginning to lose my regionalized English accent. Time divided between two regions somehow softened my accent. Between the two dialects, I found my voice that I still use today. As a child, I had no vocal training except by exposure to accents in both places where we lived. It was my ear that led me toward sounding more Scottish with a little English and completely erased how I used to talk as a young child. Without realizing it, I had acquired a kind of middle-of-the-country voice, pleasing to the ear.

When I wasn't on the fire patrol in England or living the rural life in Scotland, I spent time drawing. Drawing proved to be an enjoyable hobby for an introspective boy who was not too keen on team sports. After I saw Walt Disney's sensational feature-length animated film, *Snow White and the Seven Dwarfs*, I spent hours drawing Snow White and the dwarfs in my school notebooks. Up and down the margins, I practiced drawing these characters from memory. I still have those school exercise books with my not-very-good drawings, along with caricatures of my favorite movie stars.

Another Disney film, *Fantasia*, started me on a lifelong love of classical music. Living where I did, I had never seen an orchestra before, or a conductor, for that matter. Seeing Leopold Stokowski lead the Philadelphia Symphony Orchestra in the movie was a revelation to me. I've collected that orchestra's recordings ever since, all thanks to *Fantasia*.

My paternal English grandfather also reinforced my love for classical music. He was partly deaf. When I stayed with him one time during the war, I came home to find him with his ear cocked to the radio. He didn't want to disturb my grandmother or aunt. He held his one hand to his ear to hear better and conducted the music in the air with his other hand.

After seeing Deanna Durbin in the movies, I began drawing her in the margins of my school exercise books. She was my first crush. I really had a strong sense of longing to know her, because she was chirpy and usually played an only child who made things come out right in the end. I thought, "Gosh, maybe one day I'll meet her." I knew nothing about where she made her movies or anything.

In 1939 Robert Stack gave Deanna her first on-screen kiss in *First Love*. I was devastated. It was curtains for Deanna as far as I was concerned. "Trashy girl," I thought. "Letting a total stranger kiss you!" I was loveless after Deanna Durbin left my life. Carmen Miranda fortunately did a samba into my heart later that year.

One day my mother and I went up on the train to London just for the afternoon to go to the pictures, as we described movie-going then. We saw *How Green Was My Valley*, a very moving story. It was amazing to watch this kid about my age, Roddy McDowall, who was so

My 1939 sketch of the family cat, Timmy.

natural that it seemed as though he wasn't acting. Sitting there, I remember thinking that I would like to act and do what he was doing onscreen. He made it look so easy and touching. I cried when he cried. I felt an empathy with these shadows on the screen for maybe the first time in my life. As I watched Roddy's tender moments, it suddenly dawned on me that he might be acting. I thought, "Is he pretending?" I couldn't get a fix on how he was so effective on the screen, but it made me start to wonder about it.

I went to other films, still not connecting that I might want to act someday. I sat there thinking, "Are these people acting, being bravura and grand?" or "How do they just talk to people, making up the words as they go along?" It seemed they spoke and reacted so naturally that it might be real. That may seem naïve, but I think some people still do think actors just make it up as they go along.

Hollywood entertainment began to captivate me even more. After discovering Glenn Miller and his music, I became further enamored with American music, especially the sounds of Bing Crosby. His crooner style was so appealing. I loved listening to him much the same way the Beatles later captivated teenagers in the 1960s.

On Christmas Eve in 1941, my parents gave me pocket money to

LEFT: *Movie actresses, including Dona Drake in* Road to Morocco, *inspired me to draw.* RIGHT: *Hollywood glamour girls such as Vera Zorina had definitely caught my eye.*

spend on myself. I had heard about a two-disc set — with twelve-inch 78 rpm records — of *A Christmas Carol*, read by Basil Rathbone. I walked through the snow to the record shop where the set was displayed in the window. It was always a big deal to get a record set of 78s because most records at the time were ten-inch discs. There were very few twelve-inch 78 rpm discs; in fact, the only other one I can remember was Artie Shaw's *Concerto for Clarinet*. It was so exciting to have this set to listen to for more than fifteen minutes. My parents told me to save the records to hear on Christmas morning, so I did.

By the time I was a teenager, I started going to the movies three or four times a week. I couldn't shake the images I saw. Performances intrigued me. I grew interested in how scenes were constructed and why the story went where it did. At age fifteen, I saw a film that had a deeper impact on me, *Blood and Sand*, starring Rita Hayworth and Laird Cregar. The bullfighting scene burned into my brain. Laird was in a room with Tyrone Power and a cape lying on the floor. As he prepared to exit, Laird picked up the cape and swirled it around majestically. I was mesmerized.

As a moviegoer, I stopped paying attention to the stars or the romance on the screen. The character actors began to fascinate me: Thomas Mitchell as Scarlett's father in *Gone with the Wind*; Vincent Price playing a playboy with no money in *Laura* and then the tough prosecutor in *Song of Bernadette*. I took note of Boris Karloff and Peter Lorre.

In 1942, I saw *Now, Voyager* and focused in on Gladys Cooper. She played a mean, dominating, rotten mother to Bette Davis. I was utterly captivated. Why was she so mean? How could this real person come up with those feelings so realistically on screen? Her spitefulness just hypnotized me. That evening there was a long walk from the cinema back to my folks' house, but I thought, "I'm going to stay through again." In those days, there were double features with two movies, a newsreel, a trailer, and cartoons, but I sat through the whole show again. I thought, "How marvelous it is to be able to do what she's doing. You must be good to be rotten like that!"

After watching *Now, Voyager* twice, the hour was about ten o'clock when I got home that evening. My father had gone to bed. He had to get up very early in the morning to instruct WRNS ladies in the Navy. Next came my Scottish mother's understated reaction to devastating announcements from her only child. I walked in and she was sitting by a table lamp and darning socks. I can still see her.

"You're late," she said to me.

"I know mum, but I know what I'm going to do. I'm going to be an actor."

She didn't look up; in fact, she went right on darning. She said, "All right, I'll talk it over with your dad in the morning."

I carried on about the picture before going up to bed. When I got up the next morning, my dad had already gone to work. My mother was pouring tea, being very Scottish and laid back.

She said, "I talked to your dad about acting."

"Yes?" I asked in anticipation.

"If you feel that strongly about it, you can leave tomorrow," she replied.

"I can?"

"Yes," she said, "but you won't get a penny from us."

That dampened my sixteen-year-old enthusiasm.

She continued, "We know you're artistic. We don't know anything about acting, but we don't think it's a very reliable profession."

Even though that was a disappointingly negative response, I do believe that my parents were learning more about my interests and trying to help me find my way in the world. They thought I was artistic because of my drawing and some piano lessons I had taken for a few years. My interests had influenced them into thinking that I was artistic, which always seemed like a backhanded compliment to this "sissy, artistic son."

The Gillingham railroad platform where I caught the train.

My father had an aversion to the very idea of actors — "sissies," he called them — and acting in general. He was later convinced that I would be sold into slavery when I decamped for Tinseltown. My parents had inherited a Victorian philosophy that espoused that ordinary people should "know your place," meaning, "don't get any big ideas, kid."

In their innocence, my parents told me later that day that if I would decide against acting and not leave the next day, then they would enroll me in architecture school. Architecture school? Never in a million years would I have thought about being an architect.

My father informed me, "We are not going to throw away our hard-earned money on somebody who is just going to hope to make a career as an actor."

I went to bed and thought, "Well, I'll put acting off for a while."

I didn't know I was going to put it off until 1955! But in all fairness to my parents, there was a world war happening, and realistically, I would need to go off and serve my country as nearly all young men inevitably did in those days. If they could have seen inside me, they would have realized I was a very insecure sixteen-year-old. All teenagers go through it, but being an only child, I didn't have feedback from siblings to build my self-confidence. My parents were going to force me into architecture school, yet I hated the idea of it. I longed to be an actor but didn't know how to be one. I didn't like *me*. I was very depressed being David Frankham at the time.

Even the prospect of going into architecture school for two years, only to interrupt it for the Army, meant that I saw my whole life before me. I was going to be squeezed into professions that I had no affinity for whatsoever. It really was like fitting a square peg into a round hole. I didn't fit.

At the crossroads of decision, I took the coward's way out. The more I thought about film acting, the more I realized that I knew nothing of it, other than what I had seen in the movies. I had never

It shows that I wasn't happy about being "condemned" to architecture school at eighteen.

even seen a play. I had seen vaudeville and such performers as Gracie Fields and Tony Martin, an American singing star, but it was film that had made me decide that the simplest way to be an actor was to go where they made them. By then I had discovered that most movies seemed to be made in Hollywood. I didn't even realize that English movies were made in England. I knew as much about acting as I did about architecture.

That was the end of the discussion. I couldn't be an actor. Where would I have gone at sixteen if I had followed my parents' edict and left the next day rather than go into professional school? It was 1942, during the middle of World War II. Which repertory theatre would have taken in a kid who knew nothing about acting? I didn't even know a single real actor. I had made an almost dumb kind of animal instinct decision to be an actor in film.

I didn't know how to go about being an architect, either, but that's the road I would be taking. In England at the time, it was customary for students to go from the equivalent of American high school to the next education phase of choice without so much as a backward glance — typical British understatement.

I recall that one day I left secondary school and the next week, I started architecture school, very resentfully because my parents wouldn't let me pursue acting. I just knew that I would want to be an actor again, even though I didn't know how to go about being one. I did know enough to realize that I was going to be a miserable architect!

When I arrived at architecture school, I was situated with eleven other students. We had drawing boards lined up, six on one side, six on the other, so everybody had somebody sitting opposite him. The fellow nearest me was a Scot; I could tell by his accent. I liked him because deep down, I think I always wanted to be a Scot and not an Englishman.

His name was Jimmy Thomson. We discovered that we were actually born at the same minute, day, month and year — February 16, 1926. It was an extraordinary discovery that cemented our friendship. Jimmy and I joked about being "twins" even though we were born in two different spots of the country!

He had three sisters, one of whom I was later officially engaged to. Jimmy became my first real friend. He liked music but had not heard of Glenn Miller. Because of that, I didn't warm to him immediately, but I introduced him to Miller's music. Jimmy had a great sense of humor. I met his parents, too. His three sisters were like the *Little Women* of book and screen, simply marvelous girls. In the summer of 1943, we had to prepare drawings for our annual exam, tests administered at the architecture school. Jimmy stayed at my house doing drawings, and the next year I stayed at his house doing drawings for our tests.

We had a very nice teacher, Mr. Paine. I looked up to him. He was so elegant and tweedy-looking in a very sophisticated way. I really thought so highly of him, yet he was always exasperated with me. We would take a break in the common room for coffee between classes. There was a piano there and people played boogie woogie while the rest of us sang along.

Even though I couldn't sing, I enjoyed mixing in with the others. I had come out from the isolated only child that I was. While we sang, I didn't realize that Mr. Paine was observing all this exuberance on my part. At the end of the term, he wrote, "I wish that Frankham could be as enthusiastic about architecture as he is about the latest gramophone record." His note didn't go over well with my mother and dad when they read that. But it was a very honest evaluation of my concentration as an architecture student.

Jimmy, meanwhile, was awfully good at his work. The others also loved being architecture students, but I didn't! Once again, I was an outsider. I was really unhappy aside from my good friendship with Jimmy. I tried to

Laird Cregar sparked my interest in acting in The Lodger, *1944, Fox.*

study. I drew things, but Mr. Paine said, "Frankham, your houses always look good, but they would all fall down because you never put foundations on them!" I seemed to be doing really stupid things like that all the time there. I would draw a house and not think about what it rested on for a foundation!

I did my best, but it wasn't working. I knew I would have to push myself through architecture school. We all knew that we would be drafted into the Army for two or three years and then have another two or three years of architecture school waiting for us after our service.

While my father finally expressed a little pride at the thought that I would become an architect, acting occasionally lurked in the back of my mind. I tried to fight it by thinking, "This is my life, and it's been laid out for me. I'll just go to the movies and enjoy what I see and not have any sense of determination about wanting to act."

I felt that way until I saw *The Lodger,* with Laird Cregar, in 1944. His performance just devastated me. He was terrifying, partly from the editing, which heightened the suspense, and partly from his bloated face as the camera moved in on him. His riveting performance stopped me cold. Just as I had been fascinated with Roddy McDowall and Gladys Cooper, I thought, "I have got to do this one day. I don't know how, but I have to try this acting."

Inspired by Laird Cregar, here's how I thought aspiring, moody actors should pose in 1944.

Days in architecture school held no appeal for me. I couldn't wait to see Cregar as Jack the Ripper every day for the two weeks that the movie played. His performance is such a total leaving of the actor's own personality as he becomes Jack the Ripper. I identified with that seemingly tortured character. There were days when I felt like I was being tortured in architecture school, doing something against my wishes.

I tingled with anticipation on my way to the theatre each night. I couldn't wait to shiver again as Cregar came looming out of the fog the first time in the movie. I was hypnotized by the performance. At that time, there were no videos to watch over again, so repeated visits to the cinema had to do. There was no Internet Movie Database, either, so I had no way of realizing that Cregar had already four memorable years of acting for 20th Century-Fox. Later I would discover that Cregar was also memorable in *I Wake Up Screaming* with Betty Grable and Victor Mature, playing a sinister detective who turns out to be the killer. I also liked him as a pirate captain in *The Black Swan* with Tyrone Power; in fact, everything he did under Fox contract was just so good.

When I left the cinema after seeing Cregar, I made up my mind that I was somehow going to act. By then I had read and learned more about English filmmaking, but my sense was that English actors came into film through repertory theatre backgrounds with training and experience. I knew that wouldn't work for me. Just as there was a class system for ordinary people, there also seemed to be a kind of class thing in English films, where most of the actors sounded posh or upper class.

I knew I wasn't going to do any good in domestic pictures. I thought, "If I'm going to do this one day, I have to get to America." It was a sense in me like a homing pigeon. America was across the ocean, away from the war and a land of enchantment as far as I knew. Other American entertainment piqued my interest. I remember the first time Frank Sinatra's recordings became available in England. We had only heard remotes on the American Armed Forces Radio Network of Sinatra's time with Tommy Dorsey. There was always a lot of screaming and cheering going on, so I really couldn't tell the quality of the voice.

I sat down very critically that afternoon because I was a dyed-in-the-wool Crosby fan. I thought, "How dare this person come along and threaten Bing's stability?" I was gone the moment I heard Sinatra sing. What a marvelous voice he had. He didn't sound the least bit like Bing. "Saturday Night Is the Loneliest Night of the Week" was one of his first releases, and I became a big Sinatra fan as well. Listening to music helped me through the drudgery of architecture school. I loved to jitterbug to Glenn Miller's recordings with any girl who was handy. I couldn't stand just shoving a girl around a floor for a formal foxtrot or a waltz, but get that Miller swing beat going, and I was off.

Early into 1944, the opportunity to act came along in architecture school, of all places. All students were required by Mr. Paine, our instructor, to put on a play. Family and friends would be invited. I honestly wasn't interested in stage acting at all, but Mr. Paine was going to direct the play, and I liked him. When he chose *The Merry Wives of Windsor*, I had no interest, but he said, "No, Frankham, you're going to do this with the others." It's ironic, really, because I was the one wanting to be an actor, and he wasn't cajoling the rest of them that much!

I played a very small part of a fellow who sits at Falstaff's feet. We only had two or three weeks of rehearsals before staging the play for two weekends. Each rehearsal, I sat at the feet of a plump student who played Falstaff. Just like an old Hollywood cliché, he was drafted one day and somebody had to fill in for him!

Mr. Paine said, "Frankham, you should play the part. It's only logical. You've sat at his feet, you've seen my directions to him, and you've some clue about what this is about. You're going to be Falstaff."

They padded me with cushions and glued a beard on my chin. As I learned the lines, I waddled around the stage as Falstaff. I remember standing in what we called the wings — actually just a classroom with curtains — waiting to waddle on. I heard people laughing — all the invited mums and dads and brothers and sisters. I remember thinking that it was unexpectedly kind of exciting. That was the first time the adrenaline began coursing through me as an actor.

Because my heart was in the movies, I didn't even realize the connection to acting. There I was as Falstaff, and I never had actually seen a real

That's me on the right in costume as Falstaff in my architecture school's production of The Merry Wives of Windsor *in January 1944. It's no wonder that my father asked, "Which one was David?"*

play! I'm sure I was lousy as Falstaff. Believe it not, I still have the script. Now I can't imagine a seventeen-year-old having any sense of significance for that beautiful Shakespeare dialogue.

Yet our show seemed to go well, in spite of the constant threat of air raids all around us. In fact, our program contained this disclaimer: "In the event of an air raid alert, the action will be suspended for one minute. The play will then continue." We could have all been blown to bits, but the show would have gone on! My mum and dad came to see our show. My father sat through the play and applauded at all the right moments. Later I heard that as they were going home on the bus, my mother said in her quiet Scottish voice, "Well, I quite enjoyed the play."

My father said, "It was all right. Which one was David?" He hadn't even bothered to look at the program! Oh, well. I suppose he had never seen a play before, either!

Given my parents' philosophy about my creative endeavors and their desire for me to conform to class standards, I don't know where I mustered the resolve to haul myself up from a very un-promising environment, but I aspired to be better and not be a victim of my environment. I was single-minded about my ambition; my acting goal was to be my salvation.

I would have made it as an architect, but I would have made a very unhappy one. In a way, I anticipated at least a lull in my otherwise dull studies because like all the young men my age, I knew I was going to be drafted after I turned eighteen. If we were fortunate enough to come back unscathed after a few years of service, we would have three more years at architecture school before graduation. None of us had any income as professional students. All of our parents supported us financially as we studied.

My pal Jimmy Thomson was suddenly called up two months before we were to take our two-year exams. Passing these exams meant that you had another three years to go. Jimmy was called to Ireland to do his basic training. It took his father's influence with a Member of Parliament to get him back in time to finish his studies in preparation for the exam.

On a very chilly morning in November 1944, we all showed up around the corner from the BBC in London for our exams at the Royal Institute of British Architects. There was a big hotel opposite the Royal Institute called the Langham Hotel. I had spent three years as a devoted member of the Glenn Miller Society, so I knew that Major Glenn Miller and his orchestra had been stationed or billeted at the hotel.

We all waited around for the doors to open at the Royal Institute at ten in the morning as I just stared across at the Langham. When a GI came out, that was enough for me. I dashed across the traffic to his side of the street. He turned out to be Corporal Broderick Crawford, the actor who would go on to win the Academy Award in 1949 for *All the King's Men.*

What a stroke of luck for me to run into him. I knew he was working as the master of ceremonies and announcer for Glenn Miller.

I said, "Is Major Miller here?"

Crawford said, "No, the band is out recording because we're going overseas and we need to pile up a stockpile of recordings."

"When will they be back?" I eagerly asked.

"Maybe this afternoon," came his reply.

That news was almost the end of me at the Royal Institute of British Architects, because I didn't have my mind on that exam. All through the test, I kept looking at my watch thinking, "I have to get out of here by two o'clock."

There would be no sighting of Glenn Miller for me that day. I found out in a few weeks that I had somehow passed the exam in spite of the distraction. I think they passed us all because who knew how many of us would come back from the war in 1944. The war was still on. D-Day had happened June 6, and the allied armies were pushing across Europe.

I was sad that I had missed my second opportunity to see Glenn Miller, though. Earlier that year in August, Paramount premiered *Going My Way* with Bing Crosby in England. Through the Glenn Miller Society, I knew that Miller and the orchestra were to appear for thirty minutes, their only public appearance in England besides performing for armed services during their six-month stay in England.

When I told my parents that I just had to go, my mother asked if I had the money to attend. When I didn't, she wouldn't let me go. Besides, making a trek from Kent into London would have risked certain death from buzz bombs. I was so devastated, and that night at the appointed hour of the show, I remember thinking that Glenn and the orchestra would have been on stage and playing.

December 1944 was tough on me. On December 9, Laird Cregar died at age thirty-one. A man of great size, he had gone on a crash diet that resulted in a heart attack. The following week, Glenn Miller's plane disappeared. It was a real double whammy for me to lose a hero at eighteen. Although Cregar was dead, Glenn Miller was missing, even though that meant that he was presumed dead. Until it was official, many of us wanted to believe that there was some glimmer of hope. I would not have much time to mourn.

Early in January 1945, I got my call-up notice that I was to be drafted on January 18 into the armed forces. The drudgery of architecture school was to be exchanged for the military. Service was a rite of passage for all war-time youth my age. I was sent to basic training in Scotland, of all places, at Fort George, a dreary prison-like place near a loch.

For six weeks men screamed at us: "You're going to forget you ever had a mother by the time we're through with you!" We were brainwashed to not be the thoughtful, sensitive fellows that some of us were. We were to march in time, tote our rifles about, and shoot at targets with machine guns. I actually found it kind of interesting, a break from drafting blueprints, but I saw a few very sensitive souls who were having a terrible time. Some of the men could not forget their parents or brothers or sisters at home.

Because it was January, there were deep snowdrifts. At one point, we weren't allowed to leave the fort for six weeks. We were shown a movie every evening as a consolation. The trouble was that we saw the same movie each night. I saw *Bathing Beauty* with Harry James and his orchestra fourteen times! They changed the movie every two weeks, so if we attended each screening, we could see the picture at least fourteen times. I couldn't wait for evening to come. *Bathing Beauty* also had Basil Rathbone as one of the stars. I had seen him in *The Adventures of Robin Hood*, and he scared me in *David Copperfield* as he whacked the daylights out of poor Freddie Bartholomew. I marveled at his range, moving from those villains to a comic turn.

Six weeks passed before I was sent to different camps. The next one was located in Surrey. Again, in each transit camp, there was a film shown every evening. This time, the movie ran longer than fourteen nights. Twenty-three nights in a row, I saw another movie. Years later, I still could quote lines from the film.

In training as an army cadet near Woking, England.

At the Surrey camp, we had to pass a series of tests wearing full cartridge belts with a rifle over our shoulders and a steel helmet on our heads. All of us had to climb up a big pine tree, go hand over hand to the next pine tree thirty feet away and come down on the other side. It was a real obstacle course that required us to jump over and under things and finish by shimmying up a rope.

I couldn't master it on the first try because of the height. With one guy's rear stuck in my face and my rear end protruding into the fellow's face below me, I panicked and had to get down from there. The people behind and in front of the few of us who couldn't complete the course weren't that happy to have us climbing down them. Because the course was a requirement, I would have to try to pass it again the next morning by completely finishing the entire obstacle course.

That night they showed a movie, *Cover Girl*, with the beautiful Rita Hayworth. The movie featured a wonderful score and songs. At one point, Gene Kelly, Phil Silvers, and Rita sang as they marched down the street. Thinking ahead to the next morning's obstacle course, I got up in the middle of the song, singing "Make Way for Tomorrow." As I made my way out of the movie, I left them and went straight to the pine wood, singing and maintaining the song's rhythm as I reached the tall trees.

Since it was dark, I couldn't see the ground forty feet below. That helped quell my fear of heights. Unable to see the ground, I managed to go hand over hand, up the rope and down to the other side, without any of the equipment or passing out from fright. The next morning with rifle, attachments, and steel, I was humming "Make Way for Tomorrow" quietly to myself so the other fellows wouldn't think I was strange. It worked! I did the course!

Not long after I arrived at basic training came official word of news that most people had already accepted. Glenn Miller really was dead. He had flown off impulsively to Paris ahead of the orchestra. A perfectionist, he wanted to get everything ready, so off he went in a fog in his two-seater Piper and disappeared forever. Later, through conflicting stories, it was revealed that his plane had been bombed, perhaps mistakenly by a British plane. When I heard that there was to be no miracle for Glenn Miller, I tried not to appear emotional, so I made my way to the latrine, sat down, held my head in my hands and cried. It was just so heartbreaking to me. He may have died, but the music lived on in my heart.

I displaced sadness by getting lost in the movies. If I grew tired of watching the same film each night at camp, there was a cinema four miles away. Surrey is full of canals, so on one weekend, I followed a canal four miles into the nearby town of Woking to an ABC Cinema showing *The Picture of Dorian Gray*. I lost my heart to the English girl in that, but I'm ashamed to say I didn't get her name the first time around. I had to sit through an entire program again to find out that the lady in question was the marvelous Angela Lansbury.

The movie ran for two weeks, so each Saturday and Sunday, I walked four miles to drool over Angela's performances and then walked back. Then, glory be, the cinema immediately booked *Gaslight*, again with Angela. In complete contrast to the shy, sweet English rose she portrayed in *The Picture of Dorian Gray*, now she was a saucy tart sashaying around Charles Boyer. I marveled at her range, a word that I had learned by then.

It was back to reality when we went from Surrey to another bleak place, literally a prison located on a peninsula on England's southern coast. The

Army had moved out all the prisoners to put us in instead. Every window had iron bars, and the doors were steel enclosed. There always seemed to be a low point that every fellow reached in the Army. Some bigwig was coming to inspect us all one day. My job was to paint coal white. The path to where the brigadier would be staying had to look impressive for him to inspect the troops. I was handed a paint can and told to paint the coal leading to his door so it would look chipper. As I painted the coal, I thought that the Army was some life!

World War II was coming to an end, and I had been fortunate enough to be born in 1926, young enough to escape the harshest years of combat. Everyone was relieved that the war was ending and that the Allies had been victorious. We were invited to consider whether or not we would take commission to become officers. I thought, "What the hell? I'm painting coal. Maybe it's a good alternative."

Talking to a recruiter, I told him that I was midway in my training to be an architect. I explained that I would certainly like the advantages of being an officer, but I hoped would there be an opportunity to utilize my training by being in charge of or drawing or designing buildings for the Army.

The recruiting officer told me my idea would work and even explained which branch of the service I could go into to specialize in designing Nissen huts. I agreed to enter officer training and was whisked off with others, most of whom were rather posh-sounding. I thought that I was moving up in the world.

Officer training was nice, with weekends spent in country houses that had been given over by wealthy owners to the Army to use while they were away or staying in their country homes. Part of our training included making tents at night to show that we could survive on our own. It was sort of glamorous, and I actually enjoyed that kind of activity.

One week our coursework required us to ride motorcycles. Enormous British motorcycles were so heavy that every time I got onto one, I fell off the other side from the sheer weight. It was difficult to balance myself. We were being tested, so an understanding sergeant marked me down as sick so I never had to get on one again. I also learned to drive a jeep with a stick shift. If we jammed or stalled the vehicle, we weren't allowed to press a button to get it going again; we had to wind in the front. Motorcycles aside, I passed all of the officer training courses, and in January 1946, my group was told that we would be sent to an unspecified foreign location.

I had one day to say goodbye to my parents before getting on a plane. Wearing seatbelts, all of us sat on the floor opposite each other on the plane. We landed in Haifa with palm trees and camels. Although we were only there shortly to change planes, we found it wonderfully temperate and mild, not freezing like it had been in England.

Off again, we next landed in Persia and only spent one day there. We next came down to earth in Karachi, India, to refuel. We didn't even disembark there and next flew down to the southern tip of India to Bangalore, high up in the tea country. Once there, we each had our own tent, where we were given enough time to think and acclimate to the warm and humid climate. Just as before, time was spent by watching the same movie each night, but this time, it was a different movie, *The Bells of St. Mary's*. I was glad I liked Bing Crosby.

A brigadier informed us all that we were not going to be with the same group for much longer. I was not going to be able to serve my country or develop my skills as a draftsman; rather, I was to build steel bridges. An alarm bell went off in my head. At the end of his talk, I asked to speak to the brigadier. I can't believe my bravery, but I was only nineteen, so I told him, "I can't continue on this course, because I was promised I could utilize my architecture training."

"PROMISED?" he bellowed with a purple face. "What the hell are you talking about? What do you mean?"

I held my ground because I still thought that I would have to go home and be an architect. With the war over, it dawned on me that I had choices. I told him that I wanted to continue in the Army where I could do some kind of draftsmanship because of the career that awaited me after the end of my service.

The brigadier said, "I don't want a word of this discussion to get out because it's bad for morale. If somebody drops out of this group, quitting would permeate the rest of the dozen trainees. You'll leave tonight under cover of darkness."

Immediately demoting me to a private, the brigadier put me on a train with a sergeant who had a gun to protect me because the Indians hated the English military. We were about to hand the country back over to them, when it should have been theirs all the while. I found out that I was being sent to Calcutta as punishment for standing up to the brigadier and wanting to do something besides build bridges.

For three days on this long train, none of the Indian passengers knew that two Brits were in the caboose on the end. Wherever we stopped, we had our rations to eat. We couldn't get out, because no one was supposed to know that there was a British soldier and a sergeant on the train.

When we arrived in Calcutta, we found the city hot and humid. Many of the Indians chewed beetle juice and spat everywhere. It seemed that the streets were slathered in red stuff. I was then introduced to my new platoon, what I called the cutthroat crew. These men all looked like they were from pirate movies, real dregs of the British army. I was deliberately being punished by being placed with a bunch of losers who all looked like ex-rapists or murderers.

We were stationed opposite the beautiful Hooghly River. There had been floods and for six weeks, we would see dead, rotting cow carcasses floating each morning. The Sikhs and the Hindus were fighting, and sometimes we would even see human heads in the gutter. Talk about growing up at nineteen!

I thought, "I'm not going to die. I'll rise above all this. I didn't do anything wrong."

The commanding officers couldn't make us do army maneuvers because the weather was so muggy. At six a.m., we would show up on parade, most of the men with hangovers. There was nothing to do but go back to our *charpoi*, a bed made of wood. Instead of a mattress, ours was made of rope comparable to a hammock.

Once in awhile, we heard instructions for lunch break over a system of loudspeakers. There were thirty of us in a room. Somehow I got into the office to see the microphones used for the loudspeakers. They had two turntables and some records. I thought, "What have I got to lose?"

I asked the sergeant, "Do you play music over the system?"

"No," he said. "We have no reason to."

I inquired, "Would it be all right if I asked some of the men if they had favorite songs? We could play them here over the speakers."

"I suppose so, if you've got nothing else to do," he replied.

Heartened by his approval, I asked all the other men which songs they would like to hear. Like most people our age, we had the same favorites by the likes of Bing Crosby or Perry Como. The military had the recordings sent in batches from England, so there were plenty of records to be played.

I asked to play records at a set time in the morning or afternoon and take requests. Permission was granted, so I became a disc jockey for the first time. Each day, I took out some 78 rpm records and put on a heavy needle to play songs over the loudspeakers. The records wore out with just one play, but the military promptly sent in replacements. I was just passing my time talking to some of these deadbeats who wanted to hear a song or two. I spent six weeks that way and thought that my record playing would be the end of it all.

We were suddenly told to board the train to New Delhi where I would spend another two months. It was hotter than hell in New Delhi. Even six a.m. was unbearable. One day I was told that I would be Acting Sergeant Frankham instead of Private Frankham. Without being told why, I was given a pistol and taken to a luxurious house in a suburb and ordered to stay there until further notice. Every morning a jeep picked me up and took me to a facility surrounded by barbed wire. The facility controlled electricity in that part of the country.

LEFT: *I didn't look happy about being shipped off to India in 1946.* RIGHT: *While stationed in Delhi, I only saw one dog, which I named Skipper. Here we are, off-duty, in November 1946.*

Each day I went into this electrical compound to sit and do nothing, while four Indians were there taking care of the electrical supply going out to that area of New Delhi. Nobody told me what to do, why I had the gun or what to expect. Only one of the four Indians spoke a little bit of English, so I really had nobody to talk to.

At two p.m., I was driven back in the jeep through the blazing hot sun to the mansion that I shared with another acting sergeant. We even had a cook, so I couldn't believe my good fortune. Somehow I thought the military might be making it up to me for punishing me after I insisted on being trained as an officer as I was originally promised.

I lived out the summer of 1946 in New Delhi in the mansion until I was told to return to the Red Fort in old Delhi. The huge red fort housing us had been constructed by the moguls, Indian nobility, as a marvelous city within a city. Back I went, a private again. Next I travelled by train across India to Madras, a city in the southern corner of the country. I was put on a ship and ended up in Singapore. Ironically, we were housed in Changi, a Japanese prison camp that had originally been built for conquered British troops. Now we each had a Japanese prisoner of war to shine our boots and press our pants as punishment following the war.

A life of boredom ensued again. My friend Jimmy from architecture school had a sister who had taught me two-finger typing, so I volunteered to transcribe the results of a court-martial in which a soldier had killed an officer. Every day I typed written courtroom proceedings as a transcript. The whole trial was interesting and exciting, but I never knew how it turned out, because we were then moved again. I had been glad to look for options instead of lying around. Typing made life bearable.

Off we went again on a long train to Kuala Lumpur. The highlight was watching a tiger running at the same speed of the train on the right side as we rode through forests of rubber plant trees. The tiger kept parallel pace with the train until he finally disappeared through the trees.

When we arrived in Kuala Lumpur, I was sent to the coast to Morib. With its golden beaches, palm trees and gentle surf, it was almost like Hawaii. After enjoying the change of scenery, I was once again bored silly with nothing to do. We got up at six to report that we were all there and then returned to our barracks to lie down again. Life was so boring that we enjoyed the excitement when a group of chaps one day cornered a cobra in the camp. It was marvelous to see the hood of this enraged poisonous snake. To see a huge cobra spitting at these idiots was exciting, until they shot and killed it.

I was interested in getting to know some friendly dogs from a neighboring village as I wandered up and down the beaches. Four or five dogs and I splashed in the surf of an estuary leading into the ocean. I went out as far as I could walk into the water and then it dipped deep down, so I never went farther than that.

Interesting pools often formed in the sand. Once the dogs and I saw a snake coiled there in the water. I learned later that the venom from a sea snake is the most poisonous, but there I was blithely splashing around near danger. Later there was a report that a village boy was killed and eaten by crocodiles in that estuary. I had lived a blessed life with no idea of how dangerous it could be. I had never seen a croc there!

Around my twenty-first birthday, I had a close encounter with deathly illness. We had all been told that the jungle was out of bounds. One day

I got a stick with a piece of string and decided to go fishing in the little stream near the estuary where I found the waiting dogs. There was a tug at the string. When I pulled it up, there was a snake attached! Frightened, I dropped it and ran back to camp on a jungle path. As I ran, I sliced my leg at knee height on a banana leaf. I thought nothing of it when the wound stopped bleeding, so I didn't report it.

The next morning, February 16, 1947, was my birthday. We were sent to Kuala Lumpur, but we didn't have time to look around at this marvelous city. I remember feeling sorry for myself that morning, because I had to parade on my birthday. That's all I remember, because I next fainted dead away. After collapsing, I was shoved in a medical unit's mosquito ward. Because malaria was prevalent, the doctors thought I was ill with that dreaded disease.

A wonderful nurse going through her evening duty heard me breathing very strangely. She lifted up the tent and called over the officer. Together they stared at me. My face was turning blue. The doctor checked me out and said to her, "He's got typhus, not malaria!"

In a coma, I was sent to intensive care. While I languished, deathly ill, I had an out-of-body experience. I distinctly remember seeing myself lying on that bed, dying. I saw the nurse and the doctor, just like watching a movie. Recovering days later, I woke up to find officers at the foot of the bed with red tabs on their uniforms. These were brigadiers telling me that there was a good chance that I was going to be court-martialed. In their thinking, I had gone out of bounds into the jungle. The fact that I had been cut meant that it was a self-inflicted wound in their rationale.

Half-dead, I thought that the Army was still getting back at me for turning down that officer training. They finally told me that because I almost died, they decided not to court-martial me. If I hadn't been so ill, they otherwise would have most certainly done so. The whole course of my life had changed after being saved by this nurse who had noticed me gasping from typhus.

Because I was a skeleton, skin and bones, the Army sent me up to the Cameron Highlands. When the Brits took over half the world, they always named the places with British names. There were actually sections of Scotland named Highlands, but I was in northern Malaya on a tea plantation where I had not a thing to do but eat, get better and listen to records every day.

After I put on a little weight, it was time to go back. The Army sent me back to Kuala Lumpur but my platoon of "cutthroats" had left. Was I relieved! The Army decided to make me an acting sergeant again and placed me in charge as a drawing officer to supervise Indians making blueprints of officer quarters that were to be constructed.

I was finally where I had asked to be at the beginning of my officer training, still serving my country, just sitting and watching these guys draw their blueprints. Using my two years of architecture training, I walked by and inspected their work and placed a check mark of approval on their plans.

I thought, "This is right. This should be happening to me after what that brigadier did to me. I have what I wanted, and now I can look forward to three more years of architecture study."

Involved in blueprints and drawings, I went to the movies and sat around and socialized in the sergeant mess hall in Kuala Lumpur. Life was as good as I let it be.

One evening in the officers' mess hall in Kuala Lumpur, I enjoyed a cup of tea and walked over to look at the bulletin boards. They contained lists of houses where we could go for tea and socialize. Some of the nearby rubber plantation owners were very kind to English officers because we had helped save them from the Japanese in World War II.

I noticed an invitation to servicemen from Radio Malaya, inviting us to submit a list of our eight favorite records and our reasons for our selections. The most interesting letter would be rewarded with the opportunity for the soldier to go onto Radio Malaya to introduce the winning selections personally over the air.

With nothing else to do that evening, I didn't even leave the mess hall. I sat down and decided to enter the contest. I remember listing songs by Glenn Miller, Frank Sinatra, and "Two Silhouettes," a lovely song by Dinah Shore that appeared in the Disney animated package film *Make Mine Music*. I placed my entry in the ballot box. That was the end of it until a brigadier told me later, "You've won some sort of prize. You're to show up at 2200 hours."

With my list of eight favorite tunes in hand, I arrived at the appointed hour and was introduced to an announcer. He asked if I had ever broadcast over the air. I told him how I had announced records over a loudspeaker system in Calcutta but that I had not really ever broadcast.

As I sat down in front of the station's microphone, the moment was captured on film as the announcer snapped a photo of me to document my radio debut. I made my own little musical history as I said, "Good evening, I'm David Frankham, and this is my kind of music, and I hope this is your kind of music, too."

As I sat in that chair, I thought to myself, "I'm home. I can do this. I'm not going to be self-conscious or bombastic. I'm just going to chat, because I know that people are listening all over Malaya."

My thirty minutes of air time passed quickly. The radio station staff thanked me. I was going out the door when an announcer said that the station manager, a Mr. Jackson, wanted to talk to me on the phone.

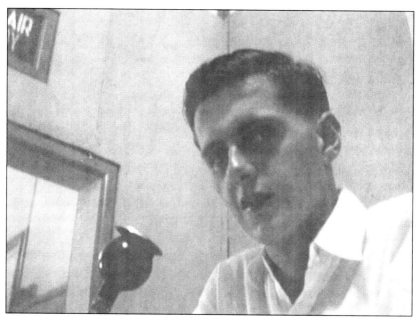

Hosting My Kind of Music *on Radio Malaya on August 8, 1947.*

"Well done," he told me. "You're a natural. It's kind of a gift to just talk conversationally into a microphone. Not everyone does that, and even the professionals can still sound slightly sleek and not warm or friendly."

When I later met Mr. Jackson in person, he said, "Would you like us to train you as a relief announcer?"

"YES! YES!" I replied without hesitation. "I would like that very much!"

The radio station employed two announcers, both of whom had girl-friends they never got to see together as a group of friends because one announcer always had to be on duty. They thought that if they could find some dummy to train, at least one could get a weekend off so they could all four be together and double date. They were willing to try me, and I was more than willing to learn. From the start, I was a willing pupil as they taught me how to read news on the air and to write scripts to be delivered live.

In the corner of the studio, there sat a teletype machine. Radio Malaya's base was in Singapore, so half an hour before reading news, the machine clacked and rolls of paper produced news bulletins. Announcers cut them up and read the Singapore news to people in Kuala Lumpur.

Who knows why we can do what we can do in life, or why we're interested in one thing more than another, but I found that I had an affinity for reading the news and being on the radio. When I started learning to be a news reader, there were many Malay names that I had not heard. Once or twice, people rang up and said, "Can't you tell that chap to say this properly?" and gave the correct pronunciation for wherever they lived. I quickly learned a lot about broadcasting.

In short time, the station gave me my own program called *My Kind of Music*. What a luxury! Once a week, I had carte blanche to pick my own records and talk about them for thirty minutes. My show debuted in the summer and continued throughout the fall of 1947 from a carpeted, soundproof studio that was split into two smaller studios. On one side were Indian musicians, sitting on the floor with sitars. Although we couldn't hear them in the other booth, these musicians performed nonstop for the Indian population throughout Malaya.

On our side, records hung on one wall. All those discs were like being in a candy store. There were even more records on the shelf in a simple studio with a desk, microphone, and two turntables. The studio was located on the third or fourth floor of a circular building where I stayed on weekends once I got confidence, rhythm, and satisfaction going with my show.

On Friday nights, I was glad that I didn't have to report back to my officer duties until Sunday night, so I spent all day Saturday in Kuala Lumpur. Using my pants to make a pillow, I slept on the floor inside the small studio. I slept soundly — I couldn't hear the sitars from the next booth at all — so those guys on the other side of the booth must have thought I was crazy sleeping there on the floors! It was wonderful to wake up, put on my pants, sit on the floor and think, "I have it made!"

I loved communicating with people via radio. On Saturday nights, I read the news, played music, and put on giant, sixteen-inch records that were transcriptions of drama programs. That was so simple, because it meant just putting the stylus onto the disc and letting a complete radio program play for thirty minutes.

On Sundays, I would get up and walk down into the markets. Malays were such gentle, nice people. They had suffered terribly under Japanese occupation during the war. Many of the locals spoke English, so I wandered around and tried their food. Nearly every vendor offered appe-tizing stir fry. I sat and ate wonderful stir fry with soy sauce every Sunday.

Eventually word got around back at the base that I was moonlighting as a weekend disc jockey, so my buddies started showing up to spend the weekend. There we were, spending Saturday nights on the floor! It was a great boost to my ego, though, because they were in awe of me as an announcer. They were better friends and peers than the cutthroats I had left behind earlier in my military service. These were decent fellows, good people. One of them, Graham Fairley, was interested in architecture, so with my background and training, we hit it off nicely. He liked watching how the radio station worked, but he was destined for a successful career in architecture after the military.

The Army made it clear that I couldn't be paid for my moonlighting, but it was fine for me to do whatever I wanted in my off-hours as long as no money changed hands. I didn't care about money, and the station manager knew that, too. The station operated with government-allocated funds, meaning that Mr. Jackson only had funds to pay his two regular full-time announcers. I was doing the station a favor, and they were doing me a favor by allowing me to enjoy something I liked to do.

Mr. Jackson and his wife noticed that I always wore olive green slacks and white shirts, so one time they took me to shop for a suit. I would hang it up at the radio station and put it on, which was dumb, really, since no one could see me on the radio. Nevertheless, I loved that white silk suit. It looked elegant and made me feel good when I wore it.

The Jacksons also took me to dinner with their friends on Sunday afternoons before my announcing duties. We enjoyed luxurious lunches with older owners of rubber plantations. One of the wives of a plantation owner told me that she personally knew the characters that Somerset Maugham had written about in *The Letter*, his 1927 play that had been adapted by William Wyler into a film starring Bette Davis.

This elderly woman told me all about the rubber planter's wife who had an affair with a lover. After she shot him, there was a trial to determine whether the killing had been committed in self-defense or as revenge for rape. She had lured him with a letter to snare him into coming to see her. She was hanged, but in the movie, Bette Davis was killed by the lover's other mistress, a concession to the censors' demands that killers must be depicted dying by the end of a film. It was chilling to think that I was now lunching not far from where the true story had happened.

I was living it up, not caring that I was working on the radio for free because I felt I was learning. My dread intensified each day as my three-year military stint grew closer to its end. I knew that I would have to go home. By the end of the fall of 1947, I was told that it was time to prepare to board a ship bound for Britain.

Radio was satisfying, so I realized that I didn't want to go home to architecture school. I loved what I was doing, so much so that even the thought of an acting career had been placed on the back burner in my mind. I knew that I was good at broadcasting, so I asked for a meeting with Mr. Jackson one evening. I asked him if I could stay on for him. He told me that he could only afford two announcers with his government allocation. I wanted to use my Army severance pay to come back and work when the first opportunity arose.

"No," he said. "You should find another job. We can't pay you. We love your work, but we simply can't pay you."

Then he said the magic words. "In England, I went to school with Wynford Vaughan-Thomas. I'll write a letter to take to him saying, 'Young Frankham shows promise. He might be of use to the BBC.'"

I was somewhat solaced by Mr. Jackson's idea of helping me. Wynford Vaughan-Thomas was a radio legend to British listeners. A war correspondent during World War II, he had proven himself extraordinarily brave by covering battles and offering commentary. On D-Day, June 6, 1944, he was on the front line with his BBC recording microphone in hand, along with the Allied forces, in the line of fire from the machine guns firing at the tanks. Protected by only a flak jacket and steel helmet, he covered the war with hundreds dying on each side of him. He literally went through bloody water to get to the sand. From then and until the Allies reached Paris, he broadcast daily communiqués about the war's progress. We all had listened to him. Following the war, he had been named a high-ranking official at the BBC. He could be a good contact once I returned home.

As I said a reluctant goodbye to Radio Malaya and my military life in Kuala Lumpur, I boarded the ship to take me back to England. On the voyage home, I had time to think about my future. The same movie was screened each night for us on the one-week trip, *Moss Rose*, with Ethel Barrymore and Vincent Price. The acting bug began to nip at me a little more. I decided that I had two options: I could take the letter of introduction to the BBC, or I could do what my parents expected of me by returning to architecture school for three more years without pay.

By the time I arrived home, I decided that I had to have a shot at auditioning as an actor. I wrote a letter to the Young Vic Company, a theatre that specialized in working with young actors. In turn, I received a letter telling me when to audition and to bring two prepared pieces, one contemporary and the other from Shakespeare.

I prepared a piece of dialogue from a Bette Davis movie, *The Corn Is Green*, a scene about dreaming of better things with which I could identify. I can't even remember which Shakespearean piece I selected. Very inhibited and lacking confidence about my prospects, I didn't even tell my parents about my audition. All I told them was that I was going up to London for a day.

When I arrived at the Young Vic, I put my name down on the book and noticed confident people my age who had been actors before the war interrupted their careers. I was twenty-two, and these competitors seemed posh and confident. I thought, "I can't do this!" Told that I would be seen in an hour, I started to take a walk. I never went back. Not only did it not feel right, but I refused to humiliate myself in front of professional actors. (It's likely a good thing that I didn't make it at the Young Vic; later that year in 1948, the director and entire faculty resigned!)

That night on the train ride back to my parents' home in Kent, I felt so dejected, yet I felt that I could not afford to give up completely on acting. I started to think that I would pursue something less grand. I saw a newspaper ad announcing that the Malvern Festival was also holding auditions for its summer of 1948 season.

I wrote to the Malvern Festival and was told the same thing — prepare two pieces — which I had already done for the Vic. Again I went up on the train, arrived early and put my name down on the log. With one hour to go, I took a walk in the Malvern Hills and never went back. The same sense of dread had happened twice. I was trying to force myself into acting in a time and manner that was not yet right for me. My gut feeling was telling me that maybe I could act later, but the time didn't seem right.

Even though I had been given a letter of recommendation to a BBC legend, I was not thinking positively in a mistaken belief that the BBC would not be interested in me. A letter of recommendation with a legend, though, was still preferable to architecture school. I had enjoyed radio broadcasting, so I relented and called for an appointment with Wynford Vaughan-Thomas.

This time around, I didn't leave for a walk. Vaughan-Thomas was very funny and jolly. The famous broadcaster fondly remembered my dear Mr. Jackson from their days at Exeter College. The whole encounter proved remarkably simple as he read Mr. Jackson's letter and looked up at me,

"I think you'd be right for the BBC's European Service," he told me.

He picked up the telephone and called a friend in charge of the European Service. He made an appointment for me and sent me to his friend. The very next day, I told this interviewer that I had done a little radio work in Malaya.

"When would you like to start?" he asked, just as simple as that. Instantly, my life unfolded in front of my eyes. There was no microphone test, no question about my radio accent.

I told him that I could start the next day, on a Friday. He told me to report at nine and that my training would start immediately. The next morning I was on the staff of the BBC as an announcer for its European Service. I couldn't believe my good fortune. Even my father thought my appointment was great. He didn't seem to mind at all that I would not be returning to architecture school because he could tell the neighbors that his son was a BBC announcer.

What a difference three years had made! The military had plucked me away from an unhappy architecture training experience. Most of my military service hadn't fared much better until I stumbled into radio. From entering a radio contest, I had found pro bono work that prepared me for the BBC. I had mastered an escape from the drudgery of returning to architecture training. Radio wasn't acting, but it still seemed like the next best thing to show business. My whole future somehow seemed brighter as I prepared to start my career as a bona fide announcer for the BBC.

CHAPTER TWO

"Here Is the News, Read by David Frankham"

Being drafted had taken care of my decision-making as to whether or not I should flee architecture for acting ambitions. Getting sidetracked into radio, no matter how interesting and stimulating the BBC, was another delay, but I never stopped believing that it was my own personal destiny to become an actor. Yet I didn't have the foggiest idea how it was going to happen. How on earth would I get myself from England to Hollywood, California?

Everything eventually fits together professionally in a pattern as years go by, but I was still too young to see that when I started at the BBC. Sometimes I felt I was even being sidetracked in broadcasting when I was either promoted or transferred to interviewing from news reading or from interviewing to script writing. Because I was a staff member of the BBC, I had little choice. Often I thought I was wasting time, but as it turned out, it was all useful and dovetailed into my own plan for reaching Hollywood. The work provided a rich background, no matter my final choice.

When I was growing up in the 1930s, there was only radio. The BBC was a government monopoly. Even though it was radio, the stiff upper lip, ruling class atmosphere around the BBC meant that one had to have a university education to be considered for speaking on the air as an announcer or a news reader.

Sitting in our little house in Kent and listening to the BBC, I thought that the announcers sounded very posh. There was once a published photograph of a BBC radio news reader sitting in a black tie and dinner jacket at his desk while he read the news at nine from London. Nobody could see him like that on the radio, but that was the rigid, compulsory approach that the BBC incorporated.

In the 1930s, my neutral accent would have never gotten me into the BBC. By the time I arrived back in England from military service in 1948, there had been kind of a change. The BBC had introduced regional announcers with dialects for the comfort of local listeners. In fact, Wynford Vaughan-Thomas, the contact who helped get me started, was Welsh. He didn't have one of those terribly correct, Mayfair-type accents that seemed to represent the southern part of the country on the BBC.

My childhood exposure to my mother's farming family in Scotland had taken the edge off my working class English accent. If my mother's family had lived in Glasgow, with its more pronounced accents, there would have been no hope for me, yet we stayed in Fifeshire, which had no extreme accent.

With my Scot mother and English father, I had an easier time of transitioning from Radio Malaya to the BBC without having to take vocal lessons. I had spent time in Scotland and had exposure to various dialects. My father had sort of a working class English accent, but if I had talked like him, I would have never had my foot in the door. My parents, though, reacted to my BBC appointment with enormous pride, really the first time they had openly expressed their satisfaction with how my life was developing. Although he was reserved to the point that he wouldn't say it directly to me, my father was always telling the neighbors, "My son, the BBC announcer." That was a wonderful feeling to me.

In hindsight, I recognize that I actually earned my living as a talker. I had a voice that was right for the times. I was coming into the BBC at a time of change. I think Wynford Vaughan-Thomas probably thought of me for the BBC's European Service because I had been overseas in India. I started very much in awe of my colleagues, because there were three lady announcers and six fellows, slightly la-di-da because the fellows were too old to have been in the war. There was a little bit of the old BBC posh-style still present with them.

The first morning that I reported to work, I was introduced to one of the news readers, who merely said, "Come with me." I sat with him while he read the news and just saw the way he delivered his copy, more or less the way that I had done it at Radio Malaya. I listened to his not-so-grand accent. No one questioned my accent, having taken off the rough edges from my upbringing. In fact, my BBC voice is still the one I have today.

The news was read live, almost the same throughout the day, except the news reader I shadowed read headlines to different countries. He talked to Poland for five minutes of news with a Polish translator sitting opposite him. The Polish announcer then did the news in Polish, and it was back to the BBC announcer for another bit of news to be repeated again by the Polish announcer.

The second day, I reported to work at 2:30 a.m., because at 3:45 a.m., we had to do a Russian broadcast live. The studio was underground in

I was delighted to join the BBC in London.

a place called Bush House, which was near Australia House in London. Because of the war and the BBC's importance to people listening under the Nazi regime, the studios were safely secured underground. Millions had tuned into England just to hear what was going on in the world. That significance had really put the BBC's European Service on the map.

The third day on the job, the announcer more or less said to me, "You're on your own, kid." That responsibility was awesome, because I had grown up seeing photos of the famous microphones with "BBC" engraved on them. What a surprise to learn that morning that those photos were just show biz glamour. In reality, the BBC had put a clip-on for the mike so would it read "BBC." Mine was just an ordinary microphone!

Sitting at a desk, my heart pounded as I said for the first time, "This is the BBC European Service. Here is the news, read by David Frankham." As news readers, we were handed items to read about fifteen minutes before we went on the air. With a hotline type of phone next to us, we would quickly look over what we were about to read live on the air. If there were any foreign pronunciations — a city or a language that we didn't know how to pronounce — we automatically picked up the hotline phone. Believe it or not, there was somebody whose job was to sit in an office all day and night — in shifts — and who knew exactly how to pronounce every single word in the English language. If, for instance, I got to "courier," and didn't how to say it, he would tell me, and I would write it phonetically over my news item, "c-o-o-r-e-a-y." The BBC pronunciation was taken as gospel by the general public in the United Kingdom. If that's how it was said on the BBC, that was the only way to say it.

I got through my first broadcast well, and in time, I became used to talking to the same regions in Yugoslavia, Russia or Scandinavia. Scandinavia was difficult, because they had some very odd or hard names to pronounce. Reading the news as part of the European Service quickly began a pattern that I followed for the next three years.

The European Service was near St. Paul's Cathedral on Fleet Street, while the BBC's Overseas Service was located on Oxford Street, right around the corner from Valhalla, which was the actual location of the BBC Home Service. The cream of the crop worked there on stations such as The Light Programme, a station that broadcast music and entertainment. It was exciting and prestigious to become part of the BBC "family."

Going from Army pay to a real salary at the BBC was my first reward for choosing to forgo architecture school and acting. I found a wonderful little flat, so I was finally on my own. Living in London was my second reward for putting my acting ambitions on hold. With shift work three days on and three days off like clockwork, I explored London. At age twenty-two when this great adventure started, I used my free time to see every play and movie. I was having the time of my life, so much so that I mostly didn't even give acting much of a thought.

On a day off, I saw Laurence Olivier and Vivien Leigh in *The Sleeping Prince,* which was later made as a film with Marilyn Monroe. To see those two great performers acting live, the caliber of their acting just wowed me. Yet I could sense that I would never be up there with them on stage. I wasn't necessarily thinking that the stage was prohibited as the right medium for me, but something just didn't seem right for me when I visualized myself onstage. Not following through on my lack of theatrical ambition no doubt helped curb my acting appetite for the moment.

My BBC experience taught me a number of skills that would later serve me well, including the most severe test of all: the ability to read "cold" and without error, hesitation, or prior rehearsal. I found early on that I loved it. Usually, we got news releases at least a few minutes before air time. I always went over them calmly for foreign pronunciations and then scribbled in a phonetic translation above the name or city so there would be no hesitation in my voice when I was on the air. I always marked the copy with a pencil stroke for breath pauses; I never stopped doing that, because it made my newscasts smoother. Of course, you couldn't do that if you were handed an item while on the air, "This just in…" Then I would be back on cold reading turf and it was challenging. The big thing was to remain calm and bear in mind that listeners wanted me to be good at reading or they wouldn't have tuned in to the station.

No matter whether news reading or interviewing, I had a mental picture that I was being listened to by a nice, sixty-ish lady. I never had an image of critical professionals judging me, although they often were, and their criticisms were of enormous value. My executive producer held an inquest on every broadcast that went out over the BBC, which is one reason that the BBC radio standards remain so high to this day. My "listener" was also alone, because people often listened solo or at most, maybe a couple per household. I would talk to him, or her, or that couple. I mentally beamed my concentration at the individual listener just seconds before going on the air. It made me feel very relaxed and secure and helped me gain confidence and stature on the BBC.

That's not to say that there weren't some funny moments. As a newcomer, I read my initial sports scores so quickly that the station switchboard lit up with complainers! In Britain, they had a sort of football lottery each Saturday night based on the scores, and listeners checked out their entries.

I screwed up that entire evening's results! The next Saturday, somebody from the BBC sports desk stood in front of me and conducted me silently as I read the scores slowly enough that everybody could mark his entry duplicates to see if he had won. I was sure that I would never be allowed to read the Saturday results again, but that humiliating lesson was all I needed — nobody had to conduct *me* again! I went right on doing the sports scores because the BBC saw the potential in me and cared enough to guide me.

I had yet to be trusted with full powers in production and interviewing, but I was allowed to tag along with producers to see how it was done. Lena Horne and her husband, Lennie Hayton (he arranged and conducted for her at MGM and in her stage shows), were headlining at the London Palladium, so I saw her two shows a night for fourteen days. Because the European Service was not too far from the Palladium, we were always welcome to see shows there free as a courtesy to BBC employees. I used this privilege to see Horne over and over again. She was sensational.

I got to be friendly with Horne's husband, who was an absolutely brilliant and superb arranger of many of the MGM musicals of the 1940s. He had been an accompanist of Bing Crosby's in the 1930s and was a very gifted man. Horne, meanwhile, was usually drenched in sweat after her shows because she strained during her powerful performances. Twice she said when I went to see her afterwards, "Honey, I look like an old crow." Nobody looked less like an old crow than Lena Horne!

I then sat in on the BBC radio interview at Horne's hotel. She was not allowed to stay at the nicer hotels, as all the other American stars did, because of hotel restrictions on non-whites. (Those were very unenlightened days and a shameful time in our history.) Yet she was gracious and charming and down to earth, and I adored her.

Her daughter, Gail, was present, and I took her on an open, double-decker bus tour of London one day. Lena seemed pleased that I took the time to show her daughter around while she and Lennie prepared for their shows. (Gail grew up to marry first the director Sidney Lumet, and later Kevin Buckley, an editor at *Playboy*, where as luck would have it, a young friend of mine happened to work in an internship. When he met Gail Buckley, he recounted my story of meeting her as a girl some forty odd years earlier. Talk about life leading you full circle!)

One night I was walking home through Leicester Square, not far from the BBC Studios. There was a great commotion at the corner of the square. I walked over to see what it was. A film crew was shooting a movie, which I had never seen being made before. The scene was a very brief one. A taxi came around the corner. An actor got out and walked into a night club. "Cut. Do it again, do it again!" I heard the director say. The poor actor did that four or five times because of lighting or sound problems. The actor was Richard Widmark and the movie was *Night and the City*. I remember thinking, "Gosh, a real Hollywood movie star." That was my first true encounter with the movie production side of show business, so the acting bug slowly began to re-emerge.

I used to walk home from work at the BBC after reading the evening news to thousands of listeners. The audience was pleased, I'm sure. My parents were proud and my bosses planned promotions for me. The acting bug began to bite again, eroding my satisfaction at working in radio. I began to think about when I would get to be an actor. I tried to remind myself that I was fortunate that so many people were taking time to advise and improve me.

Eventually, I grew restless. Once the initial thrill of being on the BBC wore off, I thought, 'This is a routine job.' It's amazing how quickly something exciting can become mundane. I loved my three days off because I would wake up and think about where I would go for lunch, which movie I would see that afternoon, or which play I would enjoy that evening. My free time was glorious, but the work began to be wearing and routine.

I had a light voice, so I wasn't given the "heavy" stuff to read. If someone of importance died, I didn't read that bulletin; instead, they got someone with a much deeper, more serious voice to deliver the ominous news in an appropriate tone. I was sent one day to the BBC's Overseas Service. Announcers would take summer breaks and so the Overseas Service would draw temporary replacements to fill in from those of us in the European Service.

Temporarily broadcasting for the Overseas Service, I got a fan letter as a fill-in announcer. A very nice person in Australia wrote, "We enjoyed the warmth of the announcer on this certain date. He was natural and relaxed." The managers traced the schedule for that date and discovered that I had been the announcer this listener had enjoyed hearing in Australia. Eight or nine weeks later, I received this nice fan letter, so I thought, "Well, I must be doing something right."

Then the BBC's Home Service borrowed me twice. I got a call asking if someone from the European Service could come over and announce an American singer. They were recording a fifteen-minute program. Once it was taped, the BBC would decide where it fit into their programming. It was no big deal to the BBC, but the singer turned out to be Dorothy Dandridge, who was not well-known at that time.

I was knocked out by her beauty and her talent and practically frothed at the mouth after the program when I told her I was convinced she was going to be a big star. Three years later she was, in *Carmen Jones*, which I still watch at least four times a year because she was that terrific. Sadly, though, that was the high point of her film career. It was still almost impossible for a young black artist to get ahead in those days, and she also chose unwisely with her marriages. I ran into her again a few years later and reminded her that I had told her she would be a big star. She smiled sadly and said, "Well, honey, you were right. Only it didn't last long, did it?"

During my little interludes away from the European Service, I was allowed to write my own introductions. I began to enjoy writing as I had done for my introductions on my Radio Malaya music program. That furthered my ambition beyond the European Service after I left the momentary glitz of celebrity and went back to my routine of reading the news.

In 1951, the BBC Home Service launched a popular comedy program called *The Goon Show*. Created by Spike Milligan, the show also starred Peter Sellers and garnered a huge rating every week. The performers were extraordinarily gifted and funny. The show featured a regular announcer, Andrew Timothy, who was almost a regular part of the Goons in that he had a great sense of humor. The performers made jokes about him and then he joked back to them.

When Andrew Timothy went on his summer vacation, the producers came to the European Service looking for a replacement. The opportunity to go to the Home Service was so appealing that several of us news readers auditioned. Wallace Greenslade competed with me. A portly man, he was very jolly and had a great outgoing personality, whereas mine was not. I couldn't force myself to be something I wasn't, so Wallace won the part.

After a few weeks, he did so well as the announcer for the Goons that Peter Sellers and the rest of the cast loved him enough that Wallace never returned to us as a news reader. He came to see the rest of us from time to time. Very social, he walked into the green room where the news readers sat between shifts and told us what a wonderful time he was having on *The Goon Show*. I thought, "Oh, God, I *must* get on something fun like that."

By then, the boredom of just sitting and reading the news each day for the European Service meant that I wanted more. Even though I enjoyed my life away from the BBC in London, my longing to communicate more than just the news eventually got to me. I came to know Hanns J. Friedrichs, a member of the BBC's German Service. Hanns spoke good English. His father had been a mayor of a town in southern Germany and was imprisoned by the Nazis for his opposition to their regime. Hanns was drafted and had to route march for Germany just as I had done for England, but his heart wasn't in it. We hit it off immediately. He had a great sense of humor, always calling me "Frankham."

We both loved jazz, so through the BBC's German Service, we were given permission to create and write a weekly jazz program called *Good Mood*, or *Gut Aufgelegt*, in German. Each Sunday night we broadcast a half-hour jazz program to West Germany, with me in the control booth manning the boards and putting on records. Hanns delivered the introduction and narration, and then at the end of the program, we each had our names credited.

A dashing Errol Flynn kind of guy, Hanns was fun to be around. He loved the ladies and they loved him. Some of the secretaries would see us sitting in the commissary as we worked on our jazz script. They would walk by and drool over Hanns. When he went away, here they came, saying, "Would you tell him that Dorothy called?" Later he would say that he was through with Dorothy or so on in a sort of charming way.

I thought he was terrific and fun, although he had an enormous lack of confidence about working in Britain. He would always say half-jokingly, "Oh, I'm just a poor German and everyone thinks I was a Nazi." No one really did, because everyone had to be cleared to join the BBC. Often he sat opposite me while I did the news in English and then he read the script in German. He was a jobbing announcer like me. Hanns was a great influence and friend. Like me, he wanted to do more with his creative impulses and talent. He later became one of West Germany's most beloved broadcasters when he transitioned to television as the German equivalent of Walter Cronkite.

I also began writing a jazz program for the BBC's Finnish department in Bush House. Finland loved Dixieland, which was not really one of my favorite styles, but I enjoyed working on the program because it gave me something creative to do. I wanted to be more involved with music, and I knew that I could not do much of that if I remained with the European Service.

I started looking on the bulletin board, which was supplied to all the BBC's regions. If there was a vacancy in any of the regions, the Midland Region, Scotland or Ireland, the vacancy was published on all the bulletin boards. Anybody could apply to transfer if they felt like it, and I felt like it. I asked the Midland Home Service in Birmingham if they had any vacancies coming up, and I was told that they would. A short time later, the chief announcer from Birmingham traveled down to London to interview the candidates.

The interviewer asked me, "What's your reason for wanting to leave London for Birmingham?" I told him, "All I'm doing is reading the news. I know it's a wonderful job, but I would love to be involved with orchestras and just more to do than I have in the European Service."

With that, I got the job. Wonderfully, the transition happened just as easily as that.

Birmingham was the "second city," a stately area with a marvelous symphony orchestra of great prestige. The city was home to great libraries and halls of education, while the other half was strictly industrial with blue collar workers employed in different trades. Listening to some of them, I thought, "Oh, God, what have I done?" thinking that I would have to adopt their regional accent in order to talk like that on the BBC.

My accent, though, was fine and got me through yet again. Nobody thought I was too posh or talking down to them, but I did not know a soul. At first, I was just reading the news, missing all my friends such as Hanns Friedrichs, missing passes to theatre, movies, London, Hyde Park, and everything that I had loved and left behind after working there three years. It was gone by my choice.

Gradually, I got to know the secretaries, Gillian Renton and Rita Arnold, and the two other announcers quite well. Initially, I read the news. Instead of learning names of foreign towns, now I had to learn all the towns in the Midlands, which extended from Oxford up to Nottingham. I was strictly studio-bound. This work was my life now, and I had asked for it.

Then my bosses tried me out for the Midland Light Orchestra, a very fine orchestra. My work took on a worthwhile meaning as I started introducing lighter music such as Leroy Anderson or Tchaikovsky. We broadcast from a huge studio called the Vestry Hall with wonderful sound and ambience. At work I looked in the bin to see my next day's assignment. I frequently found that I was repeatedly assigned to introduce the orchestra.

My light voice seemed to go well with the lighter music. I was never trusted with the City of Birmingham Symphony Orchestra because they played "heavier" fare such as Mahler, Beethoven or Bach. The BBC used announcers with deeper voices to announce such serious music. Well-suited for lighter music, I built a rapport with the Midland Light Orchestra, which was situated at one end of a long studio while I sat at a desk with a microphone at the other side without an audience. The

orchestra always rehearsed a couple of hours before I got there to introduce them over the air.

I wrote light-hearted introductions to be delivered live. The work
required me to be really on form. My mother used to do her ironings on
Tuesdays. I was actually on the air from one to two p.m. on Tuesdays, so
she began to time her ironings with the Midland Light Orchestra. That

In Birmingham, I eventually produced my own weekly BBC series.

pleased her, because by then, my dad was in the city working with his own business, having left the Navy. It was nice knowing that my mother was listening, even though I couldn't mention that on the air.

The BBC would occasionally invite a small, live audience of about forty people to sit in and listen to the broadcast, especially for *Children's Hour*. I loved those broadcasts with their simple melodies and childish rhymes.

With my friend, BBC secretary Kay Beardmore in Birmingham, 1950.

I was completely at ease with the music. The only part I never really liked about an audience coming in was when I was told to warm up these in-person listeners. That act required me to be *me* again, instead of a faceless person over the air. I hated doing that. I wasn't good at greeting a crowd by saying, "I'm so pleased you're here, and I do hope you enjoy the show."

My mother and father came up for the weekend to Birmingham one time to hear a Saturday evening show with the orchestra. My parents were proud of the work I was doing. My father sat with his chest puffed up, proud of his son announcing the orchestra. My parents' presence seemed to make me more nervous somehow, so I didn't really make eye contact with them. I just looked over their heads and stumbled back to my seat once the red light had gone on, but it was a nice feeling to know that they were proud of my work.

I began to be glad that I had left London. In fact, I built up confidence, so much so that the BBC started to send me out of the studio to work around the region for brass bands. I had always been snobbish about brass bands, thinking they served little purpose, but I discovered that they had their own very high standards with brilliant instrumentalists. They were very serious about their performances, which were all taped and subsequently broadcast.

Once I realized that I respected their work, I grew more confident and began to make little jokes during my introductions. Once in a while, the otherwise very serious brass band musicians would break up at my humor. At first I thought that I would be fired, but my bosses liked what I was doing. "That's okay," they told me. "You're lightening up the reputation of these rather straight-laced brass bands."

I delighted in getting out and about in the area. In fact, the BBC gave me first class fare to travel on the trains. I used the first class ticket the first time around, but then I noticed that there was nobody else in any first class compartment going up to Nottingham. Cleverly thinking, I got my next voucher, took it to the ticket office, traded it in for a third class ticket and kept the difference as cash for myself. I had started a little business on the side for myself that way.

My career took a major turn one day completely in the opposite direc-tion. I was sitting in the announcers' little green room with nothing to do that particular afternoon. Another producer, Peter Cairns, whom I had not met before, was responsible for interview programs. He came in and said, "Hey, what do you know about Eve Boswell?"

Being a fan of pop music, I knew that she was a singer in a band led by Geraldo, whose real name was Gerald Bright. His music was very popular and similar to Glenn Miller's music. Eve Boswell had left the band to go solo. She released some recordings on Columbia, so I knew her work as a music fan.

Peter said, "Well, tell me all you can about her, because she's sitting in Studio Four and I've got to interview her."

I said, "Well, okay, she's from South Africa, and this is her new recording that's doing very well on the charts."

He said, "Come with me and feed me this information on our way to the studio so when we get there, she'll think I know what I'm talking about."

Peter and I walked in to find Boswell sitting at the microphone. He said to her, "So sorry to be late, Miss Boswell. I'm Peter Cairns, and I'm producing the series. This is my colleague, David Frankham, and he's going to be interviewing you."

I was floored at this news. He hadn't said a word about me conducting the interview! We had walked down two floors with me yakking away about Eve Boswell's work on the way to the studio. What could I do? I couldn't very well embarrass or contradict him in front of Boswell, so I had no choice but to go along with this announcement. Peter walked into the control room and said that he would give us a few minutes to prepare as he dialed up the balances on the microphone. With no notes, I sat there with this charming lady. I had nothing prepared whatsoever as I glared at Peter through the glass. Peter said, "Okay, let's do it."

We began taping a seven-minute take, a lot of time to talk. Fortunately, she was a professional. I was learning that when you interview a celebrity, unless you really screwed up, you would usually be fine, because a professional knows how to fill in a pause. Celebrities are used to promoting themselves all the time. Boswell and I both seemed to do well together. Peter walked back in and thanked her for coming in as our celebrity guest for that week. We walked her to her BBC limousine provided by the network to take her back to her hotel.

As we strolled back to the studio, I said to Peter, "That wasn't too bad, was it?" He said, "Come with me. I'll show you what you did wrong."

We went back to the booth to listen to the acetate discs that we had recorded. "It's all right, and we can put it on the air," he assured me. "But don't keep saying 'May I ask you this?' Just ask it! And stop saying, 'I see, I see.' Nobody gives a damn whether you see or not."

He edited and trimmed the "fat" from the interview. Gone were all of those time-eating phrases that I had unknowingly inserted during my part of our impromptu interview. Peter told me that he was going to be critical to be helpful. I was incredulous that my first solo effort at interviewing went out over the air! I remember saying, "You can't broadcast that!" but the BBC did just that. I was told it was good enough by professional standards to air.

I thought the recording would be what the BBC called a "one-off," meaning that it was a one-time deal and would never happen again. I thanked him for the opportunity and experience. A week later, Peter called from a different department. He said, "I'm going out to a theatre to interview a funny man, the British equivalent of Spike Jones, at the Coventry Theatre. I thought you'd like to come along and see how I record these on location, because it's not the same as sitting at a studio."

Backstage at the theatre, Billy Cotton joined us, and once again Peter said, "This is my colleague, David Frankham, and he's going to do the interview!"

Realizing my surprise at being caught off guard twice in a row, Peter later told me, "David, I felt that you ought to do these interviews, but if I had told you in advance, you would have panicked." I probably would have. He had sensed that the less I knew about something ahead of time, the better.

Every member of Billy Cotton's orchestra was a fine musician and a comedian. Peter handed me the mike and told me that we were recording, and all the musicians came in and said funny things during our interview. There were about six of them standing around me, throwing straight lines at me. I don't know how I got through the interview, but I rose to the occasion. I started laughing when they started laughing. We recorded about ten minutes, which I knew was way too long. As we talked and laughed, I knew that we would have to edit the material.

Toward the end, it was almost like how I imagine it would be to fly on a glider. You briefly think that you might crash, but then you realize that you're gliding and not going to crash after all. I even realized that I wasn't doing too badly. The adrenaline had kicked in, and so did the interview. My whole pattern, professionally, was to throw myself in the deep end to see if I could swim. It was exhilarating!

Going back to the studio, Peter said, "You didn't keep saying, 'I see, I see.'" He never praised me, but if he said, "That's fine," then it meant that my work was really good.

Peter told me that I could be interviewing full time. I didn't see how as a news reader, but he told me that he could get me transferred if I was interested. The BBC in Birmingham was opening up television, and he was head hunting for a radio replacement so he could leave and transition into television. He was looking through different departments for somebody who could take over his job as producer, writer and interviewer on his weekly show called *What Goes On*.

A change in scenery interested me, so Peter told me, "I think you'll do as my replacement." He recommended me to his boss, who recommended me in turn to the head boss at BBC Birmingham. He agreed to give me a try. I was to transfer from news reading. With a thirty-minute program to fill up every week, I no longer had to read the news. My responsibility increased, however, because it was now my duty to find a celebrity to appear each week during the last ten minutes of the program. I also had to find other interesting people by reading the *Birmingham Post* in the morning or finding contacts from around the region to recommend others to talk to as prospective guests. The pressure was on to see if I could succeed as an on air personality!

Producing *What Goes On* involved a degree of organizing to make sure that everything ran smoothly. I found that to be successful, one must be organized — be prepared and be on time — so even my producing gave me useful insights.

When I took over the program, listeners could almost anticipate the music between each interview because the show used the same things every week. I tried to do a little bit of razzle dazzle to revamp the format. I picked out commercial recordings of instrumental tunes, and those selections did seem to perk up the program. The BBC griped, because it meant that they had to pay a royalty any time the music played, but they let me get away with it because it spruced up the program.

There were a few perks with being on the BBC. I had a secretary, Gillian Renton, to field phone calls. If I was feeling tired at the end of the day, she would sit right beside me saying on the phone, "Mr. Frankham is not available right now; may I take a message?" I would whisper in her ear: "Who is it? Do I want to talk to them or not?" Gillian was wonderful. She really spoiled me.

Movie theatre managers were only too pleased to make their weekly releases available to media professionals who might mention or write about them. This perk also made me a great hit socially; the secretarial pool at the BBC was mine to choose from whenever I wanted a date for an evening at the movies! My main motivation was the fact that I was determined one day to be involved in the movie business. I saw a movie almost every night of the week and was automatically invited to press showings as a BBC representative.

Typically at the BBC, the on-air personalities socialized with each other and not with the technicians or other employees. I found that arrangement to be a great bore and didn't care to sit at a bar with the other hosts or producers. So on Saturday nights, I invited all the technicians over to my flat. Gillian always helped me host these parties, and the get-togethers always proved to be great fun.

I sometimes grumbled under my breath at my first pay checks, considering the varied work I was doing for the BBC — writing, producing, and interviewing. Starting out, I faced a common frustration among young reporters. I would say, "God, do I really have to cover another flower show or interview somebody about his blasted prize canary?"

One assignment led me to put together a documentary about race car driving, which I was not remotely interested in, but it was an assignment. I knew nothing about cars, but I assembled some racing-style music and numerous sound clips of cars speeding past the microphone. I enjoyed putting it all together, even though it wasn't my favorite subject.

The most touching interview I conducted was at Christmas. The producers wanted a Tiny Tim-type segment for my program, so they told me about a school for blind children in Birmingham. They suggested I go and chat with a few of the kids. If I could spot someone who was at ease with the microphone, I was to ask him what Christmas meant to him.

Once I got there, I was overwhelmed as I had been told that I would be. These kids never really acknowledged they were blind. They were just running about, having a great time, all of them totally sightless. It was like kittens in a store — how was I to choose ONE? Yet one of the children just felt like the right material for me. I said to young Brian, who was about eight, "What are you going to do for Christmas, Brian?"

He said, "Oh, I'm going home to my mum and my family. I've got brothers and sisters. They can see, and they'll lead me up to the Christmas tree and we'll find our gifts. I'll have a lovely time with my family, but I want to come back here to the school because I learn a lot."

Brian was great. By then I had learned to shut up and let the guests do most of the talking. The segment went out on the air that Friday evening. The staff liked the interview very much. To my amazement, the following week the segment was picked up and broadcast in Manchester, Glasgow, Dublin, and the Home Service of the BBC in London.

Everybody broadcast it, even a prestigious daily program called *Woman's Hour*. The show's producers had said, "We want the Frankham interview with Brian." The segment played throughout Christmas week with little Brian talking about the meaning of Christmas to him. My work had a powerful impact on our listeners and me personally.

Sometimes I went reluctantly to many a political gathering with a microphone in one hand and research notes in the other, hoping that nobody would recognize that my real interests lay elsewhere. I got away with it, since I was never hauled over the coals when I got back to the studio. A few of my interviews with non-celebrities were really hard work. While it was easy to sit back and let someone famous do all the talking, I occasionally had to dig during a man-on-the-street interview. When I interviewed a man with a supposedly famous talking bird, I asked him what made the bird famous and he just replied, "Oh, I don't know." Talk about uphill work!

My broadcasting work added up to a learning experience, because I just couldn't say on the air, "Oh well, thank you for that brief chat." I had to keep going and make it interesting and entertaining at the same time. I enjoyed most interviews because many people were thrilled to be talking to somebody from the BBC. Still a monopoly, the BBC claimed enormous prestige. Doors opened to nearly everybody from the BBC. People were thrilled to see the BBC sticker on the microphone and asked when our program would air.

Once I had to go into a tiger's cage for the circus. The performers were happy to talk about the circus to promote it. The lady I interviewed outside the tiger's cage said, "It would be much more interesting to do this chat *inside* the tiger's cage!" There were three little stands with a tiger sitting there. Even though this woman assured me that I was safe, I was terrified to be in there!

I told her, "I'm really scared." The lady replied, "I imagine that it would really please your listeners very much to know that you're frightened!" I never looked at her; instead, I focused on the tiger just lying there quietly. His tail was going, which didn't please *me* too much. I was glad when that interview was over and out of the cage!

Interviewing anyone for the BBC was clumsy in those days. The BBC used modified stretch limousines that we called "recording cars" for our mobile work. There was room for the driver, a passenger, a few seats, and then the rest of the car was turned into a portable recording studio.

We recorded directly to big, sixteen-inch acetate discs, so these portable studios had built-in acetate recorders inside them. When we went to interview someone outside the comfort of our studios, we drove up in this enormous car to the parking lot outside where our interviews were to take place. If the interview was upstairs, we had to tie the microphone to a rope. I went upstairs and lowered the rope. Next we tied the microphone to the rope, embarrassing me when I started to interview more celebrities. The idea of lowering and raising our microphone via a rope seemed rudimentary to me.

When we recorded interviews, the acetate discs were awkward and clumsy because they only ran four minutes. If you were talking animatedly, you suddenly had to stop and apologize while the engineer put on another disc because the discs were one-sided. Eleanor Roosevelt was a

I'm happy because this interview with some zoo owners was moved from the lion's cage to safety.

marvelous interview, but I had to apologize when the discs were being changed. The short time span wasn't good if we were recording someone really good or someone who was thoroughly or enthusiastically talking. I would have to tell the guest, "That was four minutes — we can only record four minutes at a time."

I would wait for the recording engineer, Chris, down in the BBC recording limo, as he took off the acetate disc and put on another. He would tell me he was ready, and then in front of the guest, I would have to say, "Okay, disc two. Ten, nine, eight, seven, six, five, four, three, two, one. You were saying?" It was awful to stop someone mid-sentence when he or she was just dying to get out all the information I was asking them during the interview. It was almost like choking somebody when we had to stop to change discs.

I would go home and wait for my interviews to come on the radio that night, and the next morning at work, before my boss started in on his list of things to improve, I created my own list. It didn't take too long to get me up to standard. The only time I did a really lousy interview was with Ella Fitzgerald, because I completely fell apart sitting opposite her with my microphone. I couldn't believe I was chatting with one of my idols. I never forgot that embarrassing lesson and learned not to become *too* awestruck.

When I took over the *What Goes On* program, the BBC wanted to spice up the show by including celebrity interviews as a segment each week. Although only ten minutes were allotted for celebrities in our thirty-minute program, the BBC felt that the ratings would spike with a little star power. Most actors were only too happy to plug themselves or their product, from a play to a movie, or in the case of singers, their latest records.

After my Ella Fitzgerald experience, I taught myself early on not to be over-awed by the big names that came through Birmingham. Without any real personal power, I was simply a representative of the BBC. With the full backing of the BBC's prestige, I contacted an agent to book a guest. The agent would say "yes" or "no." If they said "yes," I showed up wherever the celebrity happened to be appearing and did my recorded chat and took it back to the studio.

Wanting to make my program a hit with listeners, I worked to secure top name chats whenever a major personality visited Birmingham to perform. Among the first was Betty Hutton when she spent a week doing a show there. One of the biggest stars of the 1940s, she was madcap, screaming and singing, an enormous movie star.

By 1952, things had slowed down at Paramount, where she was under contract. I found out later that she had ticked off so many people there. She was such a perfectionist that she couldn't help it. She was so driven. All she cared about was pleasing the audience. If the people who were doing her hair or putting on her makeup didn't shape up as she did, she screamed and hollered. When she was no longer the box office rage, Paramount eventually cut her contract one day after a good ten-year run.

I learned that her mentor, songwriter Buddy DeSylva, died one day, and Betty was out at the studio the day after. People just stopped talking to her and turned away from her. When she arrived in England, she was touring from the London Palladium to Birmingham, Glasgow, and Manchester.

My bosses all suggested that we try to get her as one of our program's first big celebrities. I hoped that she would agree. Because she was so bombastic, I didn't know what to expect or really what kind of person she was.

Her agent told me that she had contracted the flu while working in Manchester and that she would not be giving any interviews. I was such a fan of hers, though, that on my own, I took the train up to Manchester for her last performance there before she came to Birmingham for a week. I met her husband, and he said, "No, Betty's in bad shape. She's doing the show because she loves the audience, but no interviews."

Betty Hutton was the first big star to appear on my interview program.

He told me they were leaving on the train the next day for Birmingham but thanked me for my interest. Using what I had learned, I arranged to get on the same train. I walked up and down the corridors until I saw where Hutton was sitting with her husband. I beckoned her husband out and said, "I haven't really given up yet. Do you think she might change her mind?"

He said, "I don't know. Why don't you go in and talk to her?"

With my heart pounding, I sat down opposite Betty Hutton. I loved that lady and knew every recording she had done and every song note by note, so I was very nervous. She was dressed in black velvet with a close-fitting hat with sequins on it. The clothes looked terrific though she looked terrible because of her illness.

"Hi," she croaked, as I delivered my spiel and request for an interview.

"Oh honey, I can't talk," she said. "Look, I've got two shows to do, three on Wednesday and Saturday, but thank you anyway."

I told her that I would keep trying, if she didn't mind, just in case she started to feel better.

"Whatever," she nodded.

For five evenings, I sat in her dressing room. She kept her head in an inhaler to try to clear her sinuses and vocal cords for her performance. She was sweating so much that someone stood in the wings to mop her off. Betty was a POW! POW! POW! performer. She had just done *The Greatest Show on Earth*, in which she swung from a trapeze for Cecil B. DeMille. People had said she couldn't pull off such a feat, so she did it to prove them wrong.

For her vaudeville act in England, she was flying out over the audience with no net, every night, for two shows a night, with the flu! I was so impressed at her stamina and resolve that I only adored her more. She was always giving one hundred-fifty percent of herself.

She was extraordinarily kind and patient with me, even though she had a temperature of 102 degrees the entire week that she performed. In the wings, I stood and watched each of her two nightly shows as she would swing on a trapeze and sing all her big hits. She loved every moment of it, in spite of her illness. She performed all of her scheduled appearances. Finally, the night before my show was due to go out, I asked if she thought she might have enough voice to do an interview.

She said, "Gee, Dave, you've been loyal. Let's meet at the hotel tomorrow. I don't know what time I'll get up in the afternoon, but I'll give you a call." My persistence had paid off! The next day, I went to the Midland Hotel earlier than the previous nights. Her room was on the third or fourth floor. The recording car was down in the parking lot with an engineer, Chris, who had to be ready to put the stylus on the acetate disk after he heard me counting to ten on my microphone.

Betty Hutton met me in a terry cloth robe, sweating from the fever. "Okay," she said. "Let's do it!"

She watched as I started extending the rope down to the parking lot. She asked the name of the engineer, grabbed my microphone and called down to him: "Where's the mike, Chris?"

Betty pulled up my microphone. She was extraordinary. I know she was a walking disaster to everyone in Hollywood, but not to me. She wanted it done perfectly. In front of me, she demonstrated the marvelous professionalism that I would come to see in so many entertainers. She transformed herself from this poor, flu-ridden lady with a nasally sinus problem, one who could hardly talk, into the Betty Hutton we all knew.

"Hi, everybody! This is Betty Hutton!" and she just came alive once the recording started. She turned into Betty Hutton before my very eyes. There was practically nothing that I needed to say once she sat down and did this wonderful interview with me. She never stopped talking and even included songs from *Annie Get Your Gun*. As soon as it was over, she slumped back down and staggered off to her room to take a little nap before she did her theatre routine.

It was great for her to do the interview, and it meant so much to me, prestige-wise with the BBC, because they were taking me for granted before that. I was just going along, doing my job just like everyone else, but the powers that be were impressed that I had persisted in getting this interview when she had publicly announced that she would not be giving any interviews that week because she was not feeling well. It was the only time the BBC ever gave me credit in a memo that read, "Frankham used unusual initiative in securing the services of Miss Betty Hutton at a time when she was not talking to anybody in the press."

My show went out on Friday night. I went to both of her performances on Saturday. When she finished, I went back to the hotel with her. As she walked up the stairs, I told her that I was going to miss seeing her after spending so much time together.

"I want to hear from you!" she said.

"Okay," I said. "I'll write."

"I don't mean THAT," she replied. "I mean by reputation, okay?" And then she ran up the stairs. I lived on cloud nine from that interview, a far cry from my start with Eve Boswell. Betty Hutton was a big movie star.

Aside from show business royalty, there was true royalty as well. I was presented to a young Queen Elizabeth, but the meeting was not quite as glamorous. She had only been the monarch for about a year then. She and her husband attended some festivities at Bristol Cathedral. The BBC sent me from Birmingham, along with other BBC correspondents from London and Manchester.

The three of us were to do very quiet, running commentaries as the ceremony progressed. We were told that the Queen always likes to know who is muttering away within eye line of her, so she had to see who we were. That would be the only presentation, we were told.

We were also warned, "Don't speak unless you're spoken to, and address her as 'Ma'am,' not as 'Your Majesty.'" We were all primed to do just that, but she didn't speak to us at all. She was charming and looked lovely, with a wonderful complexion. Her hair at that point was quite natural and not the permanent style that she used in later years to keep it in place.

I was interested in meeting theatrical performers, because growing up in Kent, I had never seen a live play. The Royal Shakespeare Company at Stratford-upon-Avon was very adept at promoting itself. I found that it was usually easy to secure an interview from one of the Stratford per-formers. All I had to do was to call and ask for Laurence Olivier, Michael Redgrave or Laurence Harvey.

John Goodwin, head of the publicity, would just tell the performers, "Well, the BBC wants to interview you, so if you're not onstage tonight, you'd better come in and do the interview," and they almost always did!

Strangely, though, I would visit and watch theatrical performances and not be that interested in their techniques, or the stage, for that matter. I was more interested in film performers or singers. Besides, a visit to the Royal Shakespeare Company was technically embarrassing, because we had to pull our microphones through the PR man's window and then stop recording every four minutes.

Sometimes I travelled to Nottingham for interviews. Once there was a young singer who was not yet known that well. The then largely unknown Petula Clark was only sixteen or so, about to go on to fame and fortune. It was a strange interview, because I kept asking her questions, only her father kept answering them for her. I thought to myself, "She's going nowhere, poor soul." Little did I know!

Abbott and Costello once toured through Birmingham, so I interviewed them. They liked each other so much. I usually inter-

Abbott and Costello turned our interview into a comedy routine.

viewed people in their dressing rooms or in the BBC studio, but they wanted to record on stage, not with an audience, but between a matinee and the evening show. The nucleus of one of their audience skits was to bring up a member in a barber chair, lather him and do their "Who's on first?" routine as they "shaved" the audience member with a rubber razor. Because they wanted to do our interview on stage, I showed up with a portable tape recorder. To my surprise, they sat me on stage!

As Lou Costello lathered me up, I protested, "This is radio!" But the routine actually sounded good while the comic duo did their whole cross talk act with me being lathered up as part of our conversation. By then, I was skilled enough to go along with a mouthful of lather. We had a wonderful time even if we lost half of the interview's impact because the audience couldn't see it.

Abbott and Costello were so solicitous of each other. One asked the other if he was okay. Bud Abbott was always the straight guy in their skits, but he was a very sensitive man. So was Lou Costello, for that matter. They seemed to be more than the country bumpkins they had often played in their movies. They were total professionals, very warm, and that was a great highlight for me.

Another time I was on stage with the great star of the West End, Dame Edith Evans. I had seen her movie with Michael Redgrave, *The Importance of Being Earnest*, with her famous line that just rings down through the decades: "A handbag?"

She was appearing in a play written by Jean Anouilh. Doing my pre-interview research, I was put off a little because I knew very little about the show. I was in awe, because though I had never seen Evans onstage, I had seen her act in a couple of movies. She was a great actress and a very commanding presence in film. Imagine my surprise when she was not that way in life at all. After a matinee performance, she said, "Can we just sit on the set? I'm comfortable here and I'm not very good at interviewing."

Sitting in a chair on the stage at the Alexandra Theatre, Evans didn't want to talk about the play at all. She told me that she found touring to be a lonely experience. "I miss my friends," she told me, "but Dame Sybil Thorndike writes to me almost every day, and in fact, here's what she wrote yesterday."

With that, she took out a letter and proceeded to share Dame Sybil's opinions on the price of food and London! This was completely a different side of Dame Edith. Because she always played grand ladies, I thought she would have people at her command. She was just a lonely lady on tour in a play. It was very touching. We never once had to talk about the play, which was nice, because I really knew very little about it!

I never lost sight of the fact that I was, at heart, an actor, even before I became one. A parade of entertainers appeared on *What Goes On* for interviews, most good and encouraging of my personal interest in show business. At one point I asked if I could do a thirty-minute program with all entertainment industry content.

The BBC agreed to give me a shot with a monthly program to focus on the Midlands. Because London occupied much of the nation's entertainment focus, my bosses were insistent that I concentrate on the Birmingham area. I learned to get around that rule, though, because if a movie premiered in London with Doris Day or Howard Keel, those stars wouldn't come to Birmingham, so I would have to go to them. During the interview, though, I would acknowledge my home turf by saying, "Your film is playing in Birmingham, of course."

I wanted a show business theme song for my program. *The Band Wagon* had opened in 1953 in Birmingham. I used the film's song, "That's Entertainment," as my theme years before MGM used it as a title for its film musical compilation series. I'm very proud of that decision. The lively song really got the program off to a great start.

Shelley Winters appeared on my show when she was in England to film *I Am a Camera* with Laurence Harvey and Julie Harris. What a day. She was dubbing dialogue for the end of the picture. "Come on, honey!" she chirped, so I sat and watched her dub, which was fascinating to me because I had never seen that done before.

We began the interview in the dubbing studio, went right on talking when the limousine took her to lunch at a nearby pub, and downed Lord knows how many beers as we ate pork pie and fries

Shelley Winters was non-stop fun.

and went right on talking through several vodkas on the rocks. She was salty and funny. Winters was encased in an enormous mink coat, which she slung on the back of her chair as the vodka did its warming thing. The mink fell off her chair three times, and the third time she hollered, "Oh, the hell with it — let it lie there!" I was agog — a real Hollywood star, knocking back the booze with a mink coat under her feet!

She was full of anecdotes and filling me in on things about her career. She recounted her great love affair with Farley Granger. I had asked during the interview, "Will you two be marrying?" and she replied, "Well, you never know how it goes in show business." But during the lunch, she said about him, "He's not the marrying kind!" I didn't get what she meant until later. She also told me how exciting it was to film *A Double Life* with Ronald Colman. In her opinion, that movie was the one that sold her to audiences.

It was a chilly English winter, and we left the pub with Winters still chattering away non-stop. She dragged her mink coat through the wet street to the car, and we continued on and on until we had nothing left to say. She was terrific. I had such a headache that evening, but what an interview!

Another interesting interview happened when Sir Ralph Richardson pulled up to the recording session on a motorcycle. He looked just like a character from the movies with his motorcycle gear. His press agent had told me that he wasn't working that week, but that he was probably off somewhere on his motorbike. He loved driving it into the country. Richardson was a little strange but charming and kind. He was as eccentric as the characters he played. He was playing Prospero in *The Tempest*, and he was wonderful in it. I spent the afternoon doing the interview, and then he zoomed away on his motorbike. He was very jovial, relaxed, and funny.

Michael Redgrave, meanwhile, was extremely nervous when I interviewed him. I think he was just intensely shy by nature. I could tell the poor man would have rather been in the dentist's office. I don't think I was asking bad questions, because he just fidgeted and scratched his face a lot. He did a good interview, even though he mumbled. I realized then that a great actor could be painfully shy. I put him out of his misery when we finished, because he said, "Thank you so much," and practically ran out of the office!

That night, he was onstage with Dame Peggy Ashcroft in *Antony and Cleopatra*. Earlier in the day, I was sitting with Redgrave, this nervous, schoolmaster-type actor, and that night, I couldn't believe my eyes. He came out in a breastplate, ballsy, and almost shook the roof to the theatre. He was an incredible actor, very gifted, but a painfully shy human being.

I once chatted with Laurence Harvey. He had just come back from Hollywood. Because I was daydreaming so much about film acting, I thought, "The more I know about the technical side of filming, the better." I really didn't know anything about Harvey; I had gone to see his Romeo. He was very good, larger than life, and very grand. Because Harvey had just finished *King Richard and the Crusaders* with Rex Harrison, I asked him, "Did you find it challenging to work in CinemaScope?"

What a mistake on my part. I should have asked that question before or after we recorded, because he proceeded to deliver a monologue and speak, without interruption, for twenty-two minutes on the subject of CinemaScope, none of which I wanted in my interview. The first few minutes were kind of interesting, but after three or four minutes, I realized it was time to move on to another question, but I couldn't get him to stop! Imagine how depressed I was at having a lecture on a technical subject, when all I really wanted was his viewpoint about working in Hollywood!

When we got the recording back to the studio, we timed it. He had talked twenty-two minutes about the challenge of working in CinemaScope! The guys in the editing room trimmed it down to four minutes about CinemaScope, and even that was borderline boring. In defense of Laurence Harvey, though, he was very charming and even invited me for tea after our interview concluded.

A year before I had Rosemary Clooney on my show, her husband, Academy Award winner José Ferrer, was a guest. I had gone to Clooney's hotel by pre-arrangement to tape a conversation. Her husband just walked in and said abruptly, "My wife has the flu, so I'm pinch-hitting; what do you want to know?" Actually, I didn't want to know anything about him and was very disappointed that Rosemary was languishing floors above us.

Without asking my permission, Ferrer recited the entire Lord's Prayer from his movie with Rita Hayworth, *Miss Sadie Thompson*. He had played a preacher and wanted to demonstrate what he had learned; unfortunately for me, you could actually feel the show grinding to a halt. I had no choice but to be gracious about it and let him do his Twenty-third Psalm. Luckily for my listeners, the interview was taped, so Ferrer's self-indulgence didn't make it to air time; I played one of Rita Hayworth's numbers instead!

Then there were the performers for whom I shared a great personal affection. Interviewing them could be a thrill if I was mad about their work. When I met Dinah Shore, I was charmed off my feet by her southern Tennessee persona.

Burl Ives appeared on my show before he won great acclaim in *Cat on a Hot Tin Roof* or before he played a number of famously vicious characters in the movies. He had a huge following as a troubadour folk singer, so he and his teenage son were on a tour of England. He did a very fine show with all of his hits such as "Blue Tail Fly."

We went back to his dressing room to do the interview and he exclaimed, "I'm hungry! Let's send out for fish and chips." Somebody rushed off and came back with fish and chips in the traditional newspaper. He, his son, and I sat and ate fish and chips while we talked. He was a charming man.

Meeting the acclaimed actress Gladys Cooper was also a highlight of my interview sessions. After all, she and Laird Cregar had first inspired me to think more about acting. She was legendary for finding fame as a pin-up girl in World War I. Working as the only actress-manager with her own company in London, she had produced postcards of herself to send to the troops on the front, long before Betty Grable. These lovesick troops clamored for her, because she was a stunning beauty.

Cooper became a brilliant actress. I had seen so many of her films, including *Rebecca, Song of Bernadette,* and *The Bishop's Wife.* When I booked her as a guest on my radio show, I took her a bunch of roses. We weren't going to tape our interview until Friday, so I would go backstage each night to see her and Wendy Hiller in a play that was on a pre-West End tour through the UK.

We arranged to do the interview on a Thursday, the day before my program aired. I took her red roses for five days leading up to our interview. Each night there were roses for a film, the first being *Now, Voyager.* I quickly saw that she was so full of gusto. She wasn't looking back or wishing that she was still young. She was full of enthusiasm and loved that I brought her the flowers.

The next night, I brought her flowers for *Song of Bernadette,* in which she played a very mean nun. On Wednesday, I brought her roses for *The Pirate,* in which she played the dotty aunt of Judy Garland. And on Thursday night, I brought the fourth bunch for *The Bishop's Wife.* By then, we were just having a wonderful time. It was almost as though we had already done the recording. When I finally interviewed her, I asked her, "How do you create what you do?" She replied, "Well, my dear, one simply just goes on and one *is,* and that's all." She didn't know herself how she created the magic of all those movie performances.

Meeting and interviewing Dirk Bogarde was also a privilege. As far back as 1948, I had seen his movies and become aware that he was developing into a huge star. I never wrote fan letters, but I had written one to him after seeing one of his early movies. I thought, "He is really good." He did not have the bland, post-war, pretty boy, glossy 8x10 look that the Rank Organisation was promoting at that time. There were exceptions to the rule, such as character actor Richard Attenborough, but Dirk was good-looking yet not overwhelmingly pretty. To be fair, the Rank Organisation was turning out contract players such as Donald Sinden, who did become a fine actor, but when I saw Dirk, I thought that this was a guy who looked different.

I sat down and wrote him a letter, telling him that I admired his acting, that he wasn't the usual run-of-the-mill actor in his films, and that I wished him luck in his career. To my astonishment, back came a handwritten letter from him, thanking me for my encouragement and with an observation that he was doing the best he could. I thought, "Gosh, well then, he really is a human being."

When one of Dirk's movies opened countrywide, I asked my bosses about having him as a guest and got their approval. I contacted his agent, who told me that Dirk would be happy to appear on my program but that I would have to interview him at his home in Buckinghamshire. Dirk didn't like going to studios, nor did he like the BBC. He hated the BBC because the organization was so "cheap," in his opinion.

I had to then get my bosses' approval to travel to interview Dirk, because I really wasn't supposed to leave the Midlands to work. I had broken the rule a few times to travel to London to interview performers who were not coming to Birmingham or through the Midlands. So it was arranged that I would go down to London and get a customized BBC recording car. Off we drove to Dirk's residence. I had imagined it as a cozy cottage, but the Rank people had pumped him so highly into a matinee idol that he had a country estate, complete with hounds jumping around all over the place. The estate was very grand-looking, because as he told me later, he had to keep up the public image for the fans.

Dirk Bogarde became a long-time friend.

I went in, and he greeted me at the door. When I didn't see a butler, maid or housekeeper waiting to check if the lord of the manor might speak to me, I took that as a positive sign of potential hospitality. Dirk led me into his very stately house with statues all over the place and a cozy den with a roaring fire. His manager, Tony Forwood, was there, and as I learned, he was always watching over Dirk as his agent, manager, and companion.

We sat down to talk. I never usually went over what I intended to ask, but then I was exposed to the Bogarde sense of humor without being prepared for it. We got going and talked about his movie *Appointment in London*. We were chatting away and I said, "I understand you like to do painting." He said, "You mean houses, or people, or what?" and really put me on the spot with his answer. I had to realize, quickly on my feet, that he had a very sharp wit and that I would have to pull myself together and stay with him. We had a good interview, though, very funny, and I enjoyed it.

At the end of the recording, Dirk said, "I have to say, when I saw you driving up in the BBC limousine, I thought to myself, 'Good God, is royalty coming?'" He put down pomposity, and I remember appreciating that as we talked. I thought, "Here is somebody who is real, and there's nothing phony about Dirk Bogarde."

We covered about eight minutes over two discs, stopping to change from the first to second disc. He said, "My God, can't the BBC afford to do one whole interview in one piece without having to stop and change records?" He was outspoken, and I liked him for it.

When I had to hand him the BBC's standard fee — five pounds and five shillings — the same for all guests who appeared on our program, he was extremely amused. I should note that regardless of the stature of anyone appearing on my show, celebrity or ordinary man on the street, the BBC had a stupid practice that required us to give the guest a check for participating. I always had to hand celebrities their check for appearing on the show but was told by my bosses, "Don't give it to them until the end of the interview." How insulting can you get? It was like giving a waiter a gratuity at the end of a meal.

The standard fee for our guests was five guineas, or five pounds and five shillings, which was a pittance. I always had to explain to the stars, from my own sense of guilt, that the money was simply a token, an expression of appreciation for their interview. My bosses pointed out, "Look, we don't care what they're making in Hollywood; they're essentially promoting their own work and they should be paying the BBC!"

Interestingly, the American stars really didn't care. They had no idea what five guineas meant anyway, but the British actors, whether they were Hollywood based or in the UK, always commented on how cheap the BBC was. Even David Niven, who hadn't lived in England for a long time, said, "I see the BBC guys are up to their usual tricks with practically nothing for the work I'm doing for them right now." Most actors had a very cynical attitude toward the BBC and their financial arrangements, Dirk Bogarde in particular.

One guest that I didn't particularly care for was David Niven. I found him pompous and stuck up. I went to London for him. He was making a film in England with Margaret Leighton about an army trial called *Carrington V.C.* I had seen his movies and knew that he was a light comedy actor. I'd gone with anticipation, because he sounded like a charmer. He wasn't. He was deadly serious and quite condescending. I interviewed him on the courtroom set of the movie.

Where I successfully paid homage to idols such as Gladys Cooper or Dirk Bogarde, I failed with others. I expected that performers would behave off stage the same as they did when they were onstage, especially the musical performers. I found out that I was wrong. I had grown up as a fan of Frank Sinatra's back in the 1940s, and I was still such a fan that I asked to have him on my radio show.

Unbeknownst to us in England, he had been recently fired from Columbia Records and had signed a big contract with Capitol. He had also finished *From Here to Eternity* and was about to win the Academy Award for Best Supporting Actor. We didn't know that in England, though, so all I knew was that he had been fired from Columbia. I was thinking I would be supportive of his waning career, not realizing that Sinatra was about to resurrect and create an even more legendary one.

He had traveled to London to appear at the Palladium, then on to Birmingham, and then to Glasgow and Dublin. I was even more convinced that his career needed publicity because he was only filling one hundred seats or so in theatres that had sold two thousand tickets for Betty Hutton. I went to every one of his shows that week and was impressed with his singing, even though Sinatra seemed to know that he was transitioning to a new stage in his life. Each night he strolled out onto the stage with a cup of tea and asked the musicians, "Okay, fellows, what are we going to do tonight?" Then he half-heartedly sang, impressing me, nonetheless.

It occurred to me that I could help him if I devoted a whole show to Sinatra. I contacted his agent, who told me, "Well, we don't know with Frank. You'll have to contact him personally."

I was excited at that idea. He was staying at the Midland Hotel. I called the theatre first and was told that he had an early dinner at the hotel. I went over and found him in the restaurant. When the maître d' came out, I told him that I was from the BBC. I requested that he ask Sinatra if it would be convenient for me to go in and chat with him. He went over to Sinatra and said something. Sinatra listened and stood up.

I thought, "Oh, he's coming out to talk to me!"

I did not realize the significance of the fact that he carried his napkin in his hand. He was silently telling me that I had made the big mistake of interrupting him during his pre-show dinner. The maître d' brought him out to the lobby — Sinatra was still wiping his mouth with his dinner napkin as he made eye contact with me — and I did my spiel about wanting him as a guest.

"I'm a huge admirer of your music and want to devote my entire program to you on Friday night," I told him. "You pick out whatever you love best about recording for Columbia, and we'll do the show."

Looking down at the marble floor and without making any more eye contact, Sinatra heard me out in the hotel lobby.

He said, "You know, I'm under contract to the BBC dance band."

When Sinatra declined an interview, you never forgot it.

I said, "Oh, this wouldn't be live, Mr. Sinatra. This would be your favorite recordings and some of mine..." and I began to feel that I was just running out of momentum.

Sinatra took one more look at me and then just said, "F#%* off," turned, and went back into the restaurant and sat down at his table. I stood there dumbfounded and crushed as though the entire building had just collapsed on my head.

I thought, "You can't say that to me — I'm with the BBC! — and I love your music!" I was absolutely devastated. Nobody had ever turned down anybody from the BBC before!

In hindsight, I can't help but admire him. He didn't need me, and he was telling me that in no uncertain terms. Luckily my interaction with Sinatra happened on a Wednesday, so I still had time to get somebody else for Friday's program. But I still played his albums on my show.

Ironically, I didn't learn my lesson with Sinatra, though. He had just separated from Ava Gardner, whom I called a few weeks later when she was visiting London. I delivered my little spiel request for an interview. She said, "Honey, I've been through all this before. I don't really want to do this, but it was so sweet of you to even think about me. Thank you," and she hung up on me. At least she was nicer, though, than her soon-to-be ex-husband!

I also tried for an in-depth, thirty-minute interview with Sir Laurence Olivier and his wife, Vivien Leigh. They were appearing in two plays,

Titus Andronicus and *Macbeth*. I had seen both plays. Because the Royal Shakespeare Company's PR people had told the BBC that we could interview whomever we liked, it was a wonderful feeling to anticipate that I would be sitting down with the prestigious Oliviers.

The week came, and the PR agent told me that the interview would be arranged. He called back and said, "Yes, they'll be very happy to talk with you between the matinee and the evening performance on Thursday." That meant that I would sit through *Titus Andronicus* and chat with "Larry and Viv" and go back to watch them in *Macbeth* later that evening.

I walked in backstage. As I came up to their dressing rooms — Olivier's was next to Leigh's — he came out of her dressing room with her. Leigh was wearing a fur coat. Her silk scarf-covered head rested on his shoulder. I could see tears as I drew closer.

He saw me with my BBC recorder and said, "I'm very sorry, old chap, but my wife is just not feeling well. We'll have to do it another time, if that's alright." I told him that I understood. Later that night, though, when I saw the evening performance, Vivien Leigh was brilliant, an unforgettable Lady Macbeth! She was able to pull herself together. Nobody in the public really knew at that time that she was going through a catastrophic mental breakdown.

Not getting to interview them, though, was a huge disappointment to me. I think I would have been in awe had I sat with them. I was just as in awe of her because of *Gone with the Wind* as I was with Olivier. There were very few times when I was really overwhelmed with a sense of celebrity, but that couple was an exception to the rule.

I had better luck with Sir Richard Attenborough. He was wonderful, always playing cowards or people becoming unstrung. In person Attenborough was awfully nice, just "plain folks." He knew that I had done my homework, as I did for anyone I ever interviewed, with the exception of poor Eve Boswell that first time around! I think actors could sense that, and in the case of singers whose work I closely followed as a fan, preparing to interview them was never really work for me. After our chat, Attenborough signed a photo that said, "For the best interview I have ever had in my career." He may have said that to everybody who interviewed him, but it meant a lot to me!

Actor Ben Lyon had become a big silent star and then worked into the talkies early in the 1930s in such films as *Hell's Angels*, opposite Jean Harlow. His wife, Bebe Daniels, was famous as a star of *42nd Street*. They later moved to England and started a radio show about an American family, called *Life with the Lyons*. Ben wrote all the scripts almost entirely by himself.

When I arrived at the studio to interview the Lyon family, Ben had made a script of our interview, even though I always conducted my interviews impromptu and without any staging. Ben's ability as a scriptwriter was so good that I just read the script as though we had just met. He told me afterwards that our interview was a big success from his point of view. No one seemed to pick up on the fact that we had scripted the entire show.

Life with the Lyons: *Ben Lyon, Bebe Daniels, and their children.*

Both of the Lyon children, Barbara and Richard, played themselves on their family's show. I later took Barbara out for dates on Friday nights after my show had finished. Barbara, though, wanted cabs and practically the red carpet treatment, so when I kept burning through my salary, that was the end of our dates, but I did like her a lot. She later became an actress and recorded a few songs, and her brother also acted.

English singers also appeared on my show. One was Anne Shelton, much loved in the United Kingdom, but she never acquired the international reputation that Vera Lynn enjoyed abroad. She was so good, though, that when Bing Crosby entertained the troops in London in August 1944, he chose Anne to appear with him. She was only sixteen at the time, but she had the rich contralto voice of a mature woman. I loved that down-to-earth, completely unassuming London lass.

There were always eccentric performers to make my job interesting. The singer Johnnie Ray was outrageous to the point that I'm surprised that tabloids didn't write more about his shenanigans. Ray was a big singer, up there with Doris Day, Rosemary Clooney, Jo Stafford, Guy Mitchell, and Frankie Laine. He had a big hit song called "The Little White Cloud That Cried." It was in the post-war days when singers were all the rage, and they all topped the bill at the London Palladium, except Doris Day, who said she was too scared to appear in public like that. Audiences went mad for all of these sensational singers.

Johnnie Ray really rang an audience's chimes. He jumped all over the place and screamed and was a very unusual performer from that era. Now I see him written up as a predecessor to Elvis, but he wasn't really yet singing rock and roll; he was singing popular songs. He was to appear at the Birmingham Hippodrome for a week. His agent agreed to book him as a guest. My clueless bosses didn't even know who he was but trusted me with my choice of guests.

I thought spending a day interviewing with Ray would be a good idea, because it was his birthday, and he had fan clubs all over the world, with several in Birmingham alone. He agreed to a daylong visit to record his activities. We met, and he was very shy, one of those performers who is quiet until they walk on stage and then they just explode. With the tape recorder going, we started with breakfast. He was a little deaf and wore hearing aids. If he took them out for a second, he couldn't seem to hear much of anything. Strangely, he semi-joked at one point that he didn't really need to wear them and suggested that he wore them for publicity, so I wasn't sure if he couldn't really hear or not. He spoke with a bit of a stutter, so it was a little difficult doing the interview, because I had to edit that out later back at the studio.

Then we drove out in the BBC limo to his fan club for his birthday lunch. It was a fascinating day. We went to the house of a little girl who was president of Birmingham's Johnnie Ray Society. She practically fainted away when he walked in, and then she was overawed by the fact that I was following him around with a microphone in my hand. Ray seemed to calm down and lose the stutter when he talked to his fans.

After he cut the birthday cake, I took him into the BBC studio before his evening's shows. I had interviewed people at the studio but he was the first I had interviewed outside and then brought back to the studio. There was a very popular radio soap opera on the air called *The Archers*.

The cast was recording and asked if I would bring Ray into the studio at the end of the day. I brought him in, and all these middle-aged ladies fell apart over this very skinny, stuttering, shy guy who turned into a demon the moment he started singing.

I then stood in the wings for the first of his two evening performances at the theatre and recorded the audience's thunderous ovation. People just screamed and ran up and down the aisles. I never did get that. He was just okay to me, but he was almost like Elvis in the beginning of the rock and roll era.

At the end of the evening, I had switched off the tape recorder. My secretary, Gillian, a sweet, shy lady, joined me, because Ray said, "The band and I are going back to my hotel to have a few drinks. Why don't you join us?"

So Gillian and I joined them all at the hotel. The band was a few drinks ahead of us, and we didn't drink that much. Everyone was happy and high. Ray was very social, going from group to group, thanking the musicians. Gillian and I felt rather square, because the musicians were so hip.

When somebody put on a rock-and-roll type of record, Ray went into his room and came out a few minutes later wearing only a jockstrap, made of the stars and stripes with spangles. Gillian nearly had a fit on the spot. I don't think she had ever seen a man that undressed before. He began to do a kind of rock and roll gyration and paraded nearly naked through his hotel suite.

I was embarrassed, quite honestly. I hadn't been THAT close to show business. Gillian and I both looked at the ceiling and the floor. We really didn't want to be there at that point. Gillian quietly said to me, "David, could we leave?"

So we went up to this jock-strapped person and told him that we had a lovely day and got the hell out of there. We were just too square for that kind of show business. Yet it was an extraordinary day. What a character he was. He later came out as gay, although I don't think it would have been anybody's surprise if he had announced it sooner.

Another popular singer was more pleasant during our interview time together. Frankie Laine was such a dear man. He was married to one of my favorite actresses from the 1930s, Nan Grey. She had appeared in the movie *Three Smart Girls Grow Up*, with Deanna Durbin. Poor Frankie Laine. When he walked in with Nan Grey, my attention was diverted to her. I really should have been focusing on him as my guest.

He was friendly and called me "Dave," as Americans seemed prone to do. Frankie was mesmerizing to fans, even though he was middle-aged, a little portly and wore a toupee. Teenagers ran up and down the aisles for him just as they had done for Johnnie Ray. He had been a marathon walker to win contests. He told me that he supported himself with marathons when he discovered he could sing. Mitch Miller at Mercury Records got him started, moved him over to Columbia, and suddenly it was the big time for him. He recorded with Doris Day and was really a terrific fellow.

When I had Guy Mitchell on my show, my bosses began to grow suspicious. Most of my singer guests were coming from the Columbia label. The BBC was wary of payola scandals where record companies rewarded disc jockeys with money for openly promoting their records on the air. Nothing like that had happened with my Columbia guests, but I had to keep reassuring my bosses that it was sheer coincidence that most of my singer guests came to us from the Columbia label.

Guy Mitchell was short, about five feet, three inches tall, yet he was successful thanks to the same kind of promotion from Mitch Miller that had been done for Frankie Laine and Johnnie Ray. He had hits such as "There's a Pawn Shop on the Corner in Pittsburgh, Pennsylvania." Once Miller's singers had about six hits in America, they were promptly sent over to the London Palladium before touring the UK. I always seemed to get them when they traveled through Birmingham.

Mitchell had been shopping demo records around when his "Pawn Shop" song was snatched up and became a hit. I always wondered if someone had been around for years and suddenly had a hit record, how did the labels know if the artist would be good for more hit records? Guy Mitchell told me the answer was to get a better class of songwriter to submit material to Mitch Miller, who then picked out all the hits for Doris Day, Rosemary Clooney, and other artists with Columbia.

The day he opened his show, Mitchell gave a barbecue, and to us square Brits unfamiliar with barbecues, it was a treat to try spare ribs. Once again, the magic happened on stage, and just as with Frankie Laine and Johnnie Ray, short and jolly Guy Mitchell walked out on the stage and the place fell apart. I thought that his songs weren't as good as Doris Day's or Rosemary Clooney's. I felt that he would not be well served in terms of longevity by inferior songs. His career seemed to turn out that way, and other Columbia artists seemed to have longer lasting careers.

In spite of any potential worries about how it looked, Columbia Records was always nice to me. About the time of Guy Mitchell, I started getting boxes of records delivered to the studio. I didn't ask for them — I made that quite clear to my bosses — but I loved that I was getting all the new releases the first week of every month. Worried about all those stacks of records, I finally called the label and asked them to deliver the boxes to my home, which I should not have done, given even the appearance that it might be misconstrued as payola. Thankfully, it never proved to be a problem with the BBC.

Other records labels somehow learned that Columbia was sending me records, so they deduced that I must be influential, because I started get-

With singer Ronnie Hilton, the "British Eddie Fisher" of his day.

ting even more records from all over the country. Then I got really naughty. Because LPs were coming out and taking less shelf space, I requested to receive LPs instead of 78 records.

Talking to those great performers, especially Americans, I began to sow the seeds of determination that I would somehow start planning to go to Hollywood myself. Many of my best guests lived in Los Angeles, so California seemed magical to me. I instinctively knew that I was destined to work there in some capacity. The bright lights made me long to get away from the BBC.

My show's interviews were building to the point where I was waiting for the right star. I studied each guest to see if he or she might be receptive or helpful enough to answer questions about my acting ambition.

In 1953, there was a press reception for Greer Garson when she came to Birmingham to promote *Julius Caesar*. Greer and Deborah Kerr had done cameo appearances in the film for Joseph Mankiewicz. MGM had sent Greer and her mother on a tour of Britain, first in London, then to Birmingham, where I was stationed, Manchester, and then to Glasgow and Dublin.

I asked her MGM press agent if I could interview Garson separately from the press conference for my radio show. Word came back that she would be at the hotel, and I could directly ask her. When I called, Garson said, "Yes, be at the press conference at six p.m., and we'll meet and then record the next day."

Assembling in the hotel at six p.m., the Birmingham press waited for this great star to appear. As an industrial city, Birmingham was pretty glum. Most of the press members were more interested in politics or regional news and did not share my affinity for show business. I was standing in the back when a door opened. In swept Greer Garson, wearing an off-the-shoulder, green velvet gown, with emeralds around her neck and hanging from her ears. She had flaming red hair and the fabulous clear complexion that red-haired people seem to have.

"Gentlemen!" she said, and the press practically fell down on the floor. It was a big Hollywood star's entrance that astounded even me. She was a charmer, a very smart lady, educated at London University. She had years of stardom in Hollywood. She knew how to put the press at ease by somehow memorizing all the reporters' names. She answered their questions and then said to me in the back, "Is that Mr. Frankham? We meet tomorrow, don't we? Looking forward to it!"

Out she swept, and everyone sighed. I had never met anyone like her in my entire life. I spoke with her a little after the press conference and said how much I looked forward to chatting with her the next morning. I got it into my head to say to her, "Would you be agreeable to doing a 'Day with Greer Garson' with the various activities and events that are planned for you tomorrow?"

She said, "Yes, I would love to do that." MGM's public relations man then said, "Well, Miss Garson's in your hands," and he departed for London. I panicked. I knew she had planned to go to the Birmingham Repertory Theatre, where she had started her career, and to Birmingham University to make a short introduction to *Julius Caesar*, the movie, and then a little talk about transferring Shakespeare to film. She was next scheduled to visit a local theatre at ten p.m. to make a personal appearance between showings of the movie.

I suddenly realized that I was to be responsible for getting her to all these places on time! I remember waking up the next morning thinking, "Oh my God, what have I gotten myself into?" I knew I had to meet her at her hotel at ten, and I couldn't remember what the PR man had said about what time she was to show up at the various other places! I called London and fortunately got the same guy who reminded me about her appointment times.

Interviewing Greer Garson led to decades of friendship.

Much to my consternation, we had an executive producer at the BBC who didn't know anything about show business. He had no idea about how big a star Greer Garson was. I pointed out that she was the number one star of a huge studio out in Hollywood, but it meant nothing to him. His ignorance underscored my growing desire to leave the BBC.

The BBC was going to send a little car for her, but I said, "Wait a minute! You can't just send a little car; this is Greer Garson! We've got a limousine, so get the chauffeur behind the wheel!"

I showed up at the Midland Hotel feeling a little more confident, but I had never had a Hollywood star on my hands for twelve hours before! I got up to the suite, and her mother, a very nice lady, was there with her. Greer had prepared tea, coffee, and marmalade sandwiches.

She said, "I thought we would have a little light breakfast before we started." I was amazed at the thoughtfulness she displayed. As we did the interview, she was marvelous. Just as I had done with my interview with Betty Hutton in the same hotel, I had to throw a rope down through the window for the recording engineer to hook the mike in it and haul it up to the room.

The recording engineer was a very dour man with no sense of humor. He was bored silly by going with me once a week to talk to actors or actresses. Greer took the microphone from me and said, "Oh, that poor man down there in the rain. What's his name?"

"Chris," I told her.

"Good morning, Chris," she called down to him. "This is Greer Garson. How are you? Would you like some coffee?"

He too fell in love with her right on the spot. I thought, "This lady really cares about people." She had such genuine charisma, not phony, Hollywood show business stuff. She was nothing like a grand lady of the silver screen.

She told me, "MGM stands for Metro's Glorified Mother, and that's what they've made me." She was not happy with MGM at that time, and in fact, she later bought out her contract from the studio.

Because I was responsible for her time that day, I continually looked at my watch to keep her on schedule. We were off to Birmingham University, where she was to make her little speech. I stood in the wings to record the reaction of the audience.

She had a prepared speech about the challenges of playing Calpurnia, Julius Caesar's wife, opposite Louis Calhern in the movie. The very great English actor, Sir John Gielgud, played Cassius. He had been arrested earlier that week on a morals charge. It was awful for the poor man. The stunning story reverberated through the British Isles.

Greer chatted away about transferring Shakespeare to film and took questions from the audience. One of the students said, "How do you feel about that queer in the movie?"

This great actress had a fit. She said, "One moment, please! Whoever you are, would you please have the courage to stand up and identify yourself for that inflammatory comment, you coward!"

She practically spat that retort like a shot through the auditorium. No one stood up to answer her. She continued, "Well, at least have the courage to identify yourself if you believe your convictions about Mr. Gielgud. Try to realize that there's a great difference between our everyday lives with all of our failings and the roles we play. Do us the courtesy of concentrating on the work you're about to see on the screen and not some scandal you've read in your local papers."

Greer's flaming red hair just about stood on edge, and she demolished this unfortunate student. I stopped recording, because I knew the BBC wouldn't allow anything of a scandalous nature to be broadcast in those pristine days in England. I admired her so much for her passionate defense. The student ended up apologizing, and Garson admonished him to not judge anyone. Without a pause, she went right back to her prepared comments. The next day, her spirited remarks were in the papers: "Garson Defends Gielgud."

When she finished her lecture, she came back and said, "Well, I think I dealt with that!" It was great to see her in a flamboyant mood like that. She was authentic to her core. During our interview, Greer had told me about her own life. Greer Garson was her real name. She had worked in the Birmingham Repertory Theatre. They even put a plaque on the wall saying that Greer Garson appeared there. There was nothing put on about her at all, as she had demonstrated with her fiery rebuttal.

Following her lecture and screening, it was back to the hotel for a big lunch, which she said was on MGM instead of the BBC. I was enjoying my day but still glancing very nervously at my watch because we did not have to get to the theatre until ten p.m. Though only twenty-seven, I was getting very tired. It was a long day, but Greer wasn't tired at all!

She had been wearing a very pretty flowered dress for her talk at Birmingham University. She said, "Now I have to go into the other room and change into my working clothes." Out she came about a half an hour later in a velvet green ball dress, emeralds at her ears and throat; she looked like a million dollars.

We swept off in the limousine to the theatre. She walked out on stage to rapturous applause and a standing ovation and made a lovely speech as she introduced *Julius Caesar*. The place was packed because her appearance had been heavily promoted in advance. Even though she delivered nearly the same prepared speech that she had given at the university earlier that day, it was wonderful to hear again.

I finally got her back to her hotel at about eleven p.m. that night. I really was done in, but happily so, because I knew it had all gone well. I knew I didn't have to look at my watch any more. The day had gone off without a hitch. It was like a dream to me, having breakfast, lunch, and dinner with this extraordinary woman. She was only five feet, four inches tall, but my generation was used to looking up at screens with big, forty-foot close-ups of people. Back at the hotel, I said a reluctant good night to her.

Garson said, "Let's keep in touch." Her mother handed her some writing paper with an address on it. It was marked, "Forked Lightning Ranch, Pecos, New Mexico."

I remember thinking, "I thought she lived in the U.S.," because I didn't realize that New Mexico was part of the United States. Garson explained that she was married to a rancher and lived not too far from Santa Fe.

For the next two years, from 1953 through 1955, I wrote her two or three times a year to keep in touch with her just as she had suggested. She was so friendly, writing back with encouraging notes.

I had always been bothered about handing stars their BBC check in exchange for their appearance on my show. After the Greer Garson episode, I said to my bosses, "I can't go on giving these five pound and five shilling 'tips' to these famous people. Greer Garson is making five thousand American dollars a week. Can't we have the checks sent to their agents?" So from then on, we did just that.

Garson was encouraging, but I hadn't worked up enough confidence to ask her about my acting chances. I next set my sights on Doris Day. In post-war, dreary, dull England, Doris Day was like a ray of sunshine, not only to me but to everyone who went to the movies. There was always a long line around the block at Warner Theatre in Leicester Square, which was unique in that it was made up entirely of movie theatres. There was the MGM Showplace, where all their first run movies started. Warners was next door, and down the next corner was the Odeon Cinema, where all the British films previewed, and then right across the square was the Leicester Square Cinema, where all the RKO product was shown.

Doris Day was passing through London in 1955, en route to making *The Man Who Knew Too Much* for Hitchcock. I tried not to look like a drooling idiot during my interview with her. Up close, she was a refreshing mixture of the last reel of *Calamity Jane*, all freckles and a blinding smile, with some of the sass of *Love Me or Leave Me.*

I knew her work so well, so when I planned our thirty-minute chat, I thought about things to ask her. I even thought about her favorite film. I correctly guessed that it was *Calamity Jane.* So she talked a little bit about it during our interview. I knew all the numbers from the film, including the hit "Secret Love."

She told me, "Warner Bros. just didn't get behind that movie. They should have worked harder to sell it." As we recorded, I thought, "Boy, I'm getting some good stuff out of her."

Doris continued, "They just did not believe in that movie as much as I did, and if they had really promoted it, the film would have been a bigger success. It made a few million in profit, but it should have done much more!"

This was a side of glitzy Doris Day that I had never seen from the big screen. It was more of a tantalizing talk than I had expected. She talked about each song from the movie and even told me about the very bad time she had recording with an ailment she experienced at the time.

When I interviewed Howard Keel, we talked about all of his big films, *Kiss Me Kate, Calamity Jane, Annie Get Your Gun,* and *Seven Brides for Seven Brothers.* We included songs from the films to have him discuss each one. At one point, he slapped me on the back and said, "I'll tell you anything you want to know, but don't ask me about that goddamned Betty Hutton. I can't stand that pushy dame!" When I asked him about working with Doris Day, he said, "Well, she was kind of a pain because she made a fuss about a pimple!" He also proceeded to criticize Christian Science, all material that I couldn't put on the air. Besides, when he criticized Doris Day, he dwindled in my estimation, but at least you knew where you stood with Howard Keel!

Keel had an ego as big as a five-story house, but he did a very fine stage show consisting of his movie hits. I liked him without taking much of a shine to him. I admired his talent because he was very good. He didn't strike me as terribly bright, but then, very few performers were rocket scientists. He brought an amiable presence to all of those MGM musicals. He had filled an essential gap for them, exactly what they wanted, and he had a good, long run.

I managed to build a friendship with Keel's accompanist, Jack Lattimer, who was touring the country with him. I went to watch two shows a night to familiarize myself with Keel's work in advance of our interview. Lattimer told me over coffee one day, "He's always demanding and temperamental, but it's always worth it when the curtain goes up." I couldn't put that in the interview, of course.

Betty Garrett and her husband, Larry Parks, were headlining at the Palladium. Both were familiar to audiences, Betty from her MGM contract in which she began in *Words and Music*, followed by *On the Town* with Frank Sinatra and Gene Kelly, and with Sinatra again in *Take Me Out to the Ballgame*.

Larry Parks was a contract player at Columbia but not featured very much. He found overnight fame when he got to play Al Jolson in *The Jolson Story* and then in *Jolson Sings Again*. They had a charming act when I went to see them. Neither one of them was a major singer, but it was a very good show. I booked them on my program and traveled to London to meet them at the BBC's Broadcasting House.

It was a rainy day when I arrived on time. I went up to the reception desk and asked if Miss Garrett and Mr. Parks had arrived. "Yes, they're over there," the clerk pointed to these two young folks huddled in yellow rain coats. They had no entourage or studio people with them. They were delightful.

They were very brave, because I did not know at the time that Larry's career was over because of the House Un-American Activities Committee hearings in the States. During the hearings, he had managed to put off naming names. Finally, they got to him. He had broken down and said that he and his wife were not Communists, that they had gone to meetings out of curiosity as many people had done, but that was it. The committee kept asking Larry who else was there and he told them that he didn't know. Finally, he was exhausted and named names.

None of this came out during our on-air chat, though, and afterwards, I told them that I would love to move to America eventually and try my hand at acting. "When you're there," they said, "here's where we live." They told me that they lived on Nichols Canyon and that Lena Horne and her husband, Lennie Hayton, lived just up the road. Their offer was exciting and fed my daydreaming of an acting career abroad. At least they hadn't laughed at me openly sharing that I dreamed of acting. We didn't discuss my ambition in great detail, but I was encouraged enough to think about bringing up the topic more directly with a future guest.

Another time I interviewed the ravishingly beautiful Moira Shearer. *The Red Shoes* had made her an international star, and then she came to America to do *The Story of Three Loves* with Kirk Douglas. She told me that Fred Astaire had wanted her for *Daddy Long Legs*, but she had had enough of Hollywood at that point. She was married to Ludovic Kennedy, and they lived in a stately mansion on a huge estate. I went there to interview her after she told me that a studio would make her nervous. Even though she had butlers, she wasn't grand or pretentious.

Like most red-headed ladies, she had pale skin and a beautiful, flawless complexion. We had tea and sat in a conservatory for the interview. She was very frank when I asked her if she had a contract with any studio. She told me that the whole weight of the studio system depressed her. Her heart was really in legitimate ballet, not in moviemaking, and she found the whole "stop/action/cut" of the movies unnatural without the flow of theatre or ballet. A real charmer, she was quite content to be back in England.

Just as I had to take the train down to London to interview Doris Day, Betty Garrett, and Larry Parks, I also traveled to London to meet Irving Berlin around the time *There's No Business Like Show Business* opened across the country. It was spring, but he met me wearing a very heavy coat. He was a small man, so his huge, camel-haired coat went almost down to his feet.

I held out my hand to say hello, and he curtly snapped, "Hi."

Joined by his wife, he walked right past me and up the hall toward the recording studio where Peter Sellers and the Goons recorded. I thought, "Oh, this is not going to be easy. Maybe he's had a bad morning or something."

Before I could even tell him my name, Berlin said, "Can't you do something about this miserable cold weather in your country? I hate this goddamned weather. I don't even know why I come over here."

It turned out that he wasn't kidding. He was totally devoid of any sense of humor. When we started recording, I mentioned his new film and asked, "Do you expect it will be a big hit here?" There was a long pause, and he said, "Well, of course it will. I wrote it, didn't I?" From there, it was all downhill.

Maybe he was actually a charming man who was just having a lousy day, but he was non-productive as interviews go. I had to drag remarks out of him. That was an interview I did not mind trimming down; when I got back to Birmingham, I cut that one down to the bone. I thought, "I am not going to give this bad-tempered man any more air time than necessary." I still love his music, but there was such an arrogance and sullenness there with him.

In the winter, the Royal Shakespeare Theatre only used touring productions until they could resume their renowned summer schedules. In the interim, quite a few notables, including Margaret Rutherford, came through for a one-week winter run before moving onto the next city.

Rutherford was another disappointment, even though I loved her then and now. She had dithered her way into people's hearts for years. I went to interview her with great anticipation and found that she had absolutely no sense of humor. That sounds impossible, but when she was funny on screen or on stage, people had written that material for her. As a real person, particularly an older lady, she took her profession very seriously. While I nudged her to tell me something funny, she launched into a speech on "The Art of Comedy." As a potential actor, I should have been absorbing her useful lecture but it made for deadly dull interview material. I didn't get a single laugh from her. It was my fault, because I had gone with the presumption that she would be a funny lady. She was a dull interview, I'm afraid.

Douglas Fairbanks, Jr., was also a frustration. It wasn't his fault. At the time of our interview, he was chairman of the board of Cadbury Chocolates. The company was observing an anniversary or major milestone, and because the Cadbury offices were not too far from Birmingham, my bosses sent me to interview him, but not as our star of the week. I was told that I could not ask him any questions about his acting career. They told me to talk to him only as the chairman of the board of Cadbury's. With that mandate, I was restricted to asking him about chocolates and what the board was doing to make the company a great success.

Talk about boring subject matter, or at least to me! I couldn't say one word to him on the air about his movies! After the interview, I did ask him some show business questions. I remember apologizing to him and telling him that the BBC had requested that I focus only on Cadbury. He was very understanding, because he had to fulfill his duties as chairman of the board. Fairbanks was very charming, though, and pleasant in our strictly business interview.

There were so many extraordinary people that I got to meet that I had become accustomed to sitting with somebody famous. In 1955, Edmund Purdom came on my show to promote *The Student Prince* with Mario Lanza. The film was not yet in release in England, so I had to tell him that I had not seen it when he asked my opinion of it. He had several publicity people with him, and after he asked them to get a copy of the print, we sat later that afternoon and watched the movie together.

My bosses frequently reminded me that I was interviewing movie stars perhaps at the expense of ignoring talent in the Midlands. Sometimes they suggested a broader scope than beyond the type of guests that I most enjoyed interviewing. When they encouraged me to talk to local actors, I befriended a stage actress named Mimi Yarwood after I saw her in an amateur production of *Medea*.

Mimi was a tiny little lady of about five feet, two inches tall. She was brilliant, though, so after the show, I went back and asked if she would appear on my program. She was very modest and shy, so she reluctantly said yes. We had a great interview and when it turned out that she lived just around the corner from me, we became close friends. On my annual vacation to the south of France, Mimi joined me in 1955. We had a great time together and were very compatible. Life was good, yet something was missing.

As I continued to dream of an acting career, Greer Garson started writing from New Mexico with much good advice about how to get started in Hollywood. She told me how stimulating and challenging I would find life and work there. I was enjoying the challenges in radio, but I knew there were greater challenges elsewhere. I still had a restless feeling that I wanted to be an actor.

There were certainly days on end when I thought, "Oh, the hell with it; I'm sitting pretty here, acting's a pipe dream, and why don't I just forget the whole thing and live out my days with the BBC and collect a great pension at the end of it?" That's what my parents expected me to do and what my fellow colleagues at the BBC were sure I would do. But Hollywood and its stars were just too alluring, as the parade of guests on my radio show never failed to remind me.

Besides, the times were changing at the BBC. Television was just coming into the UK. The BBC was going to put on a TV magazine program of interviews. By then, I was in charge of the Department of

Recorded Programs, and each department had to contribute to the program. The new TV show was rather like my radio show, *What Goes On*, also a magazine format interviewing different people.

I was told that I had to do two interviews for this television show. One was to interview a man at a sink about a garbage disposal, a dreadful subject! The other was to interview a lovely actress, Zena Walker, who was playing Juliet opposite Laurence Harvey's Romeo at Stratford that year. I had already interviewed her for my radio show, so the BBC tried to make my television debut as easy as they could by re-interviewing somebody with whom I had already built a rapport.

I really didn't want to do television with the camera looming at me, but I had to do as I was told. Producer Peter Cairns said, "Frankham, you've talked to this girl before, so we'll get her to come in, sit her on a little couch with you, and you'll ask her the same questions that you asked her on radio. The only difference will be that there will be cameras pointed at you."

Talking to her was easy, but I couldn't get used to the big, clunky television cameras. There were two of them, and their operators couldn't get a close-up by twisting a dial. They did a close-up by moving up to a foot from my face. I was sweating, because they had put some sort of makeup paste on me. Zena wasn't sweating; she had done this sort of thing before. She looked marvelous, because she had done her own makeup.

I was very nervous about the camera trailing after me. I could always hear it, with some guy pushing this machine after me, and then the red light would go on. Then I had to cross the floor while somebody else was being interviewed, and talk to this man with his garbage disposal. I was so fatigued by the time I got to him that my voice was beginning to go. We did the interview and went off the air. The producer said, "That was good, a first for us all, and I think we all did very well."

I got on the bus to go home to my little flat and thought to myself, "I don't care what they threaten me with, but I will never do television again." I hated the experience, because I was self-conscious.

Radio would be my home for the rest of my time at the BBC, where there were some bright spots, even as I grew restless. In contrast to the rudimentary technology used in television, things were improving considerably on that front for radio. In 1954, all of the BBC's interviewers were given little satchels, which we would hang over our shoulders. Inside was a mini reel-to-reel tape recorder. We could then sit down, open up the satchel and start recording. Now I was also my own engineer, capable of recording up to fifteen minutes at a time instead of four minutes as we had been forced to do with the acetate disks.

Back at the studio, the recordings were transferred to a larger reel. Now it was much easier to edit an interview. Once or twice, I returned to the studio and sat back to hear what I had recorded, only to discover that I hadn't done something correctly. There's nothing more embarrassing than saying to a celebrity, "Would you mind doing that all over again, because there was a technical glitch." There were some horror stories among a few others at the

Improved technology made the BBC more mobile during my years there.

BBC when a significant interview was lost. I learned to make sure that my red light was on to signify when we were recording. It made a huge difference to my job when we were the first in the country to get these recorders.

By the 1950s, my friend Jimmy Thomson had finished architecture school and wed a lovely lady named Mary. I couldn't get a reprieve from my BBC work, so my parents attended Jimmy's wedding. My mother was furious — "He's your best friend; can't you show up for his wedding?" Unfortunately for me, the BBC was that strict. Jimmy and his bride hopped on a boat and moved away to Australia.

By 1955, I knew I wanted to leave England, too, but I wanted to go to America. I wanted more. I was doing a lot on the radio, but I didn't feel that I was getting paid fairly for all I was doing. Not to sound like Orson Welles, but I was writing, producing, and interviewing, really doing three jobs. I thought they could give me a promotion, but they didn't.

When I interviewed guests for my program, I particularly paid attention to film actors. By the spring of 1955, I thought, "If I talk to somebody with whom I am comfortable enough to open up to, and if they can help get me to Hollywood, I'm going." I thought about my sense of timing and planned to strike if the opportunity was right after an interview if I perceived that the guest would be receptive to giving me advice or help.

My parents at my friend Jimmy Thomson's wedding in 1955.

As soon as somebody gave me a suggestion about how to work in America, I vowed to just go for it.

When Alec Guinness appeared on my program in August 1955, I found him to be very bland. In Birmingham to promote his film *To Paris with Love*, in which he had a romantic scene, he was making a big career move at the time and would shortly leave for Hollywood to film *The Swan*, with Grace Kelly.

Before our interview, I had sat through *To Paris with Love*. He was in the manager's office to meet the press while I watched the movie, thinking, "He should go back to those marvelous, unforgettable character roles that he plays. He's not really a romantic leading man."

It was easy to talk to him, because he was very low-keyed, quiet, and shy. After the interview was over, I felt comfortable enough to ask him my million-dollar question. I told him of my acting ambition when we were off the air.

"How old are you?" he asked.

"Twenty-nine," I replied.

"Too old," he said, dashing my dream with his disapproval. "You should have started at twenty-one, carrying a spear at Stratford."

I went home on the bus rather discouraged and thought that it wasn't a very constructive opinion from somebody whose opinion I valued as one of the greatest actors in the world. It didn't put me off, though, because I still was determined to prove I could do it with just the right person to encourage me.

"He's talking about theatre," I realized. "I'm not interested in theatre!" I bounced back rather quickly from being put down by Alec Guinness. I bided my time, with little patience, I must admit.

As I had learned by playing Doris Day records, there was a lot of power with the BBC. If I had a singer on my show and only played one of his records, I was deluged with tons more records sent by labels hoping that we would promote their singers. At one point, my flat was covered with stacks of 78s.

Rosemary Clooney was appearing at the Palladium in September 1955. After my earlier attempt at interviewing her ended with getting stuck with her husband instead, I contacted Columbia to see if she would like to try again and chat with me. I was told that the record company was giving a reception for her at the Dorchester Hotel. They agreed to set aside a room for my thirty-minute interview with her.

I brought my little portable recorder to meet Clooney after I watched every one of her performances over the course of a week. She was marvelous as I had watched her. In fact, I thought, "She has got to be that nice off the Palladium stage, too." She was, as we laughed about all of her hits: "Come On-a My House" and "Mambo Italiano."

She lightheartedly made fun of some of her silly songs, calling them "kid songs." She told me, "I'm prepared for any of the stuff they throw at me now. I just go in, they point me at the mike, and I sing whatever they put in front of me, only somehow, it becomes a big hit!"

Our interview was going so well that towards the end of the thirty minutes, I instinctively knew she was the person who might help me. At just the right moment, I asked her, "What do you think of my chances of going to Los Angeles to work in radio?"

She said, "I think you would be great! If you decide to do it, just call me at Paramount and I'll get right back to you. If I can be of any help…"

Clooney gave me her contact information and told me to call her secretary. She also gave me her home phone number. "There will be somebody there, and if I'm not in, I'll call you right back."

Rosemary Clooney, whose encouragement proved invaluable in getting to America.

Those were the magic words! Going back home to Birmingham on the train that night, I formed my resignation letter in my mind and handed it in the next day at nine a.m. I got a lot of flak from my BBC colleagues. My mentor, Peter Cairns, said to me, "Why in the hell are you running after Rosemary Clooney to Hollywood?" I couldn't seem to get through to people my reason for leaving. A few of the technicians did wish me good luck, and so did Peter.

I wasn't running after a singer; I was following my own dream, but it was difficult to make others understand. England in the 1950s was very conservative and uptight, and it was difficult to find colleagues who could relate to my creative ambition.

I realized that I had needed creative support, the kind that Rosemary Clooney was showing me. For all of the salacious things written about how show business can be filled with pitfalls, the casting couch or backstabbing efforts to fight one's way to the top, creative people also understand each other and, for the most part, support each other. In time, I would come to find that people play different parts in the cast and crew, but ultimately everyone is using his or her talent to the same end, and that was the rewarding feeling I had been missing in England.

As an example of this kind of support, Dirk Bogarde proved to be an additional godsend. When I interviewed him for the second time, he was promoting *Doctor at Sea*. Although Dirk did not like to stir from his house, he thought that this new movie with Brigitte Bardot had great promise, so he reluctantly agreed to travel throughout the United Kingdom to promote the film.

When I interviewed him at his hotel room, he was still resentful of the BBC. "Am I getting another five guineas for appearing on your show?" he growled, and I sheepishly told him that he was. We did the interview, and he was very big on Brigitte Bardot. He had enjoyed working with her very much.

At the end of the interview, I packed up my portable recording gear. I told him that I would probably not see him anymore because I was off for Hollywood.

"You're leaving the BBC?" he asked.

I told him that I was indeed.

"Jolly good for you," he said. "Where are you going?"

"Los Angeles," I replied.

"Jolly good," he said again. "Do you know anybody there?"

"No," I told him. "Just Rosemary Clooney, and I don't know her well at all beyond just the thirty minutes we spent together in London when she promised to help me get established."

He went over to his briefcase and pulled out a phone book with names and addresses. He told me to write down these names: Elizabeth Taylor/ Michael Wilding, Stewart Granger/Jean Simmons, Alexis Smith, and Danny Kaye.

I said, "I don't know any of them."

"Of course you don't," he said patiently. "You're English, so you'll be good for a drink with them. You have that in common and you might meet other people through them. Give them a call when you get there."

Then he crossed off Stewart Granger and told me that the actor was jealous of Jean Simmons. "If Jean likes you, it will be bad for her, and he's not very kind to her as it is."

He also told me to write to him at his home to update him on my luck in Hollywood. That invitation started a forty-four-year pen pal friendship that would last through his death in 1999. Once a month for the rest of our friendship, I wrote a letter and always received a letter or card in return, many of them ending with "Jolly good" or "As ever, Dirk," at any good news I shared with him.

When I resigned my BBC job, I also immediately wrote Greer Garson to tell her that I was on my way to Hollywood. Before I left England, she wrote back with advice: "You will find it stimulating and challenging to work in Los Angeles. If you don't come over with a 'bowler hat and umbrella' attitude, you will fit right in."

There was a lot to do that last month when I wasn't working. I went to the American Embassy in London to get a passport. I signed immigration forms. I went on about my remaining assignments, but nobody said another word to me after their initial dismay at my news. People just assumed that I would change my mind during those four weeks, so nobody ever mentioned that I was going away to America.

When I left the BBC for the last time, I simply finished that day's work, got on the train for London, and made my way down to my parents' home in Kent. Except for Peter Cairns and Gillian, nobody said, "Well, best of luck" or "Keep in touch." Nothing. The others were shunning this "idiot" who had been given opportunities with orchestras and interviews and movie stars and limousines. They couldn't understand why on earth I didn't want to work there anymore.

The local newspaper ran a story telling listeners that I was leaving. And so, my career at the BBC came to an end. I had saved money and built up confidence to follow my dream. Through much of 1955, I had plotted and planned for the day when the time would be right for me to leave. Looking back, I still think of my seven years with the BBC as a detour from my heart's desire, but a lot of what I learned there came in useful when I was finally able to call myself an actor. Nothing is wasted.

At the time, my father and mother didn't agree, though. They, too, were shocked at the news that I was leaving the BBC. My father asked how I could give up my work and the pension that I would receive at the end of my career. My poor, insecure father was just thinking about what would happen to me when I turned sixty-five. My mother, in her quiet way, just said, "Well, if you've made up your mind, that's what you have to do."

I hadn't been told that my mother had been diagnosed with breast cancer. The doctors had said to her, "Mrs. Frankham, you must come in to attend to this cancer or we can't promise full recovery." My mother is said to have replied, "No, my son is set on going to America, and if I tell him that you want me to have surgery, he might not go." She delayed her surgery, yet thankfully recuperated.

When I told my friend Mimi that I was leaving to pursue acting, I asked her if she would consider following me to the States. I told her that if I got established in Hollywood, even in radio, my presence there could open doors for her acting career as well.

"No," she told me. "I like my job as a secretary. I love acting in amateur productions, but I'm sure Hollywood's not an easy career. There aren't any guarantees of success, so I would not be interested in working profession-ally anywhere as an actress, either in England or America."

The other memory I have about my preparation to leave for America was standing at a bus stop near my parents' home and hearing that James Dean had been killed in an automobile accident.

Those three weeks went by quickly. I gave away most of my Columbia records and packed just a bag of clothing. I didn't know what would lie ahead of me. I didn't even know what the weather would be like in Los Angeles or anywhere in America, for that matter. I had very little money because after I had paid my passage on the *Queen Mary*, I had 250 pounds left from my BBC severance pay. That would translate to $750 American dollars, or a little more than $6,000 of today's dollars.

On the day I took the train to Southampton in November 1955, my parents saw me off in London. They got back on the train and went straight to the hospital where my mother had a mastectomy that very day. Truthfully, I don't know that I would have stayed even had they told me about my mother's illness. I was so hell bent on getting to America. I had to go. I had waited so long to get there ever since Gladys Cooper and Laird

My parents, about the time I left to pursue acting in the States.

Cregar had shaken me to my timbers a decade earlier.

Everything in my background had been building up to this day. It had all started with Peter Cairns bursting into the green room and asking, "What do you know about Eve Boswell?"

Getting my own talk show interviewing celebrities at the start of 1952 had led me three years later to Rosemary Clooney. By then I was a seasoned interviewer, so my knowledge of pop music had been my ticket to Los Angeles when she was receptive to my question about my chances.

So, much to my poor parents' dismay, I booked passage on the *Queen Mary* and set sail for America and Hollywood, sight unseen, just to try my luck. I promised my folks that if I hadn't made good in five years, I would go back to the BBC for the rest of my life. Meanwhile, I had set my course and there was no turning back.

CHAPTER THREE

California Here I Come

The *Queen Mary* sailed for the States with me aboard in November 1955. I bought the cheapest seat possible in steerage, which meant that I was roughly below the water line. The porthole was painted black, so I couldn't see anything else.

My bunkmates were three very robust Irishmen, immigrating like me. As the ship began to sail from Southampton, there was a knock at the door to deliver a message. I had been invited up to dine at the captain's table. The Irishmen took a very dim view of that news and wondered why it was me getting the invitation and not them.

Passengers had to tell the purser who was sponsoring them. Sponsoring somebody meant that they were responsible for the immigrants if they got to America and fell flat on their face, which meant by extension, that if I had not started making a living in Los Angeles, Rosemary Clooney would have been forced to support me! (We laughed about that years later.) The purser saw that I had listed Rosemary Clooney as my sponsor and decided to add me to the captain's invitation list as a BBC reporter of some importance!

At the captain's table, I sat next to a lovely English lady named Rose Bligh. She also had a lovely English complexion. She was very sweet and nice, so we hit it off the first evening and spent the rest of the five days together, strolling about the deck or going to an afternoon movie. I just assumed she was immigrating like me, so on the last day, November 15, as we passed the Statue of Liberty, I asked her, "Rose, are you going to be living in America?"

Rose said, "Actually, I'm just in America on holiday, and then I have to go back to work." She was staying with friends in, as she put it, "ConneKHT-TT-KHUT."

I said, "What line of work are you in?" and she said, "Well, actually I'm lady in waiting to Her Majesty." So I was big time with this awfully nice, important person! (We later wrote back a few times when I landed in Los Angeles and she continued to vacation in New England, but we later lost touch.)

Arriving in New York, I got ripped off by the cab driver who could tell that I was literally off the boat. He took me by way of Yonkers and Staten Island to the Statler Hotel. That diversion aside, I was ecstatic to be in America at last.

Before I left England, I had cabled Gladys Cooper to let her know that I was coming. She was appearing in *The Chalk Garden* with Siobhan McKenna at the Ethel Barrymore Theatre. She cabled back to me on the ship: "Have a box seat arranged for you and supper afterwards."

Gladys was the star, and for her role, she received a Tony nomination for Best Actress in a Play. I found the theatre and settled in for a fantastic performance. She was wonderful that night, a testament to how she became one of the greatest stage actresses of her generation back in the United Kingdom.

The thrill of being in America and watching my first Broadway play was exhilarating. Following the show, Gladys greeted me with, "My dear, you're here! How exciting for you!" She decided that we would eat at the Rainbow Room, so off we went as I told her about my plans to trek westward to Hollywood.

"Can't you stay a little longer, my dear?" she asked. "There's so many people that I would like you to meet!" I told her that I had to get out to Los Angeles, because Rosemary Clooney had promised to make some contacts for me in radio. I thought that if I stayed in New York with Gladys, there was a chance that Clooney would forget me by the time I arrived. That magical evening heralded my otherwise inconspicuous arrival in the States and a welcome stopover on my way to Hollywood.

I didn't waste any time and flew to St. Louis and then on to California, where I literally knew nobody. Arriving in Los Angeles on November 16, I decided that I would pick the first hotel that the cab driver drove past once I left the airport and arrived in Hollywood. When I had moved from London to Birmingham, I had been in cultural shock, but when I arrived in America, I wasn't thinking about such things. It didn't matter; just being there was so exciting!

I knew that I had $750 and that the money would last me for some time. I asked the cab driver to take me to Hollywood. We drove along Sunset Boulevard to a motel with a garish electric palm tree blinking on and off. It looked like Hollywood, so I told him that the place would do. That motel was my home for my first night in California. The next day, I looked across the street and spotted a four- or five-story building about a block away. I walked over to those apartments to inquire about living there. The rent was $60 a month, an amount that I could afford with my savings.

The apartments were on Sunset Boulevard, not far from Hollywood High School. The building was owned by the Dolly Sisters, immortalized on film by Betty Grable and June Haver. By then, the remaining sister had retired from show business, but it was fun to say that the Dolly Sisters were my landladies.

I moved into my little apartment. Murphy beds were new to me. They had to be pulled down from the wall! The whole apartment was tacky, in reality, with a tiny little kitchen. I arranged to have a telephone installed. After the phone arrived, I remember looking at it and thinking, "Nobody's going to call me. I've got to start working on my career now."

It began to dawn on me that it was up to me to make my success happen. A little bit of luck plays such a vital part in any acting career, and that's true for any of the arts. I would need lucky breaks. Without them, it would be tough going. Over my career, I saw many actors just disappear because nothing seemed to happen for them along the way.

I don't believe in lucky accidents, though. I do believe in being in the right place at the right time as a result of one's labor and ambitions. People come into our lives for a reason, as did Rosemary Clooney. When I called Paramount, her assistant told me that Clooney was away in New York, recording with Benny Goodman. In fact, she had arrived in New York on the same day that I arrived on the *Queen Mary*! Had I known that earlier, I perhaps would have stayed in New York longer and sought out Clooney in Manhattan.

In fact, Clooney wasn't scheduled to return to California until January 7, 1956. Somehow I didn't panic. I realized that I now had seven weeks to grow accustomed to my new way of life. I spent the 1956 holiday season growing acclimated to American culture, people, and food. Being in Hollywood was like a movie coming to life. I had seen movies depicting high school life, where the girls all wore saddle shoes, bobby socks, and big skirts. I had seen and loved so many American films. People looked exactly like they did in the movies of the era.

The only surprise was the concept of a supermarket. We didn't have those in England at the time. On Hollywood Boulevard, which runs parallel to Sunset Boulevard just around the corner from my apartment, I had to go into the supermarket through a turnstile. There I saw frozen foods for the first time; I guess England was so cold that no one had thought of frozen foods before! I had never tasted Mexican food or seen TV dinners on a tray.

Everything I saw, I liked. People in Los Angeles that winter looked very happy to me. There was none of the post-war gloom that was still evident, to a degree, in England when I left. Everything was exciting to me, even American radio. Because I anticipated getting started in radio with Clooney's help when she returned, I bought a little radio and spent time listening to programs. I also bought a little television set and a small record player. With some Ella Fitzgerald LPs, time passed very easily for me. I was establishing roots.

After getting through the 1956 holidays, I had succeeded at adapting to the American, or at least Hollywood, way of life. My apartment was around the corner from the present day El Capitan Theatre. One night, I looked out the window and watched a movie premiere. Just as I had seen in *A Star Is Born*, the premiere had it all: searchlights, red carpets, socialites, and crowds pressing against barriers as they watched Frank Sinatra, Jean Simmons, and Marlon Brando walk down the red carpet for *Guys and Dolls*.

My money situation was adequate until I suddenly contracted conjunctivitis. One evening after I got home, I couldn't see well. The next day I went to a clinic and was told that if I hadn't come in when I did, I would have lost the sight in my one eye. Without health insurance, I spent several hundred dollars of what had started as $750.

With about ten days remaining until Rosemary Clooney was scheduled to return, I decided to conserve the rest of my money by just eating cereal. I called her assistant on the appointed day and heard back from Clooney on January 7, 1956.

She told me that she remembered me. "What have you been doing since you got here?" she asked.

I told her that I was getting used to American ways and listening to a lot of American radio. True to her word as she had promised in England, she said, "That's good, because I have someone in mind. I'll make a call and then get back to you."

When she called me back, she said, "I've talked to Peter Potter, and he wants to see you at nine in the morning. You'll get along with him. His show is on the air from six to ten, and he'll talk to you there at the studio."

Peter Potter was one of five popular disc jockeys on the radio in the L.A. market. Clooney had very thoughtfully remembered that he was very much an Anglophile. Potter was married to Beryl Davis, a popular English big band singer whom I remembered from her work with Glenn Miller back in England. (Beryl had a younger sister, the actress Lisa Davis, but more about her later.)

I thanked Clooney for her help, and she said, "Call me back and tell me how it went."

A kind man with a Southern accent, Potter hosted *Jukebox Jury*, a program that aired on radio and briefly on television at the height of its popularity. A small panel of actors or other recording artists listened to new records and then voted as to which ones they liked best.

When I showed up at the studio to meet him, Potter was on the air. I assumed I would talk to him after he came off the air at ten a.m. I was shown in at a quarter to nine, and I could see through the window that he was still on the air with two turntables on each side of him and buttons to press for commercials.

Outside the booth sat Al Hibbler, a blind African-American singer who was there waiting to plug his Decca Records smash hit "Unchained Melody." As we both waited, Hibbler told me about his eight years with Duke Ellington, whose music I greatly admired.

It took me a moment to realize that Hibbler was an actual on-air guest and not just waiting to talk to Potter. The host beckoned for someone to let Hibbler know that it was time to go in. The moment the record finished, I heard Potter say over the speaker in my little waiting area, "Our next guest is Al Hibbler. Hi, Al, great to see you!"

I thought, "Oh, my God. He's going to do that to me." I realized then that I wasn't going to wait until ten o'clock to talk to Peter Potter. Sure enough, Hibbler plugged "Unchained Melody" and when they finished, Potter beckoned to me while he played another record.

When I entered the studio, all he said was, "Hi." Because the record was ending, he didn't say another word to me until the song finished. He had his notes and said, "Well, folks, our next guest has just come right off the boat from England, and he's a friend of Rosemary Clooney's. Dave, tell us all about yourself."

At first, I stammered a little while he proceeded to interview me live on the air. Because I had spent seven years as a radio broadcaster myself, I went along with him. My BBC training kicked in as we talked and then stopped for commercials before resuming live again on the air. We had a good exchange about my background and the kinds of music I liked. I dropped as many musical names as I could, including Doris Day and Rosemary Clooney, telling Potter and his listeners about how I had worked with them back in England.

He put on one of Clooney's big hits, "Come on-a My House." I thanked her publicly on the air in case she happened to be listening at home. Then Peter said to his audience, "As you know, we have *Jukebox Jury* every Thursday. I'm going to ask Dave to come back and appear on the show."

I was delighted at this introduction, because it was a great way to be starting 1956. We got along well enough that I called back Clooney that night and told her what had transpired at the station that day.

"Good," she said. "Keep me posted as to whatever else happens."

I had handled myself well enough to begin appearing on *Jukebox Jury*. The premise of the series was a forerunner of sorts to today's popular *American Idol* TV series, with a panel of four celebrities sitting and passing judgment on recordings.

On *Jukebox Jury*, Peter held a mallet in his hand with a little gong, and before each record played, he said in his Southern drawl, "Will it be a hit? Or a miss? BOING!" It sounds corny today, but it was an enormously successful show, so much so, that two or three years later, an announcer from one of my BBC programs hosted the same series when it travelled across the pond to England.

That Thursday I appeared as a panelist along with three other predominantly young personalities, all of them singers. I hadn't been there long enough to know how popular they were or even who they were. My only claim to fame was that I had been a BBC radio host, but because my radio career had started by me picking my favorite top records, I fit in well enough and held my own as we passed judgment on the records.

Peter also hosted a television version of *Jukebox Jury*, so then he invited me to appear as one of the panelists for the televised show. Connie Francis was one of the judges, along with James Darren. I felt lucky that I had been included as the odd Brit, a sort of curiosity to American audiences who heard or saw me paired with three American performers with established names. (More or less the same formula would be used fifty years later to great success on the *American Idol* program, so in a way, I was an early, although less acerbic, version of Simon Cowell!)

When we finished *Jukebox Jury* and left the air, Peter asked if I knew any other disc jockeys. I told him that I didn't. He said, "I can tell you know your records. I'm putting in a good word for you with Bill Stewart and some of the other DJs."

Bill Stewart was a peer of Potter's, another top disc jockey who played LP records. His show aired from ten p.m. to two a.m. each night. On Potter's recommendation, I went on Stewart's program and shared the evening show with him. Working on his show gave me time to relax and stretch. We would play LPs and discuss each track. Stewart liked me and invited me back for three or four shows, after which time he gave me the midnight to one a.m. time slot all by myself on Saturday evening, going as far as actually leaving me in the studio alone for a bit. Once I played Frank Sinatra's *In the Wee Small Hours* album. I knew that LP backwards, so I was able to talk between the tracks about the composers and arrangers. Sinatra was a fantastic ballad interpreter. I loved his music, so I had lots to talk about with each track.

Stewart then sent me to Dick Whittinghill, another top disc jockey in Los Angeles. All of these gentlemen were very nice; in fact, there wasn't a rotten apple in the bunch. Soon I found myself working freelance, going from radio station to radio station to appear, usually for $150 or so for each show. There was a week or two in between without an opportunity, but I was building up my little bank account.

Rosemary Clooney had been true to her word. I'm not sure what she initially told Peter Potter, but I think just her clout in Hollywood and as a major recording star was enough to have him take me seriously from the moment we met. Because of her, I was able to start working enough to pay my bills.

Working in radio paid my bills and was interesting, but I still wanted to be an actor. There I was in Hollywood, and if I was going to be in Hollywood working in radio, I was only one step from becoming an actor on screen. I was frustrated, though, because I didn't know how to go about getting my foot in the door.

Dirk Bogarde had given me telephone numbers of people to call in Hollywood. Determined to see how far I could make it on my own, I had yet to contact any of them by the start of 1956. When I wasn't doing anything on radio one week, I swallowed my pride and started calling those on Dirk's list.

I first called Alexis Smith, whom I had admired as Cole Porter's wife, Linda, in 1946's *Night and Day* with Cary Grant, and for her role opposite Bing Crosby in *Here Comes the Groom* in 1951. She had worked with Dirk in 1954's *The Sleeping Tiger*. Although Alexis was actually Canadian, Dirk enjoyed working with her and thought she might be a good contact for me.

Unfortunately for me, Alexis Smith was living in the San Fernando Valley. She invited me out for a drink, but as a new arrival without a vehicle, it was too far to travel without a car, even by bus. I didn't even know where the San Fernando Valley was at the time. She wished me well and gave me some encouragement over the phone, but it was otherwise the end of the line because I couldn't get to her.

Comedian and actor Danny Kaye was next on Dirk's list to call. His wife, Sylvia Fine, answered and invited me to attend a large Chinese dinner party hosted by Kaye. He specialized in making Chinese food. He loved being in the kitchen, and he was "on" as himself while he cooked in an entertaining way.

I had seen him at the London Palladium. He was a huge hit there, and I knew how gifted he was at improvising. For some reason, I thought that he would be quiet and low-key, but he wasn't. He was exactly as he appeared onstage.

Danny Kaye was one of the first contacts I called in 1956.

The other guests were writers and producers. I just stood in the kitchen and watched him. I found him easy to talk to while he cooked. He danced around, being Danny Kaye at the same time. When he calmed down, I told him that I enjoyed seeing him in London and that it was a great pleasure to be at his house.

I enjoyed the food, which he cooked perfectly, but there were so many people there and I was so new to Hollywood that I didn't know anyone and didn't mingle that well at that particular event. I suppose I could have been more aggressive and called Danny Kaye again to talk more about my acting prospects or to ask him to point me in the right direction, but I never followed up with him.

Sitting in my small apartment on Sunset Boulevard on February 27, 1956, I was having my breakfast when I realized that I had nothing to do for the day. No one was going to discover me if I just sat in my apartment, so I decided to call Michael Wilding, the last person on Dirk's contact list. When I dialed the number, a lady answered the phone.

"I'm a friend of Dirk Bogarde's, and I was just calling to say hello to Michael Wilding," I said to her.

"Michael's filming in Africa right now, but I'm his wife," the voice said on the other end.

I nearly dropped the phone. I thought, "I'm talking to Elizabeth Taylor!"

Explaining that I had been directed to her husband by Dirk Bogarde back in England, I couldn't believe it as she turned out to be so warm and welcoming.

"Well, it's my birthday today, and it's also my son Christopher's first birthday," she said. "We're having a little get-together this afternoon to celebrate. Would you like to come up and have some champagne?"

"I would love to," I replied.

"How about three o'clock?" she asked.

"Well, being new here, I don't drive. I'll just need the address to take a cab there."

"Well, it's a little complicated," Elizabeth said. "It's a winding hill where I live. Why don't I send my assistant, Peggy, down to meet you? Meet her at the Beverly Hills Hotel and she'll drive you back here."

We laughed a bit when she said, "Will you wear a red carnation?" I stammered and told her I didn't have one, still not believing that I was talking to her.

She said, "Well, that's all right." She called, "Peggy? What are you wearing?" From the background, perhaps in another room, Peggy answered.

"Peggy will have short hair, corduroy slacks, and a beige sweater. Come up to the reception desk around three o'clock and Peggy will meet you. I'm looking forward to seeing you."

I've always wondered what Peggy thought about being asked to pick up a young import from England, sight unseen, but Dirk's recommendation must have held some sway for Elizabeth to invite me so casually. I think it also speaks well of the generosity and compassion for which Elizabeth Taylor was rightfully famous.

I selected my best outfit and made myself ready. I arrived at the Beverly Hills Hotel early enough to relax and get my thoughts together. I was walking through the lobby when I spotted Alec Guinness, his wife, Merula Salaman, and their teenage son. Guinness, who had just appeared on my radio program five months earlier, looked astonished when he saw me.

"Hello!" he said. "What on earth are *you* doing here, something for the BBC?"

"Well, Mr. Guinness," I began nervously. "I've come to be an actor."

"Oh," he answered. "Do you have time to talk about this?"

"I can't at the moment," I told him. "I'm on my way to see Elizabeth Taylor!"

A little name dropping never hurt, and that certainly seemed to get his attention. I told him that I was working part-time in American radio, that I had resigned from my position at the BBC, and that I intended to stay at least six months to pursue acting in Hollywood.

"Do you have a good agent?" he asked.

I told him that I did not.

"Oh," he sighed in pity. "You have to have an agent to negotiate for you. What is one to do with you? One can't just leave you here," he said.

"Even if I fail, then I will have tried," I told him. "I can't spend the rest of my life saying that I want to be an actor and wondering how it would have worked out if I had done it."

A fortuitous encounter with Alec Guinness led me to my first agent.

Luckily for me, he felt responsible for this wayward, stubborn, young fellow countryman who stood before him, although he truly was not responsible for me in any way. Guinness told me that he had just finished filming *The Swan* with Grace Kelly and would leave for England the next day.

"Come to the hotel here about 7:30 and we'll take the car out to MGM and talk more about what I might be able to do," he said. With that, he turned and walked off to join his wife and son.

My mind was whirling when Peggy picked me up just a few minutes later. Had I not been there a few minutes early, I would have missed Guinness altogether!

Before she became Elizabeth's personal assistant, Peggy had worked for Peggy Lee and Dolores Hope, Bob Hope's wife. As I quickly learned, she was the consummate organizer; Elizabeth didn't have to think a thing about where she was supposed to be because Peggy always knew.

Peggy drove us up to the Wildings' house in the Hollywood Hills. I no longer felt like a tourist as we drove past beautiful estates and palatial homes. The Wildings' home was a low, Spanish-style house that circled the pool in a backyard courtyard. Its procurement had been arranged for them by MGM when the two of them married. Elizabeth later told me that the house payment was deducted from their weekly salaries, hers being $5,000 and Michael's being $3,000.

Peggy had forgotten her key. She rang the bell, and Elizabeth herself answered. Elizabeth was beautiful beyond measure. She wore no makeup and needed none. With her tan, double eyelashes, violet eyes, marvelous, shiny raven hair, and an off-the-shoulder blouse, she was stunning. I melted at the sight.

She said, "Hi, come on in," with a smile.

The birthday party for Elizabeth and her son had started by the time we arrived. Although my BBC interviewing experience had taught me not to become too star struck by celebrities, I was nevertheless awed when I walked into a room and saw Elizabeth Taylor, Jane Powell, Lana Turner, and Virginia Leith.

The famous ladies were sitting at a little nook and sipping champagne. In the middle of the room was a portable carousel. A clown in full makeup entertained the group and mesmerized Elizabeth's two little boys, Christopher, celebrating his birthday, and Michael, Jr., age three.

There were no other children present, but Michael Wilding's elderly father, who lived in a guest cottage on the property, joined in the boys' fun. The senior Mr. Wilding was very nice, well-read, and scholarly, and appeared uninterested in show business. He seemed completely oblivious to the fame of these notable women at his grandson's party. It was a festive, happy scene.

Elizabeth and her famous guests were friendly and welcoming. As she headed across the room to me, Elizabeth said, "Champagne?" She stopped short, turned around and, thinking aloud, said, "No! Wrong! You're English — you want tea!" She handed the champagne to one of the ladies, and then Peggy brought me a cup of tea, even though I secretly craved the champagne.

Peggy had to get something from the car, so when I went with her, a green Rolls-Royce drove up. A sleek, elegant lady drove up, got out, and put up the hood and said, "Something's wrong with this damn car!" It was Linda Christian, Tyrone Power's wife. She slammed the hood and then joined the other ladies.

I spent the afternoon talking with these very famous ladies and enjoying cake and punch. As the afternoon wore off, the clown left with the carousel. The ladies began trickling away from the party.

It seemed like my cue, so I said to Peggy, "I suppose I should be going."

Elizabeth heard me and said, "No, stay awhile."

My heart pounded a little again at the prospect of having more one-on-one time with her. Mr. Wilding retired to his cottage, so Peggy and I sat down with Elizabeth. As she talked, I quickly realized that there was no starry nonsense about her. She was practical and down to earth. She must have been aware of her beauty, but there was no parading around like a movie star unless it was called for at work. At home, she was just folks, if you can imagine Elizabeth Taylor being that way.

Elizabeth asked about my background at the BBC. I told her about my life's true ambition and how I had arrived in Hollywood with hopes of becoming an actor.

"Well, I wish there was something I could do with you, but I'm on the outs with MGM right now over my contract," she said. "I don't have many friends there right now, but let me think about it."

She studied me for a moment and then said, "If you're going to start auditioning for parts, you need some sunlight. You look awfully pale to be an actor."

"Well, I *am* English," I noted.

"Why don't you come up here to the house and swim whenever you feel like it? You'll get some great sunlight that way. Just call whenever you want to come up and Peggy will come and get you."

Again, I couldn't believe my eyes and ears. On the same day that I had been invited to breakfast the following morning with Alec Guinness, I was being invited to swim at Elizabeth Taylor's house when she wasn't shooting *Raintree County*.

I told her that I would be glad to accept her gracious offer but I couldn't impose by being driven up whenever I wanted to use the pool.

"It's only two miles to your house," I said. "If I can do this, I know how to get here now. It's uphill, so it will be good exercise for me."

"Well, really, do call. Someone's always here," she said. "If I'm not here, Peggy's here, so just call whenever you want to come up and use the pool."

When I returned home that night, I felt so alive and full of energy that I barely slept. I must have spent hours reliving the day over in my mind as I tried to sleep. What a whirlwind day it had been, perhaps the most significant of my life.

The morning after encountering Alec Guinness and visiting with Elizabeth Taylor, I returned to the Beverly Hills Hotel to meet Guinness at 7:30 a.m. I went up to his room. Always conscious about schedules, he looked at his watch.

He said, "The car will be down now, so it's time to go." I hardly had time to say, "Here I am — I hope you remember that we talked yesterday afternoon," but he did remember that he had agreed to help me.

We took an MGM limousine out to the studio. On the way, he told me that he was going to do post-production dubbing on *The Swan*.

He said, "Now, my plane leaves at four this afternoon for Heathrow. I hope they're on schedule at MGM."

I was overawed at driving onto the MGM lot. It was the crown jewel of studios, especially for someone who loved musicals as I did. MGM's famous gate was often shot in movies; in *Anchors Away*, for example, Frank Sinatra tries to get in through that same gate that we were now entering.

As we drove, I couldn't help but wonder, "What if we see Clark Gable or another big star?" I suppose I hadn't really thought of Alec Guinness as an MGM star, but he was a celebrity, nevertheless. It's funny how one's mind processes things in those situations. We passed soundstages on each side, hallowed ground where film history had been made.

That morning with Alec Guinness, the studio was on schedule, so the time passed easily enough as he dubbed. I watched him work and was not overawed by that. Dubbing was not too unlike radio work, and I had actually witnessed dubbing back in England. When I had interviewed Shelley Winters for the BBC, part of the interview was done in the dubbing room before we left to finish our chat in a pub.

At lunchtime, Guinness said, "We might as well have a bite to eat on MGM." We went into a regular commissary. He didn't have a private spot to dine, because he really didn't view himself that way. Eating out there in the open had its advantages.

As we dined, in walked Grace Kelly, scheduled to do her dubbing work for the afternoon. I had seen *Dial M for Murder* and *To Catch a Thief*, so I recognized her instantly. She came over to the table and said, "Alec, darling!" and then followed with hugs and kisses. I don't remember what they talked about. I just stared, hoping my mouth was closed. She was so beautiful.

She serenely wafted away to do her dubbing. It was common knowledge that she was about to marry, so I said to Guinness, "Gosh, she's almost like a princess now, isn't she?"

He said, "Yes, Grace does take herself very seriously." I don't know if that comment was disapproving or not, but it stuck in my mind.

After lunch, we went back to his hotel so he could pack. He invited me to come up to the room. He asked, "Well, what kind of parts would you be comfortable playing, assuming you can be an actor?"

I remember saying, "Well, I have never acted, so I don't know if I can."

Thinking of Richard Attenborough and the types of cowardly or unstable characters he typically played, I told him, "I think I would be good at playing cowards like Richard Attenborough."

He said, "All right. I am going to give you three letters of introduction, but I can't recommend you as an actor because I have never seen you act. I don't know if you're good, bad or indifferent, but I will give you three letters of introduction."

That was a lot, coming from a great actor like Alec Guinness. I couldn't have expected more, especially when he asked me what kind of parts I would like to do and I had to think about it before I answered.

Guinness continued, "All I will say in it is, 'This young man did a very nice interview with me in England six months ago and is now in Hollywood, anxious to try his luck as an actor. If you have any advice to give him, would you be kind enough to respond to this letter?'"

He sat at his desk as he wrote. Guinness said, "I am writing now to Ridgeway Callow, first assistant director on *The Swan*, and I am sending a note to David Niven, who has his own TV show, *Four Star Playhouse*."

Back in England, I had interviewed David Niven, so I thought there might be some reaction there from his letter. He then continued:

"The third letter is to my agent here at the William Morris Agency, and his name is Peter Shaw."

I didn't know him, but a letter of recommendation is a letter indeed. Guinness sealed them up and he said, "I've just said, 'Would you have the courtesy of talking to him?' I can't say more."

I said, "Really, I'm very grateful for these letters." And I was. Guinness didn't know me very well. He had reservations about my lack of acting preparation and my age. So I had every reason to be grateful for this good turn of luck.

Having kept his promise, off he went to England. I went home and mailed the letters. I thought, "I guess I'll hear back eventually, but I don't know if this will work." It seemed chancy to wait to hear back.

I first heard from David Niven, whom I candidly did not like. When I had interviewed him in England, I found him very standoffish and dull. Naturally, he sent me a very standoffish and dull letter.

Niven started his letter with, "Dear sir." I thought, "Oh, come on; you could have said 'Dear Mr. Frankham.'" His letter continued: "My television program has ended for the season, and in any case, I don't need any extras."

Furious, I thought, "Up yours, Niven! How condescending can you be! An extra is someone who stands around and doesn't do any acting."

He didn't even finish it with "Sincerely yours," just "David Niven." I threw it away. (In fairness to Niven, however, he had started his career as an extra, so in his worldview, he still saw starting as an extra a suitable option, even though he was being adamant that there were no jobs for me in that capacity.)

I heard next from Ridgeway Callow, who was one of MGM's biggest assistant directors. He had even worked on *Gone with the Wind*.

His letter said, "I've heard from Alec. Give me a call; come out the studio for lunch and I'll show you around the back lot."

I thought to myself, "I haven't come eleven thousand miles to take a tour of MGM; I want to *work* at MGM." So I didn't respond to that letter, which in hindsight was a mistake. Who knows where that might have led!

The third letter arrived from Peter Shaw, who was a much-respected agent and vice president of the William Morris Agency. He wrote, "Alec has told me that we should talk. Give me a call."

This was a prospect I liked, so I made an appointment. Friends told me he was married to Angela Lansbury. I foolishly thought, "Gee, maybe she will be there," because I was a huge fan of hers.

When I walked into his office, the first thing Peter said was, "Hello. How are you? I want you to do something for me. Now, please go out and come in again."

I said, "What?"

He said, "Come in again. Come into my office, but this time, do it as though you mean it. You need self-confidence, because you looked as though you were coming in to ask for a job, and you never get work that way."

That was a valuable lesson, one that I never forgot, no matter how nervous I felt in the early years going for an interview. If it showed that I was nervous, I was not going to get the job unless the producers were desperate for me.

So I had gone in rather sheepishly. Truthfully, I was intimidated. I knew that William Morris was an enormous agency representing nothing but big names. I had felt self-conscious. Nevertheless, being told to come back into Peter's office was a surprise, but I did as I was told, even though I still felt a little self-conscious about it. From his expression, I could tell that I had done much better.

"That's the way to come in," he said. "If you're going to get going here, you have to have confidence in yourself."

That was a challenge to me. I said, "Peter, I know what I can do with my background, but I just don't know what I can do as an actor."

The next surprise came when Peter picked up his telephone, buzzed his secretary and was put through to Universal Studios. He said, in front of me sitting there, "Do you need a new leading man? I have a young chap out here from England just off the boat who might just be exactly right for you."

I was thinking, "Wait a minute! I haven't even acted yet, and he's talking about leading roles?" That was Peter, just no boundaries and very brave. I thought, "Wow, that's a vote of confidence!"

Unfortunately, they didn't need any English leading men, so Peter hung up the phone and said, "Well, you are unknown, so we can't represent you, but I'm going to send you to the hardest-working agent in town. She represents English actors when they're starting out, and anybody who wants to get lots of work initially should be with Maurine Oliver. Tell her I suggested that she meet with you."

I was so fortunate to have a good shove from an influential individual. In retrospect, with age and maturity behind me, I know it was very risky to just come out to Hollywood in hopes, as it were. For would-be actors who arrived without contacts, it meant possibly sitting for months without anything happening. I saw that situation with so many young hopefuls of my age when I was starting — they had great enthusiasm and high expectations, but, for most of them, nothing ever happened.

So, in March 1956, and upon Peter Shaw's recommendation, I went to see Maurine Oliver, a witty, warm Irishwoman who was also strong-willed with grit and determination. She was a real life Auntie Mame. Maurine had started out as a young actress with the Abbey Theatre in Dublin, Ireland. Known at the time as Maureen Rodin-Ryan, she moved with her mother to Hollywood in the 1930s. Changing her name to Maurine Oliver, she did a few small roles on film. She played Joan Fontaine's maid in both *Rebecca* and *Suspicion*, and she had a hilarious walk-on, again as a nursemaid, in Lubitsch's *Heaven Can Wait*.

She decided that, in her own words, she "looked like a bump on a log," so she smartly switched to the agency business almost overnight. Rather than go back to Ireland, she became an agent.

Her first client was her close friend, Sara Allgood, one of my favorite character actresses, nominated in 1941 for a Best Supporting Actress Academy Award for *How Green Was My Valley*. Sara had said to her, "Maurine, you have the gift of the gab. You should just try to start an agency. I have such confidence in you that I'll be your first client if you want to do this."

So Maurine started her own agency, and with a busy, working actress like Sara Allgood, she was able to establish herself. Once Maurine became an agent, she never looked back. By the time I met her, she had built up a good group of character actors. She even drove Angela Lansbury to MGM to audition for *Gaslight*, the movie that helped establish her as an audience favorite to this day.

Maurine was good. I could sense that at her first meeting with me. I hadn't met many agents; in fact, I had just met Peter Shaw, so I didn't know much about assessing the quality of an agent, but something about her clicked. I just liked her breeziness. I told her my story, how I was determined to be an actor, and that I was freelancing in radio.

Maurine said, "Well, I have somebody on the books who is almost a dead ringer for you, so it wouldn't be fair to him for me to represent you as an actor. If I sent you on an interview, and you got it, it would be taking away bread from him, and he's already my client. But, I'll represent you for radio. What are you getting?"

I told her $150 for an appearance. She shook her head and said in her Irish accent, "Oh, no, no, dear; we can do better than that! Who are you going to see next week?"

So she got on the phone and got me up to $200 right there. She said, "We'll sign, with me representing you for radio, exclusively."

My radio appearances continued from March to June. One day Maurine called me to tell me that her look-alike client was going to New York to do a musical adaptation of *The Importance of Being Earnest*.

"You come in and I'll sign you for acting," she said. "We'll send you out for things." Much to my relief, finally I had an agent!

Everything I eventually did as an actor happened because Maurine made it happen. She worked tirelessly every day. At night she was off to a theatre somewhere to check out a young performer. She loved the business and had a terrific reputation for integrity among her peers.

She would say, "Never go in hat in hand, deferentially, as though you're there for a job." In the daytime, she drove me around to every studio to introduce me to casting agents. Whenever I didn't get an audition, Maurine always said, "Well, that just means you're free to take whatever comes along next." Not a bad way of looking at things.

She also taught me well about expectations. Whenever I was up for something and waiting to hear if I got the part, she immediately switched my mind to the next audition so I didn't sit thinking, "Gosh, I wonder if it's going to work out?" She was awfully good about instilling mental self-discipline in me.

Who knows, too, how tough the going might have been for me but for that chance meeting with Alec Guinness. He had come through for me, directing me to a big agent who in turn found the right agent for me. Thank goodness Guinness was flexible in his viewpoint, too; had he stuck to his initial adamant belief that I was too old to act, he could have very easily refused to help me once we crossed paths.

Having been extended a helping hand, I knew that it was now up to me. If I succeeded or failed in Hollywood, it would be a destiny of my own making.

Elizabeth Taylor and Michael Wilding were very kind to me that first year in Hollywood. Without much acting experience behind me, it was to be slow going until I could get my foot in the door.

Elizabeth had invited me to use her pool to tan, so I wasn't about to let that opportunity slip through my fingers. However, the first few times I called, just as she had requested I do, I felt strange. I didn't know her that well, so I would call, and say, "Hi, it's David, I was up before and Elizabeth invited me to use the pool?"

Peggy, her assistant, usually answered the phone. The first few times she said, "Of course, come on — we told you to come up. We'll be here all afternoon."

I would take a bus to the Beverly Hills Hotel and then walk two miles up to the Wildings' home. I was welcomed as though I had been there forever. There was no formality about it. It was a very easygoing house. The children didn't even have a nursemaid.

Elizabeth was in the middle of shooting *Raintree County*, so Peggy looked after the Wildings' children when Elizabeth wasn't there. They were good little boys, and I got on well with them. One day they told me that they liked to catch bugs, so I went with them to the side of the house where there were exotic plants and flowers. The boys used a jar and caught bugs and then I helped them release the captured insects.

For someone hoping to make it big in Hollywood, it was rather ironic that every day not working in radio was spent with Elizabeth Taylor. On days when she wasn't filming, Elizabeth sat by the pool and read. She always wore a pale lemon swimsuit and tanned beautifully. She was gorgeous. I would swim laps while she read magazines or read over her lines for *Raintree County*. She didn't seem to have a care in the world.

Michael Wilding soon returned from Africa. He was full of charm, and he seemed to like me as well. He gave me suggestions on who would be filming what and which productions might be good for parts. I liked him immediately. Dirk Bogarde called him a disgrace to the profession because he had become a huge star without much of an acting ability. Michael had enormous charisma, though. He was so easy to get along with. He had enough "know how" from being a star in England.

This Raintree County *publicity photo captures how Elizabeth Taylor looked when I got to know her in 1956.* (MGM)

Elizabeth could see that I was genuinely interested in making movies and not just interested in swimming and sun-tanning, so we began to discuss acting techniques. She gave me her script from *Giant* to read and study, and I still have it today. She told me that she adored James Dean. He had given her a Siamese cat at the end of the movie, so she had three or four kittens running around her house by the time I got to know her. She asked if I would like a cat, but I was living in a small apartment so I didn't take one; otherwise, I could have ended up with one of the offspring of James Dean's cats!

Elizabeth thoroughly knew her craft and went through a list of different film shots and explained the purpose behind each one. In her reasoning, close-ups meant that actors had a chance to shine by being in character. She often said, "Save your best acting for close-ups, especially whenever you see these letters in a script: ECU, extreme close-ups. Long shots aren't worth anything."

One day she invited me to the set of *Raintree County*. I met her at her house at four a.m. and rode with her in a limousine to MGM. That day, I watched her film her death scene on the MGM backlot. Her work consisted of being fitted in her period costume and reclining in mud.

She had me sit close by, off camera, to watch her work. "They're going to be filming a long shot," she explained. "They'll be so far away that I won't have to act at all. I could be thinking about what's for dinner tonight, but the camera won't know it, and when the audience sees it, all they'll be thinking is how sorry they are to see me dying on screen."

Elizabeth introduced me to Montgomery Clift one weekend at her house. On weekends he was there to run over scenes together as I swam in her pool. Just a few years earlier in England, I loved watching *A Place in the Sun*, with its fine performances, direction, and camera work with wonderfully slow fades and close-ups. There were no more beautiful people on earth than Elizabeth Taylor and Montgomery Clift. That was still true six years after *A Place in the Sun* was released. They both were still knockouts, young and movie-star good-looking. I'd stare and think, "Why can't I look like that?"

Monty was so charming, a beautiful man in the purest sense of the word, very friendly. He was an intelligent actor and easy to talk to as he always sat on the floor, dressed in blue jeans. He was very low-keyed, always smiling. He and Elizabeth talked about shooting, but they included me in the general conversation about whatever was happening in the world. I felt privileged to be allowed into such a relaxed atmosphere, especially since I had been a complete stranger.

He never had good coordination, though, and at the best of times, Monty always reached for a doorknob on the wrong side of a door. With his bad coordination, he should not have been driving. The road down from the Wildings' house was narrow and sharply curved. On the evening of May 12, 1956, Elizabeth held a small dinner party. I was not there, but Elizabeth later recounted the whole evening's events.

Elizabeth and Michael hosted Monty, Rock Hudson, and his then wife, Phyllis, for a dinner party. Elizabeth had made *Giant* with Rock the year before. During filming, Michael would fly out to Texas on location, and Phyllis would visit Rock, too. They all remained friends after the film was finished and got together again this particular evening.

Elizabeth said no one was drunk. They had a pleasant dinner and a chat. When Monty left for home that evening in his car, for some reason, he lost control. He wasn't going that fast, but Monty hit a utility pole and smashed his face into the steering wheel. Rock and Phyllis came running with the Wildings. As soon as they saw what happened, Rock said, "The papers will be here in no time." The lights went on in the neighbors' houses. His friends wanted to protect Monty, because he was unconscious.

Elizabeth sat in the front seat and cradled his head in her arms. Either Michael or Rock ran back up to call and an ambulance was there shortly. Elizabeth famously helped pull teeth out from the back of Monty's throat to keep him from choking. I later went down with Elizabeth and Michael to see Monty, critically injured, in the Cedars of Lebanon Hospital. We visited him to keep up his spirits until he was well enough to leave. The

Elizabeth Taylor and Montgomery Clift on the set of Raintree County. (MGM)

poor guy was propped up in bed with his mouth in a cage-like device while the surgeons worked to restore his damaged upper lip.

Eventually, he began to recuperate. MGM had leased him a house, but Elizabeth wouldn't hear of him being alone. He came back up to her house where Elizabeth nursed him. His mouth was twisted on the right side. He couldn't eat through that wire cage on his jaw, so he had to drink nutritional milkshakes through a soda straw. Elizabeth hovered over him like a mother hen. We all took turns feeding him from a blender mix by a straw.

Monty initially did his best to keep a sense of humor about the whole thing. He was incredibly courageous throughout the entire ordeal. He was always smiling, but it was the pain medication. Sometimes Michael and I would put him to bed in the guest house. He would just flop around helplessly. He lived through that awful summer in sort of a haze. He was on morphine which probably ruined his life. I later heard he stayed on medicines for the rest of his life because of the pain.

Production on *Raintree County* shut down. MGM decided not to finish the film, but Elizabeth wouldn't hear of it. I was there when she said to an MGM executive on the phone, "He's got to finish it! He'll die if he doesn't have work to finish." In fact, she threatened to walk and never work again if MGM did not promise to resume production.

In time, Monty recuperated and *Raintree County* was finished. It's morbid now to see pre-accident scenes and then scenes where he's not really up to it. He never fully regained mobility in his face. Part of his upper lip was permanently numb, and his career suffered because of the change to his looks.

It's ironic that *A Place in the Sun* was based on *An American Tragedy*, because that really became the story of Monty's shortened life after that summer of 1956. Elia Kazan was quoted in Richard Schickel's biography of him that Monty was a mess in 1960 during the production of *Wild River*, but Lee Remick and Jo Van Fleet looked after him through the production and kept him away from drink until the shoot was over. Despite all the tales of backstabbing and intrigue in Hollywood, actors could truly care about and look out for each other.

In addition to Elizabeth being a loyal and supportive friend to established actors such as Monty or to a newcomer named David Frankham, she was also incredibly smart. One day I was leaving the Wildings' house for my two-mile trek home. The telephone rang. When Michael answered it, Marlene Dietrich was on the line, asking for Elizabeth. Marlene had been offered a part in *Witness for the Prosecution*. She had to decide about the script. Because Elizabeth was so adept at seeing the potential, or lack thereof, in parts for women, it turned out that other stars regularly sought her career advice.

Marlene Dietrich wanted to know if she could drop in for a quick consultation. As I was getting ready to leave, the Wildings told me there wasn't much time; Marlene was just two minutes away by a cab, and she would be there before I left. Marlene was an intensely private person, and they did not want to risk upsetting her by encountering me, having to explain who I was, and waiting to see if I was trustworthy in Marlene's opinion.

Robert Wagner, a hi-fi music buff, had recently installed hi-fi equipment in the Wildings' attic so they could enjoy music throughout their house with speakers in the walls. While Elizabeth prepared to meet Marlene, Michael hustled me up to a small space next to the hi-fi equipment in the attic. Being the summer, the attic was incredibly hot without air conditioning, but Marlene was not going to visit for very long. I heard her come in and listened while she visited for thirty minutes and sought Elizabeth's opinion of the part that had been offered to her.

I could not see them, but I overheard those two legendary Hollywood stars conferring about what would turn out to be a terrific part for Marlene. Elizabeth's advice was obviously spot-on. After Marlene left, I heard Michael call, "Okay, David! You can come down now!"

The Wildings were so kind that summer that I was too touched or awestruck to pick up on subtle clues that their marriage would soon be ending. I arrived for my swim one day when Elizabeth was discussing with Peggy what would be her friendly separation with Michael.

Elizabeth said to me, "Come with us to the airport, because Peggy and I are going to go and have a drink with Michael before he leaves for Europe." Their trial separation had all been arranged.

As I digested the news that Elizabeth and Michael could be headed for a divorce, MGM publicist Howard Strickling arrived. He was a very nice man, one who had his clients' best interests in mind. He reminded Elizabeth that she had to call gossip columnist Hedda Hopper. Hedda and her counterpart, Louella Parsons, rode herd on actors who were really wage slaves, no matter how enormously popular they were in a world-wide sense.

Elizabeth said, "Oh my God, yes," so she went into her bedroom and broke the news exclusively to Hedda, an hour before Howard generally released the news to the world that Elizabeth Taylor and Michael Wilding were separating.

Elizabeth was clearly still part of the old Hollywood system. Part of it was magic and the other part shocking. My own experience as an interviewer for the BBC had meant that the public was not remotely interested in a star's private life back in England. I had always focused on the star's work. For the most part there, the press did not cover or reveal private details. As a member of the movie-going public, I had thought that everyone was perfect, went happily to work, didn't fool around or have sexual aberrations of any kind. I wish it were still that way today, with the non-stop obsession over every bit of minutia about a star's life.

I couldn't believe that Elizabeth could be so calm about her impending separation. That evening around midnight, Peggy drove us to the airport where we were to meet Michael in the Scandinavian Airline Systems' VIP room. Elizabeth and I sat in the back of the car. We drove up to find a waiting horde of photographers. "How did they know you were coming here?" I asked Elizabeth.

She sighed. "They always seem to know," she murmured.

When I opened my door and got out of the car, the crush of cameras slammed me up against the wall while Elizabeth walked through them, refusing to comment. We met Michael for the drink, they wished each other well, and then he left for his flight.

We were able to slip out of the airport without the photographers seeing. Elizabeth began crying and said that she didn't want to go home. Friends were watching her children, so she decided to stay at Peggy's apartment. During the drive home, she could not stop crying on my shoulder, and she continued to weep once we reached Peggy's place.

I gamely put my arm around Elizabeth's shoulder in a vain attempt to comfort her. The shock of it all was so great that I truly didn't know what to say. I was so new to Hollywood that movie star romances were not my area of expertise. All I could do was to assure her that everything was going to be fine.

In retrospect, Michael was several years older than Elizabeth, so I think the age difference had something to do with the end of their marriage. Their careers were on different paths, too, and filming far apart could not have helped, either. The summer of 1956 had been a transitional one for Elizabeth. One chapter ended and led to an even more momentous one for her.

Two days later, the Hollywood press was reporting that Michael Todd had called Elizabeth. He swept her off on a worldwide tour that culminated in their marriage. She had new adventures to pursue. My summer adventure with the Wildings had ended, too, as my own career was about to take off at NBC. Looking back at the spring and summer of 1956, I will forever remain grateful to Elizabeth Taylor and Michael Wilding.

CHAPTER FOUR

Live from NBC

Believing that I was planting the right seeds to blossom into an acting career, I convinced my English friend Mimi to quit her job as a secretary and join me to try her luck in Hollywood. Elizabeth Taylor might have been encouraging to me, but Mimi and I could share more adventures together as fledgling actors who were on the same level.

I arranged to rent an apartment for Mimi above mine. I met her at the airport, and the moment that charming, sweet, cute amateur actress set foot off the plane, she hated absolutely everything about America. She was condescending about it. She hated the clothes that the women wore, she hated the food, American television — there was nothing that she liked about it.

America was appealing to me, though, and I intended to make the best of the opportunities in this exciting place called Hollywood. From some of my early auditions, no one would have believed that I ever had a chance! Prior to my signing with my agent, Maurine Oliver, one such prospective role took me to audition for a Bela Lugosi low-budgeter, with Lugosi himself.

I had gone into an agent's office on Sunset Boulevard, where all the agents' offices seemed to be located. The agent was sort of distracted by shuffling papers, so he said, "Get out to the old Chaplin studios. They're shooting a Bela Lugosi movie there. Maybe there's something there for you."

The entire experience was very strange. Lugosi was shooting a scene in a jail cell for what I believe was one of his last movies, *The Black Sleep*. The idea was exciting, talking to an agent and being sent to a real studio, which was around the corner from my apartment. The old Chaplin studio was small, consisting of bungalows instead of towering buildings.

I told somebody at the gate that I had been sent to meet the director and was pointed to a soundstage at the back. There sat Bela Lugosi. He wasn't doing anything. He must have been a very low-key kind of actor. He just sat there alone, quietly rehearsing and talking to himself.

The director shoved me in to read with Lugosi. I must say that I was thrilled! I knew nothing of his background except he had scared the living daylights out of me in *White Zombie* and *Dracula*. Wearing a dark suit, he had dark shadows under his eyes, and his hair was kind of oily and

One of my first headshots in 1956.

flattened. I don't remember even being properly introduced to him. The director simply said, "Read this scene."

Lugosi said, "Ah, which scene is this?" It was only one page. He knew everything. He didn't have a script in front of him, because he knew his part. I read my lines to Lugosi, who seemed kind of bored by the whole thing. He didn't say, "Well done," or "Do you want to do it again?" He just read the dialogue with me, but I was reading with Bela Lugosi! The accent wasn't phony. It was THE Dracula accent. I thought, "Even though it's one little scene, I'm starting my career by working with Bela Lugosi!"

He didn't move at all. It was almost like being in a wax museum in that I saw this figure and thought, "That looks just like Bela Lugosi!" There was no movement to him at all.

The director said, "Thank you." That was it. I was dismissed. I left without even the standard, "Thanks for coming in." I didn't get the part, but it was quite exciting to be sitting across from Dracula himself. Sadly, Lugosi died not too long afterward from a multitude of health and career problems later dramatized by Martin Landau in *Ed Wood*.

Thankfully, my first Hollywood work came elsewhere, on television at NBC, to be exact. As good fortune would have it, I had arrived in California during the Golden Age of television. Every network aired a number of anthology series with dramatic weekly episodes. Several of these series began airing as early as the afternoon and into evening hours as alternatives to soap operas. Because many of the major motion picture studios still feared television and withheld their films, the networks were forced to come up with dramatic programs to fill the airwaves with sixty- or ninety-minute stories that offered more substance than thirty-minute episodic fare.

With excellent scripts and dramatic parts, working on these programs was an actor's dream. Many of Hollywood's biggest stars began by appearing on anthology series that bridged the gap between stage and screen. Several of these shows were prestigious, including *Playhouse 90* and *Studio One*, and noted actors, as well as up-and-coming stars, could be seen any day of the week.

The networks were spared the expense of maintaining a full cast for recurring scripted plotlines. Adapting well-known literary works meant that audiences enjoyed a degree of familiarity with the storyline. For many episodes, teleplays were just that, broadcasts of stage plays, staged for television. Such teleplays also were vehicles for the networks to spot actors who could be cast elsewhere in regular series. It was an exciting age of television that lasted just a decade or so as the medium gained legitimacy and fully developed series became standard fare for most viewers.

NBC broadcast several anthology series, including *Matinee Theater*. Created and produced by Albert McCleery and hosted by John Conte, *Matinee Theater* ran from 1955 to 1958. Each day, the series featured original dramatic plays and adaptations of noted literary classics. There were five primary directors, one for each day of the week's hourly production. With a different cast each day, the show aired live at noon on the West Coast, with each production airing at three p.m. in the Eastern time zone. The name paid homage to the fact that the program literally aired during matinee hours in New York.

The show was a gift to actors, experienced or otherwise, because it was something different, a whole new play and cast, Monday through Friday. Broadcast live, the show was hugely successful. NBC was promoting the first color sets. Skillfully, the writers whittled down and adapted a three-act stage play to fifty-two minutes. The other eight minutes were taken for break-ins to promote NBC's color TVs. The show itself was shown in color, which was unusual, because most shows in 1956 aired in black and white.

Maurine decided to send me to *Matinee Theater* to audition because she felt I wasn't experienced enough for *Playhouse 90*, where they needed proven actors with a resume. Because my radio work made me a member of the American Federation of Television and Radio Artists (AFTRA), I could be considered for *Matinee Theater* roles. AFTRA's members worked on live television or radio broadcasts.

When I started going to NBC on auditions, I said to Maurine, "I have no experience. What am I going to say if they ask what I was in most recently in England?" Having often felt guilty about things all my life, I would especially have felt guilty if I misrepresented myself.

She said, "They won't ask you anything, because I have already told them that you have been sponsored by Alec Guinness."

"I haven't been sponsored," I protested.

She said, "Yes, you have, dear."

So she simply told the NBC people — and it was true — that I had worked with Alec Guinness and he had started me in Hollywood with letters of introduction.

I was still worried. I said, "I have to have a back-up plan in case they say, "What were you in?'"

Maurine and I sat down. She said, from right out of her head, "You've been in REP."

"But I haven't!" I argued.

"Listen to me, dear. You've been in REP. You've been with the Irene Weller Players."

I said, "Who are they?"

"They aren't!" she replied. "But THAT'S who you were with!"

I told her about my aborted attempts to audition for the Old Vic when I had to prepare a little piece of Shakespeare and another from *The Corn Is Green*.

Maurine said, "Okay, we'll skip Shakespeare. Besides, you don't look Shakespearian, dear." So she put down *The Corn Is Green*, *Rope*, and half a dozen plays that I had supposedly appeared in with the Irene Weller Players.

She said, "Now memorize that, because you're going up to NBC tomorrow. Only tell them if they ask you. You've got to believe this or you're no actor. You have to believe!"

Catching on, I said, "Okay, I believe."

I began going out to NBC. They had five casting directors and over the course of two to three weeks, I met each of them. No one asked me about the Irene Weller Players, so I never got a chance to spout off about my appearances in *Rope* and the others that Maurine crafted.

I think the producers of *Matinee Theater* were all under pressure. It was a highly organized, smoothly running organization. During the five days, one team was casting and another starting ten days of rehearsals. Another team would go in the day before the live show, and another team produced the live show that particular day. They were all in different stages of development, and the casting directors were really working very hard. Fortunately, they didn't dilly dally over my previous experience. Somebody did ask, "What was it like working with Alec Guinness?" and I said, "It was very easy," because it was — all I did was interview him!

Reading was easy for me because of my BBC news experience. For a news reader, delivering something without preparing for it first was called a cold reading. Before reading a news bulletin, I usually had time to read the items I was to announce over the microphone. But sometimes someone would sneak quietly into the news room and hand me another piece of news that I had not seen. Over the years I had become skilled enough that when it happened, I could go right from a piece that I had already seen to the new piece of paper and read it as though I had also seen that before. So I was good at cold reading.

When the NBC casting people said, "Just read a few lines from this, David," they handed me a part and asked if I wanted time to think about it. I usually said, "No, that's all right; I can do it." I just looked at it, got an idea of the character, and just read the lines.

In spite of what seemed like good cold readings, I had yet to be cast in anything. I said to Maurine, "Do I really have to keep doing this, because they really don't have anything for me." She kept assuring me that my weekly visits for callbacks would pay off soon. While I wasn't getting the parts, I *was* reading for NBC. Casting directors giving me script direction was the first real direction I had ever experienced. I must have been able to do it well enough for them to call me back.

Each time I went to an interview at NBC, I thought all the way out there, "Richard Widmark, Richard Widmark," because he had made such an enormous impression on me on film in *Kiss of Death*, his first big acting job. He had been such a skilled radio actor that there were stories of his always keeping a cab running when he finished one show to jump into the cab and do the next one. He had no training as an actor, no formal experience in theatre or anything, but he just moved right up to this incredible performance in *Kiss of Death*.

I kept thinking to myself, "Well, if he can do it, why can't I? All I'm doing really with these people is being a radio actor. I'm not made up or playing a character; I'm reading lines."

I remember leaving those auditions thinking, "God, if only there was a radio show. I know I can be a radio actor. You don't have to memorize lines. You don't have to dress up. You stand in front of a microphone and read the script. You've got it in your hands the whole time."

Yet I was aware that it wasn't radio and that if they gave me a job, I would actually have to act. I believed I could do it. I never went to Hollywood to be a movie star. I knew I didn't look like one, and I didn't have whatever movie stars had. All I wanted to be was a working actor making a good living in film. My only experience with acting was as a viewer of movies, because I had seen very few plays. I was comfortable in the language of film, and I could adjust to that.

My confidence level grew, and my exposure to the network's casting agents soon paid off. My reading for NBC continued through the summer of 1956. That July, Roddy McDowall was cast in an adaptation of *September Tide*, a play in three acts presented on *Matinee Theater*. The 1950 play had been written by Daphne Du Maurier, the author of *Rebecca, Jamaica Inn*, and the short stories "The Birds" and "Don't Look Now."

Roddy had also committed to act on Broadway in *Diary of a Scoundrel*, but he wasn't to begin rehearsals until he had finished production on his

September Tide episode. When the Broadway producers wanted to start rehearsals sooner, Roddy was forced to call NBC on a Friday to tell the network that he was off to New York. *September Tide*, however, was to broadcast live the following week.

Peter Shaw and his wife, Angela Lansbury, were long-time friends of Roddy's. In an effort to protect Roddy's reputation with the producers of *Matinee Theater*, Peter thought of me. Roddy and I were both about the same age, with a similar build and look, and English, too. Peter called Maurine and said, "Get David to NBC as fast as you can — he may be right for this. I've seen the script, and I think David can pull this off."

The studio was over a barrel. I went over and read for the part. I was so panic-stricken, though, that I couldn't remember anything that I had done when they asked about my credits, so my nervousness actually worked to my advantage. The producers told Maurine, "Okay, he'll work. We'll give him Roddy's part. Read through is tomorrow."

I thought, "Read through tomorrow? Oh, my God!" And they handed me the script. Fortunately, I had seen *September Tide* in 1950 because the BBC European Service building was right across the street from the theatre where Gertrude Lawrence was appearing. The play had been written for her. I usually had afternoons off, so I just walked across the street to see a matinee and then went back to my evening BBC shift.

I had always wanted to see Gertrude Lawrence, and she had proven marvelous in this part. In fact, I had gone to see *September Tide* three or four times. The actor playing her son was very good. His name was Bryan Forbes, and he would go on to direct *Whistle Down the Wind* and *King Rat*. Going home from NBC with the script in my hand, I tried remembering Bryan Forbes and what he had done with the part a few years earlier.

Mine was a simple role. The script was divided into four parts with commercials, and my character didn't come in until the fourth act. He was a rather grand university type who has come down for Christmas holidays, and he's had a skiing accident. His left leg was to be in a cast, which was a godsend for me, because it meant that I wouldn't have to remember marks or move on the floor. All I had to do was sit on a big couch, and the other three people in the play would come up and talk to me. In that sense, it was a shoo-in.

I realized right away that while I didn't have much to do in the way of moving, I did have a monologue. Act Four would open with the camera tight on me. I didn't have to play Hamlet. There was no great demand being made on my acting talent. I just had to learn a lot of lines.

I cannot stress enough that being in the right place at the right time is absolutely essential to success sometimes, in any profession. In my case, my breaks had started coming pretty regularly as soon as I was drafted into the military, and yet I cursed what I thought would be a waste of my young life at that time. One never knows. I always feel that luck means that if an opportunity comes to you, if you're prepared for it, then you're

My first acting job was replacing Roddy McDowall in 1956.

ready for that opportunity. It's "fortuosity," to quote a Sherman Brothers song. Do your best so you're prepared for the right moment when it comes along.

In my case, the BBC had prepared me for working in a live medium. Because I was just starting out with virtually no acting experience, I had thought I would start on television or in the movies with just a line here or there. NBC didn't know that I was a rank beginner, because the role was a starring part for Roddy! I was to have fourth billing. Maurine told me to keep my mouth shut. She said, "You don't know how lucky you are! Usually actors have to go through at least a year in small parts building up slowly to feature roles, so you don't understand the significance of this — you're starting at featured star!"

Although Roddy would have had top billing, I would have feature billing for my debut! In Hollywood, there's a gentlemen's agreement that I wasn't aware of — wherever you are, you usually don't go down. You can stay at featured, but you don't take smaller parts after being featured. You can go up above it, but not down. I was starting half-way up the ladder.

I started with a two- or three-minute monologue, which absolutely petrified me, because if I dried up, there would be no other member of the cast to cue me. I just had to keep plowing on, live on nationwide television. Quite honestly, I didn't even know if I could act. I had read lines and self-rehearsed, but my primary "training" had been to emulate and pattern myself after other actors whose performances I admired. I thought, "This is the moment of truth." I learned the lines that afternoon, because we had rehearsals the very next morning.

A little panic set in, because while I had faked it with the casting directors, I would be dealing with a director and other actors, and they would know right off that I had no experience. I wasn't intimidated by the technical aspects. I was used to the red light telling me that we were going live on BBC radio. Television was going live when I left the BBC, and I had done that once, even though I hated the experience.

Then a red light of sorts went off in my head. Unlike my aborted attempt at appearing on BBC's experimental television program, I needn't be as self-conscious because I wasn't going to be me, I was going to be playing somebody! That's how I found out the great thing about acting — I could portray a character and lose myself in the process.

I showed up for the first day of a ten-day rehearsal, convinced the others would discover I was a fake before I got through the ten days. Nobody asked me, though, if I had done anything else before. The assumption was that I had acted before. I thought, "How can I look seasoned or experienced when I haven't had any seasoning or experience?"

I was really very nervous that first day. Including myself, there were four primary stars. The cast included Irene Hervey, an MGM and Universal player in the 1930s and 1940s. The lovely lady had been married to singer Allen Jones. The mother of singer Jack Jones, she had been seriously injured in a car accident in the 1940s and spent several years sidelined before returning to acting. She was very warm, and I liked her from across the table.

Sitting next to her was Donald Murphy, who had made a career appearing on anthology series such as *Four Star Playhouse* and *Studio 57*. He was suave and very good-looking, so I was immediately intimidated.

The third star was Joan Elan, an exotic-looking beauty with dark features. Joan had been born in Sri Lanka and had worked in film and numerous other anthology series, including *Robert Montgomery Presents* and *Schlitz Playhouse of the Stars*. She was very short-sighted and had to peer at the script.

One smaller part went to Marjorie Bennett. She was very fussy, and I didn't like her. I thought, "She'll be the first one to find out that I've never acted before!" The other actor was a familiar face, Lowell Gilmore, whom I had seen play the artist who had painted the portrait in *The Picture of Dorian Gray*. He was a low-keyed, smooth-speaking English actor. I hadn't seen him in anything other than that, but I was very comfortable around him.

We sat at a table with the director, Larry Schwab, for the first rehearsal. We read, and I was fine for the reading. It was easy, because I sat for forty minutes before they got to my part in the script. The other three principals read. Then it was my turn. The director said, "Here's where we'll take a commercial break, and then, OK, David!"

And so I read. I knew that I could do the reading. The great advantage of a ten-day rehearsal was that I could grow in confidence as we rehearsed toward the culmination of a live broadcast. We didn't get up on our feet until the third day. We had to be off the book by the second day, but I had already memorized mine. I didn't want to falter on my chunk of monologue.

This new experience actually went well. Nobody seemed to say, "You've got some nerve pretending to be an actor!" My fear had been that the other actors in the cast would think I was a fraud, or the director would get rid of me when he discovered that I wasn't an accomplished actor. That fear began to dissipate. My earnestness and years of studying other actors must have paid off. At no point did someone say, "This guy doesn't know what he's doing." I felt accepted as a legitimate actor during that initial cold reading.

The Sunday night before my first full week of working at NBC, I was invited to attend a party in Ventura, north of Los Angeles. My friend from England, and now upstairs neighbor, Mimi, was invited, too. I thought that I really shouldn't go, because I would have rehearsals the next day.

The party host told me to bring my script and come anyway. We were all out having a barbecue in the garden. I told the host that I wanted to go inside for a half an hour or so to run over my lines to prepare for the next day. The window was up, and I heard somebody say, "Where's David?"

I heard Mimi reply, "Oh, he's inside, pretending to be an actor." Two groups had gone up in cars, so I made sure that I went back home that night in the second car. I never again spoke to Mimi. I arrived home first. She knocked on my door, and I didn't answer. She called on the phone, and I didn't answer.

I thought, "I need all the confidence in the world, and I do not need somebody putting me down like that." Later, mutual friends asked why I wasn't talking to her and I simply told them, "I have nothing to say to her." (In fact, I never saw her again. I was told that she got a job in a music store, met and married someone there, and moved to Long Beach. I'm assuming she must have grown to like something in America!)

My confidence level, however, was to be boosted by working with my fellow actors on my first NBC production. I began to feel as though I was part of this group of people. In fact, Joan Elan and I clicked from the start, albeit guardedly because of my recent blow-up with Mimi, another lady with whom I had hit it off. Joan, though, was the type of confidence-building friend that I needed. She played my sister for the episode, so she took me under her wing as we rehearsed lines together.

She had just come off Broadway, where she had played a role in *The Lark* with Julie Harris and Boris Karloff. Joan told me her story. She had been at dance school in England. Her parents were well to do. She had a very high class accent, so I was immediately impressed because there was still a ruling class system in England. I thought that she was high class, and there I was, working class, but she was awfully nice to me.

With her slender looks and dark hair, she had been brought to Paramount to appear in a movie called *The Girls of Pleasure Island*. Paramount had gone on a publicity tour to find three girls to play the daughters of an English plantation owner. Americans came onto the island during World War II, and the plot followed the romances between each girl and an American GI. Paramount picked Joan and two other actresses, and they were all shipped out to Hollywood with great fanfare to do the movie in 1953.

Joan was a seasoned actress and had good agents to help her freelance on television. She and I got along famously. If rehearsals were late and we didn't have to be back to the studio until noon, Joan and I started a habit of meeting at Coffee Dan's on Sunset Boulevard each morning at

My friend Joan Elan, second from right, in The Girls of Pleasure Island.
(PARAMOUNT)

ten. We sat there to chitchat and then got into her sports car to drive to rehearsals. It was the start of a beautiful five-year relationship.

We did a dress rehearsal, and then we followed a pattern that would hold for all of the *Matinee Theater* productions. The day before going on live, there was a camera rehearsal at NBC. It was a shock to go from a rehearsal hall with our marks on a bare floor to a soundstage. The lights were so hot, because the show was in color. Instead of a bare floor, there were these three enormous cameras set up in the studio. It was their day. Each camera man had a legal pad attached to the camera. The director would start and stop and say, "Say your line — stop!"

The camera man wrote down on his legal pad where he had to be with his camera at that moment. Each camera man did that all day long. We had been warned the day before that it was very frustrating for the actor because there was no continuity to our performance. We had to stop repeatedly with someone saying, "Now wait, the other camera's on over there; now it's on you." We had to look to see when the red lights went on to let us know which camera was live. All of us actors felt that it wasn't really a rehearsal. It was strictly a technical rehearsal.

The next morning was the day of the live broadcast. I got up at four, the normal schedule for NBC's live shows. It was cold and dark outside getting to NBC. In order for *Matinee Theater* to go out live at noon in Burbank, the actors had to show up at NBC by five a.m. to get into makeup and costume. We met in the dark, shivering each morning, at the studio gate. By the end of the day, live television actors were usually exhausted because we had started so early for camera and dress rehearsals.

While we ran through dress rehearsals, the crew worked feverishly to make sure all the technical equipment and giant television cameras were in working order between the studio and the control booth. Three cameras were used, and each had to be synchronized, tested and guaranteed to cooperate, or the live staging would not work.

Then we were called onto the set and did a rehearsal again with the cameras, but this time we did the show without stopping on each scene. My scene was easy, of course, because all I had to do was to sit on a couch. The rehearsal was partly for the actors and partly for the cameras.

I sat in makeup as the artist put this great plaster of Paris face on me because of the tremendous amount of heat from the lighting. Someone said, "Well, his eyes look as though they're disappearing into the back of his head." You don't want to hear that at seven a.m.! They fixed the problem by putting white makeup over my eyelids. For years, whenever I got a job and sat in the makeup chair, I would say to the artist, "My eyes disappear into the back of my head," and the artist would follow the same routine, putting white eyelids on me.

The next camera rehearsal went well as I sat on the sofa with my leg in the fake cast. There was an artificial fireplace in front of me with logs. The crew "lit" it, because they needed to test the lighting. The heat from the fireplace and from the lights above me made me sweat. That scared me, because I was supposed to be playing a terribly calm university student. Here I was on the set, and now my nerves would show.

The camera opened the fourth act right on my face and then it pulled back so I could do my monologue. It was still a camera rehearsal, but I stumbled a few times. We had to start and stop, and by then, it was ten a.m. It was time for a real dress rehearsal, no stops. Up in the booth, I heard, "Okay, folks, all the way through. If something goes wrong, just keep going."

In a sense it was like a play, because I had a character to build without interruption, other than commercials. There wasn't an audience, but there were three big cameras moving about silently on their rubber tires. I had to banish that idea out of my head to get into the part.

The dress rehearsal went smoothly with no mistakes. The director came down with a few notes and gave a few instructions to each of the actors. He never said, "You phony — you're not an actor!" So I thought, "So far, so good. I just have to get through this."

By then it was eleven a.m. My confidence had grown, until the director gave us a pep talk, as directors always do. He said, "You kids are going to be great. Everything has gone smoothly. The audience is going to love you." And then to me, he said these terrifying words: "We have twenty-five million loyal viewers watching this show every day!"

That unintentionally scary pep talk didn't help my peace of mind. I hadn't thought of how many people were watching. All I could think of was twenty-five million people looking at my face on a close-up! With one nerve-wracking hour left before going live, I thought, "David, acting is what you've been dreaming about doing for half of your thirty years. You can do this. Don't blow it."

Sensing my nervousness, Irene Hervey said, "Live television is always like this. It's like being on the *Titanic*, and you're sure you're all going to drown by one in the afternoon, but it always works out."

With fifteen minutes to go, I had my makeup refreshed. There was a little area with mirrors near the sound stage, leading to three different sound stages. Actors used the mirrors to check themselves before walking out to the set. On one of the other sound stages, they were doing a variety show. While I was standing in front of the mirror, with ten minutes to go, there was what looked like a chorus girl behind me, adjusting her feathers and fishnet stockings. I could only see her legs. She turned, and it was Betty Grable! To my generation, it was like talking to God! Seeing her completely took away all my nerves. She said, "How's it going?"

I stuttered to her, "Well, it's my first show, so I'm kind of nervous."

"You're going to be fine, honey. What's your name?"

I stuttered my name, and she told me her name, as though I didn't know what it was.

"You know, I'll bet we have dressing rooms near each other," Grable said. "You come tell me how it went."

Betty Grable calmed me down, believe it or not!

To concentrate on one member of the audience at home, I then visualized the same sixty-ish lady that I had envisioned broadcasting to back at the BBC, now transported magically to the United States. In my mind, this same audience member was sympathetically looking forward to seeing how I would do in my debut as an actor.

It worked. We went on the air, live. Terrified by my forty-minute wait before I spoke, I somehow remembered my lines, my marks, and my staging. Commercials were going on, and nobody was paying any attention to me as I slipped up and sat on my couch with a cast on my leg. I had figured out that I could sit there and run through my lines. It's a miracle that I remembered them, because as I sat waiting for my part, wondering how actors remember their lines, I thought, "When they start with me, what if nothing comes to mind?" To this day, I don't know how actors do it.

I watched the other actors do their parts. During the commercials, I could almost hear the rest of the cast sigh from the nervous tension. The commercial came on before my line. A floor manager crouched just beneath the camera and pointed at me with a sharp gesture as the red light went on from about three feet away.

I was on. The fire was roaring. I could actually hear my heart pounding. I was afraid it was thumping. How does it happen? Ask any actor, but it just falls into place or it doesn't. There was no one else to get a cue from, so I thought, "If I can just get through the first two or three lines, I think all the rest will work."

I got through my monologue. Irene Hervey then came over and spoke to me in character, followed by Joan doing her part with me as my sister. At the end of the scene, I had to get up. Donald Murphy sat at the piano as the credits rolled. He played Rodgers and Hart's "My Romance." I can't sing, but we all had to sing the song. We all knew the parts from rehearsal. As we gathered around the piano, I suddenly relaxed and thought, "I LOVE THIS!"

If I had felt at home the first time I slid behind the microphone at Radio Malaya, I truly felt at home by the time I realized that this was it — my dream of being a real actor had been realized. I sang away in character, and before we knew it, the little red light went off. A voice from the booth up in the dark beyond all the lights said, "Great show, kids!"

I was congratulated on a job well done. In fact, Irene Hervey came up to me and took my face in her hands and said, "You did very well. You have such an honest and sincere face. Don't let this town take that quality from you."

That afternoon, I rode home on the bus thinking, "I am a professional actor now in the sense that I got paid for it. I have a hell of a lot to learn, but I think I got away with it! I'm in Hollywood, in a featured role, and I'm an actor!"

I arrived home and pulled my Murphy bed from the wall. I pulled down the shades, because I was exhausted from being up since four a.m. I just fell onto the bed and felt happy.

Then the phone rang. It was Maurine, who had watched. She had immediately called the NBC casting director who had cast me to say, "What did you think of him? Was he all right?"

She told me that the casting director liked my work and would keep me in mind for other things. Then the phone rang again, and a voice I was familiar with by now said, "David, we watched. You're one of us now!" It was Elizabeth Taylor!

I thought, "My God! Then I am an actor!"

I told her, "Thank you so much. I've been up since four and I'm awfully tired."

Elizabeth said, "Go back to sleep. Rest. It's okay now."

That was the whole day of my television acting debut — going there in the darkness, being encouraged by Betty Grable, finding that I could remember lines. For my work, I was paid $350 a week, or about $2,750 in today's dollars. For my first role, I had earned almost half of the savings I had brought to America. I thought I had struck the jackpot. Because I was getting paid, it seemed like a true validation that I could now call myself a professional actor.

I had survived my live television debut, and I had Roddy McDowall, Maurine Oliver, and Peter Shaw to thank for that.

In addition to learning that I at least possessed enough acting ability and stamina to withstand the rigors of live television, I also learned something else from my role in *September Tide*.

Our co-star, Lowell Gilmore, had told me that our show was the first acting work he had done all year, eight months into 1956. That admission shocked me. I remember thinking, "What kind of profession have I picked?" If Lowell Gilmore, a well-established actor, hadn't worked all year, did that mean that acting jobs would be scarce?

I felt a little sorry for him and vowed that waiting for the phone to ring was not going to happen for me, even if it meant going back to England and begging to return to my BBC job. I took part of my $350 from my first acting job on NBC and started a savings account. I put $35 into my savings, all the while thinking, "I don't want to end up like Lowell Gilmore!"

I was young and energetic, and it turned out that I had made a good impression by taking on a featured role just a week before the whole production was to air live. What I had yet to learn in acting ability, I made up for in my willingness to work and accept a challenge. Producers and casting agents respected actors upon whom they could count when they needed them the most.

After my television debut, I continued my radio work in Los Angeles with Bill Stewart's late night DJ program, but then Maurine said to me, "David, I think it's time to give up your evening job if you can afford to. I think things are going to happen now. I'm still talking every day to the NBC people. They will have something else for you; they practically guarantee it."

I was getting $200 a week for my radio shows, before taxes and Maurine's commissions, and I had earned $350 for my first NBC show, so I said, "If you think I should not go further with the radio stuff, I won't, but I think I should wait a bit to see if I get another job." I did move over to a rental property in West Hollywood, so I felt a little more secure. Mindful of those who had helped encourage me along the way, I wrote a letter to Greer Garson in Pecos, New Mexico. She replied that she hoped it would be the first of many and sent me congratulations on getting started.

I also reconnected with a few more of my old BBC guests, including Larry Parks and Betty Garrett. When I had interviewed them, they had given me their address in case I came to Hollywood and told me that I was welcome at one of their pot luck suppers. They were just dear people. Betty's mother lived with them and their two teenage boys. Larry's American acting career had stopped because of his testimony during the "Red Scare," so he was touring Canada in *Teahouse of the August Moon*. He later became a successful building contractor before John Huston found the courage to hire him again as an actor alongside Montgomery Clift in 1962's *Freud*. While Larry toured, I became friends with Betty, even accompanying her on some afternoons to pick up her boys from school.

I began to feel a little more at ease that I was indeed going to make it in Hollywood. Getting a paycheck was a great incentive to try harder and aim higher. I was eager and excited to see where the future would lead. The following month after my television debut, the casting directors for *Matinee Theater* cast me in another featured role for a production of *Smilin' Through*, with Margaret O'Brien.

She had been born Angela O'Brien, but when she found stardom in 1942's *Journey for Margaret*, she changed her name to Margaret and became one of Hollywood's brightest child stars. I had loved her as Tootie, opposite Judy Garland in *Meet Me in St. Louis*, for which she won a Special Juvenile Academy Award. She worked for MGM throughout the 1940s, but by the time she was in her twenties, MGM's heyday was largely over and she found work in television.

Smilin' Through was written in 1919 by Jane Cowl and Jane Murfin, under the pseudonym, Allan Langdon Martin. It had been a big hit on Broadway and filmed by MGM in the 1930s and again in the 1940s. Margaret was to play a young Irish woman whose romantic attachment to my character was opposed by her father. I played Willie Ainley.

There had only been one catch in getting the part. The casting director asked Maurine, "How old is David?"

Always very cautious when that question came up, Maurine replied, "Why do you ask?"

The casting director said, "Well, he'll be playing opposite Margaret O'Brien, who's twenty-one."

Maurine said, "Well, it's perfect casting, because so is David!"

Over the phone, Maurine had lopped nine years off my age! I did have a very young face, and with not too much makeup, they believed I was twenty-one, and I believed I could be a convincing twenty-one. Makeup did the rest. The human face really looks like a road map, so the makeup artist put white stuff on to fill up all the laughing cracks, my forehead and then the base over that. It wiped out all character in my face, but at least I looked a lot younger.

Somehow, I got away with it. It was a good part for me, and for my second time around, I started to work with a little more confidence. I knew that I wasn't going to be bothered any more by the three cameras coming up to me, and I had grown used to the lights.

Margaret was pleasant but quiet. She never really progressed beyond being a child performer the way Elizabeth Taylor and Roddy McDowall had, but she was very nice and sweet. At twenty-one, she was still very much under her mother's influence. When she finished rehearsing scenes, she would often go and sit with her mother, who was always on the set twenty feet away, all in black, knitting like Madame Defarge in *A Tale of Two Cities*. Her mother seemed to be a major influence on her. She kept a vigilant eye on Margaret at all times. Margaret just meekly sat by her, without a word. She would get up and play a scene, nice and pleasant, and then she went right back to sit next to her mother. She was still like a little girl, even though she was twenty-one.

There was a sweet little love scene around a wishing well. I didn't have an awful lot to do in *Smilin' Through*, but it was very pleasant. I got $500, because Maurine was always pushing for the billing and the money.

Our director was Sherman Marks, who had excelled at directing or producing many live-action productions. In fact, the year before we worked together, he had been the primary producer of *Dateline: Disneyland*, ABC-TV's live broadcast from the opening of Disneyland on July 17, 1955. That live production may have been the most widely seen broadcast of his career.

Sherman told me that he was putting together a group of acting professionals. He asked if I would like to join. I remember thinking, "I must be lousy if he really thinks I need help!" or to take the positive view of it, he assumed I was a professional actor based on my performance. The following year, I joined his group.

Because my first shows were broadcast live, I didn't have the benefit of seeing my work to critique my performances as I had done following my recorded interviews for the BBC. The live shows were actually taped for copyright reasons by NBC, but they were on Kinescope, and I don't think they ever aired again.

When I first started working with film productions, I later watched when a show came on and really gave myself a hard time. I knew that if I didn't care about making myself better, then nobody else would, and I would just get lost among the few dozen other Brits who were in Hollywood trying their luck. I had to be my own severest critic. There are times when my work was fine for the work at hand, but for my future work, there were small-scale adjustments that I remembered to make.

When I was cast in *Smilin' Through*, I sent another note to Greer Garson. She had been working and unable to see my debut, but for my second episode, she tuned in to critique my performance. She sent me a note to say that I seemed at ease, but she noticed me blinking. She said it was a natural thing for actors to blink under stress, but I should knock that off.

With two live television productions under my belt by the fall of 1956, I decided not to pursue any more radio work. I was feeling almost as confident as Maurine that I could make a living, provided *Matinee Theater* kept going, because she hadn't sent me anywhere else. There hadn't been time, really, with two back-to-back live productions. It was just blind faith and Maurine's enthusiasm to propel my career.

Sure enough, a couple of weeks later, I was immediately offered a leading part on *Matinee Theater's* adaptation of *Pride and Prejudice* by Jane Austen. My roles on the show were becoming assignments now. I felt good about the part, even before I had seen the script, because I had seen the movie version with Greer Garson and Laurence Olivier. I had been corresponding with Greer since the day I spent with her back in

Joan Elan and I with the wife of Matinee Theater *writer Warner Law, and actor Anthony Dawson, February 1957.*

Birmingham. Again I wrote to her in New Mexico to tell her I would be appearing in *Pride and Prejudice.*

My newfound friend Joan Elan was cast as one of the sisters, Jane, while I was cast as her suitor, Mr. Bingley, an excellent role that would expand my range over two weeks of rehearsals. It was a good part for me, an interesting role, but I didn't have to carry the show. That was a relief.

Joan and I were elated, because we were still meeting every morning at Coffee Dan's. If we weren't working, we spent our days together. We just sat and talked, took a walk or drove out to the beach in her convertible. She was more active than I at that point, working in *Bat Masterson* and *Maverick.* She worked steadily but was restricted in a way because of her high class English accent. She really couldn't do any other kind of part.

The cast for *Pride and Prejudice* included Patrick Macnee, who went on to great fame in *The Avengers* in the 1960s. He was a pleasant, easygoing man, playing Mr. Darcy. The cast also included Marcia Davenport in the part of Elizabeth Bennett, the same role memorably done by Greer Garson in the 1940 version. I told her that I had heard back from Greer that she intended to tune in to watch our adaptation. Surely it would be exciting for her to know that the great Greer Garson would be watching, but she was furious with me. Marcia said, "Oh, Christ! That's all I needed to know." She was focusing on her interpretation and didn't want to know that Garson would be watching every word.

Best of all, the cast included the terrific British actress Doris Lloyd, as the mother of all the girls. She and I became quick friends and would play mother and son three or four times through the next decade. Doris was a mainstay of Hollywood's British colony in the 1930s and 1940s, and everybody loved her, both socially and professionally.

She worked in more than one hundred and fifty movies and television episodes during her career. Roddy McDowall had played her son in *Midnight Lace*. Of course, I had first seen her in *The Lodger* in 1944. Doris was brilliant as one of Laird Cregar's victims in that Jack the Ripper thriller. Her character sang in bars to make money. In her big scene, she goes home and sits on the bed, when suddenly, in a beautifully directed scene, she hears a little creak in the floor. In her performance, Doris began to shake and quiver.

Director John Brahm later told me that Doris was wonderful in *The Lodger* and the other times he directed her. "She would always come in fully prepared and do it just like that," he said. "She always did everything in just one take."

To my immense satisfaction, the Laird Cregar connection carried over to my new friendship with Doris and was something she was only too happy to talk about in between working those ten days. Cregar, who had inspired me to start thinking about acting, had been her best friend! She adored him and said he was so much fun, aside from a continuing frustration at his failure to lose weight. She impressed upon him that his size was his money in the bank, his huge "bulk," for want of a better word.

From Doris, I learned the tragic truth about Cregar's shocking death in 1944 at age twenty-eight, a really sad loss to the business. Fox realized his potential after the big box office with *The Lodger* and wanted to phase him into less sinister leading roles. He was going to act in *Laura* and was set to play the Clifton Webb role, Waldo Lydecker, a key part. He was so excited to get the role. Darryl Zanuck, though, wanted to do a sequel to *The Lodger*, and Cregar was rushed into *Hangover Square* in a fast attempt to cash in on his new acclaim. Cregar, meanwhile, was nervous that he would not finish in time to do *Laura*, and he was right. Fox started the film without him after seeing Clifton Webb in a downtown L.A. theatre production.

Cregar was very upset about losing the part. To complicate his anguish, Doris told me herself that his companion had issued an ultimatum to him, "lose weight or else." In the presence of Doris at a luncheon at her house, Cregar's partner had said, "You fat pig," or something to that effect. Cregar went on a crash diet and died from what should have been a routine operation, but he had lost so much weight that it compromised his health.

Doris detested Cregar's companion, both during and after Cregar's brief life. She told me that he was ostracized by everyone who knew him after Cregar's untimely death. Contrary to the official reports that claimed that Cregar had attempted to lose weight in order to attain leading man status, the reality was that he had a companion who goaded him into losing weight quickly through cruel taunts.

Notwithstanding learning the sad truth about Laird Cregar's death, working with Doris was a joy. She turned out to be as nice as I hoped. I stuck by her side whenever we had breaks. She was thrilled that this thirty-year-old "kid" vividly remembered her performances from his youth. We formed a great friendship.

She could also prove to be the source of unintentional merriment. When *Pride and Prejudice* aired on October 1, 1956, we learned some of the dangers of working live on television without a safety net. On the air, Doris was doing beautifully until she forgot in the second act that Joan Elan was playing Jane, and I was playing Mr. Bingley. Live, in front of twenty-five million people, she called us "Joan" and "David" instead of our characters' names! I don't think she even realized it. She went right on, even as the rest of us were horrified and tried to hide it while still attempting to act.

When we went to commercial, the director rushed over and nicely told Doris what she had done. "Miss Lloyd, you said 'Joan' and 'David.'"

"Oh, dear, did I?" she said. She apologized immensely, only to repeat the same error again on the air during the third act!

I thought, "I don't yet know this lady well, but I love her already, and here she is making mistakes — she'll never work again!"

During the next commercial break, here came the director again: "Miss Lloyd?"

"Yes?"

"You did it again."

"Oh my goodness!" she said, apologizing a second time.

Fortunately, during the fourth act, she remembered her lines and her mistake went right out of her head. Being younger, if someone had told me that I had screwed up in two acts, it would have devastated me to this day, but Doris was blithely unaware, other than being told at the moment. My heart went out to her. She was starting to be forgetful, but the real name of "Joan" sounded so much like "Jane" that it was almost inevitable, I suppose, to make that mistake. Oh, well — there were "only" twenty-five million people watching!

By the time I finished my third appearance on *Matinee Theater*, I had acclimated to the structure and pace of acting on live television. It was amazing how quickly you could get used to a routine, even if you had only acted three times. Quite honestly, I was getting a little cocky. I thought I was pretty seasoned by the third episode when I almost said to another newcomer, nervous about the cameras, "Oh, don't worry about that, because you'll get used to that in no time."

I really was on a roll, though. Even though I had yet to step in front of a movie camera, I had appeared on television three times on a series with an audience of twenty-five million people. By the third episode, the idea of a big audience no longer scared me.

My good luck and work on *Matinee Theater* continued almost non-stop. As a twenty-year-old Army man stationed in India, Winston Churchill had written a play called *Savrola*, a sort of agrarian tale set in Victorian England. The play was never produced, and Churchill had famously gone on to greater importance than that of a fledgling playwright.

More than half a century later, his daughter, Sarah Churchill, had come to Hollywood to work in television. Sarah had appeared on at least four episodes of *Matinee Theater* when a producer had the bright idea of staging her father's play for the first time on television. Sarah would play the leading lady.

Savrola was a long play, with four acts covering three hours. I could see why it had never been produced. It was a very faded, old-fashioned kind of play, but there was enough hype there to be included on *Matinee Theater*. To break up the play, introductions were written for each act. The script called for an actor to play a young Winston Churchill to introduce each act and set the scene.

Casting narrowed the part of young Winston to me and Maureen O'Hara's brother, James FitzSimons, or Jim O'Hara, as he was also known. Sarah inspected the two of us herself as she walked around, looking at us from the back and the sides. She was almost like royalty, because we were

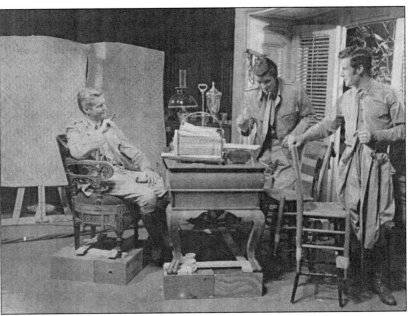

ABOVE: *That's me with my back to the camera as young Winston Churchill in "Savrola," a live episode of NBC's* Matinee Theater. BELOW: *My hair was dyed bright red to portray young Winston Churchill, at left; notice the big cables on the floor!*

told not to speak to her unless spoken to first. After great deliberation, she decided that I looked more like her father at age twenty-one. She pointed at me and said, "He'll do!" My fourth appearance on *Matinee Theater* was set.

Young Winston's hair had been red, so the makeup men sprayed my hair carrot red. Every day Sarah looked at me to see if I was authentic or not. I had to learn to smoke a cigar, which I hated, but I hoped I was convincing. I also had to rely on Sarah to see if I sounded correct as her father as a young man, although how she could have known what her father looked or sounded like years before her birth is a tad questionable, but one didn't argue with a Churchill!

As a consolation to losing the part to me, Jim was cast as another Army officer. My introduction to each act consisted of us sitting in a tent with me as young Churchill, setting the stage by introducing a bit of the plot in dialogue to interact with his officer character. The camera then dissolved into Sarah acting as the lead in her father's play.

Midway through the two weeks' rehearsal before the live broadcast, Sarah was arrested for slapping a police officer who came to her leased house in Malibu. Her habit was to go home after rehearsal and have a drink or two, study the script, play some music, and go to sleep. Her neighbors complained about her blasting her stereo with loud music at two a.m. The police were summoned, so when a young officer came to her door and asked her to silence her music, Sarah, happy after a few drinks, exchanged a few words and then punched him in the face. The officer went back to the car, called for back-up, and hauled Sarah off to jail. Promptly sprung by her lawyer, she went back home and fell asleep!

The next morning, the rest of us showed up for rehearsals and someone noticed the newspaper headline: "Churchill's daughter slugs cop!" We thought she wouldn't show up, but Sarah breezed into rehearsals at ten a.m., looking as fresh as a daisy. She acted as though nothing had happened. Not another word was said about it.

After the show aired, Sarah asked for a tape to send to her father because he had never seen his play performed. NBC worked hard on getting a good Kinescope copy to be sent to Winston Churchill so he could enjoy it. I've often wondered if I passed muster with the great man as himself when he was young.

Most people would leap for joy at the prospect of looking younger than one's actual age. I was actually thirty, playing twenty-one. My youthful looks came from being of British origin, because most of the men in my family had ruddy complexions and boyish appearances, even later in life. In fact, my father looked about fifty when he died at age eighty-three. The boyish look did help me play Winston Churchill, so maybe I shouldn't have worried as much as I did. It sure used to bother me, though. I'd stay up all night before reading for an important role, just to look older. The next day, all I looked was exhausted.

Once it became apparent that the producers of *Matinee Theater* liked me and intended to continue using me, my agent reminded me how lucky I was to be getting on-the-job training as an actor. Live television, though, meant that the chances of my luck holding out could diminish with just one slip-up. Maurine suggested that I could benefit from seeing a drama coach.

She also had another thought in mind. Because she represented so many actors from the UK, she observed that in my first three productions, I had played British parts. Maurine wisely noted that I could double my income, and her commission, if I could play non-British parts. Her goal was for me to learn to play an American reasonably well. I told her, "I haven't been here long enough to absorb enough from people around me."

Maurine sent me to a drama coach named Robert Graham Paris, who had been Shirley Temple's coach at Fox. He had then gone to Columbia as a drama coach. Retired, Paris had just completed — in longhand — a book called *How to Act*. I couldn't afford his fee for acting lessons, so we worked out an arrangement where I typed his manuscript. I wasn't that good a typist, but a friend named Betty, the sister of my friend Jimmy in Australia, had once taught me two-finger typing, and I had typed frequently at the BBC, after all.

I began typing his entire manuscript in exchange for acting lessons, all arranged by Maurine. Paris told me that as long as I was typing his book, I could come in once a week for a lesson. I shrewdly slowed down my typing to extend my time with him. Every Saturday morning for several months, he trained me to sound American by repeating a number of say-ings, including, "The quality of mercy is not strained; it droppeth as the gentle rain..." and others from *The Merchant of Venice*. He wrote them out phonetically. I had to go from an English-sounding "quality" to an American-sounding "quality" with its different inflection; in fact, at one point, he had me deliver my lines in a Bronx accent.

It worked! It turned out that I had a good ear. Maurine had been right. She began telling casting agents that I could do American parts. I was later given parts that called for me to sound like a New Englander or a WASP from the East Coast. Hollywood could be set in its ways, though, especially during the early years of television. When Maurine told one of the casting agents at NBC that I could also play American parts, she was told, "I have him in my head as British. Don't confuse me now by telling me he can do other parts! Once British, always British!"

Maurine told me, "See? I told you it was going to be hard to get them to see beyond the stereotypical 'Pip, pip, old chap' parts!"

For the next three years, I stayed rigidly British in all my parts. I mentioned my training to Joan Elan, but she just could not do it. Joan's upper crust English accent was so deeply imprinted into her that she could not change it, nor did she have an ear for different accents. For me, however, my new training would open doors down the road.

In November 1956, Maurine secured an audition for the Tab Hunter film, *Lafayette Escadrille*, a World War I aviation picture. It was to be a very brief part, but the role could help me obtain my Screen Actors Guild (SAG) membership after working only in live television and radio.

Because I had started on radio, and because my first *Matinee Theater* appearances were live, I was a member of AFTRA, the American Federation of Television and Radio Artists. Live television was a different union set-up. In order to work in filmed productions in either television or movies, I needed to become a member of the Screen Actors Guild. Without my SAG card or membership, my opportunities would be restricted to live or videotaped television. SAG membership could only be issued once an actor had a firm offer to appear in a production. Anything would do, no matter how insignificant the part.

The production was scheduled during two days off from one of the live NBC shows, but the afternoon I was to film my scene, NBC called me back off the Warner Bros. set. I had to back out from the movie and dash back to the television studio, which meant I had to wait for another chance to get my SAG card.

NBC had called me back to work on what was my fifth episode of *Matinee Theater* for a production titled *The Flashing Stream*. The lead was Grant Williams, poised on the edge of fame a year or so before *The Incredible Shrinking Man*. He was a very thoughtful, intelligent actor, and I liked him a lot. He played a president, and I played his assistant, so we had a lot of scenes together. The director suggested that the two of us get together and run lines to save the producers some rehearsal time.

Grant lived in a fancy apartment not too far from my less impressive home, so for three days, I went over to his place to run lines with him. Each time I went, he opened the door surrounded by two bosomy blondes. He said, "Okay, girls, see you tomorrow!" To this day I can't help but wonder why he had TWO busty blondes there each morning. They were very attractive, wearing tight Capri pants and tops. The fact that Grant liked bosomy ladies is about all I can remember from that particular episode of *Matinee Theater*!

Whenever I worked, I took the bus to NBC, something Maurine warned me about one day. She said that it would not be good for my career to be seen arriving or leaving by bus at a major television studio.

"Never let them see you get on a bus, dear!" she cautioned.

My headshot as I finished my first year in Hollywood, 1956.

When the rest of the cast had gone, I waited and then caught the bus, or when I was working with my friend Joan Elan, she drove me home.

Matinee Theater was the brainchild of a dynamic executive producer, Albert McCleery. He occasionally directed the show, and actually directed my *Savrola* episode because of the prestige of it being a Churchill script. One time, he drove me home, giving me sage advice all the way in his fancy convertible. He told me that he was working on a production with Roger Moore and insinuated that Moore was being difficult.

"Now, you're doing very well, son," McCleery told me. "I don't want you ending up like Roger Moore. He's getting very difficult to handle. You just take it calmly, one step at a time. You're doing very well here at NBC."

As 1956 came to an end, I did seem to be on the right track. After months of tanning with Elizabeth Taylor and using the letters of introduction given to me by Alec Guinness, I had accomplished what I had set out to do a year earlier — I was working as an actor. It was with a sense of pride that I could write my parents and former BBC colleagues in England to tell them that I wasn't a failure. Because my plan was working, I wouldn't have to return home. I could stay in Hollywood.

My run on NBC's *Matinee Theater* ended with one last episode. Joan Elan and I worked together for the third time when we did *Mr. Pim Passes By* with Edward Everett Horton, whom I had always enjoyed. The play was written by A.A. Milne, the creator of Winnie the Pooh.

Also in the cast was Reginald Gardiner, a fine comedic actor who was a very good friend of Darryl Zanuck, the 20th Century-Fox studio head. They often played polo together. Joan and I were given great parts. In fact, I had more to do than Joan, and even more to do than Reginald Gardiner, so the billing was "Edward Everett Horton in *Mr. Pim Passes By*, with David Frankham, Reginald Gardiner and Joan Elan."

Maurine told me that Reginald Gardiner, who hadn't worked as much in his later years, was incensed, or at least his agent was, when he wasn't billed next to Edward Everett Horton. Either the agent or Gardiner had gone to the casting agent and said, "Who is this David Frankham?"

Maurine informed me that this meant that I was headed in the right direction in the acting world: "Once the established actors start wondering or worrying about who you are, dear, you're moving up!"

Gardiner was nevertheless perfectly pleasant to me and very affable. The production was challenging and exciting, because Edward Everett Horton was an improviser, and I had never worked with one before. It simply meant that he got the gist of each of his speeches, his dialogue, but he would do all of his trademark stuff — he was a great stutterer — before he got to the last line and then you said your line.

This mannerism meant in rehearsal that we all had to stammer, hoping he would get to our cue. Oddly, Horton never looked at his script. He sat in the hall outside the rehearsal hall with some young fellow who read him the dialogue. He trusted this young fellow to keep repeating lines to him until he memorized them.

He then said, "I'm ready!" and we went to the set. I was very impressed. I said, "How can you trust somebody if you don't look at the printed page?" Horton was just that great, and we got through his manner of acting.

The show marked my third time working with Joan Elan, so we thought we were junior Laurence Oliviers and Vivian Leighs and that we would work forever. Joan and I had some fun times as we both became younger members of what was left of the British colony of actors in Hollywood.

There once had been a bigger group of British actors working in movies, but by the late 1950s, the group was either shrinking or assimilating. Back in the 1940s, David Niven and C. Aubrey Smith generated much of the social activity for British actors. They were famous for playing cricket on the green in Beverly Hills. Ronald Colman would come down and socialize. During the filming of *Gone with the Wind*, Vivien Leigh was very much part of the colony. The studio system had sustained much of this activity, but as that system began to disintegrate, people went where the work was, and there wasn't as much work for Brits under contract for forty weeks a year.

By the 1950s, many of the British actors were better assimilated. Doris Lloyd and her best friend, Gladys Cooper, were very social and leaders among the older set. After I worked with Doris in *Matinee Theater*, she invited me out to her house for tea. I took the bus to her home in Santa Monica. From working almost non-stop in Hollywood since the early 1930s, she lived in a beautiful, two-story Spanish house. Doris lived with her sister, Milba, who had been married to one of the great silent comedians, George K. Arthur of "Dane and Arthur" fame.

Together the sisters hosted monthly dinners or lunches as part of a very active social life. Doris set up tables in a room going out to a patio. She grouped two or three people together to stimulate conversation. Hillary Brooke was there a lot, as was Robin Hughes, who was very good as a kind of lazy poet in *Auntie Mame*.

On Saturdays, one could find the likes of Leo G. Carroll visiting Doris. Both Doris and Gladys were great friends with Carroll, a very dry, austere Brit, who was one of Alfred Hitchcock's favorite actors. Hitchcock thought he was perfect with his low-keyed style.

Usually there were actors or people associated with the business around Doris. At other times, Doris came to visit me, while on other occasions, Joan Elan and I would go visit for private lunches with Doris and her sister when nobody else was around. It was actually rare for jobbing actors to socialize frequently; you would see someone more on the set than you could socially if you were busy with work, but we did see Doris whenever we could.

Doris was so sensitive and warm. You really just wanted to hug and protect her. There was a wonderful vulnerability about her. She was one of the dearest people I have ever known, and I loved her very much. Working with her began a friendship that lasted forever, and still does, as far as I'm concerned.

Doris was immensely social and seemed to know everyone. One day in 1957, she asked me if I would like to have tea with her friend Jimmy Whale. She was returning some books to him. I said, "Of course," but the penny didn't drop. It was only on the way to his house that she mentioned that we were going to visit the director of *Frankenstein, Bride of Frankenstein,* and the 1936 version of *Show Boat.* I realized we were on our way to meet a legend, James Whale, some forty years before Ian McKellen portrayed him in *Gods and Monsters.*

Whale was charming, handsome, very aesthetic, and rather cynical about Hollywood in general and full of cautionary advice to a thirty-one-year-old novice. A quiet man, he lightened up considerably when I sincerely told him that his *Show Boat* was easily the definitive version, and he chatted animatedly about its production. I felt quite comfortable with him. I knew he was retired, so there was no point, as there so often is with actors, in thinking I might get a job out of meeting this person. I didn't feel that with him.

We sat for tea out near his pool. He went back and forth and brought out sandwiches. He was a relic of the original English colony and time had seemed to pass him by. We left him smiling and waving, rather sadly. A month or so later, he drowned himself in his pool. Doris was devastated.

Ian McKellen was eerily accurate in his performance, and really caught the man's isolation and frustration at time passing him by. I did not see, however, a Lynn Redgrave-type housekeeper lurking about; in fact, Whale served the tea by himself that day. He was my first real connection to my favorite genre, as it turned out.

The great bonus with Doris was that her best friend was Gladys Cooper Like Laird Cregar, Gladys had inspired me to think about acting when

I saw her onscreen in *Now, Voyager* back in 1944. Gladys was well established as an international performer. Doris was known primarily for making movies, and although her acclaim may not have been as great as the type enjoyed by Gladys, you would never have known that to see them together as great friends.

Gladys often breezed in to visit. One day Doris was making marmalade from the oranges in her garden. Full of authority, Gladys marched in and tasted it. In a kind of charming way, she said, "Doris, this is much too sweet, and we'll just have to start over," and proceeded to dump the whole pot down the drain!

Off she went with Doris and me, meekly following along to the orchard in the back, plucking oranges off the trees to make more. Doris was saying, "Oh, dear, Gladys," while we picked.

"This will be right now, Doris, you'll see!" proclaimed Gladys as we made a new batch of fresh marmalade.

Doris usually got a bit dithery around Gladys, who just had inborn energy, because Doris was more shy, gentle, and sweet. Gladys wasn't unpleasant, but she just breezed in as a lady of great friendly, social authority while people just automatically gathered around her. She was just energy on wheels. I never saw her when she was less than energetic.

Gladys and I unfortunately never had the satisfaction of working together, but she did teach me how to drive. "You don't drive, my dear?" she asked incredulously one day. She promptly offered to teach me how to drive her car. Even though Gladys was in her seventies, she owned a Thunderbird, which she used to go tearing along Sunset Boulevard.

One time I was with her when she was pulled over by a traffic cop. Her whole glove department was stuffed with speeding tickets!

"Oh, dear, what have I done, officer?" she sweetly asked. "I really must take care of those," she promised. Off we went, speeding again as she drove me home! She was not the ideal person to teach me to drive. She eventually gave up trying after I had the general hang of it.

She was young at heart and loved show business. Just being around such a vivacious personality was uplifting. Her tremendous energy was shared by all of those character stars from the 1930s and 1940s. They all seemed to exude great energy and enthusiasm, something I would need as I attempted to establish myself further as an actor.

Actors will always look for commonality to share with each other, so even though the British Colony in Hollywood might have been fading, building relationships with the likes of Doris Lloyd and Gladys Cooper did much to build my confidence. Their friendships were important, too, because I had grown up drawing inspiration from their performances. I'm very fortunate to have arrived in Hollywood in time to know them in their golden years.

As 1957 developed, Maurine grew fidgety and wanted to get me into the Screen Actors Guild so I could audition for movies. She also wanted to move me beyond *Matinee Theater*, because I had more or less done one each month for the last six months of 1956. With six episodes under my belt, I learned that the producers planned to mount a production of *The Importance of Being Earnest*. I thought I would be a shoo-in to play the part of Algernon, the aristocratic young Londoner. I felt I was born to play the part, even though I had never read the play. I had seen the Michael Redgrave movie, however, so I thought I could do the telefilm with my hands tied behind my back.

My confidence level was so artificially high that I thought I would get the call to start production as had happened on my earlier episodes. It was a surprise instead to get a call to come in and read for the part.

"That's odd," I thought. I knew I had won the other six roles without even reading. By then, I knew all the directors who rotated on *Matinee Theater*. For this production, however, it was a new director for whom I had yet to read. Since he had not worked on the show before, he wanted to meet the actors that he had in mind for the part. He was English, though, so I thought we would share an affinity.

Roger Moore had already been cast as Ernest, and Hermione Gingold was cast as Lady Bracknell. With that casting, I thought they were aiming for very broad comedy. I also thought it was just a courtesy to go in and read for the director. I met him, and he seemed pleasant enough. He asked me to do a cold reading, which I could do well, so I read Algernon, very effectively, I felt.

"Nice to meet you, and thank you," he said to me. Off I went. Most actors used an answering service before the days of answering machines or voicemail. I anticipated a call waiting for me when I got home to tell me that I would start rehearsals the next day. When my phone failed to ring, the next day I called Maurine, who also had not heard anything.

Everyone in Hollywood read *The Hollywood Reporter* and *Daily Variety* each morning. Another day passed, and on the third day, I read in the trade papers that the director had completed a full cast with an American actor, Robert Chapman.

I thought, "Well, there's only the part of a minister in there for him," so I called Maurine. She phoned NBC, and they said, "No, he's playing Algernon."

I felt as though NBC had slapped me across the face. I couldn't believe that I didn't get the part, especially after coming to NBC's rescue when Roddy McDowall had cancelled and inadvertently launched my acting career. Not only that, but I had proven myself time and again on live television.

I didn't want to watch the show, but I couldn't resist. It turned out that the director had his own concept of *The Importance of Being Earnest*. He didn't want it done in the traditional way. Robert Chapman had an almost impish, Tommy Steele kind of feel to him. He was fey and sort of unworldly. That was the slant the director had decided to use.

The thought of an American playing Algernon insulted me, yet Robert Chapman was better than I would have been. He was perfect in the role. I learned a lesson there. Pride goes before a fall. My assumption was that I was a shoo-in for Algernon. Ironically, I later worked with Robert Chapman. I marched right over to him and said, "I really enjoyed you as Algernon." He said, "No, no, YOU should have played the part." That was very kind. But he was right for the part, and I was wrong for it.

My let-down taught me a valuable lesson. Actors will drive themselves crazy if they count on parts too soon. Sometimes dozens of actors, if not hundreds, are up for a part, and the odds almost become casino-like. Show business is just that, a business, and just as a manufacturer's part may not be right for another company, sometimes an actor isn't right for the role. Producers and directors also come and go, and it's easy to find yourself headed down as soon as you think you're headed up.

What was especially challenging for me in 1957 was that I had been spoiled by NBC. By the time I appeared on my last episode of *Matinee Theater*, I had received second or third billing. I had been feeling pretty good, except now there were no more parts for me on that show, and Maurine was correctly pointing out to me that I was limited to working live or on videotape as a member of AFTRA.

To get the Screen Actors Guild card that could expand my work possibilities, Maurine said, "We'll get your union card by just throwing you into anything that comes along at first. Don't be too concerned if there isn't much to do." What a blow to my ego!

Having missed my chance to earn my SAG card on a Warner Bros. movie when NBC called me back to live television, my film debut would actually happen at Disney. Although I would later enjoy some fame among animation enthusiasts because of my voice role as Sgt. Tibs the cat in *One Hundred and One Dalmatians*, my Disney debut was one that I would have just as soon forgotten; in fact, for years I didn't talk about it or include it on my list of credits. Enough time has passed that I now have some perspective to see that the experience was entirely necessary to get me started on film in Hollywood.

One day in early 1957, Maurine called to say there was a very small part in Walt Disney's *Johnny Tremain*. Based on a well-loved book by Esther Forbes, the story focused on the American Revolution and young Johnny Tremain, a silversmith's apprentice who gets caught up in the historical events unfolding around him.

By taking this small part, I could become a member of SAG. I first refused, because my roles on live TV had all been featured parts, and I didn't want to start playing small roles. It's very hard to get out of that once producers think that you only do small parts. Maurine persisted, though, and in those early days, she never, ever, made a bad career move for me. I put my faith, however grudgingly, in her judgment. So, two days later, I found myself in a Redcoat uniform, leading my troops down a country lane on the Disney Ranch out in the San Fernando Valley.

I had one line, delivered through a nearly obscure long shot. I thought, "This is a bit of a comedown after pages of dialogue on a live show." I didn't enjoy working on the movie, certain that when the film came out, all my hard work in television would mean nothing because I was appearing in such a small role. I never saw Walt Disney on the set, and if I had, I probably would have hidden from him because of my embarrassment over working in such a tiny role.

The film came and went, though, and though I continued in television, I could now work on filmed TV as well as live. And with my first true feature film role just a year or so away, *Johnny Tremain* did me no harm.

Because I didn't enjoy my experience, I never saw the film; however, during a visit to the Walt Disney Studios' Archives in Burbank more than fifty years later, some friends paused and stopped each second of the film on DVD in an attempt to spot my scene. We gave up, but when I returned home to New Mexico, I finally watched the film in its entirety. One of my eagle-eyed young friends helped to locate the shot, one hour, fifteen minutes and forty-five seconds into the movie. I'm the man leading a group of Redcoats in the distance who turns back and says, "After them!"

Watching the film more than fifty years later, my reaction was, "I wish I had more to do in this." The experience reminded me that almost every time I got a script in my early years, I almost always said that! I really shouldn't feel that bad about my one line, because Walt Disney's daughter, Sharon, also had a bit part in the film, and she, too, delivered one line! In my case, though, those two words, "After them," earned me my SAG card!

From an ego point of view, 1957 was proving to be tough going after ending a six-episode run on *Matinee Theater*, but I slowly made the transition from working live on television to doing everything on film. Maurine was as good as her word, and gradually, the billing, the parts, and the money got better.

In spite of my television work at NBC, I knew that I needed some acting lessons. Director Sherman Marks had told me that he was forming an actor's group, so Joan Elan and I decided to join. Sherman's group was really a scene study class. Joan and I both took the weekly class for a five-year period from 1957 to 1962. The only essential requirement was that one had to be a working actor. Actors in the group invited other actors to attend during breaks from filming. I was enthusiastic, but Joan was nervous about being critiqued by the other actors.

We met each Saturday morning at ten a.m. For homework, we prepared a scene. Over four hours, each of us stood up and did our scenes for the others. We were then critiqued by Sherman and the group. If we were lousy, they told us, which was a little nerve wracking, to say the least. The experience offered me great training, because I had to learn how to do scenes to my peers' suggestions.

Sherman tried to encourage Joan. He said to her one time, "I don't know what it is that you have, Joan, but you've got something." The something she had was that she was very short-sighted. She had tried contact lenses to no avail; one of her lenses had fallen into her soup, and she gave up on them. Her eyes were never wide open because she had to sort of squint and peer to see. It made for a sexy look to the casting people or the actors who critiqued her!

Richard Bull, who later became a long-running member of the *Little House on the Prairie* cast, was in the group, along with his wife, Barbara Collentine, or Bobbie, as we called her. The three of us became good friends and encouraged each other. Every so often a guest was invited to sit in and offer comments to our class. Invited by Bobbie and Dick, one day Joseph Schildkraut visited, and I did what I thought was a pretty good scene with Bobbie from *The Philadelphia Story*. When I was done, Schildkraut drew himself up to his full height and said, "I'm afraid I can't comment on the scene because I couldn't hear a word they said." If I had only had a knife handy…

Shirley Knight was a regular, and I remember that she cried the first time she was critiqued, but she had the last laugh. In short time, she received two Oscar nominations for Best Supporting Actress, for 1960's *The Dark at the Top of the Stairs*, and again, for 1962's *Sweet Bird of Youth*.

Another member, Ray Stricklyn, received a Best Supporting Actor Golden Globe nomination for 1961's *The Plunderers*. He later achieved great acclaim on stage playing Tennessee Williams in *Confessions of a Nightingale* and became a top publicist in Hollywood, even representing Elizabeth Taylor. (Years later, Ray remembered those early acting classes and mentioned me in his autobiography, *Angels and Demons*.)

Paul Burke from *The Thomas Crown Affair* was also a member, as was Robert Ridgely and Mark Herron for a year or so. Very slender, slightly fey and a bit exotic, Mark later married Judy Garland. I ran into him at a screening after Judy divorced him, and he looked as though he had barely survived a shipwreck. I asked how he was and he shook his head and sighed, "Don't ask."

One year, Marni Nixon joined our group. She was a sweetheart. We did a song and dance number for the group. She was wonderful, but I never sang or danced again! Another member, Irene Tedrow, was a very talented, no-nonsense lady from the Mid-west in the Jessica Tandy mold and while she never achieved Tandy's acclaim, she certainly was much appreciated within the Hollywood community.

Our meetings were really wonderful times to share; everybody was auditioning every week for something, and we were very supportive of any member of the group who was having a slow time of it. Many in the group, particularly Irene Tedrow, Ray Stricklyn, and Shirley Knight, introduced me to positive thinking, the idea that nothing really happens by chance if one believes that something spiritual is active in one's consciousness. I found it terrifically effective in coping with the vagaries of the actor's life, and it certainly brought results. Such thinking really kept one "primed" or ready for a challenge. Believing that we were ready for the best, and believing that we were going to get a part, gave us that little something extra.

Still, Joan and I sometimes laughed at the whole absurdity of the cattle call mentality often evident at auditions. While much of the work was genuine, much of Hollywood seemed like a sham, especially when we heard somebody speaking Hollywood talk: "You're the greatest" or "I've never seen anything better!" We often laughed at the ridiculous aspects of working as actors at the end of the day. We collapsed and laughed at the absurdities of what we had to endure to succeed as professional actors.

In my early filmed television roles, I continued to play British while I worked with my vocal coach, Robert Graham Paris. I spent hours reciting lines for him phonetically in an Eastern American accent. I thought I sounded really weird and that the whole thing was a waste of time. It began to pay off, though, when TV casting agents and directors accepted that I could play American as well, so I have him to thank for a lot of work over the years.

I became good enough with my own accent that Paris called one day to put me in touch with Zsa Zsa Gabor. She was about to act in a Noël Coward comedy in Palm Beach, Florida, but was intimidated by the script and the idea of acting on stage. She had asked if Paris could recommend an English actor to help with her accent, and he recommended me.

Off I went to a big mansion in Beverly Hills, where a maid showed me in that morning. Zsa Zsa was upstairs, sitting in bed, enjoying her breakfast and coffee. "Hello, darling!" she said, as she invited me to sit on the edge of her bed. She asked if I would help her improve her English accent. I agreed, so I was to be her devoted coach for the next three weeks. I accompanied her everywhere, even when she went to have her hair dyed and to get her car repaired.

My attempt to help Zsa Zsa with her accent was in vain.

We sat together seven days a week, for three weeks. Down in Florida, the posters were out and ticket sales were going well. For all her work on her accent, though, I noticed that she hadn't got anywhere by way of memorizing her script! I kept reading the first act to her, but she never seemed to move beyond that part as she sat by the pool.

After three weeks of accent coaching, she told me that she just wasn't up to it. She picked up the phone and cancelled just like that. As we parted at the front door, she said, "Well, darling, it's been wonderful."

I said, "So you'll be sending my $600 check?"

"What check, darling?" she replied. "We didn't do the play!"

Her thinking was that she wasn't going to do the play, so she shouldn't have to pay me! (Four years later, I mentioned the incident to Alec Guinness, who reminded Zsa Zsa about the incident over my protests and secured my $600 check, ending years of waiting for payment!)

Eva Gabor, meanwhile, was preparing for a movie role that required her to lose some of her Hungarian accent and sound more English. She had visited her sister from time to time during my three weeks with Zsa Zsa. They were like kids in school, yakking or squabbling away in Hungarian and then giggling up a storm. Eva was a very fine actress, awfully good in *Gigi*. I liked her more than Zsa Zsa, because she was a real professional. She asked if I would help her. Her sister's lack of payment notwithstanding, I agreed to coach Eva.

As part of her preparation for her role, she had to go to Jax, a famous women's store in Beverly Hills, to get some clothes. Eva said, "Come in with me." I really didn't want to go, because some of the lady customers were standing around in various states of undress. One lady was standing not too far from me in her girdle and bra.

Eva whispered to me, "Look — that's one of Hollywood's best-kept secrets." This lady was very bow-legged; she looked like a cowboy. I didn't recognize her immediately, so Eva said, "That's Norma Shearer, and she has to be very carefully photographed so she doesn't look as though she's just hopped off a horse."

Working with Eva was satisfying and fun. She was apartment hunting at the time, so I went with her as she searched. As we drove along, we practiced lines from her script. When we finished, she paid me promptly, unlike her sister.

Getting established, I really couldn't afford to shop in the manner enjoyed by the Gabor sisters, so I drove around Beverly Hills and window shopped! Eventually I was able to buy my clothes at Dick Carroll's on Little Santa Monica Boulevard and Rodeo Drive.

What a challenge it was for me throughout much of 1957. After I received my Screen Actors Guild card by swallowing my pride and delivering one line in Disney's *Johnny Tremain*, I began to work more in filmed television series. Most of my early parts were usually featured appearances on episodes of existing shows. I was feeling pretty good about my prospects as I started out, but now, those second-billed *Matinee Theater* parts were gone. Episodic television meant that established programs always starred regulars who received top billing. Guest stars of a certain magnitude might be introduced at the beginning. Featured parts typically meant receiving credit at the end of the show. The bigger the part, the bigger the billing. I would have to work my way up from small parts to guest star.

One of my first filmed parts on a television series came on *Navy Log*, an anthology series about World War II Navy stories. My episode was titled, "P.T. 109" and recounted the true heroism of a young John F.

Kennedy during World War II. At the time we filmed, he was still a U.S. senator from Massachusetts and three years away from being elected president. I only had a line or two at the end of the program as a British soldier who greets Kennedy and his fellow survivors when they finally make it to safety. My line was, "Glad you're okay — won't you have a cup of tea?"

When it aired, there was my name, buried way down on the cast list. Higher aspirations aside, I really didn't mind. Working in Hollywood was a great adventure for me, having come from the closed-up studios of the BBC. There we had no windows and just sat in a room reading the news or interviewing the guests. Everything was a great lark in Hollywood for me. We filmed *Navy Log* on location in Long Beach, about forty minutes south of Los Angeles. I didn't get paid very much, but I was working. With a script based on JFK's first-hand account of his military service, it was a high profile episode. It wouldn't have surprised me to learn that the Kennedy family, and perhaps the future president himself, tuned in to see the program.

Another early appearance came in an episode of *The Silent Service*, a dramatic anthology series about Navy submarine adventures. The cast had fun going off into the Pacific to work a week on location. Working on location was a treat. I had naively assumed that being an actor meant going to exotic locations such as Hong Kong or Paris. Instead, I went to San Diego for *The Silent Service*.

In early 1958, I appeared with a very unpleasant Peter Lawford in an episode of *The Thin Man*. Lawford wasn't friendly at all. Even though my early parts were small, they offered me an opportunity to interact with established performers. I could learn so much from them from just interacting between takes, but Lawford wasn't open to chitchat or much conversation.

I had always enjoyed his work. He was good at being somebody pleasant or charming on film, when in reality, he was neither. In fact, Lawford was a complainer. He kept complaining about the cold, even proclaiming loudly, "Could somebody warm up this f@#ing studio? I'm freezing!" Phyllis Kirk also was in the episode, and she complained about the cold almost as much as Lawford.

Lola Albright was the primary guest star. A stunning blonde who had started as a model, she had made some early film appearances that included small parts in two Judy Garland films, *The Pirate* and *Easter Parade*. Lola was onto Lawford's behavior right away. He walked away from us one day and she whispered, "He really is a jerk, isn't he?"

The episode was called "The Tennis Champ." It was a scary week of shooting for me. The script required me to play a very competent tennis player, the champ himself, when in reality, I had never actually played the game! Nobody had bothered to ask if I could play tennis when I read for the part. Lola took pity on me, and we went over to a soundstage several days in a row to play tennis during lunch. She gave me pointers and helped me learn to play well enough for the episode's montage of tennis shots.

I returned the favor by helping out Lola. She was in the process of divorcing Jack Carson, who had appeared in *A Star Is Born*. A Warner Bros. contract player, Carson was a funny man and a fine actor who had a disastrous, would-be romance with Doris Day. When he and Day had filmed *Romance on the High Seas*, Carson had fallen in love with her. She knew nothing about making movies, and he spent so much time mentoring her on her first film that he predictably fell in love with her.

Lola was in the process of divorcing poor Jack, who was in the throes of heartache over the whole matter. He didn't want the divorce, so he came on the set every day at lunchtime. She was able legitimately to say, "Jack, I'm sorry, but David and I have to go off and rehearse some tennis." She told me that they were legally separated, but that he was breaking the requirement by coming to MGM to plead his case to her to reconsider the divorce.

So, Lola helped me with tennis, and I helped spare her from having to deal with Jack. Fame can sometimes be waiting right around the corner, and Lola made a great impression on audiences as a nightclub singer on *Peter Gunn* later that year. She was an excellent actress who was never given her full due, in my opinion.

I next appeared in my first of three episodes for the very popular *Alfred Hitchcock Presents* series. First airing on June 22, 1958, my Hitchcock debut episode was titled, "The Impromptu Murder." Hume Cronyn played a crooked bookkeeper who silences and kills a client after embezzling some money. I had a brief scene as his clerk, another one of my early "Here I am and then I'm gone" parts.

I very much enjoyed filming it. Even though we shared no scenes, my newfound friend and mentor, Doris Lloyd, also appeared in the episode. Perhaps best of all, a legendary actor directed us. Paul Henreid had appeared in *Casablanca*, *Now, Voyager*, and *Goodbye, Mr. Chips*. He had turned to directing, and in fact, he directed more than two dozen episodes of the Hitchcock series. There were always plusses, even when the parts were otherwise small.

Hitchcock never directed any of the episodes that I did for his series, but I did see him. He sometimes walked on the set because we filmed next door to his office. He seemed to be exactly as he appeared in those introductions he filmed for the series. He never smiled, but the crew said he was a wonderful man to work for. When it was time to film his introductions, he had done all his preparation beforehand and simply sat there as the director said "action" and then "cut" at the end of the scene.

My parts gradually improved. Appearing on the Hitchcock program and other high profile series meant that casting directors looked at the credits I added at other studios. Maurine was working hard on my behalf, especially at Warner Bros. Later she concentrated on Universal, and after that, Fox. She went to elaborate lengths as my agent to do whatever was necessary to secure work. She always was one step ahead of the game, scouring the trade papers and thinking of inroads she could make.

One of my earliest TV roles was for Alfred Hitchcock Presents.

I couldn't sit in the back of Maurine's car because it was always filled with scripts, piled so high that we couldn't see through the rear view mirror. She also seemed to have learned to drive from Gladys Cooper, speeding or making crazy U-turns with little notice. Sometimes she drove and reached into the back seat to rummage around for a script that she wanted me to see.

She also had a way of getting in to see casting agents, often saying to them, "Well, since we're here ..." and then seizing upon the occasion to introduce me in the process. She would even boldly walk into producers' offices and announce, "I want you to meet my client here," and then shove me forward to make an impression on them.

The night before an audition, Maurine called and said, "Well, dear, you have to be at Universal tomorrow afternoon." I showed up a half an hour before and then sat there looking around to scope out the competition and to see if I knew anyone else competing for the part. If I knew that some of the other actors weren't very good, it was a signal that I might get the part. Newcomers meant a little unease for us actors because we didn't yet know how well these unproven commodities could act. There was always a lot of insecurity while we sat there pretending to study our lines before going in to read for the casting agent and director.

The audition process got my adrenaline going each time. As a working actor, I had to keep up the energy level during the times I wasn't working. That meant for auditions, walking in with high energy. Actors had to walk in as though we meant to get the part. Without the energy, there would be something lacking, and that usually meant that nine times out of ten, an actor wouldn't get the part.

Maurine looked out for her clients' best interests, even if it meant turning down a role that she felt was not right for us. Michael Wilding called one time to tell me that he was doing an Alfred Hitchcock episode and wondered if I would like to come in and play the head of a jury pool. He was playing a defendant on trial and thought the part would be good for me.

I liked the idea, but Maurine immediately said, "You certainly are not. I've seen all the scripts, including that one. You're not going in there and setting yourself back a year by doing just three lines as the foreman of the jury." In other words, she got irritated whenever an actor suggested another actor for a part. She was right, though. Had I done small bits for the money, it would have been an easy way to regress.

Thursday was Maurine's day to meet with the casting agents at 20th Century-Fox. For a whole year, at the end of her business at the studio and sessions of shoving me into doors to network and meet new contacts, we had a standing four p.m. appointment with Lee Wallace, head of Fox's feature casting. Maurine just knew that I would end up in a Fox feature film.

Wallace was an Anglophile. He loved to talk about and hear about England. For a few Thursdays, I enjoyed talking about myself, thinking that it would lead to a part. The Thursday sessions eventually seemed like a chore. I said to Maurine, "Do I have to come with you today? I've run out of social things to say to this man, and he's obviously got nothing for me."

"Yes, he will," she told me and urged me to keep the appointment with her. She knew that this process could take a long time to interact with these people on whom it was important to make a positive impression. I eventually got to know all the major studios' casting agents.

Success meant knowing them personally. Maurine and I rarely socialized with casting agents, but everybody knew everybody in the business.

They knew what I was right for, what my range was, and what I felt comfortable doing. I didn't mind reading for anybody. Because of my BBC news reading experience, I was always very comfortable reading on an audition. I could do cold, or sight readings, by picking up a script and falling right into character. A shy person by nature, I would get myself excited about auditioning by thinking, "Well, I came thousands of miles from England to do this, so I can't just sit here and mumble!" My motivation was to forget the shyness and let the directors see that I was a professional.

To improve my chances, I thought about the things that might be seen as potential negatives during an audition. The worst thing that an actor is ever asked during an audition is "Tell us a little about yourself." I was never good at that, so I psyched myself up in the shower that morning by thinking of things I could tell them or parts I had done.

I had yet to do live theatre and was reluctant, but Maurine told me that acting on stage would increase my chances of getting my foot in the door. As she explained it, many casting agents, directors, and producers frequented plays throughout Southern California to spot potential talent for film or television.

My first stage audition was in 1957. A very prestigious theatre-in-the-round, the Player's Ring in Hollywood, staged *A Look Back in Anger* under the direction of a very fine actor, Paul Stewart. He was a protégé of Orson Welles who had appeared in *Citizen Kane*. At the time, *A Look Back in Anger* was all the rage. Maurine encouraged me to read for the hero's best friend, the kind of part I was playing frequently on television. I reluctantly read for Stewart, who said nothing to me other than "Thank you for coming in." That was the end of that experience.

I wasn't too upset about not being cast in the play. Even if my television parts didn't bring top billing, the late 1950s were good years to be a jobbing actor. If I didn't get one part, it was very feasible to get another. It seems hard to believe that with just three major networks there were that many scripted programs, but aside from quiz shows, television was filled with different types of programs.

On November 16, 1958, I appeared in an episode of *Northwest Passage*, a drama based on a frontiersman character played by Spencer Tracy in the film of the same name. The show starred Keith Larsen and Buddy Ebsen. It was back to British Redcoat territory as I played a lieutenant who came to the aid of Carol Ohmart and Paul Cavanagh as they battled villainous guest star Pernell Roberts. Just a year later, Roberts became a star on *Bonanza*.

It may not have been *Bonanza*, but even I appeared in a Western, an episode of *Death Valley Days* titled "Ship of No Return." The program was one of the longest-running syndicated programs ever. Even in syndication, television was creating opportunities for actors. I played a sailor, but other than that, I can't remember much about the plot. The big thrill was that the show's host, Ronald Reagan, came in to film his

With Nira Monsour on Death Valley Days, *1958.*

introductions for the shows. I remember the future president of the
United States hovering about the set.

Working on *The Gale Storm Show* took me to the Selznick Studio, a
mile down the road from MGM. It was great fun to join Gale Storm and
Zasu Pitts as we dressed up in a number of costumes.

I don't quite recall the plot, but there were a number of publicity stills

I'm dressed as Henry VIII on The Gale Storm Show.

that showed me dressed up as Henry the VIII. Gale Storm was very kind,
but what I most remember about working on her show was wandering
around the lots to see where Atlanta burned in *Gone with the Wind.* Those
sets had been left over from *King Kong.* I was especially excited to see the
Tara exterior still standing, yet looking forlorn. The studio was so historic
that the property went back as far as the Keystone Cops and the silent era.

Maurine, meanwhile, read that Burt Lancaster would be making a
movie based on the play *Separate Tables.* She urged me to read for a stage
production at the Steve Allen Theatre in 1958. Most of the film's leads had
been cast for the movie — Deborah Kerr, Gladys Cooper, David Niven,
and Rita Hayworth — but there were still the parts of the young hon-
eymoon couple to be cast. Maurine believed that appearing in the stage
production while casting continued on the movie was a great opportunity

to boost my chances of getting noticed for the film. Reluctant to audition after my previous year's stage audition had gone nowhere, I nevertheless read for the play. To my surprise, I got the part.

I had seen the play in London with Eric Portman, whom I always thought was copied by David Niven in the subsequent film adaptation. My part wasn't challenging because it was an easygoing role. The

I look as though I've seen the ghost of Henry the VIII, The Gale Storm Show.

experience was kind of like working in my live television plays, but those were finished sixty minutes after they started. This project was a bit daunting because I didn't know if I could sustain a performance for more than an hour. We had good rehearsals, though, and my qualms diminished soon enough. By the time we finished rehearsals in the evening, I wouldn't get back to my apartment until one or two a.m.

Ben Wright was in the cast as the lead Eric Portman/David Niven role. Irene Tedrow, from my Saturday morning acting group, was also in the cast. She and I became great friends during our time together because of the encouragement she gave me. I looked up to her as a seasoned pro, and her work was a great example for me. I told her how frustrated I was feeling, stuck playing the hero's best friend nearly every time I acted. It hadn't taken me long to get bored with the status quo.

Doris Lloyd brought Leo G. Carroll to see me in the play. They sat in the front row so I could see them. I kept looking at Carroll and wondering, "Is he liking me or hating the show?" It turns out that his impression was somewhere in the middle. Doris came backstage without him, so I thought, "That's not good," even though she told me that Leo had said, "Jolly good" about me in his brief post-show reaction.

Doris told me later that on their drive back home, she bombarded him with questions about my performance, looking for advice that could be passed onto me. "Hmm," Carroll told her. "Needs experience, needs experience." So I suppose I wasn't all that great, but he was right. I did need more experience; after all, I had only been acting for two years.

Over my three-week run, Maurine assured me that it would be worth the effort. She twisted the arm of Max Arnow, a legendary casting director who had discovered Rita Hayworth, Glenn Ford, and Jean Arthur. Arnow had gone to work for Burt Lancaster's production company, Hecht-Hill-Lancaster.

Maurine told him, "David's doing *Separate Tables*, so please come and see him. If you think he might be a good candidate for the movie, let us know." Good old Max came and saw me. He liked me well enough that I was invited to read for the movie. My work had paid off, because I can't say that I did the play for love of the theatre; I was hoping to get a part in the big movie adaptation. By then, I was dying to do the film because I wanted to work with Rita Hayworth. I read for Burt Lancaster himself, one of the film's stars. He seemed to like my reading and sounded very encouraging about my prospects. I knew I'd made a good impression. As I left, I saw Rod Taylor waiting for his turn. I knew right then that the part was his. Sure enough, Rod was cast.

When she learned of my disappointment at not making it into the movie, Irene Tedrow gave me good advice. She said, "David, you should have more self-esteem. You're doing fine. You need to learn that you have a cushion of self-regard beneath you that will support you whenever you take the time to recognize it."

She was taking a class in metaphysics, which might just as well have been Swahili as far as I was concerned. She explained to me that we each are representatives of the Universal Living Spirit which expresses itself through us as we recognize it. By affirming its presence at our center, we help manifest it in our individual lives as creative achievement, loving relationships, vital health, and energy. Well, that was a heck of a lot for me to swallow, particularly as Hollywood then, as now, attracted all sorts of oddball organizations peddling self-help solutions "guaranteed" to make you a star. That wasn't the case with Irene, though. I could see her putting her beliefs into her work and happy family life.

Irene invited me to the Hollywood Church of Religious Science. She told me that Glynis Johns, Peggy Lee, Eve Arden, and two or three other dozen working actors attended. I was dubious, but I went. Indeed, I was impressed that I could sit next to Eve Arden or Peggy Lee. It was known unofficially as the actors' church because so many went there to be spiritually refreshed. The church was not to be confused with Christian Science, which had always intimidated me with its do's and don'ts method of instruction. Science of Mind refers to "the Divine discontent," that urge within us to strive to be better, more successful, more loving, more creative, and expressing more of Spirit.

I took to Irene's way of thinking and decided, as I have done with all new adventures, to jump in and see what happened. I made a real commitment to that mindset. Fifty years later, I still read, study, and meditate and it works. I have days — don't we all? — when all the consciousness-raising I've done flies right out the window an hour later, especially when I'm confronted with something that really irritates me, but that doesn't happen very often.

The pastor of the Hollywood Church of Religious Science, Dr. Robert Bitzer, became a real friend and a wise one, too, along with his wife. Sometimes the teaching went over my head, but then Dr. Bitzer would say, "It's all right, David; you've been practicing what we teach, only now you KNOW it."

I went privately to twice-weekly sessions with Dr. Bitzer. My self-image improved. I could see myself getting the parts I wanted. In essence, I set my mind to achieving the outcome that I needed to happen. The power of positive thinking gave me great confidence. I was able to look at myself objectively and see where I needed to channel positivity into constructive work as an actor on the set.

Surprisingly, there was a lot of humor attached to it. At our church, Eve Arden stood in the lobby afterwards and made wisecracks. There was fun to be had in believing in myself. My experience was a vast contrast to the Presbyterian Church in which I was brought up in England and Scotland. I've always been so appreciative to Dr. Bitzer. I went to him privately and talked about parts or scripts. I'd negatively say, "I don't like this director," and he would say to me, "But David, it's all right. It's okay to be upset sometimes."

He really had much to do with me having confidence as an actor. It was Robert Bitzer who kept assuring me that my career would work out. It was never gooey like a Hallmark card, but very practical. Dr. Bitzer lived to be ninety-eight and spent decades teaching in Hollywood. He and his wife celebrated fifty years together by inviting the whole congregation to the Beverly Hills Hotel for a gala supper. Glynis Johns sang "Send in the Clowns" to them from the role she had created in *A Little Night Music*, with just piano accompaniment. It was magic.

Sometimes the early acting challenges weren't all that demanding, because most of the parts inevitably cast me as the best friend to the hero or a supporting type who reassured the protagonist that he was doing the right thing. There's not much drama in being affirmative.

In fact, there were even opportunities in radio in the late 1950s. Although television was firmly establishing itself as the preferred broadcast entertainment vehicle of choice for most Americans, many radio programs still competed for audiences. Some of the programs were transitioning to television, while other long-running radio shows seemed destined to go as long as they could, even if it meant a decline in the number of listeners.

It was a business decision, really, on the part of the networks and sponsors. While television sets were selling at a rapid clip, there were still radio listeners who were older or in rural areas yet to be reached by television's permeation. One of these radio programs was a long-running soap opera called *One Man's Family*. Created in 1932 by Carlton E. Morse, the show holds the record as the longest-running, uninterrupted serial in the history of radio.

One Man's Family, too, had seen a television version in the 1950s, but the radio show's great number of fans made it one of the last series to keep going even as television grew in popularity. The show was set in San Francisco and followed the exploits of a stockbroker and his family. J. Anthony Smythe starred as Henry Barbour, the patriarch of his family. The shows were written, cast, produced, and directed by Carlton E. Morse himself.

Performing on stage in *Separate Tables*, I came to know one of the radio serial's long-running performers, Ben Wright, who was also English. All of us younger actors revered Ben. He looked like a businessman. He wasn't very outgoing, but he was soft-spoken and kind. He called me one day to go see Morse about working on *One Man's Family*. Maurine was very annoyed with Ben, because he was always telling me about jobs. As my agent, looking out for my best interests meant that sometimes she would not just say yes to any part that came along. Ben, however, was a working actor like me, so if he knew of a part, he told me about it.

"Why doesn't he mind his own business?" Maurine said one day in her frustration. Actually, I didn't mind the work at all, so I quite appreciated Ben thinking of me when he heard that an actor was needed to step into the part of Andy Barbour, or Skipper, as he was known, a twenty-one-year-old English cousin to the Barbour family on *One Man's Family*.

I met Morse, the show's creator, whom I found to be a rather eccentric man. He was wiry and wore a black beret. He also was very nervous and agitated, which actually didn't bother me. I always felt secure with someone that creative. Morse often came down from the booth and gave the actors little instructions, but he was a gentle man.

After he cast me in the role of Skipper, I was the fourth person in the show's history to play the part of the twenty-one-year-old. Playing that age was no stretch for me, because I had pretended to be ten years younger a few times on television. To sound a little younger, though, I did pitch my voice a little higher when I was in character.

The show centered around a family crisis each week. Because the show had started while I was a young boy on the other side of the ocean, I really didn't have much insight into the long-running plotline. It was well enough written, obviously, because audiences had loved it since 1932. The plots reminded me of the Andy Hardy stories, the type that seemed to resonate with American listeners.

Working on *One Man's Family* was a low-keyed experience. Unlike other soap operas, there weren't many times when performers had to burst into tears or scream. The show aired daily, but like television soap operas, several episodes were recorded at one time. For a whole year, I worked one day a week in good company with accomplished radio pros.

Gradually, I realized that I had joined a prestigious show, albeit at the end of its record-setting run. The show finally ended in April, 1959, after more than three thousand episodes.

During the show's run, Ben was always thinking of me whenever he heard of acting possibilities, no matter what Maurine thought about it. One such prospective part introduced me to Marlon Brando, who had just returned from making *Sayonara*. Brando had become interested in Noh Japanese poetry. At that stage in his career, he only had to lift his little finger and studios gave him whatever he wanted. He contacted the *CBS Radio Workshop* program and said that he wanted to do a program featuring recitations of Japanese poetry.

One of his friends, Abraham Sofaer, volunteered to put together a cast for Brando's radio poetry reading. Sofaer was a very fine actor who had a good long run on English radio. Ben called and told me that Sofaer was putting together a small group of actors to meet at his apartment to help Brando do a poetry reading. As odd as the job sounded, no actor would turn down the chance to work with Brando, even for poetry!

We all assembled early without Brando so we could go through the script. Abraham designated poems for each of us to read. In strolled Marlon Brando, quietly and casually greeting everyone. To spend an evening in a modest apartment chatting with him like one of the guys was a big thrill to me. He was modest and considerate.

Brando talked about why he wanted to do the show, and said that CBS was being very cooperative. He said, "Shall we just run it through to time it?" He introduced each poem, which was then read by one of us lesser known actors. He then delivered the next introduction and the pattern repeated. We read through the thirty-minute show twice so Abraham could time it.

Brando was scheduled to go overseas to film *The Young Lions* with Montgomery Clift and Dean Martin. Unfortunately, his film took precedence and I'm afraid the thrill of rehearsing with Brando overshadows my memory of actually doing the program. Without Brando, it seemed anticlimactic to the point that I don't remember much more about it.

One door closing inevitably led to another opening, however, because Ben then led me to work on one of the greatest motion pictures of all time, *Ben-Hur*. He called one day to tell me to go to MGM. As it turned out, when the film finished production in Italy, director William Wyler discovered that many of the Italian actors' accents were too thick and could not be understood. Extensive dubbing was needed for the lesser parts.

Ever the protective agent, Maurine didn't like the idea of me working on the film. "It's just a lot of dubbing, but you might as well go since Ben mentioned your name," she said. That was a little short-sighted on her part, because dubbing nearly the entire picture led to week after week of work — and pay!

Margaret Booth was one of the great technical ladies of Hollywood's Golden Age. She had edited the 1935 version of *Mutiny on the Bounty* and had worked on Greta Garbo's *Camille*. She wasn't actually editing *Ben-Hur*, but she was in charge of dubbing in the voices. William Wyler had tasked her to find the right people. Margaret and I hit it off immediately when I auditioned.

She gave me some pages of dialogue, and after I read them, she said, "Yes, I think you'll do very well as a voice, so we'll set up a schedule for next week. Mr. Wyler will be in charge." That news was a big thrill. I showed up to find about eight of us trying out before Wyler appeared. Margaret was responsible for narrowing down the field. Two of the actors were so nervous that they started talking too soon in the dubbing process. They were thanked, and then they were on their way out of MGM.

I felt a sense of pride when I realized that I had quickly picked up the technical aspects of dubbing. I was less nervous than the other actors who were sent home. Dubbing involved enormous pressure as we watched white lines go across the screen to cue us when to speak. My heart almost skipped a beat as the cue appeared. The slightest hesitation meant losing the sync with the image on screen.

The group was finally narrowed down to me, Ben Wright, and a young lady whose name I no longer recall. In came William Wyler, this smallish man who had directed *The Little Foxes*, *The Best Years of Our Lives*, and *The Heiress*.

Dubbing meant that I was getting to see *Ben-Hur* first, months before audiences flocked to what was hailed as an epic masterpiece. I knew the movie was destined to be huge, because everyone had read about its making in the trade papers. When I wasn't in front of the microphone, I just enjoyed watching Sam Jaffe or Stephen Boyd giving their performances.

The dubbing room was small. I couldn't help but feel a sense of satisfaction when I realized that the booth was the same one I had accompanied Alec Guinness to when he invited me to MGM with him shortly after I arrived in Hollywood!

I quickly learned that dubbing was a visual process. I either stood or sat behind a microphone with a music stand holding the words in front of me. When the picture was projected, it was not full sized, and the room was dim so we could see the picture. First, I was shown a clip of the actor on the screen to give me an idea of what he was talking about. Then I was shown the same clip without sound. That part of the process could be a little disconcerting, which is why many people who auditioned for dubbing couldn't get hired. Three vertical lines crossed the screen — white

After he had directed Charlton Heston, William Wyler, right, personally directed my dubbing on Ben-Hur.

lines, from left to right — and as the third line reached the right side, that was my cue to start talking. If I started talking right on the beat, my voice matched the actor's lip movements. I had to get a rhythm that went something like, one, two, three — speak!

When it was time to take the actor's voice off and start recording mine, it was easy to get thrown off without being able to hear anything. Seeing lips moving on the screen, however, meant that I had to talk to match those lips. Once I had the hang of it, the work was easy, especially since I had recorded for the BBC and was familiar with the technical aspects of putting my voice onto tape. I learned that many film actors had to at least be able to do dubbing for their own parts, especially for outdoor scenes when the sound could not be properly recorded.

Director William Wyler was very quiet and business like. He first directed Ben Wright, and then me. Sometimes we recorded little bits or phrases. Wyler would say, "Good. Next." Up in the booth, the next clip or scene played on screen. We then came to one of my lines early in the picture when a Centurion approaches Stephen Boyd's character and announces Ben-Hur. I can still remember my dialogue:

"There's a Jew outside. He wants to see the Tribune Messala…He says he's a prince, Prince Judah Ben-Hur."

I followed the on-screen cue lines, hit my mark and said the line. Wyler stood right in front of me, between me and the screen, and said, "No. There's got to be more disgust. You despise this man because he's a Jew and you're a Roman."

So we did it again, and he said, "No! Look. I'm a Jew. Now you hate my guts. Now say it!"

I said the line. "Repeat it," he ordered. "Let's have another take."

That line was repeated for more than thirty minutes. I began to fear losing the job, but Wyler knew exactly what he wanted and was going to work me to get the performance. I was amazed at his level of direction, down to the dubbing!

The Italian actor I dubbed for was like an organ grinder. There was no confidence in his voice. We could see it even in his stance. Wyler wanted me to make up for that with the dialogue delivery. Eventually, we got the line exactly as it appears in the film.

Ben and I next played lepers for several days. The work was good money, $750 a day. The work seemed to stop, and then we were called back. One day we had to dub on an actual sound stage for some reason. Stage One had been used for some of MGM's classic musicals, so that was hallowed ground for me. From the dawn of talkies, all the marvelous MGM soundtracks had been recorded there by the likes of Judy Garland and Mickey Rooney. A piece of flooring about ten feet by ten feet marked the spot where Fred Astaire and Ann Miller had dubbed their dance steps. It was a big privilege for me to be on the spot where Conrad Sallinger had just scored *Gigi*.

Actors love working with directors who shake you by the shoulders to get it out of you. For the scene where rowers in the boat are drowning,

I dubbed a number of voices in this scene from Ben-Hur. (MGM)

I spent an hour under Wyler's direction just getting the anguish right on the line, "I don't want to die!" I could somehow feel the water by the time we finished.

Wyler was relentless. I loved working with him on every single line. It's a strange thing to be in a fairly small room with a great artist like William Wyler or Margaret Booth. There's tremendous excitement and envy, in a way, when you realize the creative talent of the great man or woman you were dealing with each day.

Ben Wright and I did so many voices in *Ben-Hur* that it's still fun to run the movie today just to listen for which voice is mine or his. The film went on to win a record eleven Academy Awards. I may not have acted on screen in the film, but I did contribute my performance to an epic masterpiece, the highest-grossing film of 1960 and probably second to only *101 Dalmatians* in having my voice so prominently heard in a blockbuster movie. Margaret Booth liked me enough that I would return several times to MGM throughout the 1960s for more dubbing projects. I always thought that if MGM loved my dubbing enough perhaps they would put me into an on-camera part, but they never did. My first big feature film role was waiting for me at 20th Century-Fox, but first I was to do my second stage play.

Early in 1959 Maurine strongly encouraged me to do Somerset Maugham's *The Circle* at the Pasadena Playhouse. Maurine knew that 20th Century-Fox was about to start casting for a sequel to one of its current hit movies. She wanted Lee Wallace, head of feature casting at the studio, to see me in the play. Maurine said, "This is a good credit, and it may help you get your first big feature. You *must* do this play."

I was cast as the young romantic lead. Rehearsals were arduous, though, because it meant that I had to take a bus all the way to Pasadena after spending the early part of the day reading for television roles. The female lead was initially Joyce Taylor, but we had barely rehearsed when we learned that she was gone. She had been cast in a movie role. Jennifer Raine, whom I knew, was brought in as the female lead for my second week of rehearsal. Then one morning we assembled to learn our director had quit. His replacement was introduced, an energetic Ralph Senensky.

Ralph said, "I'd like to see what you've done so far," so Jennifer and I got up and did our thing. He said quietly to someone, "Well, I'll take the fellow, but the girl has to go." So I started the third week with a third female lead, Rachel Ames. Ralph approved of her, and I hit it off with her as well. We began rehearsing. An immensely pleasant man, Ralph and I worked well together. I respected his direction because he was the kind of director from whom I could learn more about acting by listening to his suggestions.

Students at the Pasadena Playhouse were required to attend productions to help fill seats and learn from the experienced actors onstage. My idol, Laird Cregar, had trained there. Two of the young actors who likely saw my stage debut were none other than young Gene Hackman and Dustin Hoffman. I've often wondered what those young "novices" thought of me in the cast, because they most likely had more stage acting experience!

One of the stars in our play was Estelle Winwood. She was very kind to me initially, telling me that I was young and cute. She said, "It doesn't matter how many young girls we audition, because David's charm will carry it off."

Then, inexplicably, she didn't speak to me for the next three weeks. The rest of the cast followed her lead, and so through our rehearsals, I was mostly snubbed for a reason no one would tell me. Everything grew very tense, but neither Rachel nor Ralph knew why everyone else was siding with Estelle. She would even walk right past me in rehearsal without acknowledging me.

One morning this strange treatment really got to me. I was so fed up that I decided not to go to rehearsals that day. "This is so unprofessional that I can't deal with it anymore," I told Maurine over the phone before I went back to bed. There came a pounding on my door about twenty minutes later. It was Maurine. "I will not have Estelle Winwood make my client a frightened little rabbit," she told me.

She turned her back and said, "I'm not going to look. Get dressed and shaved, and I'll sit in the car and wait for twenty minutes, so you'd better be ready by then!" I did as I was told, and she drove me to the Pasadena Playhouse that day. She told me that she was going to stay there in the auditorium until I finished rehearsing, and she did just that. Thank God for her, because she believed in me.

Ralph and I never knew what had happened, or why the rest of the cast wouldn't speak to me. Ralph theorized that I possibly wasn't paying enough attention to Estelle or "kissing her rear enough," to put it vulgarly. She wasn't Greta Garbo, though, so I didn't think I should be fawning over her, especially when nobody else was either. On opening night, Estelle brought a lovely gift to my dressing room, told me that she just knew I was going to be perfect, and all was well, as though nothing had ever happened.

A few weeks later, I was at the supermarket and saw her struggling with her cart on the way to her car. I went up and said, "May I be of assistance, Miss Winwood?" She turned and said, "Oh, yes, how helpful and thoughtful, young man!" She never recognized me from having just worked together onstage a few weeks earlier!

For the most part, I enjoyed working at the Pasadena Playhouse, but it was a bad time for me because I had just moved into a guest house near the beach. It took me an hour to get into Los Angeles and then another forty-five minutes to get out to Pasadena on the bus. After the curtain came down at 10:30 p.m. and by the time I had waited around for bus connections, it was usually two in the morning before I got back home. It was really not much of a pleasure because of that.

Yet there was a great tradition at the Pasadena Playhouse. All the actors' dressing rooms opened up in the green room so the audience could come in to talk to us after the show. Sometimes no one visited, and we thought, "Oh, God, we must have been terrible tonight!" One night, though, Fay Bainter came in. The Academy Award winner said that she loved my work. I damned near fainted dead away, so I knew I must be doing something right!

Always heeding Maurine's advice that casting directors attended our productions, I also tried out for a stage production of *Witness for the Prosecution*. I was named the understudy for the leading man, Jack Cassidy. Shirley Jones told me that her husband had never missed a performance in his entire thirty-year career in theatre!

So I resigned, thinking, "I'm not going to sit there every night and never get a chance to play the part." Who knows who might have seen me in that production, but thankfully, Lee Wallace, head of 20th Century-Fox feature casting, saw me at the Pasadena Playhouse, just as Maurine had wanted. My feature film debut was about to happen in a very big way.

CHAPTER FIVE

Channeling My Inner Villain: *Return of the Fly*

My first three years in Hollywood were always spent playing the hero's best friend on television series. There I was, usually smiling in the background, or saying to the hero, "I'm your friend, so I'll stick by you." After two or three years of that, you're ready for the funny farm. *Return of the Fly* liberated me from those goody-goody parts.

From an actor's point of view, it's wonderful to play villains. They're just more challenging. Over the years, big stars who played variations of themselves all said that it's just as hard to play what looks like you as it is to play very dramatic parts. I don't know that I agree. I played myself when I started in Hollywood and that didn't seem too challenging to me. Playing the villain in *Return of the Fly* and being convincingly evil was very challenging, and from there on, I enjoyed those kinds of roles more than the standard bland parts.

In 1958, 20th Century-Fox scored a major hit when it released *The Fly*, starring Vincent Price and David Hedison. The film was based on an original story published in *Playboy* and written by George Langelaan. James Clavell had adapted the script, and the story seemed to resonate with audiences in an era when science fiction and monster pictures were popular, especially with teenagers and at drive-ins. As the space race began in the late 1950s, audiences were fascinated with technology and the implications of it being abused, so with its plot about a man whose experiments result in him being genetically scrambled with a fly, the movie combined modern science with horror and broke new ground in the genre.

The Fly was so successful that Fox quickly gave the green light to a sequel. The first film's director, Kurt Neumann, had died shortly before the movie's general release, so Fox chose Edward Bernds to direct the sequel. Bernds had worked as a sound man for many of Frank Capra's films in the 1930s before moving over to Columbia to direct a significant number of shorts starring the Three Stooges. By the 1950s, he began directing features, including a number of science fiction or B horror pictures that included *World Without End, Space Master X-7,* and *Queen of Outer Space.*

Ed thought there was potential for a sequel, and the production heads at Fox were thinking the same thing, so he got the job. I'm not entirely sure why he was also chosen to write the film, but I imagine that it made sense to have Ed write and direct the picture in order to expedite the production and capitalize on the first film's success while it was still fresh in the minds of the public.

Ed set the sequel's plot several years after the first film's conclusion. In *The Fly*, David Hedison played a scientist, Andre Delambre, who met an awful end after accidentally mixing himself up with a fly in a teleportation experiment gone awry. Vincent Price was the only star from the original film signed to return for the sequel, and because he was a top star, I'm sure that it made sense for Fox to include him for continuity and his box office draw. In the original, he plays Andre's brother, Francois Delambre, a witness to the horror depicted so memorably when he discovers his brother's head on the body of a fly saying, "Help me!"

Brett Halsey, who had previously worked with Bernds on a couple of pictures, was cast as Phillipe Delambre, Andre's son, now grown, and planning to resume his father's experiments with disintegration-reinte-gration. Being a sequel, the same horrific effect was bound to happen again, but this time, a villain was added to the plot to spice up the action. It was to be a good part, because the villain, Ronald Holmes, alias Alan Hinds, was to work as Phillipe's assistant while simultaneously double-dealing and trying to steal the secret of the Delambres' invention.

Just six months after *The Fly* was released to theatres — in fact, I believe it was still playing in some parts of the country — pre-production started on the sequel. Fox signed Brett Halsey and Vincent Price, so the search began for an actor to play the villain. In February of 1959, the studio compiled a list, supplied by the various Hollywood talent agencies, of young actors who might be right for the part in the film to be called *Return of the Fly*. Lee Wallace, head of feature film casting at Fox, attended theatrical productions and saw me at the Pasadena Playhouse, thanks to the urging of my agent, Maurine Oliver. He also knew me from a whole year's worth of going with Maurine to see him every Thursday on the Fox lot.

Fox wanted somebody who was going to be a double-dealing crook and villain but who didn't look like it; the actor had to have sort of a fresh-faced kind of honesty about him. That's how I had been typed in so many television shows, which I enjoyed, but I felt that I could still

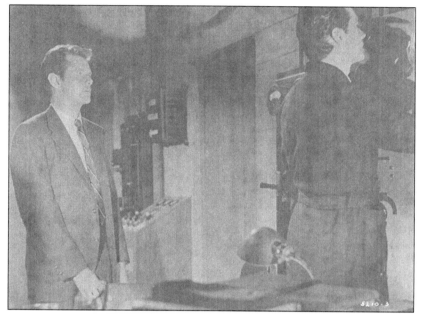

Playing the villain versus Brett Halsey, right, in Return of the Fly. (20TH
CENTURY-FOX)

stretch my range a bit. I wanted to investigate playing different kinds of parts, but when I was sent to audition for *Return of the Fly*, I had no idea that I was really going to be reading for a villain. I thought the part was going to be just another hero's best friend, so it was a mixed bag at first. I was excited about the prospect of a big part in a feature film produced by a major studio, but I wasn't all that thrilled at the idea of playing another bland pal to the hero.

So I showed up at Fox and read the script. As I sat there reading, I thought, "Holy smoke, this is a wonderful part!" The idea of playing a villain was just dawning on me as I read, so I think the adrenaline got going, and I really put my heart and soul into my audition. Mustering every bit of positive thinking I could, I went into it with a sort of confidence that I don't really think I had exhibited before. It must have worked, because I was selected and told rather quickly by both the producer and the director that the role was mine.

Ironically, Ed Bernds later said that he chose me because I looked as though I would be very convincing as the sincere hero's best friend, but in my reading, it seemed to him that I could also be very convincing as a really sneaky, underhanded kind of two-timer, which hopefully was just a nice thought about my acting the day of my audition and not the way I really was!

Not only was I pleasantly surprised to find myself cast as a villain, but I was ecstatic to find myself in a leading part in a big movie at a major motion picture studio. Arriving in Hollywood three years earlier, the plan in my head had been to start gradually in television, get small parts in movies, and maybe I would get featured in movies, and then one day I'd get a leading part in a movie, if I was lucky. To get a leading role in one whack like that, I can still feel the rush that I felt going every day to work.

Vincent Price was one of my film idols.

Eager to start production, I was just as thrilled at the prospect of working with Vincent Price. As a teenager in the 1940s, I had been such a fan of Vincent when he did so many fine movies under contract for Fox, including *Laura*. When I saw him in *Leave Her to Heaven* and *Song of Bernadette*, I realized his enormous range. I even stood in line with everyone else to see him in the 3-D *House of Wax*. I never dreamed that he and I would be making the first of what would turn out to be three movies together.

Nor did I dream that fifteen years after being inspired by Laird Cregar's memorable performance in *The Lodger*, I would end up filming scenes on the same soundstage where he gave the performance of his life. It was almost too good to be true, but there I was, at 20th Century-Fox in March 1959 as we started work on my first feature film.

On the first day of filming, David Hedison came on the set at eight a.m. to wish us all a good shoot. I've never forgotten that very supportive gesture. In addition to Vincent, we now had the blessing of another of the original film's stars, so spirits were high, even though the budget was smaller for the sequel.

Director Ed Bernds addressed the tight budget while we were being fitted for costumes the week before filming was to start. He told us that there was no time or budget for read-throughs, so he hoped that the principals could get together over the weekend and run through our lines. I remember taking a cab that weekend to Brett Halsey's house in the Hollywood Hills, where we enjoyed the read-through, even if we weren't being compensated for it.

Widescreen staging was needed for CinemaScope in Return of the Fly. (20TH CENTURY-FOX)

In fact, the smaller budget meant shooting in black and white, and in later years, Vincent still grumbled about that choice. It didn't make much sense to him to film the sequel to a major hit in black and white when the original had been in color, but at the time, we couldn't be too unhappy, because Fox did opt to shoot in CinemaScope.

Fox owned the rights to CinemaScope, so they used it quite extensively in the 1950s to double the size of the projected image on the movie screen. Studios were employing all sorts of gimmicks to counteract the popularity of television, but CinemaScope was actually a real innovation, and widescreen movies were becoming mainstream.

Working in CinemaScope, however, was a real challenge. All of us actors had to do a lot more walking about in a scene. It was a bit daunting for directors to keep the cast moving in scenes in which we really should not have been moving. Vincent and I had our first scene where we were talking in the lab. We really should just have been standing next to each other, but we had to keep moving around to fill up space in order to work with that long letterbox shape that the audience would see on screen.

In that particular scene, Ed Bernds had me pacing up and down while I talked, and I thought, "It's hard enough for me to remember the lines and to realize that I'm finally working with the wonderful Vincent Price; I've also got to remember that I'm working in CinemaScope *and* I have to keep moving, thinking, and talking at the same time, which isn't as easy to do as it sounds." And it wasn't easy, especially since I had only worked in television at that point and television is much more intimate for actors in a studio.

Vincent, however, put almost anyone at ease. He was warm, funny, encouraging, and super professional, very relaxed. He, too, didn't find CinemaScope the easiest thing to stage, and I heard him mumbling about having to do a lot of walking around. A very tall man — I think he was six feet and three inches — he was very charming. He didn't like uptight people working with him. In fact, he straightened me out the very first day of shooting.

I was understandably nervous; after all, it was my first feature film after working exclusively in television. Before we started shooting, we first met during makeup and wardrobe sessions. Vincent had pointed out to me in a very friendly way that, as he put it, "You lucky SOB, you got the best part in the film!" That was his way of making me feel confident. I'm sure he could tell I was a mixture of excitement and nervousness.

On the first day of shooting, I was aware that I had this wonderfully written part to which to do justice, so as soon as I finished each scene, I went straight back to my little dressing room and sat there and went over the next scene in the script. I knew the lines, but as I waited to do close-ups, I welcomed the chance to look at the script one more time.

Vincent joined a group with the rest of the cast in chairs that had our names on the back. My chair sat empty because I was in my dressing room. The other actors were all chatting away and reading the trade papers about what was new in Hollywood. So finally, Vincent stuck his head in my dressing room and said, "What the hell are you doing in here?"

I said, "Oh, Mr. Price, I'm going over my lines for the next scene."

He said, "Get the hell out of here. There's a chair out there with your name on it. Come and join the rest of us on the set between scenes and be sociable. I like a social set!"

With that, Vincent laughed and thumped me on the back. He didn't mean to scare me; that was just his way of encouraging me to socialize and have fun, because camaraderie was important to cast and crew morale. Not only did the social chat relax him, but it served to put the rest of the cast at ease, too. And from that day forth, whenever I worked, my preparation was done at home. I never saw him look at his script, so Vincent taught me to enjoy the social company of all the other actors. I went and joined him with the rest of the cast, and we all sat around in our chairs and had a good time between scenes.

Working on the same soundstage where Laird Cregar was so sinister in *The Lodger*, I naturally started asking Vincent about him. Vincent, who had delivered the eulogy at Laird's funeral in 1944, spoke very highly of this immensely talented actor. He told me what a popular man he was and that he was a happy man, full of fun and humor until his last film, *Hangover Square*, which he hated. In many ways, Laird and Vincent played similar roles in suspenseful films, and after Laird's untimely death, it was just Vincent left to play those particular kinds of roles.

As I sat there and wondered, "Am I really working with the star of *Laura* and *The House of Wax*"? I also quizzed Vincent about his work at Fox. He never told me exactly what it was about, but he did mention a big run-in with Darryl Zanuck over something related to renewing his contract at the end of its seven years. A furious Zanuck barred Vincent from the Fox lot and wouldn't even let him back on the property to retrieve his personal things from his dressing room. Vincent told me that he drove to the lot in the dead of night and climbed over the fence to get his clothing and belongings and then drove away. That was all in the past, though, because Zanuck was gone and Vincent was back working again at Fox.

From that first day on, I couldn't wait to get to Fox in the morning to start to work. I really loved working on *Return of the Fly*. For a film with a dark, serious plotline, it was hard to keep a straight face with Vincent because he delighted in all of these strange-looking people who were coming out of the teleporter machine with mittens shaped like rat feet on their hands.

Vincent also loved to tell a very funny joke about thirty seconds before the cameras rolled. He would get to the point of the punch line just before Ed Bernds said, "Action." Inevitably, his humor always happened during a serious scene, and he did it just to break me up or to relax me. There were a couple of times when I would be doing this very intense scene, and the joke would just come to me. There are a few instances where you can see the smile on my face that showed up on film. I said, "Vincent, please don't kid around," but I loved him for it. I was glad he brought a sense of humor to put me at ease.

It was equally wonderful working not only with the man who had written the script but who also was directing it, because if we had any problems as we went along with dialogue, we had only to turn to Ed Bernds, who took off his director's hat, put on his writer's hat, and straightened us out

Vincent always found fun in his work.

on what we were supposed to be doing. Ed was a great big bear of a man, warm and kindly, very funny. When I learned that he had worked with the Three Stooges, it amazed me that he could write and direct a fairly serious science fiction film along the lines of *Return of the Fly*, but he later told me that he had seen *The Fly* and thoroughly enjoyed it.

In addition to Vincent, there were several other notable veterans in the cast. John Sutton was cast as the inspector familiar with the horrific plotline from the first film; the part was very similar to the one played by Herbert Marshall in *The Fly*. By the time we started production on the sequel, Marshall wasn't well, so Fox supposedly said that the insurance company wouldn't pass him. Had something happened to him during production, Fox would have been liable for the money and would have possibly even had to re-shoot the film. That was a tough break in the business part of show business, but Fox just said that they couldn't risk using him.

John Sutton had worked with both Laird Cregar and Vincent Price in *Hudson's Bay*. He and Vincent had also made a number of other films together, including *The Three Musketeers* and *Tower of London*. Sutton acted a little frosty toward me at the start of our shoot, and I wasn't sure why until he told me that he had wanted my role for himself. He confessed that he had not been honest with himself about the fact that he was too old to play the part. He was having a little difficulty adapting to the idea that he was then playing older characters, but we worked well together.

Several days into production, I read the next day's call sheet and it said that I would be working with Dan Seymour. How excited I was to have two key scenes with him in the film. He was an actor who had held his own with Humphrey Bogart in *Key Largo* and *Casablanca*, among countless other movies. Working with gifted actors always brings out the best in the others. Dan was a smoothie, the ultimate pro.

Our biggest scene was the one where my character, Ronald Holmes, aka Dr. Alan Hinds, reveals his villainous intention during a visit to a sleazy mortician, played by Dan. The mortician is moonlighting as the "fence" interested in ill-gotten microfilm with blueprints of Delambre's fantastic integrator-disintegrator device. Dan shot all of his scenes in one day, from seven a.m. to ten p.m. that night. I was even more in awe as the day went on, because he never once looked at the script. He knew his part and never needed one line of direction. In fact, he was ready to go from the start and flawlessly did everything right the first time.

We both sensed that we had a good scene when my character tries to convince his of just how valuable the teleportation device plans will be on the black market. He's messily eating crab or lobster in the offices of his funeral parlor, and here I'm an equally sleazy, smarmy young villain threatening him to do business or else. It was a well-written scene that we both relished filming. It was also a lengthy scene in the sense that it lasted more than two minutes — that's a long time to be on screen. That was a challenge to us actors, because we had to sustain that energy and focus throughout to keep the audience's attention.

In this particular scene, we each sparred in a give and take maneuver as two disreputable men would do, and then my character exited while his still chomped away on his dinner. I heard Ed Bernds say, "Cut!" from his director's chair, and then I heard applause. I went out and joined in the applause, and Dan said, "No, David, this is for you, too." Our scene together was the only occasion in my career when the crew applauded the master take, and Dan really was the reason for it.

As part of a breakneck production schedule, and likely to save a little money on the salary of a veteran like Dan, Fox crammed all of his scenes into one very long day. By late in the evening, Dan worked with me again and still gave his all. We had a night scene that we filmed at ten p.m., and Dan never complained, even after working all day. There I was in between takes, pumping him about what it was like to work with Humphrey Bogart

My big scene with Dan Seymour, seated, in Return of the Fly.

and Claire Trevor. He loved to talk about his career and never seemed to tire of my questions or our work. The next day, I was sorry that he wasn't back on the set so this film buff could ask him even more questions.

The special presence of one other cast member should be noted. In the final shooting script, there was a scene where my character returned to the lab to steal some plans or blueprints. One of the scenes called for me to be discovered and then deal treacherously with the interruption.

Michael Mark was cast as Gaston, a night watchman. When I was introduced to him, I instantly recognized him as the actor who had played the father of the little girl who gets thrown by Boris Karloff into the water and drowns in *Frankenstein*. Mark's big scene involved him walking and crying through the town with the little girl in his arms.

"Were you in *Frankenstein*?" I asked.

He was so moved by my question that his eyes filled with tears.

"Yes, sir, I was," he replied. "How very kind of you to remember."

He was so polite that he insisted on calling me "sir" as one of the leads, when in reality, I was the newcomer and he had worked in Hollywood for years. He mostly had played small parts, many of them uncredited, but he had steadily worked in a number of films, including *Casablanca* and *The Ten Commandments*. He was very grateful to be working on our movie.

Mr. Mark and I filmed a rather chilling scene that was cut. The scene was set at the lab when my character secretly sneaked back to steal the teleporter plans. Discovered by the night watchman, my character fought with him, knocked him out, put a rope around his neck, and then hoisted him up over a beam.

I remember telling him to let me know so I didn't tie the rope too tightly, and, of course, he was rigged so as not to be injured. At the end, Mr. Mark thanked me profusely, more so than even our director, because I had remembered him. An actor's life can be so frail. Unless you're a big movie star, you can go along all your life without very many people saying, "Hey, weren't you in…?" When you are recognized, it's an overwhelming feeling, as Mr. Mark was a testament to that.

I'm not entirely sure why the scene was cut, but I suppose it was because we had already established my character's villainy and the hanging could have been one gruesome killing too many on screen.

Return of the Fly involved more special effects work than I had previously encountered in my television roles. Actually, I had very little to do with the special effects, most of which involved the transporter disintegrating and reintegrating animals and people. All I had to do was to look down at an "X" on the ground and act horrified because there was nothing really there to see.

Then Pat O'Hara, who played a nosy detective trying to arrest my character on a murder charge, came back in wearing a guinea pig's hands and feet to finalize the effect of me crossing him with the animal a little

It's always more fun to play the villain, Return of the Fly.

earlier in the plot. Although there was a special effect showing a guinea pig reintegrated with human hands, that really was a live guinea pig working with me in between special effects shots in the final film. To tell the truth, the guinea pig scene was hard to do because I love animals. Then, as now, the Society for Prevention of Cruelty to Animals was always on set to be sure that the animals were treated in a very humane and kindly fashion.

The hero's "best friend" shows his true colors, Return of the Fly.

A movie set can get very hot, and the animals, once they worked their scene, were taken to where it was cooler, because most of them, rabbits particularly, can start panting in no time under the hot lights. They had to be treated very kindly, but at the same time, I had to look as though I didn't give a damn about them. I hope that was good acting, because I hated lifting up an animal by its ears. The handlers told me it was okay to do that to a rabbit, but I wouldn't like to be a rabbit picked up by my ears.

You know you're truly a rotten villain when you kill a man by crossing him with a guinea pig and then you stomp and squish the poor guinea pig-hybrid sporting human hands. That's a real gross-out scene in the movie, but no harm came to the guinea pig. It was realistic enough, though, that the scene was censored and shortened for the British release, so my friends and relatives back in England were spared the sight of villainous me killing a strange-looking guinea pig. When I wasn't pretending to be diabolical, there were refreshing breaks while some of the other actors worked on scenes without my character. For this movie fan-turned-actor, roaming about the lot on lunch breaks was a delight. Chicago had memorably burned down around the 20th Century-Fox Lake in 1937's *In Old Chicago*, and I delighted in walking around and spotting familiar scenery.

Poor Pat O'Hara, crossed with a guinea pig, Return of the Fly.

The mansion façade used in the film was very realistic on the outside. When I opened the front door and walked through, it was all two by four planks and scaffolding. Just the year before, it had also been used in *The Fly* and in *The Long Hot Summer*. The mansion exterior was just around the corner from the Fox soundstages and only yards from Wilshire Boulevard, one of the busiest thoroughfares in Los Angeles. When Fox sold off the

Perfecting the art of disintegration and reintegration in Return of the Fly.

real estate to pay for *Cleopatra* a few years later, I think the mansion went, along with the lake, as well as the Bernadette Village and several other spots familiar to film buffs.

On the soundstage next to where we were shooting *Return of the Fly*, Frank Tashlin was directing one of my teenage idols, Bing Crosby, along with Debbie Reynolds and Robert Wagner, in the musical romance *Say One for Me*. My encounter with him was just a little embarrassing for me.

One evening we were outdoors filming the scene where I shoot Vincent Price and then hop into his convertible to escape with the blueprints for the teleportation device. It's an action scene and important to the plot as the villain rushes to get away and take the plans back to the funeral parlor headquarters of Dan Seymour's character.

If memory serves correct, the beautiful sports car in the scene actually belonged to Brett Halsey in real life. Brett had grown up in California and had been working steadily, so a convertible was natural for him. Having used public transportation or a taxi cab in London and Hollywood, I had not yet really learned how to drive.

As the crew prepared to film the scene, Brett handed me his car keys and said, "You do know how to drive a straight shift, don't you? Be really cautious with this car." Wanting to look as suave and cool as Brett, I calmly replied, "Oh, sure, I know what I'm doing."

In reality, I couldn't even figure out how to brake, so I sat there fidgeting with the car and quickly tried to learn where everything was located. When Ed and the crew asked if I wanted to rehearse the getaway drive, I said no. I knew that would mean that I would have to do it all over again, and if I couldn't figure out how to drive the car the first time, I wasn't about to embarrass myself twice.

About the time we were set to roll film, production stopped on *Say One for Me* at the next soundstage. Out came Debbie Reynolds, followed by Bing Crosby. It turned out that Brett's sports car caught Bing's eye, and evidently he, too, liked sporty little cars. There I was, sitting, waiting for Ed to roll film and also trying to focus on acting and driving at the same time, and there came Bing Crosby strolling right over to the car.

"Say, fella, what kind of car is this?" Bing said in that famous smooth baritone voice.

I nearly lost it, as I nervously sat there looking up at a boyhood idol, a crooner whose records I had bought as a teenager and an actor whose performances I had enjoyed for years. Nervously peering up at that famous face, I stammered, "Mr. Crosby, I really don't know."

Luckily for me, Bing suddenly realized that he was holding up the shot, although our crew didn't seem to mind waiting for a big star like Bing. He excused himself, got out of the shot and stood over to the side and watched as I prepared to kill the crew and wreck Brett's car — and my career.

The camera was straight ahead of the car, which meant I was driving right up to camera. I thought I was going to hit the camera crew positioned just three feet away. Shaking head to foot, I somehow did the scene, and I managed to pull it off by reasonably driving. When you watch the scene in the film, you can see me driving very cautiously so I don't hit anyone. For a villain who had just shot Vincent Price and was supposed to be making a quick getaway, I'm a very careful driver!

There was also another long shot where I had to drive in, stop the car, grab the blueprints, and run into the exterior of the funeral home where Dan Seymour's character awaits. Thank God we did the car shots in one take, because I couldn't have done it again.

Aside from my car phobia, shooting the rest of the picture was great fun. Brett Halsey and I had a big fight scene when his character, Phillipe,

Disposing of my crime against nature, Return of the Fly.

discovers that his assistant is secretly using the transporter machine in the laboratory. Brett and I fought all over the set and nearly wrecked it. Brett had made a number of movies with plenty of fight scenes under his belt, but this was a big one for me, staged all around the lab set for the maximum effect of CinemaScope.

We had a stunt choreographer who helped set up the action. Had the

LEFT: *Now it's Brett Halsey's turn for teleportation,* Return of the Fly. RIGHT: *A stunt double has helped me subdue Brett Halsey.*

picture enjoyed a bigger budget and more production time, I think we could have done a better job. Even though we were working for a major studio, the movie was a B picture with its limited budget, and it was hastily made in the sense that when I look at it today, I can see that my punches were sloppy in the fight scenes.

We never could have foreseen that one day, DVD would enable me to slow down the action and spot the stunt doubles. I have done that several times over the years whenever I've watched the film, but I'm always interested in seeing the finished result on film and how effective it was — or wasn't. Because we were filming a black and white movie, I think they used chocolate sauce to simulate the blood coming from my lip.

The conclusion of that fight scene was a lot of fun. My character remembers that Phillipe is afraid of flies whenever he recalls what happened to his father in the first film. After Alan knocked out Phillipe, I had to drag Brett into the teleporter device and toss a fly in with him to mutate him. The memorable result was a man wearing a giant fly head and arms, all part of a costume designed by Hal Lierley, who had done makeup for Olivia de Havilland and Miriam Hopkins in *The Heiress*.

Brett had wisely negotiated his contract so he didn't actually have to

Literally time for the Return of the Fly.

wear the fly mask as David Hedison had done in *The Fly*. A stuntman named Ed Wolff wore the giant fly costume and went thrashing about the set and in several outdoor scenes. It meant that instead of working more than two weeks as I did, Brett got to do all his scenes in one week but was paid for the rest of the time. Very smart!

On the other hand, I had more scenes to film, including a creepy segment when Alan goes back to Dan Seymour's funeral parlor. Phillipe, now the mutated fly, first strangles Dan's character and then waits for me in a darkened building filled with caskets. Phillipe the fly gets his revenge by lifting me off my feet, choking and then breaking my neck. It was fun to pretend to have the life choked out of me at the hands of this larger-than-life creature. Inside the costume, though, Ed Wolff had a weak heart, so I was amazed that he could put himself into potential harm's way by doing such stunts.

For an added chill, Ed Bernds had the idea of getting an extra fright from the audience. Because the scene was set in a funeral home, Phillipe, half-man, half-fly, stuffs my seemingly lifeless body into a casket and closes it. Bernds thought that he could scare the audience by having my dead body experience a reflex movement. When a policeman searches the room, I raised the lid and extended a shaky hand before finally collapsing dead back into the casket.

Before we filmed the scene, we rehearsed Bernds' idea. Vincent, who wasn't in the scene, came up to the coffin after I had made my last movement. He closed the coffin with a click and said, "One hour to lunch!" I pushed the lid and it didn't move! We were using a real coffin, lined with silk, and rented from a local mortuary. I couldn't open the coffin. With blind panic, I began thumping as I heard Vincent laugh. His idea of a joke nearly scared me to death. Not too many live people ever climb inside a casket, so I had enough of that to last for one lifetime.

Critics and even people working within the movie industry can be snobby about certain genres, especially horror or science fiction, but I think it's a challenge to do a horror film convincingly without being laughed at or being hammy. You rely upon your director to tell you if you're overdoing it or underdoing it.

Up until that point, I had used my television roles to get experience working in front of cameras. It had been an education for me, but it was pretty routine stuff: Brit versus Yank, scuffle, shake hands, and make up, nothing very exciting. But to play a villain in a feature at Fox, co-starring opposite Vincent Price and a giant half-man, half-fly? I was in heaven.

While *Return of the Fly* may have been considered a minor Fox film, a number of the studio's resident crew members, top professionals in their field, worked on the movie. There were *several* Oscar winners who worked on our film. For example, art director Lyle Wheeler was one of the top all-time Academy Award winners with twenty-four nominations and five statuettes to his credit. He won Oscars for *Gone with the Wind*, *The King and I*, and in the same year that he made *Return of the Fly*, he earned his fifth award for *The Diary of Anne Frank*.

So for the film buffs, myself included, or for the critics who sniff that we only made an insignificant monster movie, it's important to remember that some remarkable people with great pedigrees worked on *Return of the Fly*. For a young actor starting out in Hollywood, the movie meant the opportunity to learn from professionals. Even though by 1959 the studio system was largely over for most movie stars, working on a major studio lot still offered steady employment for the behind-the-scenes technicians assigned to work from one production to the next. Working with these talented individuals made a lasting impression on me, and I loved every minute of it.

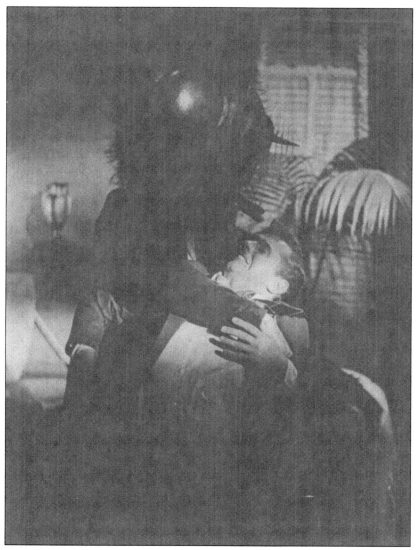

That's Ed Wolff strangling me from inside the fly costume.

If making *Return of the Fly* sounds like fun, that's because it was. I wish it had lasted forever. I would have preferred a shooting schedule of three or four months instead of thirteen days, including fitting for wardrobe. How we accomplished all of that in thirteen days, I don't know, but the combined effort of so many talented people must be the answer. Many one-hour television shows during the era required as many as eight

Lobby card, Return of the Fly, *1959.*

shooting days, so I think we did well to produce an entire CinemaScope feature that quickly.

As we wrapped up the film, I realized that making the movie was truly my first big break. Because I had joined an acting study group a year or two before, I felt that I knew more of what I was supposed to do as an actor, especially with Vincent Price encouraging me. As we worked to finish the movie, I remember thinking, "I can call myself a professional actor now."

It was rewarding for me to play a villain, because I got to do and depict things that most actors will never actually do in real life. I had a very hard time of convincing my mother about that. She was always delighted to see that I was making good in Hollywood when she saw the films over in England or my name out in front of the cinema, but when *Return of the Fly* came out, she said, "David, I really didn't know whether to invite my friends to see you doing all of that."

Return of the Fly opened on August 26, 1959, without a big premiere, in Los Angeles and across the country. On the first day, I went to two screenings on my own. At ten a.m. the morning of opening day, I went downtown to catch the first showing. I was so nervous that I was shaking by the time I saw my name up on screen. The movie started and I relaxed. For the most part, I liked what I saw and thought we did a pretty good job to have done the film so quickly and on a tight budget.

When the lights went up, my self-esteem was soaring. Later that evening, I went to a theatre near a college, and it was filled with college kids watching the movie. At first, they didn't react at all when I was pretending to be a good guy, but once I turned bad and started killing animals and police officers, they hissed and booed. To this day, I don't know if they were booing my character or my work, so that was a little unnerving and it actually depressed me that night.

I remember reading the trade papers, and while the box office didn't set the world on fire, we ironically were beating *Say One for Me*, the Bing Crosby picture that had filmed simultaneously on the next soundstage at Fox. *Return of the Fly* opened wider and made more money, so to take part in something that bested my idol Bing Crosby, I was pretty proud.

The film's influence even spread abroad. One day I received a call from my old BBC colleague, Hanns Friedrichs, who by then had become a German television broadcaster. He said over the phone, "Frankham, you're famous!" He had seen the movie and thought it was funny to hear me dubbed in German.

My mother had to twist my father's arm to get him up to London to see my movie debut. That was my father's attitude when I began appearing in movies. He never seemed impressed by anything about my movies, although I'm told he did point out my name on the poster to the cinema manager. Inside the theatre, though, he was probably still asking my mother, "Which was one was David?"

Return of the Fly resulted in a Fox contract for Brett Halsey as a result of his high profile exposure in the movie. Brett was a good actor, and went on to do *The Best of Everything* and later played Mary Astor's son in *Return to Peyton Place*. Not too long after we worked together, he was married to a really stunning Italian actress named Luciana Paluzzi. Years later I saw Brett in *The Godfather III*, looking very distinguished as Diane Keaton's husband.

I was in the process of being offered a Fox contract as well, until a falling out with a Fox casting director ended that. Even though I was disappointed that a disagreement meant no contract, I had to look out for my own best interests, and what was being offered to me was not what I wanted for my career.

After I was interviewed for *Starlog Magazine* in 1990, I had a very nice letter from Ed Bernds, my old director. He wrote, "Your career should have gone further at Fox, and I don't understand why it didn't." He must not have known about my disagreement with the Fox casting director. When I watch Fox films made immediately after 1960, I sometimes find myself thinking, "I wonder if I would have been up for that part under different circumstances?" Well, it's all water under the bridge.

Nevertheless, *Return of the Fly* opened doors for me. From a purely financial aspect, it doubled my income and my acting opportunities. I would still occasionally play rather bland best friends to heroes, but I was soon afterward offered a part in a Disney film as a cowardly drunkard Englishman, a role that certainly would not have been suggested for me prior to proving the range of my acting abilities by playing a villain for Fox. The film enabled my agent to get her foot in the door for good parts by saying, "Well, David has just played the villain over at Fox in *Return of the Fly*. Will you please consider seeing him?"

For a film that could be dismissed as a monster movie, producers or casting agents always remembered the film; I suppose anything with "The Fly" in the title would be difficult to forget. Over the following years, numerous parts went back to my role as the villain because it was a big film. It was wonderful to have stretched my horizons as an actor.

In the 1980s, the *Fly* films were remade for new audiences. I went with an open mind to the remake of *The Fly* with Jeff Goldblum. I was impressed, because technically, the special effects had come along so well. It was a good film. On the other hand, I thought *The Fly II* was just bad. When imagination goes out the window and you have nothing but gore, lost is the creative and imaginative control essential for any kind of film to have quality. I just don't think that one had anything going for it.

Return of the Fly has lasted with fans, thanks in part to interest in the first film and greater appreciation for Vincent Price and all of his work. I've seen the movie play frequently on AMC and the Fox Movie Channel over the years. In August 2010, the Fox Movie Channel ran the film all month long as part of a salute to the *Fly* movies. It's still fun to watch.

Fox put out a terrific DVD boxed set showcasing all three of the *Fly* movies, including a third film, *Curse of the Fly*, from 1965. I had a lot of fun looking at all the publicity stills in the bonus features. There has also been a book published called *The Fly at Fifty*, covering the legacy of the original film with some coverage of the sequels and fans' continuing interest in the story.

There was a great publicity shot taken of me being strangled by the fly. Friends framed it for my birthday a few years back, and that's a point of

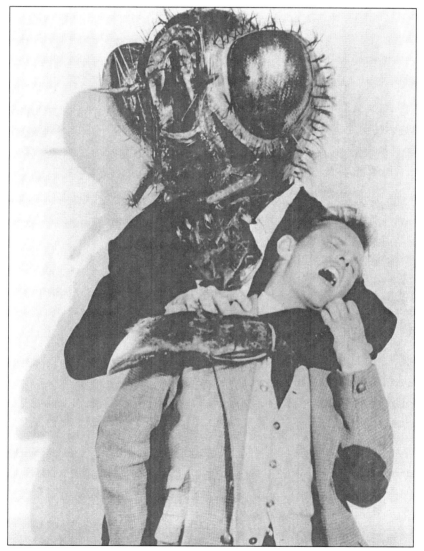

Villainy rarely pays, Return of the Fly.

pride in my collection. I even have a few lobby cards in Spanish and other languages, so I think the film had reach outside America.

In 2002, the Memphis Film Festival invited me to attend a retrospective weekend dedicated to the *Fly* films. I was in the middle of moving, so I unfortunately couldn't attend, but David Hedison and Brett Halsey represented the films rather nicely. In fact, another retrospective screening of the first two films was held in Los Angeles shortly after Labor Day in 2008. I was in L.A. for a Disney event the week before and didn't know about the *Return of the Fly* screening until friends called shortly after I returned home and asked why I wasn't there. Maybe if that teleporter ever gets perfected, it will be possible for actors to be at two different industry events at once!

I am often asked why I think the movie has held up so well. I think part of why it worked was the basic premise of how new technology in that era could be abused. When we made the film, we were all living in the atomic age, and there were great moral implications of how nuclear technology could be abused — and still is today, for that matter.

There's also the element of intrigue with my character out to steal the technology's secrets. The villain is on the run from the British police, and he's clearly willing to steal and sell the teleporter plans to anybody willing to pay the highest price. So, there were shades of the Cold War in there; much of the paranoia from that time period was based on fear of the Soviets or double agents working for evil syndicates or rogue elements, not too far from what the James Bond pictures later incorporated into their plotlines. It's also interesting that the first two *Fly* films were set in Canada and not the United States. It could have been very easy to set the film in Mayport or some all-American location, so the French-Canadian elements add some layers to it, I think.

While the special effects have since been surpassed by today's standards, I like to think that *Return of the Fly* represents a pretty good effort for what we set out to do. We entertained the audience, gave them a plot that seemed at least theoretically feasible in the scientific realm of the era, and kept an interesting story alive. The cast and crew were dedicated to making it the best we could with the budget and production time allotted, and I'm proud that it marked my feature film debut.

Return of the Fly helped solidify a career pattern for me, which I appreciate more in retrospect than I did at the time. That dabble in villainy helped consolidate my diversion into bad and not-so-good guys as opposed to the white-bread heroes that I had been portraying in my first few years in Hollywood.

The door that director Ed Bernds opened for me stayed open for decades to come. Just a year later, Vincent Price recommended me for another genre picture, *Master of the World*, and second only to that film, *Return of the Fly* remains the happiest film experience of my career.

CHAPTER SIX

A Cat Among *101 Dalmatians* and Working at Disney

Actors looking to be forever remembered, or at least rediscovered later in their careers, should follow this one simple piece of advice: voice a Walt Disney animated character. My journey into the wonderful world of Disney has never really ended, because my voice will likely live forever as new generations of children — and the young at heart — embrace Disney animation anew.

I was fortunate enough to win the approval of Walt Disney himself when I was cast as the voice of Sgt. Tibs, a scrawny, yet brave, Cockney cat that nearly single-handedly saves scores of puppies from certain doom in the clutches of Cruella deVille's henchmen in the 1961 animated classic *One Hundred and One Dalmatians* (aka *101 Dalmatians,* to simplify the title, and I should note that Sgt. Tibs is sometimes spelled in Disney publicity materials as Sgt. Tibbs).

Dreaming of an acting career back in England, I never envisioned providing voiceovers for animated characters as a career possibility, although the notion would not have proven too far a stretch given that I was making a living through the use of my voice on the BBC. Playing Sgt. Tibs was as fun as one might imagine, and working at Disney stays fresh in my memory as an exciting experience. I had been brought up on *Snow White, Fantasia, Bambi,* and *Pinocchio* as a child in England; of course, I saw them all in their first release!

At age eleven, I particularly fell in love with *Snow White and the Seven Dwarfs.* My exercise homework books, which I still have, were covered in the margins with my not-very-good drawings of the dwarfs. It was seeing *Fantasia* that first exposed me to classical music in general and the Philadelphia Orchestra in particular. I had never seen an orchestra before or a conductor. From then on, I collected every recording they made. I owe years of listening pleasure to that movie.

I had only been living in America and working in Hollywood for three years when I got the call to audition for *101 Dalmatians*. I had

Model sheet with alternate spelling for Sgt. Tibs. (© DISNEY ENTERPRISES, INC.)

just finished my first leading role in a movie, playing the killer in *Return of the Fly* at 20th Century-Fox, so I knew that my parents wouldn't be too enthusiastic about my work in the United States if that role was an example. I was relieved to be able to write them that I was being considered for a Disney feature. My friend Doris Lloyd had also done the voice of a character for a Disney film back in the 1950s, a flower in *Alice in Wonderland*. Working at Disney would be a good career move, I decided.

About half a dozen of us actors had appointments in the spring of 1959, at a huge recording studio on Disney's lot. The recording studio was about the size of a barn and large enough to accommodate a full orchestra. It stood empty that day except for a microphone suspended from the ceiling, a stool and a music stand on which were displayed a few pages of dialogue from the film. Around three sides of the walls were pinned dozens of rough sketches of various sequences still to be animated, and all showing Sgt. Tibs in various situations.

I was introduced to Wolfgang "Woolie" Reitherman, who was in charge of the animation as one of Disney's directing animators, one of the nine master animators that Disney referred to affectionately as his "Nine Old Men" in later years. I was excited to talk with a man who had helped create so many of my favorite Disney movies.

As we walked around the walls looking at all the sketches, Reitherman explained what Sgt. Tibs was all about and what the animators were looking for by way of a voice for him. He told me to take my time thinking about a characterization as I studied the dialogue and then to let them know in the control booth when I was ready to try for a take.

Luckily my training in England had been in radio, and I had already done *One Man's Family*, a Hollywood radio soap opera, because recording the voice for a cartoon character was exactly like doing a radio play — the actor had to convey everything with the voice alone at that stage of production. It's only later that the full resources of the Disney craftsmen came into play, and by then, of course, the visuals were much more important than the soundtrack, although both were vital to the film's effectiveness.

I tried a few tentative takes, very conscious of the fact that I was standing on hallowed ground. This was, after all, the same studio used by all the other fine performers over the years who had provided voices for the Disney characters, not to mention several musical greats and favorites of mine who had recorded at Disney just a decade or two prior. Those performers had included the Andrews Sisters and Dinah Shore for pictures such as *Make Mine Music* and *Melody Time*, as well as my idol, Bing Crosby, who had narrated and sung for the Ichabod Crane segment of 1949's *The Adventures of Ichabod and Mr. Toad*.

Woolie Reitherman guided me into making Sgt. Tibs as peppy and excitable as I could, and that was that. I thought, "Even if nothing comes of this, I'm relishing every moment of it." I left the studio knowing that I had at least one chance in six of being part of a Disney film, and was delighted to hear a few days later that the role was mine.

I was told that Walt Disney's practice was to listen to all the audition tapes at his leisure, by himself in his office, and then he made the final selection. Woolie said that Walt had an infallible ear for the character's voice and wanted to be completely objective about his selections. When he heard the various voices, he didn't want to be thinking about what the actor looked like.

Voicing Sgt. Tibs was a different kind of experience for me, so I was very excited. My diaries from the time record that I contributed my part in two recording sessions, on May 1, 1959, and one month later on June 1, working closely once again with Woolie and the talented story editor, Bill Peet.

Once more there were dozens of sketches of Sgt. Tibs sitting all

The famous "Twilight Bark" sequence from 101 Dalmatians. (© DISNEY ENTERPRISES, INC.)

around the studio walls. With so much stimulation, it wasn't too difficult to imagine myself as a skinny Cockney cat. An added pleasure was working alongside an old friend, J. Pat O'Malley, who was providing the voice of a blustery sheepdog named The Colonel.

Pat was jovial. He looked like a sheepdog, and that's not because he was recording the voice of a sheepdog! He was very jowly, and he possessed a lopsided grin to the way he talked. I liked his great warmth and joviality. He really got into the part. I later learned that most of Disney's voice actors rarely recorded together, so it was truly a treat to be there at the same time with Pat.

After Pat recorded his part, the microphone swung over to me. Woolie Reitherman personally directed me. He kept telling me to make my voice a little more Cockney. That bothered me, because if I had been authentically

Cockney, I believe it would have been hard to understand. Having lived in London, I had been in parts of the city where Cockneys lived and worked. I love their accent, but it can take a little time to get used to the dialect. I thought I had better refine my accent a bit, so Woolie suggested a light-hearted, cheerful approach. He then spent so much time with me, sentence by sentence, explaining what was happening — visually — to

J. Pat O'Malley voiced the Colonel to my Sergeant. (© DISNEY ENTERPRISES, INC.)

Sgt. Tibs at that point in the picture.

Sometimes I had to add a few words to make it sound authentic, so when I went back again, the writers sometimes had incorporated that into the final version. You didn't change a script at Disney once it was in final draft, so they liked your input while you worked on creating the character. The Disney people cared deeply about their work; there was never any sense of tension or pressure on the actors, as there is so often in other movie-making. It was all very low-keyed and relaxed, a lot of laughter as I recall, between takes, and a great feeling of innocence about the whole project.

As I had found during my earlier dubbing work on *Ben-Hur*, when it's just you and a microphone, some actors get a little self-conscious or even nervous. Thanks to my radio background, I felt no self-consciousness while recording my part. I was so delighted to be working at Disney; it wasn't high pressure work in any way or sense. They regarded me as a vocal artist, and that was a wonderful feeling. The animator who brought Sgt. Tibs to life was John Lounsberry. He actually sat there sketching while I recorded the voice, so I was very keen to see the results.

Several of the film's voice actors recorded more than one character's

It's heroic Sgt. Tibs to the rescue of 99 puppies. (© DISNEY ENTERPRISES, INC.)

voice in the film. For example, in addition to recording the voice of the sheepdog, Pat O'Malley also voiced Jasper, one of Cruella's henchmen. Betty Lou Gerson, the voice of Cruella, recorded a few lines as Miss Birdwell, a quiz panel judge on a television show watched by a room full of puppies. The directors even asked me to record a small, secondary part while I was working on my Sgt. Tibs performance. I contributed a few lines as a Skye Terrier who excitedly yaps early in the film's Twilight Bark sequence as word spreads about the "dognapped" Dalmatians.

During my audition and recording visits, the Disney studios them-selves looked (and still do) like a quiet college campus, not at all like the rather grey factories of MGM or Universal. Every day was a picnic with people eating their lunch on the ground or on benches throughout the property. Each street on the lot was named after a Disney character, and all employees — including actors hired for each picture — were reminded that if they happened upon the boss strolling around the grounds, he was to be addressed as "Walt," never as "Mr. Disney." All very informal. I must say I found that difficult. I had such a reverence for the man that I found it almost impossible to say, 'Hi, Walt' while we were making *Ten Who Dared* later that year!

One of the interesting things about animation is how much time can

Poor Sgt. Tibs finds himself in a very funny sequence with Jasper Badun in 101 Dalmatians. (© DISNEY ENTERPRISES, INC.)

pass for a voice artist between recording work. After my first two initial recording sessions in 1959, I was called back for further recordings on January 29, 1960. Over the course of one year, my work as Sgt. Tibs was finished. Interestingly enough, because most of us rarely recorded our parts together, I worked on the film without much awareness that many of my acting peers and fellow Brits were also voicing other parts. For the most part, nearly all the roles in *101 Dalmatians* went to English actors, many of whom I knew or worked with, including Frederick Worlock, the voice of Horace, George Pelling, the voice of Danny in the Twilight Bark sequence, and especially my dear friend Ben Wright, the voice of Roger Radcliff.

Toward the end of his life, Ben went almost entirely deaf, but he enjoyed one last hurrah when he returned to Disney animation as the voice of Grigsby, the manservant to Prince Eric in the 1989 smash *The Little Mermaid*. He was so typically modest that he went through his audition for that film without telling them that he was a Disney alumnus from

101 Dalmatians. Ben and I had worked in a stage production of *Separate Tables*, and when I auditioned for a role in the 1958 film adaptation, it was Rod Taylor who beat me for the part. Although Rod was actually Australian, he was very good as Pongo in *101 Dalmatians.*

I had also worked alongside Lisa Davis, the voice of Anita, Roger's wife and the owner of Perdita, the mother to the original brood of Dalmatian

Sgt. Tibs has a little trouble with Rolly, 101 Dalmatians. (© DISNEY ENTERPRISES, INC.)

puppies born early in the movie. Not too long before the start of our work on *101 Dalmatians,* Lisa and I played a dotty English brother and sister on an episode of *77 Sunset Strip.* Lisa had followed her sister, Beryl Davis, to America from England. (A big band recording star, Beryl married Peter Potter, the L.A. disc jockey whom Rosemary Clooney directed me to when I arrived in Hollywood.)

Tom Conway, who voiced both the Collie and the Quizmaster in *101 Dalmatians,* appeared with me in a 1961 episode of *Adventures in Paradise.* Tom's younger brother was George Sanders, who later voiced Shere Khan in Disney's *The Jungle Book.* Both of them were blessed with rich, smooth tones to their voices. Tom Conway's wife, Queenie Leonard, also voiced one of the cows who nurse the puppies after Sgt. Tibs helps rescue them and then leads them to the shelter of a country barn.

I think it's interesting to note just how many of us from Hollywood's "English colony" worked on the film. As one of the surviving voice actors from *101 Dalmatians*, I can look back all these years later and appreciate just how lucky we all were to take part in something that continues to hold such meaning for new generations of children and long-time fans of what became a well-loved classic film. I'm sure I speak for all of my fellow

Many fans often comment on Sgt. Tibs' bravery, 101 Dalmatians. (© DISNEY ENTERPRISES, INC.)

countrymen when I say kudos to Disney for giving authentic English actors a chance to play most of the parts!

Because my encounter with Sgt. Tibs occurred just as my television career was taking off, I honestly didn't think too much more about *101 Dalmatians* after I left the recording studio for the last time in 1960. I had seen a rough cut with my character, but for some reason, I missed seeing the film upon its original release in January 1961, and I didn't get around to seeing the film until its third re-release in December 1985. I went to a children's matinee on an impulse, dreading the racket that I was sure would be going on all through the screening. I couldn't have been more wrong — the six- and seven-year-olds all around me were as quiet as mice during the right spots, laughed during the appropriate parts, and applauded at the end. I really felt so proud to see my name on a Disney film, as only one of the dozens of people who contributed to the final result.

I must confess, though, that I was amused when I saw the film for the first time and spotted my name listed as "Dave" Frankham in the credits. I can't imagine why Disney did that, because I had worked for them before in my very brief part in *Johnny Tremain*, and even though I received no

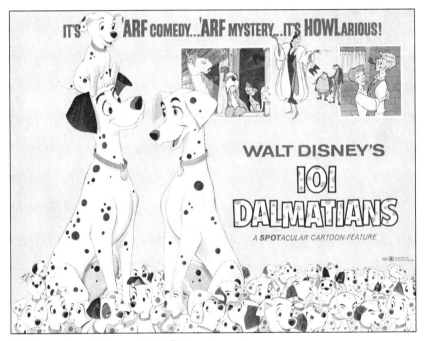

1969 re-release lobby card, 101 Dalmatians. (© DISNEY ENTERPRISES, INC.)

billing for that picture, I was, as usual, "David," for legal and compensation purposes. Maybe Disney was more informal in the animation division!

Upon its initial release, *101 Dalmatians* became one of Disney's biggest animated box office hits, and successful theatrical reissues followed in 1969, 1979, 1985, and 1991. The film always was skillfully reissued at appropriate intervals by the Disney marketing experts. The 1991 reissue was one of the top-grossing films that summer, and I did a newspaper interview about my part in the film to celebrate its thirtieth anniversary.

When the film was finally issued onto home video, I added it to my library to relive the happy times of making it. *Entertainment Weekly* once reported it as one of the top-grossing films of all time, adjusted for inflation, and illustrated the story with a color photo of Sgt. Tibs protecting the puppies underneath the stairwell in Hell Hall; I had the article framed.

Like most other actors who were working prior to the home video market, I could never have foreseen being blessed with the opportunity to actually own video or DVD copies of my performances. Thank goodness these mediums came along, though, because I have met a number of *101 Dalmatians* fans who weren't even born in 1961 when Tibs first tip-toed into Hell Hall on his reconnaissance mission to search for

That little cat remains popular fifty years later! (© DISNEY ENTERPRISES, INC.)

stolen Dalmatian puppies!

Several years ago, I rented a movie at my neighborhood Blockbuster video store and struck up a conversation with the young lady working behind the counter. We began talking about movies, and she told me that Disney films were among her favorites. When I told her that I had voiced Sgt. Tibs, she shrieked and called all of her young co-workers over to meet me. I heard the same reaction another time during a doctor's office visit when a technician alerted all the other nurses to come meet the voice of Sgt. Tibs.

In the early 1990s, Disney mailed me a release to sign for a TV compilation show in which they used a tiny clip of Sgt. Tibs. For that clip, I got several hundred dollars in a royalty check! Not bad at all. In later years, I've also received a surprising amount of royalties for clips of Sgt. Tibs that were used in the popular *Disney Scene-It* DVD and the *Disney Bingo* game series. The games have sold so well that consenting to let them use my voice through the Tibs clips proved to be a remarkable investment; in fact, I think I may end up making more from those royalties than I first did for my work back in 1961!

Although I later worked for Disney in a live-action role, Sgt. Tibs remains a proud highlight of my Disney cinematic experiences, one that

Visiting the spot on the Disney lot where I recorded for 101 Dalmatians. (TODD SAWVELLE)

continues to write new chapters in my life's story. In the summer of 2008, I visited the Disney Studios in Burbank for the first time since 1970, when I had auditioned for the title role in Disney's animated version of *Robin Hood*. (Thinking that I was a shoo-in with Sgt. Tibs on my list of credits, I lost the part to the Shakespearean-trained Brian Bedford, who did a terrific job when the film came out in 1973.)

Three Disney voice artists: Mary Costa (left) from Sleeping Beauty, *me representing* 101 Dalmatians, *and Kathryn Beaumont from* Alice in Wonderland *and* Peter Pan. (TODD SAWVELLE)

Accompanied by several young friends who found me through their love of Disney and Sgt. Tibs, I was privileged to walk those beautifully well-manicured, campus-style studio streets once again and reminisce about my happy times at the studio in the early 1960s. I met Dave Smith, the founder of Disney's Archives, and he graciously asked me to sign the Archives' guest book. The tour included lunch and a trip up the steps to the building that housed the same recording studio where I voiced Sgt. Tibs nearly fifty years earlier. It was an emotional experience for me, as the original studio grounds haven't changed that much through the years, even though the backlot area now houses modern administration buildings.

Earlier that year, Disney had hosted a special screening of *101 Dalmatians* at the El Capitan Theatre with Lisa Davis representing our voice cast. I was unable to attend, so the evening of my later visit to Buena Vista Street and the Disney Studios, I was privileged to sit in a similar audience for a special fiftieth anniversary screening of Disney's *Sleeping Beauty* staged to promote the film's re-release to DVD and its debut in the Blu-Ray format.

In attendance were several others who had worked on *101 Dalmatians.*

Holding publicity stills from my role in Disney history. (TODD SAWVELLE)

Walt Peregoy, a color stylist largely credited for the distinctive look of *101 Dalmatians,* was there, as was Blaine Gibson, who worked as a character animator on the film before going to work for Walt as an Imagineer and sculptor for Disney's theme parks. Mary Costa, the voice of the princess in *Sleeping Beauty,* attended to talk about her film's production during a question and answer panel.

After the screening ended, word spread that there were several other Disney "voices" in attendance, including myself, June Foray, and Kathryn Beaumont, another English native who voiced the title role in Disney's

Alice in Wonderland and Wendy in *Peter Pan.* For some time that night, I sat in my seat and signed autographs for a number of enthusiastic fans. It's always gratifying to meet a Disney fan, because the Disney films have always set such high standards of good taste — that's not true of many studios these days.

During that same visit to California from my home in New Mexico, I

Signing autographs with Lisa Davis. (TODD SAWVELLE)

also visited Disneyland for the first time in years. I was touched to meet several Disney fans there who told me how much they liked my character. When they learned of my Sgt. Tibs background, Disneyland's cast members treated me like Disney royalty by granting me a pass to ride the Lily Belle car on the Disneyland Railroad.

In March 2010, *Cat Fancy* magazine readers ranked Sgt. Tibs as the fifth most popular cat in pop culture, so I cherish and appreciate my part in a Disney classic. You're never too old to enjoy any of the Disney magic. My young Disney friends have helped reawaken my own childhood love for Disney, and today I often find myself listening to Disney soundtracks, especially the score from *Pinocchio,* one of my favorites. In later years, I started a collection of books and toys of Sgt. Tibs collectibles, some of them originating from as far away as my native England and purchased via eBay.

Just as I was finishing this manuscript, Disney scheduled a fiftieth anniversary screening of *101 Dalmatians* in January 2011 at a theatre on the studio lot in Burbank. The event marked an emotional highlight of my half-century association with the Disney classic. Arriving at the studio, Lisa Davis and I reunited more than fifty years after working together on an episode of *77 Sunset Strip*. The years just melted away as we quickly caught up on old times.

Following a screening for several hundred fans, Disney historian Les Perkins interviewed Lisa and me about our voice work on the movie. When we completed our Q&A session, Lisa and I sat for more than an hour as we signed autographs for dozens of members of D23, Disney's official fan club. Fans of all ages posed for photos and expressed their appreciation for *101 Dalmatians*.

A commonly used expression reminds audiences that the Disney success story all started with a mouse. In my case, my happy association with Disney really started with a cat. It was one of the most exciting and fulfilling jobs I ever had.

Nobody sets out to make a bad picture. That's an old Hollywood axiom, but it's a true one. During the same time that I worked on *101 Dalmatians*, one of Walt Disney's most critically and financially successful films, I also worked on what has been called one of Disney's least well-received live-action films, the 1960 western adventure *Ten Who Dared*.

The film was based on the true story of Major John Wesley Powell, the Civil War veteran who led a rugged group to complete the first successful trip on the treacherous Colorado River through the Grand Canyon in 1869. *Ten Who Dared* began with the best of intentions and high enthusiasm from Walt Disney himself, but the end product was, I believe, a rather dull movie. But at least the scenery was sensational!

About the same time that I auditioned for the voice of Sgt. Tibs in *101 Dalmatians*, I visited the Disney lot on March 30, 1959, to meet Jack Bauer, the head of casting for the studio. He told me that I was being considered for one of the leads in a two-part television film, to be called "The Colorado River Story," which would be seen on *Walt Disney Presents*, the studio's Sunday night TV show on ABC.

Studios loaned clips to other studios, and someone had seen a clip of my recently completed part in *Return of the Fly*. Lee Traver, a Disney casting director, thought I might be right to play one of the ten main characters in *Ten Who Dared*. Sounded good to me — I was to play a cowardly

Englishman who drank too much and who finally left the group when the going got rough on the Colorado. I thought it would be a nice acting challenge, if it worked out that I got the part. The following week I returned to meet director William Beaudine, and we hit it off well. Beaudine was a wonderful old guy who had started in silent pictures and most recently directed the *Spin and Marty* serials for the *Mickey Mouse Club.*

One of my publicity portraits of me in costume from Ten Who Dared *(1960).*
(© DISNEY ENTERPRISES, INC.)

I visited Disney that summer to provide my Sgt. Tibs voiceover work on *101 Dalmatians*. Script revisions were being made to the plot of *Ten Who Dared*, but the project seemed to be in limbo throughout the summer. I didn't mind the wait, because each time I returned to the Disney lot, I was excited at the mere possibility of seeing or encountering Walt.

Later that fall, on October 6, 1959, I heard that Walt Disney had given his approval to go ahead with the TV film. I had mostly completed *101 Dalmatians* by then, although it would be January of 1961 before it would be released. After I learned that *The Colorado Story* had been given the greenlight, I tried on my costumes. Our company was scheduled to fly to Utah for location shooting two weeks later.

Before we left for location filming, Disney mailed the script to me. The part was interesting — a beat-up, Errol Flynn-type who was sort of dashing but had a bad streak to him, not to mention a penchant for alcohol. The idea of going from playing a killer in *Return of the Fly* to a rotten Englishman in this Disney film was very fun.

Disney also mailed an acetate disk with the lyrics and music of two songs written by Stan Jones for *The Colorado Story* as it was called then. Stan was another one of the "Ten Who Dared" and a gentle man; we became good friends all through the production, and I told him in person how much I enjoyed another of his songs, a huge international hit back in the fifties called *Ghost Riders in the Sky*.

It was exciting to have to learn songs for a Disney movie. Each of us had been sent a disk with songs on it to learn. The songs were to be heard in a scene on the river and another around a campfire. We actually gathered to record the songs at the studio, where Thurl Ravenscroft was also on hand to add his incredibly deep, rich voice to the real chorus that also recorded the song.

In addition to myself and Stan Jones, the other eight daring actors included John Beal as Major John Wesley Powell, Brian Keith, James Drury, Ben Johnson, L.Q. Jones, R.G. Armstrong, David Stollery, and Dan Sheridan. It was a fine cast; John Beal had appeared in the 1935 version of *Les Miserables* with Fredric March, Charles Laughton, and Cecil Hardwicke. Brian Keith was making his first of what would be several films for Disney. James Drury would go on to star in *The Virginian* on television, while L.Q. Jones and R.G. Armstrong later became part of director Sam Peckinpah's group of stock actors. L.Q. was one of those natural actors who didn't seem to act. Between scenes, he seemed the same as he did on film. He and I got along beautifully.

Dan Sheridan was a TV western staple, while Ben Johnson had been a rodeo cowboy and a stuntman before working on Howard Hughes' controversial Jane Russell picture *The Outlaw*. David Stollery was familiar to Disney audiences from his role in *Spin and Marty* on the *Mickey Mouse Club* serials. He was to be paired with a little dog in the film when his character smuggled it on the trip. I thought the dog was going to steal

All ten of the Ten Who Dared *(1960)* (© DISNEY ENTERPRISES, INC.)

the picture, because Disney dogs are always very cute.

Of the ten principals in the cast, I was the newest to Hollywood with three years of acting experience to my list of credits. I was a little intimidated by the number of western-style actors when I was playing a boozy Brit, but I was ready to tackle my second feature. I had just completed an episode of *Maverick* and the year before, an episode of *Death Valley Days*, another western, so this English import was ready for a little desert sand. Between the ten of us, there was quite a bit of great potential. Disney had assembled a large, accomplished and capable cast, most of whom had done some notable western film or television work.

Our company flew on a Disney jet from Burbank to Utah. There we drove to Moab, where we would be based for about a week while we filmed on the Colorado River itself. After we arrived on location, we posed for production stills and publicity photos on the first day of shooting at a place called Green River, where the Green River flows into the Colorado. I believe that's where Major Wesley Powell truly began his actual journey depicted in the film. We then filmed an exposition scene where our characters are all introduced to an inquisitive newspaper reporter. I wouldn't be back in costume for several more weeks or so until they got to my part.

After production started, each day the completed film was sent back to Burbank for Walt Disney to see. The third day we were there, William Beaudine gathered us together and told us that Walt had phoned the night before to say footage of the canyons was sensational. Walt loved the panoramic shots of the Arches National Monument and the Moab area and decided to abandon the idea of just a TV film; we were to proceed with what would now be a major theatrical release in widescreen, re-named *Ten Who Dared*.

The budget was increased and the schedule lengthened to include much more work on location and additional filming to be completed later back at the studio. I was happy at the prospect of an expanded shooting schedule — it was guaranteed work! Everyone in the cast had to buy more clothes, because we had all planned to be there at our hotel for only two weeks, but we were now going to spend twelve weeks on location. I had to call my agent, Maurine, back in Hollywood to look after my houseplants and then mailed my house key to her so she could let herself in for the watering.

My pals on the movie were the very serious-yet-gentle John Beal, Stan Jones, and especially Ben Johnson; we were the quiet ones! I didn't take much of a shine to Brian Keith on location. He was too blustery for my taste. Most of the others went off carousing in the evening, but I'm not a drinker, so that was sort of boring to me. Ironically, I was playing a boozer in the film! James Drury caused a little commotion one evening when he played around with a pistol and fired it into the ceiling of his room, but for the most part, it was fairly quiet.

I was alone for several weeks, just enjoying Utah, because they didn't get to my scenes until late in the shooting schedule. At five o'clock in the morning, I could hear the Jeeps all driving away with the rest of the cast and crew to location, so I rarely got to mix with the other fellows during the day. In the evenings when the company returned to our motel, I usually had dinner with John, Stan, and Ben. When the production had yet to get to the rest of my scenes, I was fearful that when it was my turn, the crew would say, "Who is this British actor and where did he come from?"

The wait time wasn't in vain, though, because our director encouraged me to eat more to add the weight suggestive of a boozy character. In addition to our salaries, all the actors had a per diem. To fatten up, I ate hamburgers all over Moab. In fact, I got to know people around town during those several weeks of doing nothing but waiting to film. Sitting at a restaurant counter munching on four hamburgers, I got to

The costumers wanted me to grow a mustache and put on weight for Ten Who Dared. (© DISNEY ENTERPRISES, INC.)

know a lady who was known as a "princess" of the Ute Tribe. Non-Native Americans were rarely allowed onto the Ute reservation, but because I became friendly with her, she took me out to meet many of them.

During my three-week hiatus, the costumers also told me to grow a mustache to make me look a little older. They had stuck on a fake mustache for my first day's shooting and decided I needed a real one. I always had a boyish look; it was my curse when I started in Hollywood at age thirty. As we neared time to resume filming with me, it was decided that my real mustache wasn't working, so they shaved it off and brought back the fake one to stick on my lip each morning at six a.m.

When it was time for my part, location shooting meant that I had the time of my life. I was afloat each day in the Colorado River. We filmed at daybreak, very cold indeed at six a.m., and fairly dangerous too. L.Q. Jones and I had a fight scene in our boat and actually had to fall into the river, so we wore "wet suits" under our costumes. Wet suits are made of rubber, and the idea is to pour cold water down inside them from the neck, so that one's body temperature soon warms it up; entering the freezing river water then isn't so bad!

Whitewater rapids lurked just beyond where we filmed. As a precaution, real boatsmen waited on either side of the river, just out of camera range, to catch us if we were carried away by the swift current. As we filmed, we saw that ice had formed on the banks. In fact, the cameras couldn't get close-up shots because the weather had turned so cold. As soon as Beaudine yelled, "Cut," we were back to shore.

William Beaudine was called "One-Take Beaudine" because he was so efficient at setting up and getting exactly the shot he needed. He had started back in the silent era and actually still wore the silent film director's wardrobe, just like Cecil B. DeMille! Beaudine went through the rest of our scenes very quickly.

I think the three-week period between starting and then waiting for my scenes undermined my confidence a little. I never felt really comfortable, because everyone else had done westerns. My character's introductory declamatory scene never quite felt natural for me, and because it was the first scene we filmed, I thought that it could be better written and acted. I felt that I could have done a better job. John Beal was always so calm that just spending time around him increased my sense of security.

After nearly a dozen weeks on location, we returned to the studio to shoot interior scenes. Working on the Disney lot was just as exciting as being on location surrounded by all the beautiful scenery. I would drive up to the guard shack and say, "David Frankham, for makeup and wardrobe at 7:30," and the guard would say, "Okay, drive on." Going into any other studio was almost like visiting a prison; everything was gray and concrete, nothing at all like Disney.

When Walt Disney himself visited the set, I found him absolutely charming and modest and much liked by any employee I spoke to; he was Walt to one and all. It was impossible to talk even briefly to him without

Location shooting in Utah really was great fun. (© DISNEY ENTERPRISES, INC.)

being completely in awe of the man's accomplishments over the years. A very sensitive artist and a legend in his time, he was so quiet and modest you'd think he was just a minor member of the crew as he stood quietly in the background watching scenes being filmed. I never got over the excitement of seeing him on the set or wandering around the lot.

The first time I met Walt, L.Q. Jones and I were up in the boat filming

James Drury confronts David Stollery over a contraband dog as John Beal and I look on. (© DISNEY ENTERPRISES, INC.)

our fight. The boat was suspended high in the air, with the rapids of the Colorado River being projected on film behind us on a blue screen. That was how they filmed our close-ups; our long shots were done on location, but the weather had been too cold for many close-ups. Some of our river footage had to be re-shot as well.

I'll never forget being way up high in our boat. Crew members rocked us realistically to and fro, when suddenly, production stopped. L.Q. and I looked down and there was the legendary Walt Disney shaking hands with the rest of the cast and crew. Because we were so high up, all he could say was, "Hi, fellows!" As L.Q. and I stared down at him, I said, "Hello, Mr. Disney." Later, the director said, "No, you always say, 'Walt.' No one is allowed to call him Mr. Disney."

A few more times during production he came onto the set to watch us. It was still very difficult to call a living legend — as he was then — "Walt." He had been Mr. Disney to me since I was eleven years old, but I managed. When we completed the interior scenes at the studio on November 24, 1959, I think each of us believed we had a winner for Walt. The film had been fun to make, and we all got along well together.

A Disney artist created each of the ten actors' likeness for a lobby card on Ten Who Dared. (© DISNEY ENTERPRISES, INC.)

When I flew home to spend Christmas with my parents in England, and I still had my western hairstyle, my father was appalled: "You're not going out looking like that, are you?" he said. Imagine his reaction when he saw the film and me playing an alcoholic, blowsy, unshaven ne-er-do-well!

I was called back for further recordings on *101 Dalmatians* on January 29, 1960, and already the buzz around the place was that *Ten Who Dared* looked great at preliminary rough-cut screenings on the lot. And when it was screened for its first real audience at a preview a few months later, it did indeed look great. But there was little or no energy in the acting, scenes played listlessly and without much involvement, and the journey down the Colorado was a dull one indeed.

Walt Disney hosted the screening at the studio with a chili dinner in the back of the theatre following the screening. I went with Maurine. None of us had seen it. When I came on, I was so embarrassed, especially by my final scene, a declamatory, over-the-top speech that made me cringe, because I felt lost. When my character cowardly

The one-sheet poster for Ten Who Dared. (© DISNEY ENTERPRISES, INC.)

decides to leave the expedition, I bid the others farewell in a blustery pompous speech. I thought I wasn't up to delivering dialogue like that with just three years' experience and always believed that a thespian like Richard Burton could have pulled that off better.

After watching that part of the film, I said to Maurine, "I'm leaving." She said, "You can't. Walt's sitting back there, and there's supper afterwards."

I said, "He'll think I've gone to the restroom."

I left because I was really so depressed. I thought I wouldn't work at Disney again. And I thought I was a lousy actor, stretching my range beyond my ability. I went home in a moment of self-doubt, a story I shared fifty years later with an audience of Disney fans in the same theatre at a special screening of *101 Dalmatians*.

Disney promoted the film on his television show, especially focusing on the dangers of filming the whitewater rapids sequence. When the film was released, it didn't fare too well at the box office. With the passage of time, I will concede that the movie plays better on the small screen. Disney did run it that way at least once after its disappointing theatrical release — we all got paid all over again! — when the movie was edited

Artist Stacia Martin did a wonderful job on this fantastic painting combining my two Disney characters from 101 Dalmatians *and* Ten Who Dared. (TODD
CAMVBLLE)

down to Disney's one-hour television anthology series format for that 1968 showing. While I did not see that airing, perhaps the production worked better in an abbreviated format without the lengthy exposition at the beginning.

I actually didn't see the movie again after the preview until I watched the video in 1989. To my surprise, I wasn't as bad as I remembered! It's a

I'll always have fond memories working for Walt Disney. (TODD SAWVELLE)

pretty dumb role, a boozy Englishman walking around spouting poetry. It would take a Laurence Olivier or an Alec Guinness or a Peter O'Toole to bring that kind of part off successfully, and Lord knows I was certainly never in their league.

All things considered, I thought I didn't do too badly, bearing in mind the fact that I'd only been an actor for three years when we shot it. I certainly was chubby, though! Disney had me eating for weeks on location to look as though I'd been on the booze — I got *that* part right! That's probably why I walked out at the first screening. On the big screen, I must have reminded myself of Oliver Hardy! And that moustache looked pretty phony to me. I once read where Leonard Maltin called the film a "bomb." It upset me at the time, but I must say I pretty much agreed with his general comments the first time around — it is just a routine programmer, fairly dull except for the great scenery.

On my seventy-sixth birthday in 2002, I found myself sitting in bed and watching *Ten Who Dared* on video. There was a book published around the same time about the real life men who dared, and the author wrote that the Englishman was the only sane guy in the bunch. Vindication! In May 2012, I attended the Memphis Film Festival, where I was reunited with two of my fellow "ten," actors James Drury and L. Q. Jones. Together again after more than fifty years, we reminisced about the fun we had making the movie. I was quite touched to recall the special bond that we shared with our memories from making the movie. I'll always enjoy looking at it on DVD, released by Disney in 2009, because it revives so many warm memories of a very exciting time in my life.

CHAPTER SEVEN

A Maverick
on 77 Sunset Strip

I like to reminisce about 1959. That was the year that I made my movie debut as a villain in a major motion picture, *Return of the Fly*, dubbed on *Ben-Hur*, began voice work for an animated Disney character in *101 Dalmatians*, and traveled to location work in Utah for a Disney western, *Ten Who Dared*.

During the spring of that year, I was invited to attend the infamous Academy Awards telecast, forever known as the time the show under-ran by about twenty minutes. Jerry Lewis simply brought several big names back on stage at the Pantages Theatre for a sing-along to fill up time. *Gigi* was the big winner that year.

It was bittersweet to see David Niven win for *Separate Tables*, a film that I had read for but lost to Rod Taylor. I've always been convinced that Niven patterned his acting after Eric Portman from the stage play. The upside of seeing Niven win the Oscar in person, though, is that just being there was my revenge, of sorts, after he slighted me a few years earlier by writing to me that he had no need for "extras" on his television program.

I was making it in Hollywood, no thanks to David Niven, because 1959 also brought me several good stints on television. Leading roles in movies meant that my agent, Maurine Oliver, could legitimately promote me for bigger television parts, including guest-starring roles.

Early in the year, I appeared on an episode of *77 Sunset Strip* called "The Secret of Adam Cain." I'm glad director Edwards Bernds didn't see *77 Sunset Strip*, or he might not have considered me for *Return of the Fly*! I played a silly, spoiled English chap who gets mixed up in a Maltese Falcon-style plotline involving a stolen family heirloom. It's all part of a big game involving him and his sister, played by Lisa Davis.

Once or twice the part was borderline Franklin Pangborn, the character actor who always played fussy parts for Preston Sturges's screwball comedies. I think Hollywood usually assumed that you were a twit if you played a twit. In a sense, I think they thought that they were typecasting me, but at the same time, it was fun to play, although the goofiness could have limited my career to comedy.

Lisa Davis and I look ready for a swim on 77 Sunset Strip *(1959).*

I did enjoy working with Lisa Davis, though. Lisa is a lovely woman. Ironically, when Rosemary Clooney got me started in Los Angeles radio in 1956, she sent me to Lisa's brother-in-law, disc jockey Peter Potter. It's a small world, sometimes. The same year we worked together on *77 Sunset Strip*, Lisa and I were both cast as voices in Disney's *101 Dalmatians*. In January 2011, she and I reunited after fifty years for a special fiftieth anni-

Lisa Davis and I on 77 Sunset Strip *(1959).*

versary screening of *101 Dalmatians*. We later joined a group for dinner and then spent an evening of reminiscing at a post-dinner gathering. We exchanged stories about working with Zsa Zsa Gabor, being directed by Ed Bernds, and remembering how Hollywood was essentially a small town where everyone knew everybody in the 1950s.

Efrem Zimbalist, Jr., the star of *77 Sunset Strip*, was such a wonderful man, the Rolls-Royce of actors. The episode is bittersweet because it marked the last time that Joan Elan and I appeared together on the same show, even though we didn't actually appear together on camera. Our careers seemed to be headed in opposite directions.

New friends were always waiting to be made, though, whenever a guest-starring spot led me to another series. That same year on an episode of *The Further Adventures of Ellery Queen*, I had the pleasure of working with George Nader. He had been training at Universal at the same time as Rock Hudson and Tony Curtis; the three of them were being groomed for stardom. Nader was a little behind them in terms of success, but he was making good films, including *Away All Boats*.

Nader was good, a very serious actor. His seven-year contract would have been renewed until a very sad scandal happened, one that became

In 2011, Lisa Davis and I reunited fifty-two years after working together.
(TODD SAWVELLE)

legendary in Hollywood. A tabloid magazine called *Confidential* "outed" stars through news about drinking, drugs or sexual affairs. The magazine contacted Universal to say that they had a story prepared to run on Rock Hudson's private life.

The studio, which had spent millions to build up Rock's career, panicked. They requested an agreement that ultimately meant sparing Rock's

With Efrem Zimbalist, Jr., a true gentleman, on 77 Sunset Strip *(1959).*

reputation and giving up George Nader instead. Universal was always arranging for Nader to go with premieres with Lori Nelson on his arm and trying to convince him to get rid of his companion, Mark Miller. Nader had been willing to go along with the public charade, but he absolutely resisted giving up his personal life, so Universal sacrificed him to *Confidential* magazine in order to spare Rock.

It was a shame that Nader's career was ruined that way, because he was a very nice man. He ended up working where he could get it, so that's how he came to act on *The Further Adventures of Ellery Queen*. People cared enough about him because he had a great following as a result of his sincerity and kindness. I enjoyed working with him that week because of his fantastic sense of humor. He also was willing to talk about acting and offer advice to a newcomer.

I admired George because he had this kind of dignity that enabled him to rise above the way he had been treated by Universal and the tabloids and somehow managed to keep on working. When the television series moved to New York, he didn't follow. He went to Rome and made several pictures there.

Like George Nader, Richard Webb was also supportive of young actors when I worked on a 1959 episode of *Border Patrol*, directed by Richard Whorf. I didn't have a big part and the series wasn't that popular — it only lasted one season — but encouragement from more established actors meant a lot to me in those early years.

Thanks in part to my high profile role in *Return of the Fly*, Warner Bros. brought me onto an episode of *Maverick* as part of its effort to reign in Roger Moore, who was playing Beau Maverick. Moore's character was supposed to be an English cousin to Bret Maverick, who had been played by James Garner for the first several years of the series before leaving the show.

Eddie Rhine was Warner Bros.' television casting director. He told Maurine that Roger Moore was allegedly "misbehaving" by coming in late to work as part of his effort to improve script quality and other demands. Having previously lost James Garner over a contract dispute, the studio took Moore seriously. They threatened him legally by telling his manager that they were bringing in me, also English, to play a guest-starring role and that I might replace him if he didn't shape up or if the situation didn't improve.

Warner Bros. always went all out with the *Maverick* episodes. I think it was the most popular of the half dozen or so shows the studio had on the air each week at that time. James Garner got a hefty paycheck, Jack Kelly a little less, and they were reasonably generous with one-shot guests. It was the younger contract group, including Roger Moore, who got "slave" wages, so for all I know, Moore may have been within his rights to press for better pay and working conditions.

The writers created a new character for my guest-starring role as Captain Rory Fitzgerald, a conniving Irish gambler and swindler. The part was considered a screen test with a sixty-day option should Warner Bros. decide to add me to the regular cast, especially if Roger Moore were to be replaced. It wasn't often that I would be given such an outstanding character to play. It was a big part with some action and a great bit of dialogue. Although I had lived in England and Scotland, I thought I could reasonably do an Irish accent. I had a good ear and usually was adept at picking up accents.

My episode was called "Royal Four Flush." The production was almost a disaster from the start, for me at least. Our director was Arthur Lubin, who had directed the 1943 version of *The Phantom of the Opera* with Claude Rains, the *Francis the Talking Mule* pictures, and a number of Abbott and Costello comedies. He was easy to work for and had a great sense of humor.

On our first day of shooting, I was doing my best. At lunch time, though, Lubin took me aside and invited me to join him in the commissary. I was

My first really big guest-starring role came on Maverick *(1959).*

thrilled to be joining this great director for lunch, until we sat down and he said, "David, we're in big trouble."

"What's the matter?" I asked.

"Yours is the worst Irish accent I've ever heard," he replied. "We'll have to replace you if it goes on like this."

As I stammered and prepared to defend myself, he calmed me down. "We've called your agent to come and help you rehearse. She's Irish, so we hope you can pick it up."

I was embarrassed that he found my Irish accent lacking, especially in light of the fact that it was also a screen test in case the studio needed to replace Roger Moore. Joining a hit series meant steady pay and employment, and my lousy Irish accent was standing in the way.

Maurine quickly arrived. What better person to get me through the ordeal and coach me? "David, don't worry," she told me. "We can do this together."

So there we sat, Maurine reading my lines and me phonetically repeating them back to her. The big moment arrived, and we started production again. Lubin listened and nodded. "Much better! That will do."

Just to be safe, Maurine stayed with me that whole week, coaching me in the accent before I started each scene. I listened to get the cadence of the part, and it seemed to work. My job was safe.

It turned out that Roger Moore returned to the show that season before finally leaving for good. Ultimately, the studio replaced him with Robert Colbert as Bart Maverick's brother, Brent. Between Bret, Bart, and Beau Maverick, there were almost too many Mavericks to keep straight! Alas, Rory Fitzgerald was not meant to become a permanent addition to the series.

When I watched the episode later on television, my faux Irish accent wasn't as bad as I remembered. My first scene came with Jack Kelly in a carriage. The studio kept in long shots where he talked and then replaced my bad accent scene with the re-take. I was pleased with what I did, accent notwithstanding. Ironically, Roger Moore's character was supposed to have a slight English accent from his character having lived in England. In reality, it was a pretty authentic English accent, so I suppose there were two of us struggling with accents, albeit in different ways.

I don't think the studio was serious about the episode being a screen test for adding me to the series. Rather, I think they used me to convince Roger Moore to get back to work. Maurine finally called the studio and told them that I was dying on the vine while we waited to hear if I was joining the show or not. Moore had evidently mended his ways, so that put a damper on my chances. While my appearance may not have led to joining the cast as a regular, *Maverick* was a top-rated series. Ratings were — and still are — to a series what box office receipts are to the movies. The viewers tune in to enjoy the program and rarely know about the behind-the-scenes work involving contract disputes or accents, unless the press agents or studios get involved for publicity's sake.

With Jack Kelly on Maverick *(1959).*

With increased confidence and paychecks in 1959, I rented an apartment from a good friend, Jack Lattimer, a fine arranger and conductor who toured England with Howard Keel. I first met Jack when I interviewed Keel for the BBC back in England. Jack had built an apartment underneath his house up in the Laurel Canyon area of Hollywood. I went up to visit and liked it so much that I moved in before the apartment was completed. There was one unfinished door that let a raccoon come in and surprise me one morning, but the beautiful apartment was worth it.

I lived there for about a year. Jack was a vocal coach at his home above my apartment. One of his regular students was Maureen O'Hara. Jack had air vents going from his place down to underneath the apartment I was renting. Listening from below through the air ducts, I could hear Maureen singing her scales. She had a very good voice.

Whenever Jack worked with her, I was tempted to go upstairs to meet her. I resisted, though, because they were working and didn't need me intruding. After eavesdropping on one of her lessons, I asked Jack if he thought she was a good singer. He said, "Yes, she has a lovely voice. What a shame that Hollywood hasn't taken advantage of that in her movies." A year or so later, Maureen sang one song onscreen in Disney's *The Parent Trap*. Jack also told me that she had been thinking of doing an album of Irish songs one day.

I recorded some record albums myself in the late 1950s and early 1960s, although the work never required me to sing. I did a series of Standard School Broadcasts with singer Norma Zimmer, one of Hollywood's leading chorus vocalists who had backed up Bing Crosby and dubbed on several soundtracks, including *Seven Brides for Seven Brothers*. We sat across from one another and read poems and short stories. It was a pleasure to work with her, and she was a real charmer, going on to become the Champagne Lady on Lawrence Welk's long-running musical TV program *The Lawrence Welk Show*. Fifty years later Norma and I were reunited at a party, and I enjoyed visiting with her and her husband, Randy, for dinner.

Meanwhile, as my work steadily increased, acting offers diminished for my friend Joan Elan. She hit thirty, which was a glass ceiling for many young actresses during that era. Casting directors didn't know that it was her birthday or that she was now "over the hill," but her work began to slow down drastically. Hollywood seemed to turn off the opportunities for actresses over thirty, unless they played mothers or grandmothers. So many fresh-faced, eighteen- or twenty-year-olds were arriving to take their place that the opportunities simply dried up. Men could keep going past thirty, so it was really a very sexist atmosphere, in many regards.

The slowdown was hard for Joan's pride. She went on unemployment, but that ran out over time. What a difficult spot to be in as a friend. When I started in Hollywood, Joan was more experienced and working. As I added credits to my resume, her career was drying up in Hollywood. The trajectories of our careers signified the up-and-down potentials of show business.

I was very fortunate to be riding an upward ascent in 1959. My old friend Hanns Friedrichs from the BBC visited me when he was sent by German television to profile Billy Wilder during the production of *Some Like It Hot*. Every day we had dinner together, because Hanns stayed in a hotel not too far from my place. Each night over dinner, he fed me Billy Wilder anecdotes from the day's filming as well as stories about Jack Lemmon and Marilyn Monroe.

Hanns told me that things were going well for him back in Europe. He had married and seemed happy. After he went back, he called one time to tell me that he had hit the big time on the ZDF network in Germany. In fact, he was doing so well that he was living in a castle on the Rhine River. We both seemed to be doing well a mere five or six years after pining for something more than just our jazz program on the BBC.

That Christmas, I traveled back to England for the first time since leaving. I had filmed two feature films that year, *Return of the Fly* and *Ten Who Dared*, so it seemed like a good time to go home and "boast" of my success to my family and friends. Better to go home working than not, I reasoned!

I called Michael Ford, an old BBC friend who had taken over my program when I left. I said, "I'm home, Mike, and it would be nice to see you."

Mike said, "Come up and we'll make you a guest on your old program." My ego was thrilled, I must confess. Because I had just finished two features, four, if you counted my voice work on *Ben-Hur* and *101 Dalmatians*, I spouted off the possibilities that were ahead of me — more movies, television, etc. I had left any modesty behind in the States for that trip!

Back at the BBC, I loved seeing the recording guys, because they had saved me so many times. Every week, they had edited out all my rubbish or mistakes to make me sound terrific. They were such good people. After I had appeared on my old program, I went in to see them.

One of them was also named David. He said, "I've got a lot of your old stuff here," and handed me about two dozen acetate disks in a big bag. What a kind gesture, offering me recordings of my old programs. I had gone up by train, so I lugged the bag of recordings back to my parents' home in Kent. I treasured having these interviews with Greer Garson, Betty Hutton, Doris Day, and Rosemary Clooney.

My dad, though, wisely realized the trouble I would have toting those back to America, so he asked what I planned on doing with them. When I moved to America, I had left behind an old reel-to-reel recorder at my parents' house. I dusted it off and recorded my disks to tape by putting each one on the phonograph player and holding the microphone to the loudspeaker. The result was a very poor reproduction, but I managed to tape them pretty well.

My dad said, "Now what are you going to do with all of these records?"

That was a good question. I couldn't take them back to the BBC since they were technically stolen property, given to me by well-intentioned former colleagues as a souvenir of my time there. I told my dad that we could put them in the trash, but he had a better idea. He went out behind the garbage heap and dug a big hole to bury the disks. To this day, I imagine that there are two dozen acetate disks still buried three feet under in my father's old garden, now owned by someone else.

While I was home in England that holiday season, I also called on Joan Elan's parents. Her father was considerably older than Joan's mother. Both were terribly concerned. Joan had made me swear that I would tell them that she was working all the time in America.

Her mother asked, "Are you sure she's okay?"

"Oh, yes," I assured her, lying through my teeth to protect Joan. "She's busy all the time in one acting project after another."

Returning home at the start of 1960, I couldn't help but feel sorry for Joan, because I was winning television or movie roles while her acting offers nearly stopped. For a jobbing actor, appearing on television meant steady work for me. Industry paychecks paid for my first car, my first color TV, fancy dinners, and trips back to the UK.

Going home to England that Christmas cost me a role in what would have been my third feature, and a Frank Sinatra one at that! Prior to my trip, I had been cast as Mike Island in *Never So Few*, a Sinatra vehicle that also starred Steve McQueen. Unfortunately for me, shooting started ahead of schedule, so the casting director had to ask Maurine, "Where the hell was David?"

Because I was away in England, they gave my part to Richard Lupino, Ida Lupino's nephew, whom I frequently saw at auditions. Strangely, he always seemed nervous or negative whenever we ran into each other, so I was surprised whenever he got work. One time I asked him, "Are you busy all the time, Richard?" and he told me, "No, actually I'm an ambulance driver by trade." He seemed more enthusiastic about driving ambulances than acting.

My first celebratory trip back to England had cost me a film role, but it had been worth it. My parents could see that I was doing well for myself and I never had to worry about returning home in failure or shame ever again.

For my friend Joan, though, the frequent rejection had taken its toll to the point that she was unable to work at all. We still met for coffee or for dinner, but I was working all the time. At one point, I offered her the chance to move in with me to share expenses.

"No," she told me, "because when one of us slows down and the other is working, that's just an impossible situation." Sadly, that's what Joan's acting career was becoming. One morning, she called me before our get together at Coffee Dan's.

"You've got to help me, David," she said. "I've got a part at MGM."

"Great!" I told her.

"No, it's not great," she replied. "I've got to play a Cockney bar maid."

"Oh God," I thought to myself. Joan was terrible at any accent other than the upper-class English accent that she normally used. The way she spoke was a reflection of how she had been raised, and she could not shake that accent no matter how many attempts were made to teach her in our acting classes.

She had been beautifully educated and brought up properly speaking in an Audrey Hepburn kind of accent. She did not have an ear for speaking any other way. It was hell working with her that day. The pressure was on, because she had to start shooting the next morning. Just a few years earlier, she frequently was a show's guest star with the whole week to work, and now it was a one-day shoot as a Cockney bar maid.

Joan went through the same kind of agony as Audrey Hepburn is reported to have endured in trying to get her accent right for *My Fair Lady*. Afterwards, Joan said she had great difficulty all day at her shoot as she vainly attempted a Cockney accent. If your ear doesn't tell you that it's right, there's no way you'll ever get it right, I found in my experience.

That was one of the last jobs she ever got. With the writing on the wall, one day she said, "I have to leave. It's like the old cliché — if you're not working, Hollywood is the worst place in the world to be when everybody else is working and you're not."

Joan had friends in Malibu, so she gave up her apartment because she could no longer pay the rent. She wouldn't accept any help from me.

"No," she told me. "This is just an indication to me that I've had a good little run out here and it's over."

She drove off in her little MG to Malibu. Her leaving was a huge loss for me, but I respected her for the decision she made. She had to do things her way, because she was so independent. She felt that she had done her best work, and if acting work was slowing down, then it was time to quit.

One day she called from Malibu and told me that she had found a job as a cashier in a flower shop. She had never even been able to balance her checkbook, so her cashier job didn't last very long.

Dick Bull and his wife, Bobbie, had always joined Joan and me for dinner. One night, Joan drove from Malibu for old times' sake. I encouraged her to get there early so we could visit ahead of dinner. She had to have a couple of drinks to steady her nerves, even though she had never been much of a drinker before that.

She had acquired a huge Russian wolfhound named Hayley. Joan's MG didn't have a top on it to keep Hayley safely inside while we visited, so I said, "You can't bring Hayley into my place because I have two cats!" Even in the saddest times, we could laugh at such episodes. Hayley sat tied to the wheel inside the sports car so no one could steal her. The next morning, Joan had to go out to untie Hayley so the dog could heed nature's call, and poor Hayley went all over my two neighbors' lawns. When they asked if I knew the guilty dog owner, I lied and said that I didn't.

Joan finally moved to New York to live with her sister. We still talked every day by phone. She lived above her sister in an apartment on the fourteenth floor. Hayley had to be walked, of course, so Joan had to get into an elevator for fourteen floors. Joan, however, was claustrophobic, so she had to be talked into getting into the elevator each time she had to leave the building. Every afternoon at one o'clock L.A. time, my phone rang, and it would be Joan saying, "David, it's time for Hayley's walk. You have to help me!"

I actually had to talk Joan into mustering the courage to make a run for the elevator with Hayley on her leash. Sometimes she just couldn't. She said, "All right, we'll talk tomorrow," and then two minutes later, the phone would ring again. "I can't do it, David, I can't do it! I can't get into the elevator!" and again, I would talk her into it.

Joan eventually overcame her fear of elevators, but we still talked several times a week. She seemed relatively happy. She met a writer of TV commercials, a man named Bud. He loved her more than she loved him, but she told me that she was going to make a go of it. They later came to visit for two days while I was shooting a show. Bud had written a television commercial that was being filmed, so Joan came, too.

After they left, I never saw her again. We wrote letters and started them with "Ullo, Ullo" — just as we had heard many radio comedic English cops say, as in "Ullo, Ullo, what's all this?" and then we ended our letters with "TTFN" for "ta ta for now." Eventually, Joan and I lost touch. Years later, I learned from a friend who had encountered a mutual friend that Joan had died in early 1981 after suffering a heart attack during a minor operation. Hearing that news, I was so upset that I had to pull over my car. It was very hard to take, even after twenty years. Joan and I had spent so much time together during my early years in Hollywood.

Where Joan's career had fizzled, mine flourished. By 1960, I was making $750 a week for television work. In today's dollars, that would translate to $5,400 or so per week. Working actors who found themselves in dry spells without work could always count on unemployment. In fact, most working actors went to unemployment the day after they finished a job if another acting role wasn't waiting.

I first learned of unemployment from other actors when I started on *Matinee Theater*. Unemployment benefits for actors were based on the work we had just done. For most actors who did guest-starring roles or supporting roles in feature films, the day after a wrap meant seeing each other in the unemployment line. Sometimes I was surprised by those I saw at the unemployment office. Adolph Menjou, one of the biggest stars from the silent era, was in line one day.

The first time I went for unemployment in between jobs, I thought that my parents would have been so ashamed of me to know that I was "on the dole," as it was called back in England. Actors never thought that way, though. Unemployment meant that actors could keep going until the next part came along. We weren't there that often, because if we worked, we went in to the unemployment office to record that we had acted in a production so our earnings could be noted. For actors to earn unemployment, we had to have an agent, which was easy to prove. If we had worked the previous week and didn't have a gig the next, we were eligible for unemployment.

Luckily for me, I never had to rely on unemployment too frequently or think about going into another line of work. With my indomitable agent, I was able to work and live very comfortably. Maurine also represented other aspiring actors, some of whom I met. Through Maurine, I got to know Harold Lloyd, Jr., son of the great silent comedian, and Lorraine Bendix, the daughter of William Bendix, who enjoyed success in film and on radio in *The Life of Riley*.

Harold, Jr., and Lorraine put on a nightclub act in Beverly Hills. Maurine attended on opening night and invited me along, enticing me with the news that both Harold Lloyd, Sr., and William Bendix would attend. I thought we were in for a funny evening because both of those great performers were known for their humor.

What a downer the evening turned out to be! I'm not sure if they were dour because they were nervous parents watching their children's nightclub debut. Harold Lloyd turned out to be a sullen, mean-spirited kind of man. There was just an aura of depression about him. Maurine, for all her sparkle, never seemed to get him up from his gloom. She gave up trying as the nightclub act started.

When the evening was over and we all told the kids how wonderful they were, Lorraine went off with her dad. Harold Lloyd, Sr., left with Maurine. I was about to catch the bus home when Harold Lloyd, Jr., offered to give me a lift. It turned out that he disliked his father, which I wasn't prepared to hear! He told me that they didn't get along that well. In his opinion, his father kept him under his thumb and didn't allow him to express himself creatively. He parked outside my house and unburdened himself. I could tell that he needed to get that anger out of his system. I tried to be supportive and wished him well. That was the last time I saw him, and sadly, he died not too long after his famous father's death.

I'm glad to say that I was better adjusted by 1960. Working in Hollywood had taken me to most of the major studios. I had familiarized myself with sites that were like historical landmarks because of their associations with the Hollywood memories they held for me and other film buffs.

The 20th Century-Fox lot was rather like the Disney lot, with well-tended lawns and trees. Paramount's lot was more industrial looking, as was Columbia's, mostly because they didn't have the real estate space. Right across the street from Paramount, tucked away, was The Producers' Studio, a slightly ramshackle collection of sound stages where I later filmed *Tales of Terror*. It was a busy old lot in those days. Universal, unfortunately, was like a factory. It stretched all the way over to a golf course next to Warner Bros. It's interesting to watch a film like *Spartacus* and forget that it was filmed on the Universal lot just over the hill from the Hollywood Freeway.

Once in a while, a major name visited while making a movie. Alec Guinness didn't have time to be a part of a social circle, really, but he came from England to do *A Majority of One*, in which he played a Japanese business man. Warner Bros. gave him and his wife a huge mansion to stay in up in the hills, as they did any big star coming out to work.

I wanted to let him know how well I had done since he had helped me get started five years earlier. I was not a household name, but I was making a good living. He had taken a chance writing those letters of introduction for me, so I thought it would be closure to let him know that his effort

One of my early 1960s headshots.

had paid off and that I was doing well. I came to know a writer who was doing touch-ups to the script on *A Majority of One*. Wyatt Cooper was a gifted writer who later married Gloria Vanderbilt. (Their son, Anderson Cooper, is now a notable CNN journalist.) I asked Cooper to call Alec Guinness and pass on my phone number.

Guinness promptly got in touch with me to say that he had a tight shooting schedule with very few days off, but he invited me to Warner Bros. for lunch. When I arrived, it was a most unusual lunch, because Guinness was wearing his Japanese costume from the movie. The effect was disconcerting. I knew it was Alec, but he looked like a Japanese man.

Over a good lunch I told him what I had been doing for the past five years since arriving in Hollywood. I think he was pleased to hear about my success and that his letters of introduction to his agent, Peter Shaw, had amounted to something after all.

At one point he told me that he was meeting Zsa Zsa Gabor for dinner later that evening. I told him that Zsa Zsa didn't pay me when I coached her English accent for a play she intended to do in Florida a few years earlier.

He said, "As I'm dining with Zsa Zsa this evening. I'll bring it up."

"No, no, please don't," I implored.

"Did you get paid?" he asked. "Well? I shall bring it up."

The next day, he arranged for me to pick up a check signed by Zsa Zsa Gabor!

We had such a good time together that he told me that Tuesday was his day off. He suggested that we could meet the following Tuesday at the Villa Capri. The restaurant was near my house, so I walked up and met him for lunch. The restaurant was quiet, and nobody made a fuss over him.

As I got to know him better, I realized that Guinness was a little eccentric. He said, "This very table is where I had lunch with James Dean when he insisted that I come out to see his new car, the same vehicle he would die in two days later." He was so dramatic about the whole anecdote that he almost gave me the creeps.

Odd comments aside, our get-togethers became a weekly habit when he had a day off and I wasn't working. In addition to his enormous film salary, Warner Bros. gave him a $500 per diem that he had to spend or give back by the end of the week. One day he called and told me that he wanted to buy some records with his per diem. He asked for a recommendation for good record stores, so I told him about several locations. We went to one store in Beverly Hills where many of the staff members were out-of-work actors who either couldn't get an agent or found themselves between jobs.

People ordinarily walked by Guinness without recognizing him because he was a very boring-looking man in reality. Actors knew who he was, though, and I could hear an intake of breath when we walked into the record store. He dithered around, buying classical albums while the staff wanted to wait on him hand and foot. Because I was a record lover and a former disc jockey of sorts, he asked me if his record selections were any good.

He picked out a stack of discs and insisted that I buy an album for helping him. I bought Ella Fitzgerald's two-disc set of *Ella Sings Cole Porter*, paid for by Alec's per diem from Warner Bros. As we left, somebody behind the counter said, "It's a great pleasure serving you." Alec loved that. He was upset if he wasn't recognized and didn't like to go unnoticed.

We became pretty good friends, sometimes going to lunch on Saturdays or visiting different spots around Los Angeles. His wife and son were also friendly, a devoted family. I enjoyed asking Alec questions about his work on a more personal level; back at the BBC, I had to ask fairly formal questions. He was a big star, so I benefited from him sharing his perspective on acting techniques with me.

Alec called one day and told me that he wanted to drive down the coast to spend some of his left-over money. He picked me up at my little house in a huge stretch limo provided by Warner Bros. The chauffeur next picked up two ladies that Alec somehow knew, one of whom was the southern-born actress Joanna Moore. (She later married Ryan O'Neal and became Tatum O'Neal's mother.) She kept erroneously calling our star "Alex" instead of Alec in her southern drawl. I expected him to say in a very British way, "My name is Alec!" but he never did. He just smiled and seemed amused whenever she said his name wrong that day.

We all enjoyed a very nice lunch where Alec spent more of his $500 per diem from the studio. Then we drove down to San Juan Capistrano to visit the famous Catholic mission there. Alec had just done a movie called *The Prisoner*, about a Catholic priest in Communist Europe. As a result of making the movie, he converted to the Catholic faith. He told us he wanted to go into the mission for a visit.

A few people were sitting in the back of the church when we arrived. He walked up to the front and made the sign of the cross. The young priest immediately recognized him and became sort of flustered. The other parishioners left, so the ladies and I just sat in the back. We couldn't hear what the conversation was between the priest and Alec. When they finished, he just smiled and walked back as we left for the drive home.

That evening, we dropped off the ladies. Alec asked me to go to dinner with him at Chasen's. Ronald Neame, who had produced *Oliver Twist* and *Great Expectations* back in the 1940s, had also directed Alec to good reviews in *The Horse's Mouth*. He and his wife were planning to meet Alec at Chasen's.

Alec told me, "Ronnie's having trouble casting the female lead in *Escape from Zahrain*. You might know some girls who would be right. Come dine with us and give him advice."

Before we went to dinner, Alec and I enjoyed a few drinks. It was my opportunity to talk to him actor to actor and pick his brain about his wide range of acting techniques. I remembered that Dirk Bogarde had told me that he started the process of acting when he put on a costume. I knew that Dirk didn't care for Alec, and Alec found Dirk pretentious, so I set out to get Alec's take on acting.

I asked Alec, "How do you start creating a character? What do you go about preparing first?"

He told me, "Reading the script, the voice always comes to one."

Alec had done a stage production about Lawrence of Arabia, called *Ross*, to great acclaim with director Terence Rattigan. On a record, Peter Sellers created a sketch imitating Alec Guinness by calling himself Eric Goodness, billed in a play called *Smith*. I owned that LP, so over drinks, I thought it would be fine to ask Alec what he thought of the impersonation since he was talking about the role of the voice when creating a character.

I said, "What did you think of Peter Sellers playing you on that record album?"

Very quickly, he said, "You do realize that he wouldn't have done that without my permission." That was that. I thought, "He's not very jolly about that one."

Luckily for me, he moved back to acting techniques. He continued: "The voice comes to me when I read the script. Let me show you what I mean."

I thought, "Oh, I'm going to get some marvelous insight here, something rare and unique!"

He reminded me of our trip earlier in the day to the San Juan Capistrano mission where the priest had recognized him. He told me that the priest had told him what a privilege it was to have such a famous man in his mission.

Alec said, "I'm going to ring him up now." As he went to the phone, I just sat there, agog. Without telling me what he was going to do, he sat down next to me with the phone in his hand and requested the operator to put him through to the mission in San Juan Capistrano.

Alec then vocally became somebody else as he used a higher register and an Irish accent to pretend he was a higher-up Catholic Church official. It was really uncanny.

I thought, "How wonderful. He's going to say something funny and nice to that young priest."

Instead, Alec said in an unrecognizable Irish accent: "I am on a hiatus from Boston and visited your mission today. I'm Bishop O'Connor and I just noticed, quite frankly, that the mission was filthy outside. There were newspapers everywhere, and I really think this ought to be taken care of."

I don't know what the poor priest said on the other end of the line, but he could not have known it was Alec Guinness, because this Alec did not sound like the real Alec Guinness who had been inside the mission with him just four hours earlier. Alec didn't look like himself any more as he chewed out this young priest in this made-up, impromptu character.

He continued, "I don't know that I will have the time to be down in that area again, but I do hope that if I do, I will see some improvement in the look of the mission. After all, it's very important for the church. That's about all I have to say."

The priest on the other end said something back, and then Alec said, "I bid you good evening," and put down the phone.

I said, "That's amazing. I don't know how you can do that! Of course, you're going to call him back now and tell him it was a joke and apologize, aren't you?"

Alec said, "No! That would spoil the joke." That was the end of that. That episode showed a mean side to his nature and made me nervous. He normally just smiled that kind of gentle smile I had seen in *Kind Hearts and Coronets*. I had presumed he was a completely unassuming man with a great gift. I was used to encountering performers who could suddenly switch personalities and let their public persona disappear completely. Those episodes usually happened in a work context, though, but this side of Alec happened in a social situation.

"This is a part of Alec Guinness I haven't seen before," I thought. I wasn't sure that I liked that side of him. Then he grew affable again as the limo returned from dropping off the ladies. On our way down to Chasen's, he said something that will always stick with me. We were talking about Ronald Neame and what a great producer and director he was. Alec said, "I like working with Ronnie. He always does what I tell him to do."

I was astonished to hear him say that. I thought, "What an extraordinary thing for an actor to say to a director. Unless you're Laurence

Olivier directing yourself in *Hamlet*, why would an actor like working for a director who does what the actor tells him to do?"

Alec's comments were the first intimation that I had of his power. To a degree, it had gone to his head. He felt that he was all powerful, and that directors acquiesced and did all he told them! In my experience, actors always relied upon the director. Even if halfway through a film you decided that the director wasn't very good, he was still the boss.

At dinner Ronald Neame was a gentleman. I did my part and suggested four or five names of actresses whose work I knew. Later he saw them all and chose one to be his leading lady in his movie.

Chasen's was a wonderful old place where the Hollywood elite dined. Everyone who was anyone could be found there. Someone had pre-ordered for Alec, Ronald and Mrs. Neame, and me. I experienced great discomfort during the meal, because I had never eaten crab legs before. What looked like claws sat on a dish in front of me, and I didn't have a clue as to how to eat them. The others used tweezers to yank out the meat as they chatted. With butter on my chin, I thought, "I'm such a rube."

Crab legs aside, I relished the chance to dine with both Alec and Ronald Neame. I remember thinking about the film history on display that night. Alec had played Herbert Pocket and Fagin to Ronald Neame's producing. English movie history was on display right in front of me.

Alec was always a great finger wagger. When we got to dessert, he wagged his finger at Neame and said, "Ronnie, I think David has been a great help to you this evening. You might find the girl you're looking for from his list of suggestions, so the least you can do is find him a good part in your next film."

Neame said, "Oh, yes, Alec, you're quite right. David, come see me tomorrow at 10 o'clock." I could see that he was as in awe of Alec as the rest of us were.

I didn't have much hope of going to see Neame at Paramount and getting a good part, because to give Maurine credit, if there had been any parts for me in any script at any studio in those years, she was aware of roles that were right for me. I wasn't that thrilled at Alec's suggestion, because in my experience, I hadn't had much luck with parts recommended by other actors, other than some work that Ben Wright recommended, such as dubbing on *Ben-Hur*.

Later that evening after dinner, I had a pointed disagreement with Guinness, so upsetting that I never bothered to visit Ronald Neame the next day. Coupled with his mean sense of humor directed at the priest during his prank phone call, I decided that I was seeing a side of Guinness better left unexplored. He was not the type of friend I envisioned him to be, and it was best that I not pursue a deeper friendship.

Decades later, I can watch him in a movie and still admire his marvelous talent and acting ability. Unfortunately, I discovered the human side of him that I had not anticipated. I never saw him again, but I still appreciate his assistance when I arrived in Hollywood. He did send me to his agent, Peter Shaw, who in turn, led me to my agent, Maurine Oliver, so I owe him that debt of gratitude.

As my fledgling friendship with Alec Guinness met an abrupt end, I was fortunate enough to foster a better friendship with Dirk Bogarde. We had corresponded fairly frequently for several years since I interviewed him back at the BBC. He had given me the numbers of contacts to start with when I arrived in Hollywood, including his friends, Elizabeth Taylor and Michael Wilding.

Dirk was a prolific letter-writer, so in 1959, he told me that he had been reluctantly cast to play Franz List in Columbia Pictures' musical biography, *Song Without End*. Production started in Europe under the direction of Charles Vidor, a director with a reputation as a task-master. He had directed *Cover Girl*, with Rita Hayworth, and was partly responsible for her becoming a superstar.

On location in Vienna, Vidor was tense and acted unpleasantly toward the cast and crew. He had a quick temper and directed it one day toward one of the stars, Cappucine. She was very nervous about her first movie. Dirk told me that "Cappie," as she was known, made some mistakes, and Vidor began profusely cursing at her. She fled in tears to her dressing room as the crew stood there, silently loathing his behavior.

Later that June night, Vidor died suddenly of a heart attack. Dirk told me that when the news was announced on the set, the crew broke into applause. Vidor had not been well-liked on that shoot, and the tension lessened after he was replaced by the legendary George Cukor. After location work finished under Cukor's direction, the production moved to Hollywood.

Early 1960 allowed me to get to know Dirk better after he called and said, "We're here," referring to himself and his agent and companion, Tony Forwood. He was staying at the Bel Air Hotel with real swans outside his suite. I went up right away when he called.

"I want you to look at this suite," he said. Each of the four rooms contained a piano. Columbia had given him strict instructions to get to the keyboards and practice playing. He would be faking on screen, of course, but Franz List was a virtuoso pianist, and the picture had to provide audiences with a realistic impression. Although Dirk used a dummy keyboard on screen, he more or less had to learn the music. He didn't read music, but renowned musician Franz Aller was his coach. They started rehearsals with a few preludes and then went into Hungarian rhapsodies.

Columbia had done a picture with Cornel Wilde called *A Song to Remember* in 1945, shot strictly across the piano so audiences could not see Wilde faking the key work. Dirk agreed that for his film, it was important to be shown realistically playing the piano. The work was so stressful that he actually suffered a breakdown. No one knew about it, but in the middle of the picture, Dirk said, "F#%@ this, I'm going home." He left mid-picture, flew home to England for three days, and then realized that he would be broke by the time the studio sued him for breaking his contract, so he got on a plane and came back to finish the picture.

Every weekend was open house at his home on St. Ives Drive up in Beverly Hills after he moved into more spacious living arrangements. Getting inside meant descending wooden stairs that led from the road and into the house. Big studios provided luxury homes for their stars. The studio also placed a piano in every room, or as Dirk put it, "There's one in every room but the loo." Columbia was not about to let him forget why he was there.

He invited close friends to visit. To my immense satisfaction, he enjoyed our letter-writing friendship enough to invite me, too. Guests casually dropped by for drinks and to sit around the pool and chat. One weekend the visitors included Leslie Caron, Ingrid Bergman, and Cappucine, Dirk's co-star in *Song Without End*.

I got to know him better, building upon the letter-writing friendship that had blossomed since I left England. Dirk made me feel safe and secure as a friend. I knew that he would never lie, never make up anything, never be pompous — it was a laser-like stare you would get from him, almost defying you not to be phony in return. If you said that something was wonderful and it was not, he could see right through that and did not hesitate to tell you so.

I learned that he had served in World War II as an officer in the army. He worked as a sketch officer, and during the D-Day landings, he was among the first to jump onto Omaha Beach with a sketch book to do pen and ink sketches of the drama around him. Some of those drawings ended up on display at the Royal Academy years later, although I'm not sure if they were included because of his fame or because of his artistic ability. I thought they were good when I saw them.

He had been through the responsibility of a war in a position as a captain. I think that contributed to his integrity. There was absolutely no nonsense about him whatsoever. He felt like a real human being, not somebody dazzled by his own importance. Dirk disliked Alec Guinness for that reason, because he found Guinness to be self-impressed. There was no sense of that about Dirk; he was always down to earth.

The early 1960s saw wonderful parties thrown by my friend Dirk Bogarde.

The day before his birthday in March 1960, Dirk invited me to his birthday dinner. No one was to bring any gifts, though, because it was just a get-together sort of evening. I had already agreed to go with Maurine to see a casting director.

"I'm sorry, Dirk, but I can't go," I told him.

"Oh, but you can't miss Judes," Dirk replied.

"Who's Judes?" I asked.

"Judy Garland. Judy's coming," he said.

"What a terrific blow to miss meeting her," I thought, but I just couldn't break a commitment. I apologized again and told him that I couldn't attend.

"Well, just stop in for drinks on your way," he told me. "Meet her and then go on to whatever you have to do."

He warned me about Judy's husband, Sid Luft, whom Dirk referred to as a "used car salesman." Dirk said to me, "All Sid cares about is Judy, but when you think about it, Judy is his meal ticket. I don't know how deep that devotion goes."

Dirk also cautioned me: "Don't tell Sid you're an actor. I want him to think that you're very rich and that you have so much that you don't know what to do with it."

I asked him why he wanted me to put up such a charade.

"Just do not tell him you're an actor!" he said. "It will drive him crazy wondering who you are and how much money you've got."

When I got to Dirk's birthday party, Roddy McDowall attended and brought Gladys Cooper as his guest. By then, Gladys and I were friends, so it was great fun to see her whenever we could get together. The occasion marked my first time meeting Roddy, who was nice and easygoing. In a way, I owed him my first role at NBC on *Matinee Theater*, the one I gained after he left for Broadway.

Like Dirk, Roddy was a man of no nonsense. He was so enthusiastic about everything that he was almost like an eager puppy. He was very down to earth and didn't carry himself like the big star he was. In reality, there were several of us who were often up for "Roddy-type" parts, and we knew that we only got those roles if he was otherwise engaged. That's how it should have been, too, because he was that good.

Dirk had arranged the evening for just a few friends, so in addition to himself, Tony, Roddy, Gladys, and me, we were only missing two more guests. Sid Luft and his wife, Judy Garland, arrived. She wore a black mandarin outfit, her outfit of choice during that era. She wore no makeup, and her dark hair was pulled back. She was very quiet, gentle, and sweet. "Hi," was about all she said.

Just as Dirk predicted, Sid Luft watched me as I selected food from the buffet table. He came up and asked, "So, are you staying out here very long?"

"I don't know," I told him as I played along with Dirk's request to act rich and important. "I'm just here to get the feel of the place."

"Ah," he said. "So do you invest?" He really pumped me to see if I would invest in Judy's next project. I managed to get out of that inquisition, but he continued to follow me around as we ate. He was truly trying to find out if I was there to invest money in show business. Dirk, meanwhile, enjoyed the humor of the situation!

Even though he had requested no gifts, I had thought I would be cute. I gave Dirk a copy of Judy's latest album, *The Letter*. The album contained some spoken word passages with narration by John Ireland and Judy singing a song or two. Dirk was delighted and had me write a message on the cover.

Always wanting to deflate pomposity, Dirk said, "Come on, David, you've always wanted to get to know God, so here she is." He sat me down next to her. What a thrill! Sitting next to this magic lady from *The Wizard of Oz* and knowing the work she had done in her career and how she managed to survive, I was mesmerized.

As Garland and I chatted, Dirk moved across the room. He held up the LP and said, "Look what David's brought me!"

She promptly shrieked at me, "Why the f#$% did you give him this f#$%-ing album? I HATE this f#$%-ing thing!" Then she jumped up, grabbed the LP, and hit me with it over the head! I was devastated, but Judy's husband and Dirk assured me that this behavior was par for Judy's course and that the storm would soon pass.

"Come on, Judy," Luft said. "He didn't mean it."

"Well, I don't care! I hate that f#@%-ing thing!"

Luft said something quietly to her, so she said, "Well, OKAY!" Dirk helped Luft as they guided Judy upstairs to the restroom. The house had a cantilevered staircase. Judy muttered away to herself and held onto the walls as they climbed the stairs.

I thought, "She's going to fall off that cantilevered staircase and die, and it will be my fault!"

I apologetically told Dirk that I would leave, but he explained that her temperamental behavior happened all the time and that one could never tell what might set off one of her squalls. Sure enough, a few minutes later as I nervously watched, Judy came down smiling like a saint.

I was backed up against the wall from fear of her, but she seemed to have no memory of what had just transpired ten minutes earlier. She smiled and patted the sofa and said, "Come sit by me and we'll chat. What were we talking about?"

Whatever she was given in the restroom had calmed her down and erased an emotional crisis. It no longer existed in her mind. She was fine as we chatted. In fact, we started to get along so well that I hated leaving for my standing engagement. In reality, I was afraid that I might miss Garland singing, because Dirk had said to me earlier, "Don't ask her to sing. If anybody asks her to sing, she'll just walk right out of the house because she hates for anybody to think that she's been hired to sing for her supper."

Sometimes, though, I was told that she would sing on her own accord if she felt like it. I called the next day to ask if I had missed a performance. Dirk told me that she did not sing after I left.

"Do you think she's gotten over being upset with me?" I asked.

"Of course she's forgotten," he told me.

And she had forgotten, because over the next several weeks, the Lufts turned up again at Dirk's. The next time I saw her, she was sitting by the pool. "Hi, how are you?" she asked. I don't think she knew me from a hole in the wall. She was never unpleasant again, and I took great care never to bring a Judy Garland album to Dirk's house! So, one never knew with Old Judes, as Dirk called her.

Garland's outburst aside, weekend visits to Dirk's house were so pleasant. Sometimes he knew who would be coming, and he would preview the list over the phone. Other times people just showed up for a fun afternoon. One day I saw a tall lady coming down the staircase. Dirk said, "Oh, it's Ingrid."

"Ingrid Bergman?" I asked. Sure enough, Bergman herself visited that afternoon. Another day Leslie Caron came down the wooden stairs toward the house and Dirk said, "Let's see what kind of mood she's in today. She can be a real bitch!"

They had made a film together in England called *The Doctors' Dilemma*. They got along well, but on some days, she became "MGM Grand," as he called it. As she walked closer to us that day, he looked at her and said, "Oh, I think she's okay today."

She was charming, so much so that she took off her dark glasses and hat when it was time to eat. Dirk told the group, "I don't think there's much in the fridge."

Caron said, "Well, if you have a ham, I can prepare it for you." So Leslie Caron cooked a ham for three or four of us that evening!

Another time, Nancy Olson was there. She was a fine actress whom I admired from *Sunset Boulevard*. Olson was married to Alan Livingston, an executive at Capitol Records, and before that, she had been married to composer Alan J. Lerner. The Lerners had stayed at Dirk's Buckinghamshire estate when Alan composed the score to *My Fair Lady*. Dirk said that on one Sunday morning when the Lerners emerged from their cottage, he was the first to hear "On the Street Where You Live" played on his piano.

All good things inevitably come to an end, so after Dirk finished his work on *Song Without End* and returned home to Europe, Maurine got the word from Columbia that extensive dubbing work was needed because of some of the heavier European accents. Because I had dubbed for William Wyler on *Ben-Hur*, I was invited to come to audition.

Two of us finalists were to read for George Cukor. He would pick one of us to dub for Albert Rueprecht, an Austrian actor who played Prince Felix Lichnowsky. Rueprecht had a very strong Austrian accent, so much so that Columbia felt it was too strong for American ears, so the poor guy's entire performance had to be dubbed. I honestly thought he sounded fine, but his delivery had too many "Ve vill go to ze voods..." sounds for Cukor.

Both of us actors read for Cukor, an awe-inspiring task given the number of cinematic masterpieces he had directed — *Little Women*,

Camille, The Philadelphia Story, Gaslight, Adam's Rib, Born Yesterday, and *A Star Is Born.* I was elated to learn that Cukor ultimately chose me for the part.

The next day we started the dubbing sessions. Cukor couldn't have been more affable. He arrived with his lunch in a little picnic basket that he placed on his desk in the dubbing room. Originally during my audition, Cukor hadn't been overly friendly. I had felt if you weren't a star, he looked right through you. My theory is that he was a great snob about people who weren't stars. I picked up that impression from him when he directed our audition with, "Alright, he can do this, why can't you?" and remarks like that.

Luckily for me, I had become friendly with Cappucine during those weekend visits at Dirk's rental home. As a famous model in France, she hadn't acted very much, but she was very vulnerable, sweet and nice, so I was delighted to see that she was there dubbing when I arrived. Cukor was laughing and chatting away with Cappucine. When I walked in, she came over and hugged me. Cukor noted this affection with great interest and became very pleasant to me throughout the dubbing. It didn't change my belief that he was otherwise snobby to people who weren't stars. That was just my gut feeling.

Under his direction, my dubbing sessions went well. We were there for a whole week as I dubbed that poor actor's voice, virtually replacing his performance with my voice. It was a big part in the movie. Like every actor, I had wanted to work with Dirk, but he had finished his work and left Hollywood. Working on *Song Without End* meant that I worked with him in a way, or at least on a Dirk Bogarde movie. In fact, when I watched the movie, it did sound as though we're acting together because in some scenes, my voice came out of the actor opposite Dirk! If I closed my eyes and listened, the effect was almost like acting with him.

I wrote Dirk to tell him that I had done some dubbing work on his film, and he wrote back and naturally replied, "How jolly!" which was often how he ended his letters to me. Dirk hated making the movie so much that he vowed never to return to Hollywood. He had worked hard on the picture, and it opened well enough at Radio City Music Hall, but he felt working in Hollywood exposed actors to the phoniness and business side of moviemaking, something he detested.

In the course of one year, I had been personally directed by William Wyler and George Cukor on dubbing for two different movies. Unfortunately, *Song Without End* didn't perform that well, and it paled in comparison to *Ben-Hur.* Nevertheless, I could truthfully say that I had been directed by George Cukor, a happy memory that would last until a disastrous experience with him a few years later.

Going from working with George Cukor to appearing on television might otherwise seem a little disconcerting, but by 1960, television was blossoming into a more sophisticated medium. Production values improved, and the studios more openly embraced the medium after they realized that the movies weren't too threatened by TV. In fact, Warner Bros. had six or seven series on the air at one point.

There was a lot of work for working actors who could adapt to different television genres, depending on the series you were cast in at any given moment. Most series ended production after thirty-nine weeks in May, leaving June and July to relax on the beach, or if you had a hard-working agent as I did, summer hiatus meant touring the studios to get your name out there while the producers began pre-production on the next season with guest-starring parts in mind.

Summertime always meant the possibilities of feature films, but there never seemed to be enough of those in production to go around for actors. Maurine reminded me that scripts were prepared for the fall season during summer. She sometimes took me with her instead of me going to the beach. We would sit in the commissaries at different studios. "Hello," she would say to directors going by our table. "Do you know David Frankham?" She was constantly showing me off and working on my behalf. Maurine inevitably had a head start on all the other agents whose clients were sun-tanning and swimming in June and July.

There were usually about three or four resident Brits in my age bracket at any given time. Some stayed in Hollywood for a year or so, only to decide the living wasn't so easy. They would depart as other faces took their place. I'd meet them all at auditions, and they were a friendly lot on the whole. It took time to build up a reputation for dependability at the various studios, and some of the lads, or their agents, hadn't the patience for that.

Once in a while, an actor arrived and whizzed right past me — David McCallum, for example. He had a special look and charisma. Oddly, I never felt any resentment when I watched somebody get a series or make more movies than I. If they were good, they deserved it. I guess I never felt rejection because there was always "the next one." Whenever an audition wouldn't work out, Maurine always said, "That just means you're available for the next role."

When I didn't get a part, I handled rejection well. I loved going to bat. I always wanted to beat the three or four other English actors always up for the same parts. Sometimes I did, sometimes I didn't. I was determined to work and sometimes knew that a part was mine. I knew that I could do a good job.

Today's actors enjoy the benefits of cell phones, voicemail and text messages to keep them in touch with their agents. For my generation, a Hollywood answering service was a critical lifeline. Nearly every working actor subscribed to one called Registry. I still remember the phone number, Hollywood 34811.

No actor could safely go out and enjoy an afternoon without checking in with Registry every couple of hours to see if there were any messages. There would be callbacks or I was told I got a job and to report to work. We greatly depended on Registry, located in a huge office just off Sunset Boulevard at an area quaintly called the Crossroads of the World.

There was a busy actor called Steve Franken, and Registry was always getting me mixed up with him. I would come in at the end of a nice afternoon and say, "Any messages?" I got all these calls about starting work somewhere in a couple of days, but the messages weren't for me at all; they were for Steve Franken. Registry was a little disorganized, but none of us could have survived without those services back then.

Thanks to tireless Maurine, I never worried about rent or food on the table. Each time I finished a role, she said, "Good. Now on to the next one!" and for twenty years, she made that happen. It was only later that I realized I had taken so much of it for granted. She was really my acting manager as well as my agent. She was a very rare lady.

My television roles continued at a good pace, and I enjoyed most of them. In 1960, I did an episode of *Men Into Space*, a program that glamorized astronaut adventures during the dawn of the early space race. I was reunited with John Sutton from *Return of the Fly*. We formed a good friendship during that brief shoot. He explained that he had really wanted my villain role in *Return of the Fly* but had made his peace with me playing the part. He even helped me find a tax preparer. After I arrived at the accountant's office, I discovered that he was in Suite 1313 on the thirteenth floor. Every time I went with things for him to work on, I peered down at the ground and imagined the building slightly swaying.

Another of my co-stars on *Men Into Space* was Robin Hughes. He had made a good impression as one of Rosalind Russell's "kept" artists in *Auntie Mame*. I remember Hughes saying that he was a bit fed up with Hollywood by 1960. I think the episode was also the only time I worked with the enthusiastic Roy Dean. He had Shakespearean training but never really got a momentum going in Hollywood. He recorded albums and sang a line — "You are in Iowa" — at the beginning of *The Music Man*. He was a gifted photographer as well and published a number of books. I think he co-owned an antiques store in West Hollywood.

Working on one of Ernie Kovacs' shows allowed me to do comedy for one of my first times as an actor. Back with the BBC in Birmingham, I knew that I could be funny after I made little jokes that cracked up the orchestra I was introducing. One of my colleagues had gone off to announce for Peter Sellers and his Goons, so I knew it was possible to put a sense of humor to good use.

The year before, when I did my Somerset Maugham comedy at the Pasadena Playhouse, a member of the board — this sweet little old lady planning the next season — came to me and said that she intended to invite me back the following year for a production of *Hamlet*.

I said, "What part?"

"Hamlet," she told me.

I had to keep a straight face — I would have looked ridiculous in tights — so I told her I was flattered and that we would have to see how it went. So, imagine the laugh I had the following year when I found myself playing Hamlet in a funny skit for Ernie Kovacs. Kovacs was wonderfully funny, and I loved working with him. For my Hamlet skit, the costumers gave me a beautiful, dark black velvet hose. All I had to do was to memorize "To be or not to be" and deliver it seriously. Kovacs stood behind me making faces, an old vaudeville routine. I loved it.

Louis Jourdan was the episode's main guest. Kovacs devised a comedy skit with André Previn conducting, no less. Jourdan sat beside me as we both "fiddled" in the skit. We all gathered around a real orchestra with violins to play, part of Kovacs' surreal sense of humor. Our violin bows were made of spaghetti that just wrapped around the instruments, a very funny sight gag. I found that I loved comedy as well as villainy or dramatic parts.

Gigi had been a very big hit, so I was interested in hearing Jourdan sing the title song. When he did, it sure didn't sound like the MGM soundtrack. I had a feeling that Bill Lee or one of the great singing dubbers had somehow helped Jourdan with his high notes on that film.

As a working actor, I was always observing and learning from established pros. One was Lucille Ball, whom I met in an odd way. My friend Patricia Houston was in Lucy's comedy class for a year or so, around 1960. I would stop by Lucy's studio, Desilu, to collect her. I was usually early, so I sat way in the back of the rehearsal hall. It was fascinating to watch

Lucy put them through their paces. She was tough and would not accept excuses for shoddy or lazy work. Patricia used to walk over to me, wiping her forehead with a towel, as if she had just gone fifteen rounds with a champ. In a way, she had. Like every actor, I hoped I would do one of Lucy's shows but never did.

The start of the 1960s brought some wonderful years for me personally. I think most people who lived through that era recall that those years were exciting, full of promise and hope. The American prosperity that fueled the 1950s continued with the start of a new decade, the election of a young, vibrant president with movie star looks, and a space race to the moon. In 1960, I had finished my work on *101 Dalmatians* early in the year, spent many happy weekends with Dirk Bogarde and his friends, and even dubbed a part in one of his films.

That fall reunited me with Vincent Price on what would become my favorite feature film experience of my Hollywood career. What an exciting time it was, a real adventure for me!

CHAPTER EIGHT

Master of the World

Some actors dream of working in big feature films. Many of us worked hard to land big parts in feature films, great or not. But for all the dreaming or planning, sometimes a feature film just lands in your lap, literally out of the blue. That happened to me in the early fall of 1960, and the film turned out to be my favorite feature film experience from my entire career.

I have director William Witney and Vincent Price to thank for me getting my role in *Master of the World*. Based on a 1904 Jules Verne book, the movie was adapted for screen by Richard Matheson, a gifted writer who specialized in science fiction and fantasy stories, most famously for some of the better *Twilight Zone* episodes.

Disney had found success in 1954 when it adapted *20,000 Leagues Under the Sea*, so American International Pictures (AIP) decided to bring *Master of the World* to the big screen. Many of the elements were parallel — a mad genius who invents a fantastic transportation machine to travel and wage his campaign against war. AIP, known for lower budget fare aimed at teenagers, opted for a bigger budget with elaborate period piece sets and costumes.

Vincent Price was cast as Captain Robur, the mad genius who travels the world in his airship, bent on destroying war machines to bring about his idealized view of world peace. Henry Hull, Charles Bronson, and Mary Webster were also cast, while Mark Damon was set to play Philip Evans, a spirited leading man who jealously does battle with Charles Bronson's character.

Right before the production started, AIP found itself over a barrel. Mark Damon opted out from the film on a Friday, supposedly upset at losing the girl to Charles Bronson. His agents had belatedly advised him to turn down the film, the idea being that it wasn't good press for a rising leading man to lose the girl on screen.

Panic ensued, but Vincent recalled my double-dealing character in *Return of the Fly* while he was at the studio to fit for wardrobe. He suggested me for Damon's part, so director William Witney quickly got a print and watched my work from the previous year. If Vincent hadn't been there at that moment, I wouldn't have got the role. I don't think James Nicholson, the head of AIP, or Witney knew who I was, but they

Posing in a great period piece costume for Master of the World, *1961.* (AIP)

trusted Vincent's word and liked what they saw from my first feature film.

Maurine called to say, "Get out to American International! It's a crisis for them, and if you're right for the part, you'll be starting on Monday! Be sure to get a script to clinch the deal!"

I rushed out to the studio late that Friday afternoon and met the direc-

Vincent Price and the rest of us in the first scene we filmed for Master of the World, *1961.* (AIP)

tor. William Witney told me that Vincent had said good things about me and that he had been impressed with my performance in *Return of the Fly.* After we chatted, he said, "Go to wardrobe and we'll have a script ready for you when you're finished."

I was to be in the first shot on Monday morning, so I hardly had time to feel excited about working in a second movie with Vincent Price. As I was fitted for the Victorian costumes, I knew that I would have fun just from looking at the period costume pieces. *Master of the World* was a color film with a three-week shooting schedule, which meant that the production was of a higher quality than *Return of the Fly.* The film seemed like a good career move, and working on it would prove to be a delight from the start to finish.

Maurine correctly observed that just as Mark Damon had AIP over a barrel, I, too, was in a position of advantage. She managed to get a two-picture deal from the studio, which meant that I would be working there again on another film after our production ended. The deal was a "pay or play" arrangement. AIP had to put me into another film by December of the following year or pay my fee.

I learned my lines over the weekend and arrived on location for work on Monday morning. According to my 1960s appointments book, we

The crane in the background hoisted us to film the conclusion of Master of the World, *1961.* (AIP)

started *Master of the World* on September 7, 1960 in 110-degree temperatures on the back lot of the old Republic Studios in the San Fernando
Valley. The entire shoot was so hot that the moment we finished a scene,
the studio doors were flung open so everyone could run outside to sit and
wait for the next shot to be set up. Our authentically woolen Victorian
costumes turned out to be less fun in the heat than I had imagined!

Henry Hull, Mary Webster, Charles Bronson, and I between takes on Master
of the World.

On our first day of shooting, we filmed the scene where the primary
protagonists are unconscious in a crater with Vincent standing over us
with his cape, the symbolic "Master of the World." After we filmed that
scene, we were driven up the coast to an ocean area called Leo Carrillo
State Park to film the ending of the picture. So, we shot the film's beginning in the morning and the ending in the afternoon. We all walked into
the sunset, and I walked off with Henry Hull. That would be the only
time we were out of the studio.

As we shot the film's conclusion out of sequence, our characters had
to shimmy down a rope from the airship to the safety of a beach. A crane
hoisted us to provide the illusion of the air ship's height, and we actually
had to move seventy feet down the rope. There were no stunt men, so
Charles Bronson and I both had to do our own stunts on that scene.

Once again, I was playing a good character part I had to be defiant,
because my character had a jealous, mean streak; at one point he actually

starts to stab Charles Bronson in the back. Maybe those backhanded qualities had prompted Vincent to say, "Try David Frankham — he's done that
kind of thing to me before onscreen!" Unlike Mark Damon, I didn't mind in
the least losing the girl. I thought the part was challenging and interesting.

Richard Matheson is still legendary for his quality writing on science
fiction and fantasy productions during an era where many rotten or low-

Henry Hull, left, led community singing on the set.

budget projects gave the rest of the genre a bad name. Matheson wrote a
good script for our movie, and the actors owed him for that. Without a
good script, actors will always be in big trouble. Unlike some productions
where the writers are banished from the set, we saw Matheson from time
to time. He and I were the same age, with me being just six days younger.

In spite of how I came to the picture at late notice, there remarkably
was no more panic. We were just getting the work done without fuss over
our three weeks of shooting. A film's director — and its lead — sets the
mood on any picture. On a Vincent Price movie, everything was jolly and
happy. We were actually so relaxed, that I look back at the movie as my
favorite of the three films I filmed with Vincent.

In fact, we were so relaxed that we engaged in community singing
on the set. All the cast and crew sat around and sang with Henry Hull
whenever we weren't in front of the camera. Hull would start singing old

songs like "East Side, West Side, all around the town," and "Daisy, Daisy, give me your answer do …" wonderful old sing-along songs. Hull was an old character actor from the 1930s. I had enjoyed him as the werewolf in *Werewolf of London*. I think he was a much underrated actor. With years of excellent work in so many movies, he was an absolute delight.

I didn't know Mary Webster, but when we started working, I liked her

Henry Hull, myself, Charles Bronson, and Mary Webster.

very much, because she was feisty and fun. Mary and our other co-star, Charles Bronson, both went to the Pasadena Playhouse for training. Some nights after we finished filming, we went off to the Tahitian Room, a restaurant across the street. Everyone but Charles enjoyed drinks together. Charles was very shy and private. One time Vincent said to me, "That guy baffles me!"

I didn't share Vincent's opinion, though. I don't think he understood that Charles was shy or private because he had started as a coal miner and had yet to become a star. One of nineteen children, he started getting small parts. We could see his potential to become a great star. He, too, had worked with Vincent before, playing his assistant in that wonderful 3-D horror film, *House of Wax*, and had come a long way in five years.

Bronson may have been a man of few words, but he possessed great strength as a person and as the character he put onto film. No matter how much acting I did in a scene, when he walked onto the set, I knew that any scene we shared meant that I could just forget it. Perhaps that's why Mark Damon decided to decline the role that passed to me. I felt as though I was there for window dressing, because all eyes went to

Charles Bronson told me that he preferred contemporary scripts over period pieces.

Charles Bronson. I simply knew he was going places.

Yet he didn't enjoy doing *Master of the World.* He said, "I'm not comfortable in this kind of Victorian set-up." He was a very contemporary actor and had a close friendship with Steve McQueen, who was on the next soundstage filming *Wanted Dead or Alive.* The moment our director said, "Cut," Charles was off to visit his friend. When the rest of us lunched together, we always knew he was off lunching with Steve McQueen. He had to do our film to finish his contract with American International and go on to bigger and better things elsewhere.

Vito Scotti played our cook in the movie. He was a very funny man. William Witney liked his work so much that he built up a slapstick scene for Scotti in his cook's galley. His antics took a whole morning to shoot while the rest of us stood by enjoying the fun. Richard Harrison, who played

Charles Bronson and I did our own stunts hanging from ropes in front of a blue screen.

the shirtless muscled steersman showing off his physique, caught the eye of the daughter of the studio boss, married her, and moved to Italy, where he did a couple of American International's sword and sandals minor epics. The movie set was as impressive as the actors. The actual airship's set piece was built up on giant rollers. Crew members moved it about like a see-saw to simulate motion during takes. Like my boat scene in Disney's

Vincent Price, still in bloody costume bandages, with Henry Hull, our publicity rep Hilda Black, and I at lunch.

Ten Who Dared, we filmed many of our aerial scenes above the stage in front of a blue screen. It was amazing that none of us fell on our heads three feet off the ground, including the big climatic scene where I had to attack Charles Bronson as we both dangled from ropes. We did some of our own stunts as permitted, but thankfully Bronson and I didn't harm each other. For such serious subject matter, our director and Vincent Price kept everyone jolly and happy on the set.

Because we were shooting at the old Republic studio, quite a few television productions were also being shot at the same time as our movie. One day Vincent was talking about making *The Three Musketeers* with Gene Kelly and June Allyson.

I told him, "I love June Allyson! She's wonderful and turns me to water, she's just so marvelous and cute."

She was shooting *The June Allyson Show* on the lot, so I mentioned to Vincent, "I think she's here. Do you like her?"

"Oh, yes," he told me. "We got along famously."

A few days later as we enjoyed a twenty-minute morning break, Vincent said, "David, we need to do some publicity shots over on this other set." I followed him, and when we got to the set, a sign read *"The*

Mary Webster and I were frequently in stitches whenever Vincent Price made us laugh.

June Allyson Show" on the outside. I thought the show wasn't filming that day and that we would use the set to take our publicity shots.

We walked in and Vincent yelled, "Junie!" as he embraced her. Her guest star that week was Van Johnson, with whom she had made several films. Vincent, who just loved to play tricks, told June, "This is my friend, David Frankham, and he's absolutely nuts about you. Don't ask me why. David, you've got ten minutes," and then he walked off, leaving me to stand there with June Allyson!

Thank God this movie star was so cute in person. I can't even remember what we talked about, but in my excitement, we managed to fumble through a conversation. Vincent had planned the whole thing and just wanted to see the expression on my face when he introduced the two of us.

Just as I had found the previous year on *Return for the Fly*, Vincent's sense of humor carried over to *Master of the World*. In one scene, Vincent wears blood-stained bandages on his head and down his back. After we finished filming, off we went across the street to the Tahitian Room for lunch. Vincent stopped traffic as we crossed Ventura Boulevard. We could tell that motorists recognized Vincent with his bloody bandages. He loved the whole spectacle of it.

There is a scene where we're walking into the airship. I'm not proud of my work in that scene, because it was unprofessional. Vincent told Mary Webster and me a very funny joke as we prepared to shoot film for the scene where his character showed us the various workings of the ship. He told the joke, the three of us laughed and suddenly William Witney said, "Action!" In the final scene, you can actually see Mary and me smiling as we come into view, but our characters were supposed to be terrified of being kidnapped aboard the great airship. That little goof was Vincent's doing. The editors somehow passed it through while looking at the rushes. I marvel that nobody said, "Why are those two idiots laughing so much on camera?" I suppose it was all right, but I can see us breaking up every time I watch the film.

One of my favorite scenes came when my character walked away from his group and confronted the captain's villainy with "You're not frightening me, sir!" I had few moments of asserting myself like that, so I enjoyed such an interesting part.

The gossip columnist Sheila Graham came out one day to interview Vincent. She was rather grand and condescending to the rest of us, quite rightly, because she had driven out to interview Vincent. He insisted on introducing the rest of us to her, however, although Bronson wouldn't talk to her. I was only too willing to talk. In fact, because Charles Bronson was so shy, I got a lot of press coverage whenever he didn't want to participate in the movie's promotion. He would tell the interviewer, "Oh, just ask Dave," because he simply refused to talk about himself.

One day Mary Webster and I posed for a publicity shot as we drank Coca-Cola. I think we made more money from Coke than we did on the movie! We were backstage near our dressing rooms and someone told us to hold a few Cokes for the ad. Both Coca-Cola and our movie got some mileage from the ad, and our names were credited, so that was fun to do.

My work on the movie even brought me an award. A movie publication announced that I was chosen "Promising Newcomer of 1960," along with beautiful Leslie Parrish from *L'il Abner*. We were presented at the Coconut Grove to Joan Crawford, who handed each of us a scroll with our names engraved. She scared us both to death, so imposing, but she was an

enormous star. We felt about two inches tall next to her. She signed our
scrolls as a souvenir. She pushed in a cart with vodka and said, "Okay kids,
we've earned this!" I really loved her so much for being down to earth!

AIP also utilized me to promote the movie as part of its publicity
campaign. While I wasn't as shy as Charles Bronson, I soon found that I
wasn't that good in massive social settings. The studio had moved to new

Normally publicity-shy Charles Bronson gets the best of me in this publicity shot.

offices on the Sunset Strip. They asked Vincent and Charles to promote the movie and the studio's new location, but both of them declined, citing other obligations. Maurine insisted that I could benefit from the publicity and told me to work the room.

I'm not sure why Mary Webster wasn't there, so it turned out that I was the only actor from *Master of the World* at this big publicity event. I

Mary Webster and I enjoy a Coke and a smile.

had to shake a thousand hands and be "on" at all times. I very quickly grew tired in social situations and found myself drained. James Nicholson, the head of the studio, was there, so I couldn't sneak out from the event. Being there was part of my job to represent the movie. As a contract player for the studio, I found out what royalty must feel, worrying about what to wear and how I looked.

I'm not sure which book I was supposed to be reading in this publicity photo.

My date was Patricia Fitzgerald, a tenacious press agent who eventually opened her own offices. She was so driven that she loved this affair. The whole thing was like meat and potatoes to her, and she stayed at my side the whole time to keep me smiling and going as we greeted the public. I don't know that I shook one thousand hands, but it felt like it.

It was a wonderful sense of security to have a contract that outlines another picture lined up for me. I had begun to think, "Gee, maybe I won't have to do television anymore," because back in the 1960s, there was still a dividing line. I always sensed that some people felt that actors who worked in movies existed somehow in a more rarified atmosphere than those who "just" worked in television. People sometimes said to television actors, "Oh, you mean you're not in pictures? You're not in movies? You're just in television?" That conversation sometimes even happened actor to actor.

When I finally got into the movies, I was very proud, given that snob-bery about only working in television. By the middle of the *Master of the World*, I started thinking, "I'm going to hate to end this movie."There were other television offers ahead of me, and I was feeling my oats. After all, over the course of one year, I had acted on camera in three films.

I remember saying to Vincent, "Do you think I should just hold off

Mary Webster and I with producer and AIP co-founder James Nicholson.

and wait for another movie rather than do television?"

He looked at me as though I was a blithering idiot. He said, "You do what I do. I did it when I started; I'll do it until the day I die. You do everything you are offered. Why on earth would you deprive yourself from the experience of working in different shows and television?"

He explained that he was involved as a spokesman in the Sears Art Program for that reason. An art lover and expert, he was paid by Sears to discover art and promote affordable prints to the public. Vincent said, "I even do commercials because I get paid well for them. What's so god-damned special about just being in movies?"

I said, "I don't know. I'm just asking."

Vincent told me, "Whatever comes up, if it's worthwhile, if the part is good and the money is good — those are practical considerations — then do it. You do everything!"

And so I did. In fact, his sage advice is one reason I branched out into the lucrative world of commercials just a few years later. Because he gave me such good advice, Vincent truly was like an older brother to me. He was to all actors. He loved the whole business of being in show business. He encouraged everybody who cared as deeply about it as he did. He was very special.

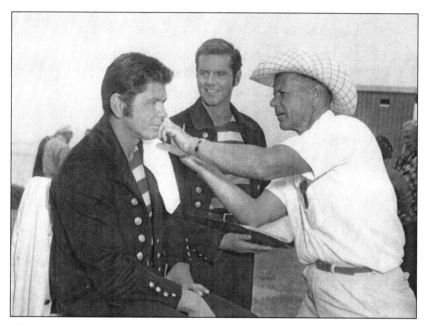

Watching Charles Bronson in make-up.

When we were filming *Master of the World*, Vincent overheard me telling Mary Webster that I was about to move into a one bedroom, one bathroom, one kitchen, little house. Because I was gaining more space than my apartment, the house would be underfurnished for a while. I told her that I planned to spend the weekend going around town to pick out some furniture.

On Saturday morning, the phone rang. It was Vincent. He said, "I understand you need some furniture. If you're free, come on out. We have a huge basement with furniture hanging up on hooks that we'll never use. You're welcome to it. When can you get here?"

I said, "Well, I can take a taxi."

"You don't drive?" he growled.

"Not yet, I don't," I told him.

"Okay," he sighed. "I'll come and get you. Where do you live?"

Vincent promptly collected me in his enormous station wagon and took me over to his huge mansion near Beverly Glen and Sunset Boulevard in Beverly Hills. His then wife, Mary Grant, wasn't there that morning, so Vincent said, "Come on, kid."

He led me down into his spacious cellar, crammed with wicker furniture. He insisted that I select whatever I needed as a gift. He acted as

James Nicholson and I with a visitor from the French consulate.

though he might be impatient with me to mask his good deed. Looking at his watch, he said, "Let's get this over with!"

Vincent's put-on gruffness was his way of helping me but preventing me from fawning over him with gratitude. He didn't like being thanked and immediately switched into his curmudgeonly mode if anyone got too profusely thankful. It was hard not to do because we wound up making three trips for furniture — a fold-up table, wicker chairs, other chairs for the living room, a little table for the kitchen, a little cupboard for the bathroom — he furnished my entire house in three trips!

When we finished, I said, "I really do appreciate this." He interrupted and said, "Okay, kid, see you Monday!" We never mentioned it again, and I knew that he would not want me walking up on the set and thanking him for the furniture. What a man. I enjoyed one of his pieces of furniture for years until it finally fell apart. He also gave me a painting by a student of

Monet's. I still hang it wherever I live, and it's always the center of attention when people stop by. I think of him each time I walk by and see that painting. That's why he was one of the most admired and loved actors in Hollywood.

After three weeks, we wrapped production. I eagerly awaited the first screening of *Master of the World*. The first time I watched the film, I nearly had a stroke when I saw myself blinking continuously in a confrontation

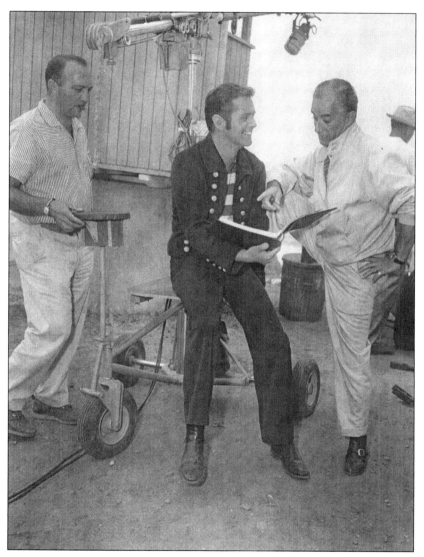

Going over my script.

scene early with Henry Hull. I just stood there and blinked in widescreen! Nobody told me, because I guess the director figured I was playing a nerdish character and nerds must blink a lot.

Greer Garson had once warned me about blinking too much. It was one thing to blink on live television, especially in a production that would air once and not come back to haunt you in reruns. Blinking on the big

Mary Webster, Vincent Price and I visit with composer Les Baxter.

screen, larger than life, taught me a lesson. I couldn't necessarily count on the director or producers to clean up such nuances that I failed to control. Believe me, I didn't blink again in a production after I realized that I did have a tendency to blink when I was disturbed. I also didn't notice that I was clenching my fists, but it's too late now!

Otherwise, I enjoyed the movie very much. AIP's staff composer, Les Baxter, did a fine score. I later had the soundtrack transferred from LP to CD so I could enjoy listening to it frequently. A few years ago, Intrada released a limited edition CD version with a few more cuts than the LP originally contained; the CD was so popular that it sold out almost immediately.

Baxter had his own career going with his orchestra in the 1940s and 1950s before becoming the in-house composer for American

ABOVE: *Charles Bronson, Henry Hull, and I in* Master of the World. BELOW: *I'm about to attack Charles Bronson.*

International. He was right up there with Nelson Riddle with huge hits. I met him a couple of times on the set and enjoyed talking about his music. He recorded big hits, including "Wake the Town and Tell the People," and he had been a member of Mel Torme's Mel Tones group, a really excellent sound that they worked out between them.

Although the movie wasn't an epic film by Hollywood standards, for its

This publicity photo of Mary Webster and me appeared on sheet music from the film's title song.

budget, it gave its money's worth. AIP spent more than usual, and the money showed on the screen as an overall good production. The film was popular enough, and our goal had been to set out to entertain. You can't really ask more of a film than that, provided that it does it fully, and I think it did.

In fact, with a pacifist antihero, albeit twisted by using violence to end violence, the film was ahead of its time with that specific message. By the end of the 1960s, that theme was more commonplace with young people. *Master of the World* also is a great adventure film. For all his fretting about appearing in a period piece, the film certainly didn't hurt Charles Bronson's career. His stature only grew as he became one of the *Dirty Dozen* and then the star of his *Death Wish* pictures.

The movie later acquired a bit of cult classic status. There was a novelization and comic book adaptation. In the 1970s, a Super 8mm digest version was released with some of the film's more exciting action sequences. MGM owns the rights to the film now, so it shows up from time to time on Turner Classic Movies (TCM).

Mary Webster and I didn't see each other again until May 2012, but we've stayed in touch and enjoyed speaking with one another by telephone through the years. A few years ago, the movie aired on TCM,

Mary Webster and I had fun making Master of the World.

and the next morning Mary and I talked about our mutual experience of watching the film again. Mary agrees that the cast did a fine job, and as actors, we're pretty pleased with our performances whenever we see the movie.

When we talked, I said to Mary, "Why doesn't MGM contact us for commentary for a DVD?" She's open to the idea as well. Let's hope that

Costume portrait from Master of the World.

the movie gets an official Blu-Ray release someday. I'll treasure a copy just to relive the happy times we all had making the movie.

America got a new president in 1961 as JFK ushered in a new era. I got my second wind, working more than ever, almost non-stop in television and movies that year. Maurine's

effort of introducing me to casting agents and getting me into good movie and TV roles really paid off. I also used the metaphysical teachings I learned at church with Eve Arden and Glynis Johns to muster the confidence and self-belief in my abilities to win roles.

I heeded Vincent Price's advice from the previous fall when we worked on *Master of the World*. "Do everything," he told me, and 1961 proved to be the embodiment of that philosophy. I worked in nearly a dozen projects, more television work than ever, and even went back to MGM for dubbing on

Boris Karloff in a Thriller *publicity photo.*

some major motion pictures.

Shortly before the start of that new year, I filmed my first episode of *Thriller*, "The Poisoner," and it aired January 10, 1961. *Thriller* was an anthology series in *The Twilight Zone* vein. William Frye was the producer. He seemed to like my work the way the producers and casting directors had five years earlier at NBC's *Matinee Theater*. In fact, I filmed four episodes of *Thriller* over a year and a half. Some episodes were set in contemporary times, while others were staged as period pieces, all with plots involving suspense or horror.

The hook that got the public watching was to hire Boris Karloff to introduce each episode. Having Karloff host the shows was kind of a con job, because audiences sometimes tuned in expecting to see the star of *Frankenstein* act in the shows, but he really did nothing more than introduce each episode. Whenever there was a cops-and-robbers modern plot, it almost seemed incongruous to have Karloff introduce such fare.

By then Karloff was a retired country squire living in England. Universal flew him out to Los Angeles to film three or four introductions once a month after three or four episodes were in the can. He filmed his introductions over a day's work and then flew back home to England.

One highlight of working on *Thriller* was the fact that Karloff always mentioned the cast as part of his introduction. He spoke with a slight lisp, so I delighted in tuning in to hear him read my name whenever I appeared in a featured part. "... And Mr. Dahvidth Franktham," he would say. It was a personal thriller to hear him lisping my name!

My first *Thriller* episode was directed by Herschel Daughterty, who directed more than a dozen of the *Thriller* episodes. "The Poisoner" episode starred Murray Matheson as a man poisoning those around him, along with Sarah Marshall, Herbert Marshall's daughter, and Jennifer Raine.

Only in 1961 could an actor go from having Boris Karloff read your name to Shirley Temple doing the same thing, all in the same month! Airing January 29, 1961, I appeared in an episode of *Shirley Temple's Storybook Theatre* titled "The Terrible Clockman."

Shirley Temple's program was largely regarded as a children's show, but one thing I've learned about my work on her series was just how much of a profound impression the program made on grown-ups who watched as children. The series was one of the first to be broadcast in color, and NBC's production values incorporated colorful costumes and detailed sets. With superior production values, great storylines and her own fame and reputation, Shirley attracted top-named talent to guest star in adaptations of fairy tales and morality plays each week.

Shirley herself was unpretentious and giggly. America's little sweetheart had grown up and married, and her two pre-teen children came to the studio when school finished at three p.m. each day of rehearsal all week long. They sat and watched their mother work and laughed with her when she wasn't working. If you didn't look when Shirley laughed, you could just hear famous little Shirley laughing. It was just uncanny how her laugh seemed to bring back little *Curly Top* again from the 1930s. She was delightful, and there was a nice, warm family feeling about the whole show. I told her one day that we had been trained by the same vocal coach, Robert Graham Paris.

I played opposite Shirley as her betrothed. She and I both loved Sam Jaffe, who was cast as her father and my prospective father-in-law. I can still see his wife, Bettye Ackerman, tending lovingly to him every evening when she stopped at the rehearsal hall to take him home. She brought him there in the morning, too. She was always there when we went over to a restaurant opposite NBC. Over dinner or drinks, Jaffe was generous with many anecdotes about working in Hollywood.

Bettye was thirty years younger than Sam, and their devotion was palpable. She loved listening as much as I did to his wonderful stories about working on *Ben-Hur, Gunga Din* and *Lost Horizon*. What a marvelous career he had. I think part of the fact that he was such a lovely man to know was his basic happiness with his wife. He was just totally at peace with himself.

English actor Eric Portman played the villain without any condescension to what was essentially a children's fantasy. Portman had started in Shakespeare back in the 1920s. By the 1940s, he was one of Britain's top money-making film stars. I had interviewed him back in London. He told me how exciting it had been to tour America in the stage production of *Separate Tables*.

Portman was a brilliant actor but sort of a sad man. I liked that he wasn't being condescending playing on Shirley Temple's show, which might have been easy for a distinguished British actor to feel, but he didn't. He took it as seriously as an actor should. We had little talks about many things. He told me that he had taken in a young Laurence Harvey when the fledgling actor arrived in London from Lithuania, only to have Harvey leave the home they shared to move in with Hermione Baddeley. "Larry broke my heart," he told me sadly. He seemed like a desperately lonely man to me.

Publicity photo of Shirley Temple for her Storybook Theatre *show.*

When I was fitted for my wardrobe for Shirley Temple's program, I decided to channel Dirk Bogarde. I had seen photos of him with his hands always in the pockets of his riding britches, so I copied the look. Later I told him that I had employed his technique, and he wrote back: "We all borrow from each other at times; at least you took from an expert!"

I had to wear bright yellow tights, something guaranteed to make one self-conscious in living color on NBC. My comfort level was considerably aided and abetted by Michael Wilding's jockstrap, which he used when he filmed *The Glass Slipper* with Leslie Caron. Thank God he had saved it and suggested using it when I hadn't a clue what to wear underneath the tights. (I still have it, but I doubt there'll be any call to put it to professional use again!)

One day we had a little disruption on the set. Some of the actors who played townspeople had a few lines, but one of them just kept cutting up and not being in character. The director, Allen Reisner, said to him, "Look — if you keep this up, we're just going to replace you. Calm down!" When someone had to shout that across the set to an actor, it made the rest of us just freeze and think that this poor guy might never work again. We needn't have feared, though, because he was John Astin, who went onto fame in *The Addams Family* and enjoyed a long acting career.

I managed to lose a little money when one of the other actors in the cast told me that he was short of funds. I was taken in by his story of how his yellow Thunderbird would be repossessed if he didn't come up with money. I gullibly asked him if I might be of help. When he asked to borrow $500, I gave it to him. We drove to my bank, I got the money, gave it to him, and he drove away as I caught the bus home.

My naiveté was on full display after we received our paychecks. A little time went by without hearing from him, so I called him. He denied that I had ever loaned him the money! A lawyer told me I needed some kind of proof. Because I had given him cash, I had no proof. The moral of that story is neither a borrower nor lender be, or if you do, get the deal in writing and have it notarized or witnessed!

A year later I was up for an excellent role in a TV series at MGM. I walked in to read for Allen Reisner, with whom I had worked on Shirley Temple's show. Thinking it would bolster my chances if I let the producer know that I had already worked with the director, I enthusiastically said, "Allen and I did the *Shirley Temple Show* last year!" Reisner glared daggers at me. He obviously didn't want it known that he had done anything so "frivolous," so I didn't get the part. Our Shirley Temple work was released onto DVD a few years ago. I hold fond memories of working on the show, aside from the loan incident.

A month after working with Shirley Temple, I was over at Warner Bros. to do an episode of *Surfside 6*. Warner Bros. was prolific in its output during the early 1960s. The studio filled television with a number of series that featured jazzy theme songs and hip characters in exotic settings. *Surfside 6's* adventures centered around three handsome private detectives who worked from a houseboat in Miami and lived the good life the rest of the time.

Our episode, "Black Orange Blossoms," aired February 20, 1961. The episode allowed me to play a villain intent on killing his brother in order

Troy Donahue, Lee Patterson, and Van Williams, stars of Surfside 6.

to steal his wife and inheritance on a plantation in Haiti. Part of the plot involved my character staging a murder by placing a poisonous snake in a bed.

I became something of a real villain to the crew. Kathleen Crowley, another of the guest stars, was a method actress who asked me to slap her for real in one scene. She told me not to fake it, so when we did the scene, I smacked her. The crew thought I was a total jerk and didn't speak to me the following day. I finally had to ask her to let everyone know that she had requested me to smack her for realism. She did, but I think she got upset at me for setting everyone straight!

Troy Donahue, one of the three primary leads, shook all the way through *Surfside 6.* I finally asked him if he was okay, and he said, "Just exhausted, man — these bastards don't give us a day off, ever." I think he was doing *A Summer Place* about the same time. There was always chatter in the press and the industry that he was no great shakes as an actor and got by on his looks. That undertow to his career no doubt added to his stress.

Three other English natives with whom I enjoyed working on this episode were Alan Caillou, Lester Matthews, and Jack Livesey. Jack had a disability and limped quite noticeably. I remember admiring his determination not to let it slow him down. He died suddenly from an aneurysm later that year, not too long after we worked together again on an episode of *Alfred Hitchcock Presents.*

Our director on *Surfside 6* was Robert Sinclair. Everyone really liked him because he favored close-ups of actors, and actors always enjoyed seeing "CU" for "close-up" in the script! Sinclair was married to the English-born actress Heather Angel and guest directed many episodes of Warner's television programs. Sadly, he died too soon when he was killed in 1970 as he defended his wife from a burglar who had broken into their home.

From *Surfside 6,* I went to MGM to shoot an episode of *The Best of the Post* called "Brief Enchantment," which aired March 4, 1961. The show was a syndicated anthology series that adapted stories published in the popular *Saturday Evening Post* magazine.

My friend Doris Lloyd worked on this episode with me, one of the several times we were paired together on screen. Seeing Doris was almost reward in itself for working. She was keeping as busy as ever, having played Mrs. Watchett the year before in *The Time Machine* for George Pal.

Our director was Don Taylor, who had started as an actor in *Winged Victory* and *The Naked City* and played Elizabeth Taylor's husband in *Father of the Bride.* He had become one of TV's in-demand directors. When one of our scenes called for me to drive a sports car up a gravel driveway to a beautiful columned house exterior, I still hadn't learned to drive that well, in spite of my near disastrous on-camera driving during *Return of the Fly* two years earlier.

As I fiddled with the gears, I ended up driving all over MGM's carefully manicured lawns and flower beds instead of the driveway. After my several attempts and nearly ruining the lawn, Taylor practically pulled out his hair and said, "Let's not fight City Hall." He ordered the car attached to a cable that slowly pulled me in neutral to fake the appearance of driving. Talk about humiliation! I was supposed to be playing a dashing Englishman, but there I was, in a sports car and being pulled on a rope. Luckily for me, I didn't have to drive that often on camera during those days.

The next month took me to NBC for an April 3, 1961 episode of *Tales of Wells Fargo* called "The Remittance Man." The popular western starred

Dale Robertson as a troubleshooter for the Wells Fargo company. The only other TV westerns I had done were *Death Valley Days* and *Maverick*. Being English, I thought, "Well, there's not much call for English types on westerns," but the writers had written an Englishman into the episode, so that happily meant work for me.

I didn't even read or audition for the show, which meant that someone had asked for me. I wondered how I got the part, so when I walked onto the set, there was William Witney, my director from *Master of the World* just a few months prior! Witney had thought of me when he read the script and said, "I just worked with this English actor, David Frankham. Let's get him for this part."

Seeing and working with him again made me appreciate the great feeling actors get whenever a director thinks of us for a role. Witney had directed a lot of westerns and specialized in them, really, going all the way back to the early movie serials, including *Zorro* for Republic and a number of *Zorro* TV episodes for Disney. If my memory is correct, his son also worked on *Tales of Wells Fargo* as well while I was there.

The other guests were Yvonne Craig, who later became famous as Batgirl on *Batman*, as well as Ron Soble. A college football player and Golden Gloves champion boxer, Soble played a villain with whom I had an extended fight scene, which we rehearsed thoroughly. On one of the takes, I hit the poor guy right in the stomach by mistake, but Witney went right on filming. Years later I saw Soble coming out of the supermarket. He reminded me that I had punched him in the stomach and said that he was still having trouble from it. I apologized again and vowed that I would leave the dangerous stunts to stuntmen.

My steady work continued throughout the spring of 1961. Next it was over to Fox, the first time I worked there since my falling out with a studio casting director after *Return of the Fly*. When he transferred to Paris, I started working at the studio again, this time for an April 24, 1961 episode of *Adventures in Paradise* titled "A Penny a Day." The program starred Gardner McKay as the captain of a boat that sailed the South Pacific on adventures.

Water scenes were shot around the Fox lake. I had roamed around the area two years earlier during *Return of the Fly*. Because the show was set on a ship, in the backgrounds on the set were long pieces of aluminum foil. Stagehands stood out of frame to move these pieces about to replicate water. They looked exactly like waves, simply an amazing effect!

One of the other guests was the Academy Award-winning actor Thomas Mitchell, who had famously played Scarlett O'Hara's father in

1939. Mitchell had just returned from a 1961 revival of *Gone with the Wind* in Atlanta. I couldn't believe I was spending a whole week with the star of what was the highest-grossing movie of all time!

When I mentioned *Gone with the Wind* to him in wardrobe, he told me about his Atlanta trip. He was a very quiet man who almost downplayed his fame and made other actors bend in to listen to his low voice. Not only did I fulfill my ambition of becoming a jobbing actor, but working in those days introduced me to performers who were genuinely part of film history. What a treat for a film buff like me as I listened to Mitchell talk about his career. In addition to playing Gerald O'Hara, he appeared in some of the cinema's all-time great films: *Lost Horizon, Stagecoach, The Hunchback of Notre Dame, Mr. Smith Goes to Washington, It's a Wonderful Life,* and *High Noon*. He only worked a few times after our show together and died the following year of cancer.

My romantic pairing on *Adventures in Paradise* was with Fintan Meyler, a dark-haired beauty from Ireland. Estelle Winwood was also guest-starring, but she didn't seem to remember me from working together at the Pasadena Playhouse. By then, she was nearly eighty, although she continued to act until she was close to age one hundred, and she lived to 102! Others in our cast included Reginald Denny and Tom Conway. Conway was married to Queenie Leonard. Conway had a drinking problem, and I remember his wife hovering nearby and attending to him, almost as though she had to keep an eye on him during production.

Working on *Adventures of Paradise* was one of my more enjoyable guest-starring television roles. Gardner McKay was a ruggedly handsome actor whose leading man looks were envied by the rest of us. My character was put into glasses for our episode. At age thirty-five and with already boyish looks, I think the effect somehow made me look even younger. When I watched the episode on video a few years ago, my vanity got the best of me because I thought I looked rather cute! Actors tend to know when they look their best, so I think *Adventures in Paradise* and Gardner McKay succeeded in making us all look great.

As the 1960-1961 television season came to an end, I did one more episode of *Thriller*. Called "The Prisoner in the Mirror," the episode aired May 23, 1961. Herschel Daugherty directed me for the second time on the series. I played an artist who, upon being driven mad, commits suicide by leaping through glass.

Others in the cast included Lloyd Bochner, Marion Ross, and Frieda Inescort, who played my mother. I really liked working with Frieda. Born in Edinburgh, she had found success on Broadway and then in a number of Warner Bros. movies back in the 1930s. Sadly, our episode together was one of the last times she worked. She had started to experience dizzy spells. After the doctors diagnosed multiple sclerosis, Frieda quickly became incapacitated to the point that she could no longer work.

After months of working non-stop, I auditioned for a few movies during the summer of 1961. That summer marks the only time I ever really had a bad audition, and that was for horror director William Castle when he was making *Homicidal.* Maurine accompanied me on the audition.

Castle asked me, "How old are you?"

I said, "Thirty-five," and Maurine said, "Twenty-five" at the same time!

"Look," Castle said. "You two had better make up your minds!" I didn't get the part. Because Maurine sensed I was a little nervous next to her, she didn't accompany me on too many auditions after that.

I added two more feature films to my list of dubbing credits that year. Because I had dubbed on *Ben-Hur,* I had little trouble getting hired to dub for another epic, Samuel Bronston's *King of Kings.* Margaret Booth, MGM's legendary editor, actually sent for me. The good rapport we had enjoyed on *Ben-Hur* paid off when she thought of me.

After *Ben-Hur* and *The Ten Commandments* had been critical and box office hits, the story of Jesus was adapted in an effort to produce another success in *King of Kings.* Directed by Nicholas Ray, the picture required extensive dubbing, just as *Ben-Hur* had, to remove some of the heavier accents. A number of performers had their entire vocal performances re-dubbed. In fact, Jeffrey Hunter had to post-dub his part of Jesus; Agnes Moorehead helped coach his dialogue.

Nicholas Ray, who had famously directed James Dean in *Rebel Without a Cause,* personally directed me as I dubbed the roles of a Roman soldier and a couple of men during the Sermon on the Mount scene. "If you can do miracles, call upon God to send hosts to destroy the Romans and free our people from bondage" and "Teach us to pray" were among my lines shouted by the characters on the hillside to Jesus. I found that as a director, Ray was very pleasant as long as I did my job well.

I was there one day when Jeffrey Hunter came in to dub his work as Jesus. What a sight! With a crew cut and blue jeans, it was so funny to see "Jesus" standing beside me dubbing his Sermon on the Mount dialogue, looking as though he had just come off the football field. In fact, some of the critics derided Hunter's casting as "I Was a Teen-Age Jesus" in their reviews.

MGM had more or less watered down the story in order to adapt the life of Jesus for *King of Kings*. The film was plagued with script problems, although it was nice to know that I had recorded my parts in the same booth as the movie's narrator, Orson Welles. Perhaps the best thing about the movie was the music. Composer Miklos Rozsa had also scored *Ben-Hur* and other epics, including *Quo Vadis* and *El Cid*.

I dubbed a number of voices in this scene shown on this lobby card from King of Kings, *MGM, 1961.*

Although *King of Kings* wasn't a big box office or critical hit, Rozsa's music has stood the test of time, and today the movie typically shows up at Easter on TCM.

Working at the request of Margaret Booth led me to another dubbing project for MGM. Margaret directly called Maurine and said, "We're dubbing on *The 4 Horsemen of the Apocalypse* — is David free?" Seeing Margaret again made me feel good because I had earned a reputation as a reliable dubber.

I became immensely excited with the project when I learned that I was to be directed personally by Vincente Minnelli. Not only did I love musicals, but I really loved his — *The Pirate, Meet Me in St. Louis, The Band Wagon, An American in Paris* — I worshipped the man's work. Working

with Minnelli was even better than working with William Wyler on
Ben-Hur. In Minnelli came to the recording studio, a bundle of nerves.
He was so full of imagination that energy came pouring out of him. He
couldn't get the words out fast enough, so the result was a bit of stuttering when he talked.

Some of the European actors in *The 4 Horsemen of the Apocalypse* had
delivered thick accents that needed dubbing for American audiences. One
of the principals spoke with a strong French accent, so Minnelli wanted
him to sound less French. I hadn't done a French accent before, so I went
to work on a "slight" French dubbing voice as Minnelli started throwing
up scenes on the screen in front of me.

For several days Minnelli stood in front of me as we worked. William
Wyler's method had been to get me going, but then he stood at one side
so there was only me looking up at the screen as I dubbed. Minnelli,
however, stood right in front of me — almost conducting me. I thought,
"This is how he must have worked with Judy Garland!"

There was nobody left dubbing but me by the third day. What I didn't
know was that on days when the rest of us weren't dubbing, Angela
Lansbury was coming in to dub Ingrid Thulin's entire performance in
the movie. Like me, she received no credit, and her dubbing work wasn't
publicized originally. Because Thulin's Swedish accent was so strong, her
voice had to go. (When I visited Angela at her home in June 2010, we
talked a little about the film. Angela told me she was paid a pretty penny
to dub on that one.)

When I finished my third day's work, Minnelli placed three script-
sized pages in front of me.

"I want you to try this dialogue," he said. "It's like at the beginning of
An American in Paris — did you see it?"

Of course I had seen it — twenty times, I told him! That pleased
Minnelli as he explained that he had Gene Kelly do a voiceover right after
the title credits as the camera panned around Paris in that film.

"This is almost a similar opening for *4 Horsemen*," Minnelli told me. "I
actually just wrote this dialogue this morning, so I just want to see how
it sounds. Can you read this for me in a slight French accent?"

I was really nervous about attempting those French accents because if
they're bad, it's a terrible effect. I remember thinking, "But there are lots
of French actors in Hollywood. Why me?"

One didn't say no to Vincente Minnelli, though, so I took his pages of
dialogue and prepared for a cold reading. I think I showed off a little for
him, because as a news reader back at the BBC, I was used to someone

coming in with a bulletin while we were on the air and slipping another page underneath the ones I had already looked at before starting. If a page came up that I had not seen before, I was usually able to breeze right through it. You can either do cold readings or you can't, and I could do cold readings.

As we prepared to record, Minnelli asked, "Do you want to look through this?"

I told him, "No, I'm ready for the take."

For three pages, I did a French accent non-stop. "Just enough," I thought.

"That's very good, thank you," Minnelli told me. He didn't even ask for retakes. As we finished, I had a feeling that I wasn't going to see him anymore, so I shook hands with him, thanked him for the opportunity and left as he turned his attention to something else in the little dubbing room.

As I walked out toward the parking lot, one of his assistants came running after me and said, "Mr. Minnelli wants you to know that he's sending a memo about you to the front office. He's very pleased about your work over this past week."

That was a wonderfully nice thing for him to do. I automatically assumed that I would be cast in the next Minnelli movie but that was never to be. The movie became a major dud at the box office. When I rushed out to see it, the credits faded and the picture started. I thought, "Here I go now," but there was nothing of what we had done. The introductory French dialogue had been cut completely. As often happened in the editing booth, Minnelli clearly had more work to do and decided not to use what we recorded.

The movie fared poorly in part to unfavorable comparisons to the 1921 original with Rudolph Valentino. Dirk Bogarde later told me that he had turned down the lead role, and I can't help but wonder what a different movie Minnelli could have made with Dirk in the lead instead of Glenn Ford.

Years later in the late 1970s, the Vagabond Theatre in downtown Los Angeles was showing two Minnelli movies as retrospectives, *The Pirate* and *Meet Me in St. Louis*. I went to see both on the big screen again in those days preceding video or DVD. Minnelli himself was there, introduced by Robert Osborne of today's TCM fame. At the end of the evening, Minnelli sat near the manager's office as well-wishers came by to greet him. I reminded him that I had worked with him on *The 4 Horsemen of the Apocalypse*.

"I'm so sorry," Minnelli told me. "That was one of my disasters, wasn't it?"

After two back-to-back dubbing projects at MGM, I returned to television as the 1961-1962 season started. I went back to Universal to film my third episode of Boris Karloff's *Thriller* anthology series. Titled "The Closed Cabinet," the episode aired on November 27, 1961, and became my favorite of the four that I did for the series.

Each time I worked on *Thriller,* I had to read for either the producer, William Frye, or the episode's rotating director. When I got the call for my third *Thriller* episode, I went out to read. The door opened and in walked Ida Lupino!

"I'm reading for Ida Lupino?" I thought. "I HAVE to get this part!'"

I gave the reading my all. I got the part, which meant that I could relish in working six days for an hour-long episode with Ida Lupino. All the actors would have jumped off a roof for her. Actors who direct are so marvelous to work for because they know more of what to communicate to actors on the set. There's just a connection there. In my career, I worked for three or four actors who also directed. Ida was a wonderful director, and I have no doubt it was because she had been one of Hollywood's best performers.

The cast also included Olive Sturgess, Jennifer Raine, Peter Forster, and my friend, Doris Lloyd. Olive was another working actor who always seemed busy. She went from show to show because she was always so reliable. Jennifer Raine and Peter Forster were married at the time, so I didn't have as much interaction with them; they paid a lot of attention to each other.

The plot focused on a ghost story and a hidden message inside a closed cabinet. The ghost is unable to find peace until the message is delivered. Ida wasted no time in telling us that she found the script wanting. Each day before we shot a scene, Ida called the cast over to her.

"Now darlings," she said. "We have to do something with this crap. What do you think your character would really say?"

She gave each of us ten minutes to write our own dialogue and then read it back to her. If she didn't approve, we refined the lines and then acted them out for her. Working this way, however, meant that she frequently had to give the crew ten-minute breaks while we improvised by writing our own dialogue.

"Write that down!" she said about a good line. We literally rewrote our roles, unheard of for most actors! Line by line, she gave her approval or sent us back for another rewrite.

The big-shot executives at Universal got word that the crew was frequently being given ten-minute breaks on the Lupino set. In no time at all, four ominous young fellows in dark suits came down to the set.

"What seems to be the problem?" one of them asked Ida.

"The problem is that this should have never gone into production!" she told the production executives. "The script is nowhere ready to film!"

Pointing over to her actors cringing offstage, Ida continued, "Look, our actors are having to rewrite their parts!"

One of the executives started walking toward us to ask us for our take on the problem. Ida instantly flew into a protective mother hen role. She literally stood between the executives and in front of us and barked, "Don't go near my actors! Get off the set! This is my show! I'm directing!"

Not only was she looking out for the actors, but when we went home, Ida was still there, rewriting the script and improving it for the next day. We had all seen her in her movies and shows, and I believe that her actors would have done whatever she said. What courage and integrity she demonstrated!

Each day, she dressed in a different pant suit, usually Capri pants and high heels and a little hat with cherries in it. Her outfits were green, mauve or pale blue. She made herself look as feminine as she could until she got to work and then the sleeves were rolled up. It was her way of saying, "I know I'm a woman in a man's world, but hell, I can hold my own with anybody."

Not only was she tough, but she had a heart of gold. Isobel Elsom had been a fine British actress. She scored a major Broadway hit in *Ladies in Retirement* and then repeated it famously on film with a plot about ladies planning to murder a trusting, wealthy woman in remote England. Ida played one of those ladies in retirement.

Her husband, actor Carl Harbord, had died. Isobel had fallen on hard times, Ida told me. To help this grand lady get a much needed surgery, Ida devised a plan that she told me about when she called me at home one night during our shoot.

"We're putting in an extra scene that I've written for you and Isobel in a railway carriage," Ida said. "We're going to shoot it at eight in the morning. Now, the scene will probably be cut, but we'll film it so Isobel can get her medical insurance to pay for the operation. We'll put her in, and she'll get payment. Don't say a word about this to anyone, because we'll film it, I'll cut it, and then say that it was extra film we didn't need. No one knows about this but her, you and me."

Ida's plan worked. Isobel had her surgery, thanks to the thoughtfulness of our director. That was her love of actors. Ida's heart of gold was also on display with our dear Doris Lloyd. As long as I had worked with her, Doris had demonstrated problems with her ability to learn dialogue.

Doris told me that she usually prepared for parts by running lines with her sister, Milba, a successful sculptress. Doris had a scene in this episode of *Thriller* that required her to find and read a poem hidden inside a cabinet. A curse of sorts, the lines were pretty routine as monologues go.

We rehearsed it for camera and then Ida said, "Action."

Olive Sturgess and I were directed by Ida Lupino in "The Closed Cabinet"
episode of Thriller, *1961.*

328   WHICH ONE WAS DAVID?

The whole scene was on Doris and the cabinet, and she just couldn't do it. As she stuttered over the first line, I saw panic on her face. She started up again and fell apart in the second line. Ida, however, was marvelous with her, a soothing influence as Doris grew upset.

"I knew it at home with Milba this morning," Doris said. "I'm so sorry!"

Ida calmed her down and helped her greatly. Not only did she love Doris just as the rest of us did, but Ida had great empathy for her because she had been through learning lines herself.

"It's all right, Doris," Ida told her. "We'll just do one line at a time."

She proceeded to direct Doris line by line. Ida said, "Action!" and then Doris did her line. "Cut!" Ida said, and then it was on to the next one, delivered and filmed one by one, about a twelve-line curse. The finished scene looked great, because it appeared that Doris knew exactly what she was doing. Ida used different angles to get the scene right. That was her concern for her actors.

"The Closed Cabinet" episode was a very gothic-style show. I remember Ida suggesting I underplay my scenes because of the corny dialogue. I think I overdid the underplaying whenever I watch our episode.

Her memory troubles aside, on the set Doris Lloyd was always social. She knew everyone. Just as she had introduced me to her friend, James Whale, the director of *Frankenstein,* she also knew Boris Karloff, Frankenstein's monster, himself. One day she invited me to join them for lunch in the Universal commissary. I sat there in awe of the great man.

Karloff was a shy Englishman whose real name was William Pratt. Doris had got to know him back in the 1930s when they both worked non-stop, usually at Universal. As we lunched, I saw he was nothing like the man who had scared many of us as children. He had even starred in some movies that I couldn't get into as a kid because I was under eighteen, the cut-off age imposed by the British censors.

I was in awe of him, not only because of the iconic image of him clunking around as Frankenstein's monster, but also for what he brought to the role under that makeup. He was a man of great sensibility and talent. He wasn't just making monster noises in that role, which was part of the acting job, to be sure, but he brought sensitivity to the monster. I could not shake the fact that I was talking to a film legend, an icon. I recalled that James Whale had complimented Karloff when Doris and I had been to tea with him. Whale told us what a marvelous pleasure it had been working with Karloff.

Of all the major Hollywood studios, Universal was the least actor-friendly working environment. The office suites overlooked the lot from a high black tower, not at all friendly like Fox or Disney. History, though, took the edge off the unfriendly lot. The *Thriller* episodes were shot on the same Universal soundstage where *The Phantom of the Opera* had been filmed with Lon Chaney. The studio had turned the stage into a soundstage and closed the curtain. One of the chandeliers was still there, wrapped up in the ceiling. The studio had movable boxes to use looking down on the stage.

I had such a marvelous time working on *Thriller*. The next year, 1962, I made one more episode with Suzanne Lloyd, Leslie Howard's son, Ronald Howard, and Robert Douglas. Best of all, Doris was also in the cast again. I always welcomed any opportunity to spend time with her, socially or working.

Our episode was called "The Specialist," and it marked the last episode of *Thriller*. The storyline was about a group of specialists on the trail of criminals. The plot had been written to launch a pilot for a series but when the show failed to be picked up, the story was used for our *Thriller* episode.

Our director was Ted Post, a prolific television director who later helmed a number of big feature films with Clint Eastwood, including *Magnum Force*. Unlike Ida Lupino, Post didn't have patience for Doris's memory problems. We were filming a scene where she had to open the door and greet me when she forgot her lines being delivered to my character.

"Come now, Miss Lloyd," Post told her. "We're wasting time!"

It was the wrong thing to say to her, because she fell apart. Luckily, I was able to comfort her and calm her down enough for her to get through our scene, but it was tough.

Working on the last episode of *Thriller* was a privilege. The show only lasted a couple of seasons, and the word on the set was that the production had suffered because Alfred Hitchcock often stole away the best writers or directors for his anthology show. Many episodes are considered classics because of the drama and horror they delivered. The show is remembered by many fans, so much so that the whole series was released to DVD in 2010 for new audiences.

Having Boris Karloff introduce the episodes was a class act in itself. When he died several years later, I wrote his daughter and told her that meeting him and hearing him announce my name four times as a guest star meant the world to me. She wrote back and told me that my words brought her a lot of comfort and that she was hearing the same sentiment from many other actors as well.

The fall of 1961 was a fun time to live in Hollywood. At the corner of Doheny Drive and Cynthia Street there was a small, four-unit condo where Marilyn Monroe lived. Friends of mine occupied a house next door. I used to sit on their patio, which backed up to Marilyn's. I could often hear her giggling and visiting with Joe DiMaggio, who had come back into her life by then.

As I learned on more than one occasion, many of the biggest stars, such as Rock Hudson, were genuinely good people to know. Maurine had introduced me to William Batliner, a casting director at Universal, when I started making the rounds in the late 1950s. Several years of networking finally paid off when she called and told me to go see Batliner about a Rock Hudson movie. Batliner explained that the company had just returned from shooting in Indonesia on a film called *The Spiral Road*. The picture was about a missionary who loses his faith deep in the jungle.

Burl Ives was a co-star, along with Gena Rowlands as Rock's girlfriend. If I got the part, I was to play a missionary assigned to replace Rock Hudson's character when he gets sent away for rest and relaxation. I was to have three scenes, so I read the second scene for the director Robert Mulligan, who next directed *To Kill A Mockingbird*. He and Batliner liked me, so they arranged my fee with Maurine. Mine was a small part, but the pay was excellent because it was a Rock Hudson picture for Universal.

That night I read the script. The first scene was just greeting dialogue. The second scene was a discussion over a drink about faith with Rock's character, helping him unload his confusion onto my character as an impersonal listener. It was very well written. The third scene depicted his character returning from his rest and relaxation.

I went to the studio the next day for wardrobe and then to the set the day after that. Wearing my khaki pants and shirt costume, I showed up at Universal to find a very convincing camp set constructed on the back lot. Bamboo and palm trees had been placed to match the Indonesian location shooting.

Rock Hudson had an enormous trailer with great big loudspeakers booming out big band and pop music. I heard Henry Mancini, Frank Sinatra, and Ella Fitzgerald — my kind of music! Between takes, he just sat on the steps of his trailer and listened to records. The crew liked him, because he was very affable.

He introduced himself to me. I was a little nervous, because this film would be my first work with a really huge, contemporary box office star. Rock, Tony Curtis, and George Nader had been put under contract at Universal about the same time, with each of them being built up in larger parts with each subsequent movie. After 1954, he had filmed *Magnificent Obsession* with Jane Wyman to great success and had co-starred with Wyman again in *All That Heaven Allows*, which really launched him into super stardom.

When Mulligan wasn't quite ready to direct my first scene, I got to watch Rock film another scene with Burl Ives. I saw that he was a natural actor without any hint of arrogance about him. I had interviewed Burl on my radio show in England. I didn't dare remind Ives of this fact or that I had shared fish and chips with his son. On my first day on the set of a major movie with the two stars, I was too afraid to make conversation.

Judy Dan, Rock Hudson, me, and Karl Swenson in The Spiral Road, *Universal, 1962.*

Besides, he was in character, and I didn't want to break his concentration.

Another actor, Karl Swenson, was also in my first scene. Earlier that year, Disney had released *101 Dalmatians* with my voice as the voice of Sgt. Tibs the cat. Karl was working on Disney's next animated feature as Merlin the magician in *The Sword in the Stone*. It was a small world after all, or at least in Disney's world!

I note this coincidence because when Rock, Karl, and I shot a scene, a plane went over and we later had to dub our dialogue again. Mulligan didn't like that much, but I was only too happy to dub because it meant another contract for dubbing at the same daily rate as my on-screen acting contract. Altogether I worked a couple of days on the jungle scene with Rock and Karl.

Rock impressed me because he didn't seem to demand or expect all the close-ups. At one point, Mulligan shot over Rock's shoulder and onto me. I got a close-up in the first scene, so I was enjoying my first day on *The Spiral Road*.

On our second day of shooting, the scene required Rock to deliver large chunks of dialogue in a very spirited manner, indicative of his character's moral struggle with his faith. As I watched him, I thought, "He's doing a damn good job with this!" I had very little to do except to feed him his cue for his explanation about his lack of faith.

Because it was a long scene and took most of the morning to shoot from different angles, we had a lot of time to talk. It turned out that we had a mutual friend named Patricia Fitzgerald, which was funny, because Rock's real name was Roy Fitzgerald, but there was no connection between the two.

I had known Pat for some time. She was an aggressively ambitious public relations professional. She worked for a PR office but planned to open her own publicity firm. Other friends would say, "She's so determined to be *the* PR lady in Hollywood that she just walks over people." I didn't see that side of her, but she aimed high with her ambition.

Rock told me that he had started playing bridge with Pat and another PR lady named Lynn every weekend at his beach house. "Do you play bridge?" he asked.

I told him that I didn't. He said, "You don't have to. You can be the dummy. We just lost our other dummy, the fourth person in the game."

He asked if I wanted to join his weekend bridge games. I never would have thought he was so passionate about bridge, so I said yes. He told me that the games usually started on Friday night, resumed on Saturday night, again on Sunday, and then it was back up to Los Angeles on Monday morning.

Since I knew Pat would be there, and I liked her, it seemed like fun. Rock also told me that he was having a surprise birthday party that weekend. His friend, Marilyn Maxwell, had arranged the party, but he wasn't supposed to know about it.

"Give Pat a call, and she can be your date, if you like," he told me, "and then we'll all walk in and act surprised at my party."

Given her love of publicity and stars, Pat was only too glad to go. Rock's birthday party turned out to be a lot of fun. A mariachi band strolled around Rock's two-story mansion as guests sipped margaritas. Dina Merrill, who was married to Cliff Robertson, was among the guests, along with Edie Adams, Ernie Kovacs' wife. She had been in *Lover Come Back*, the film Rock finished just before going to Indonesia for *The Spiral Road*.

The evening marked my first true "Hollywood" party. I had been to weekend gatherings at Dirk Bogarde's house when he was filming *Song Without End*, but this was the first big party such as I had seen in the movies, with the house beautifully decorated with candles and a live band.

Marilyn Maxwell asked me to do the cha-cha, and when I told her that I didn't know how, she grabbed me by the waist and we did the dance

together. She was a very sexy girl and a great dancer. She had been marvelous as a predatory blond in *Champion* and in the MGM musical *Summer Holiday*. She was building up a fine resume until the other, more famous Marilyn came along.

Maxwell was separated from her writer-husband and maintained a friendship with Rock. He told me later that he was providing for her teenage son, and he was determined to keep her in the public eye because he loved her caustic wit. By keeping her on his arm at industry functions, she could stay visible in Hollywood. Marilyn was very much in love with Rock, even though he had been married once

Rock Hudson and his convertible.

before in a studio-arranged marriage.

As Pat and I left Rock's birthday party, he said, "Are we on for bridge this weekend?" We both agreed to the bridge game, and that first weekend started a weekly routine that would last almost a year for me. That Friday, Rock called again to confirm that we were still on for bridge and then came by my house to pick me up.

For nearly a year, Rock called every Friday night around 10:30 to see if I was game for a weekend of bridge. If I was, he told me that he would be there in thirty minutes. He had an enormous convertible that he drove for about a one-hour trip down to Newport Beach, where he owned a condo on an island.

Every Friday night without fail, he stopped about halfway to Newport Beach and went into a supermarket. Putting on dark glasses so no one would recognize him, he then bought a pound of hamburger. Back he came with hamburger meat, and as he drove, he opened up the paper with his right hand and ate the raw hamburger using his left hand. He was a fan of steak tartare to give him energy for marathon bridge games that inevitably went on until two in the morning.

As we drove, Rock also liked to play word games. He invented words, and one Friday evening, he used the word, "runcible." It sounded real enough to be believable. For him, the word meant "a pleasant time," so if he was having a good evening, it was a "runcible drive down to the beach." He used that word frequently throughout the year I knew him. I never saw him quoted in print using the word, so I think it was just a social thing he did with friends.

At his condo in Newport Beach, Rock had a patio wall where he parked, with an open courtyard between the wall and the condo. Every Friday night when we arrived about midnight, waiting was a sack of mail thrown over the wall by the Newport Beach post office. Rock literally received enough fan mail to fill up a bag.

Once inside, he fixed vodka and tonics for me and anyone else who might be there and then opened up his mail bag. Most of his mail was simply addressed to "Rock Hudson, USA." So great was his international fame that the post office sent the mail down to Newport Beach for him. He picked out a few samples and read them, many of them from Germany. He didn't seem to understand how he was bigger in Germany than England since his movies were dubbed there.

Every Monday he put the sack into the trunk of his car, drove back to the studio and handed it over to the press department at Universal to stamp his signature on autographed photos that had been requested. Getting a weekly sack of fan mail was simply amazing. As I got to know him better, I learned that most of his close friends called him by his real name, Roy. Personal friends felt ridiculous calling him "Rock" because it sounded so artificial and part of the Hollywood PR machine.

Roy liked to play movies on Friday nights to unwind after working on a current film. He used the space between his garage and living room as a projection room. "What will we watch?" he would ask, perusing the 16mm prints he owned of all of his films, including the not-so-really good ones such as *Taza, Son of Cochise*.

Memorably, the one I most enjoyed watching, although it lasted into the wee hours of the morning, was *Giant*. Rock did a running commentary on the film. With all the DVD extras today, can you imagine hearing Rock Hudson do a commentary on *Giant*? It would have been wonderful to record, because he commented on every scene.

Almost of all his comments were flattering, with the exception of his opinion of James Dean. Roy could not stand him. He called him a pretentious little jerk. That was one of the few times that I ever heard Roy really put somebody down like that. He intensely disliked James Dean because of the famous scene where Dean took out a lasso and twirled it to upstage Roy during some important dialogue. Roy thought their director, George Stevens, should have shot that over again because the energy level was redirected to the rope and not his speech.

Reviewing his film work, Roy spoke very warmly of Jane Wyman and said that she was most responsible for giving him confidence to step up to full stardom in their two films. Both of their pictures together were produced by Ross Hunter. Roy and Ross, however, had an uneasy relationship. Ross always said that he jumpstarted Roy's career, and Roy went around saying that he made Ross Hunter's career, because it was their two pictures that also gave Ross industry recognition. I didn't know him too well, but he was pleasant enough the few times I was around him.

Roy's friends stopped by for drinks between six and 7:30. They all knew to get out of there by eight, because that's when we were ready to go to war across a bridge table. Claire Trevor lived nearby and came over one night. She had won an Oscar for playing an alcoholic singer in *Key Largo*. I hated to seem as though I was loitering about in the background, so I asked her if I could make her a drink. "Oh yes, honey," she said. "I'd like a martini!"

I went into the kitchen. I didn't know anything about martinis other than that I needed gin and vermouth. I was supposed to make a martini with a lot of gin and just a whisper of vermouth, but I got the proportions the other way around! I handed the "martini" to this Academy Award-winning actress, who spit it out and said, "WHAT IS THIS?" She took my hand and said, "Come on. I'll show you how to make a good martini."

Saturday evening's pre-bridge games were spent pleasantly after everyone left Roy, Pat, and Lynn to play bridge with me as their dummy. I could see that these three really got into their games. I found myself playing from eight p.m. to two a.m. and learned a lot about the game. They never played for money, but I could almost feel knives at throats. They were so focused and intent on winning. I eventually graduated from being the dummy to rotating in the group, and Roy said that I became quite a good bridge player.

He and the ladies drank bull shots made with beef broth. They would play a little and then drink a little. It was not like me to stay up past ten p.m., so I often felt tired. Sometimes we went beyond two a.m. if the game went long. We were all fueled by bull shots made in a big tumbler with ice. The drink contained vodka and beef broth with salt around the rim of the glass. Remarkably, nobody ever got drunk. By sipping at these things — whoever was the dummy got up and made a fresh batch — it kept us focused on the game.

Early on Monday mornings, we all drove back up to L.A. after spending a whole weekend together. Those weekends were great fun and lasted for me well into 1962. There were some memorable moments that stand out. One weekend as we drove down, we heard on the car radio that Ernie Kovacs had been killed in a traffic accident. When we got to his condo, Roy called Ernie's widow, Edie Adams, and asked if she wanted him to come up and console her.

I completed my part in *The Spiral Road* after several days of shooting. A few months later, Roy called one Friday and said, "The girls are meeting us at the theatre near LAX. They're previewing *The Spiral Road*."

Off we went, the four of us in a row with the bigwigs from Universal sitting behind us. Up came the picture. It looked good. Roy looked great, and there was my opening scene. But then my middle and closing scenes were missing. Both of my interior scenes were cut. All that was left was my outdoor scene that I had been forced to dub. If you sneeze, you miss me.

My part got whittled down because it was a long, sprawling movie. Something had to give, and it was me. As an actor, I couldn't take it personally because I got paid, but it was still disappointing to act and then have my scenes trimmed. The movie's editing made my part look almost like an extra.

"Oh well," I thought as the credits came on at the end. "It's only a movie." I remembered that when I signed the SAG contract, I was getting seventh or eighth billing, but now my name was at the end of the credits! I thought, "Oh great, I've just done some movies as a lead and now I'm at the bottom of the cast list with one little scene in this."

The four of us went into the manager's office because it was a preview, meaning the audience marked preview cards to rank the film as good, great, bad, or indifferent. The Universal executives looked through them. The general consensus was that the film was good. It wasn't to be a big hit, according to the preview audience, and they were proven right. I don't think it was a big moneymaker because at the time, Rock Hudson's audiences were used to frothy comedies with Doris Day. The movie offered him a chance to expand his dramatic range, though, with a deep, agonizing kind of role to play. Roy did very well and became a better actor a decade or so later, but he was already good at that stage in his career.

After the preview screening, Roy said, "You're very quiet. What did you think of the movie?"

I said, "Well, you're a big movie star; you don't know what it's like when you're struggling to get good billing and five years after you started, suddenly you wind up at the bottom of the cast list."

"What do you want to do about it?" he asked.

"Well, I can't do much of anything about it," I told him. "It's done now, but it's frustrating for me professionally."

He proceeded to set me straight on how he had started in Hollywood, laboring in tiny parts before finding stardom. He told me that after leaving the Navy following World War II, he had been drinking beer with his buddies as they discussed their plans. "I'm going to Hollywood and be a movie star," he told them.

Roy recounted to me how he was driving a delivery truck, trying to get started as an actor. He told me that every lunch time, no matter where he was making deliveries, he always parked on Washington Boulevard outside MGM. He visualized himself over the wall, starring in an MGM movie. He did that every weekday to build his confidence.

In 1948, Roy went onto the set of *Eagle Squadron*, starring Edmond O'Brien. Raoul Walsh had him read for a very brief speech. Walsh saw promise in him, with his great looks and height. He felt that Roy might amount to something, so Walsh put him under personal contract.

When Roy got his script, he had one page of dialogue. In his brief scene, Edmond O'Brien was at a blackboard. They all played pilots as O'Brien's character outlined information on the blackboard. When O'Brien's character runs out of room to write, Roy's line was, "Hey commander, you better build a bigger blackboard."

That's a hard line to say, and it took Roy fifty-seven takes to get it right! The studio came down onto Walsh and asked why he was spending all the time on the unknown kid. "Can't you get somebody else?" they asked.

"No, he'll get it," Walsh told them. "I see a lot of personal promise in him."

As Roy told the story, he got his line right after all those takes. Walsh put him under a personal contract and later sold it to Universal, where he enjoyed a seven-year contract. I heard this whole story from Roy as we drove. "So you see," he said, "I know all about working my way up to bigger billing."

I apologized for forgetting his rocky start, but stuck to my point that unlike his start with one line, I had just done two big features with co-star billing only to be reduced to a small part in his movie.

Nothing more was said about it. Six weeks later, as we drove down to Newport Beach on a Friday night, Roy said, "Oh, by the way, your name is off the credits on *The Spiral Road*."

"What do you mean?" I asked him.

"I had Universal reshoot the end credits. Isn't that what you wanted?" he said.

"But how can you do that?" I replied.

"Simple," he said. "I just told them to take your name off the credit title."

I've never forgotten that amazing gesture on his part, which was probably an expensive one because they didn't yet have digital editing to erase a name and had to reshoot the credits. But he did it. That's the kind of man he was.

As my agent, Maurine was more pleased than I was that my name was removed from those prints. "Thank God," she said, "or it would be back to square one again with casting agents wondering what Frankham was doing at the bottom of the list!"

Roy was one of the most unaffecting superstars that I've ever met. He and Marilyn Monroe had been voted by the foreign press as the world's top box office stars because they made more money than any other star at the time, but it had not gone to his head.

Pat Fitzgerald, one of the bridge club regulars, was driven to be the best-known PR lady in Hollywood. She was opening a new office, so every weekend after a bridge game and a bull shot, she said, "Oh come on, Roy, you've got to be my number one client. If I get you as a client, I'll have no trouble with my business!"

"No, no," he told her. "We're too close. I have to keep it as a business deal where somebody can look at me objectively without friendship involved." He never budged to her repeated requests to represent him.

When Pat finally opened her PR firm, Roy told me with a laugh, "She's got this swanky office with a reception desk, and right behind the desk is this enormous blow-up of me." She never claimed that Roy was her client, but anybody walking in to consider signing with Patricia Fitzgerald automatically assumed that her number one client was Rock Hudson. In her determined way, she achieved her objective.

One time the bridge club ladies went off to Hawaii together. On a Friday night, Roy picked me up to see the girls at LAX before they left. Ordinarily, all he had to do to avoid being spotted by the public was put on his dark glasses. With the glasses off, you could tell it was him, but if he put them on, he got away with it.

After the girls were off, we walked back through a long tunnel from LAX to the parking lot. He forgot to put on his glasses, because it was late at night, around eleven. Somebody recognized him as we walked. A woman screamed, "There's Rock Hudson!" and from nowhere, about a dozen people suddenly crowded us against a wall. He was very good with them, greeting them and saying, "If you don't mind, I have an appointment; I can't stop and talk."

Because I was not Rock Hudson, somebody pushed me back and ripped the arm off my green sports jacket. It just hung on my arm. The crowd trailed us back to his car as he calmly handled the situation. I learned something from him that night. If you can be nice to a rather belligerent crowd, you can communicate an attitude that everything is okay. Roy handled the crowd so well that they calmed down and respected him more. Not me, though — I was hanging on to my jacket when we got in the car. Roy laughed about it and said it was the price of fame.

About a week later, a surprise package arrived at my house — it was a new sports jacket. He was a very thoughtful friend. Over the Christmas of 1961, we exchanged LPs, which were then $3.98 each. He was kind enough not to throw some big expensive thing at me because I couldn't reciprocate. He gave me Dave Brubeck's *Take Five*, a huge hit at the time, and an Ella Fitzgerald LP. Christmas at his house saw him hosting a small get-together that included Glynis Johns. He was so kind to include me as a guest that year.

On February 16, 1962, Roy and I joined the two ladies on our way down to the beach for the weekend's marathon bridge sessions. They were aware that it was my thirty-sixth birthday, so Roy said, "Let's stop off and have a bite to eat." It had all been pre-arranged but I didn't know it.

At the LAX airport, there was a revolving restaurant that employed a three violin orchestra and piano to play soothing music. As we dined, Roy and the ladies each handed LPs to me as gifts. The whole evening was quite subdued and soothing. Suddenly in the background, I heard musicians start to play "Happy Birthday."

I was so shy. In fact, I rather am to this day. Everyone turned as the band walked through the tables to surround me. I wanted to die as everyone looked at me. I remember the occasion with enormous fondness and gratitude now, but I was just so embarrassed at the time. I wanted to crawl away from there.

Over the course of 1962, I was able to see the real person and not just the Rock Hudson image that the public knew. When I became part of Roy's bridge club, I found that Marilyn Maxwell wasn't usually invited down for the card games. She would inevitably call during the middle of the game and irritate Roy. I heard him take calls in another room, saying, "Marilyn, damn it, I am NOT going to marry you!" I was privy to some tension between them even though they cared for each other very much, just on different levels.

Because Roy was private and reserved — not all friends and associates knew his personal details — the one downside is that so much has been written or rumored about a man who was a gentleman and a loyal friend. Hollywood was less enlightened in those days, and people could be unkind. Roy himself told me that his feelings were hurt at an industry event just after his success in *Pillow Talk* when he was introduced to Cary Grant.

Roy said he held out his hand and Grant just looked right through him and walked past without any reaction. He could only speculate the reason, either from rumors about his personal life or perhaps a little professional jealousy from an aging Grant, but nevertheless, that's not how he liked to treat people or to be treated himself, and it hurt coming from a brilliant actor like Cary Grant.

Roy also was candid about his feelings for his ex-wife, Phyllis Gates. He said that she had taped private conversations in which he made some frank admissions about his personal life. She in turn threatened him with media exposure unless he agreed to her divorce terms. He had grown to detest her by the time he told me these details.

Phyllis had been the secretary to Roy's agent and manager, Henry Willson. She was privy to all the negotiations in Willson's office and knew Roy's reputation. The magazine called *Confidential*, the biggest gutter rag of all time, was successful by outing stars about their sexuality, drug habits or alcoholism. The press knew what went on through contacts around Hollywood. Universal was told that *Confidential* would be doing a story on Rock and some of his male "friends." I don't know if they had anything incriminating. I don't think they could have, because he was very discrete in all his dealings, in my observation of how he dealt with his personal life.

Phyllis knew all about this. Either the studio or Henry Willson told Roy that he needed to get married to quell the rumors. Phyllis was there at Willson's office and agreed to enter this arranged form of marriage. They married and had a beautiful house in the San Fernando Valley, a kind of Cape Cod-looking house with trees all around it. Subsequently, the magazines got the feed about the happy couple and everyone was satisfied.

After awhile, Roy and Phyllis privately went their separate ways. Lawyers came into the situation, but Roy told me that negotiations were all in his wife's favor. She was getting the house and some other property; successful actors often invested in real estate, even if it was a piece of barren land. Roy wisely bought quite a bit of land with his earnings.

They were getting nowhere with the divorce proceedings. Negotiations were not coming to a friendly end. One evening Phyllis called and said, "We don't need all of this; just come over and we'll have a friendly chat without the lawyers and end this amicably. Whatever we agree about, that will be the end of the whole thing."

Roy went over and said Phyllis seemed affable. He admitted having differences and male friends, named names, parted agreeably and that was it. He left thinking everything was going to be fine. He told me that he thought her lawyers would call his. A few days later, Roy got a look at what she was demanding: a percentage of his earnings, not just as a movie star, but all of his holdings in perpetuity so long as she lived; if he died, she would continue to collect a big portion of his estate. He called her and said, "What the hell is this all about? We didn't agree to this."

He told me that she said, "I know, but I taped our talk the other night. It's in a deposit box at the bank. If you don't agree to my demands, I'll release the tape to the media." Then she hung up on him.

Roy was stuck. Phyllis got everything she wanted, and they never saw each other again. Obviously she didn't have to work for Henry Willson again, because now she was set for life. Roy confessed to me that one day he was at the Beverly Hills Hotel for a publicity lunch. After he finished and got into his car, he was about to drive away when he saw Phyllis drive up to another section of the parking lot, not too far from his car. She got out and started walking into the hotel. He told me that he could barely resist putting his foot on the accelerator. "It was all I could do to not run her down," he said.

I also learned that Rock Hudson and several other leading men had been discovered by the very strange Henry Willson. At Thanksgiving in the fall of 1961, I was among the guests at Roy's house. Willson drove down to Newport Beach, had a drink and left. I thought he was creepy and pitiful. I asked Roy what Willson was doing, leaving to go out on Thanksgiving.

He said, "He's doing what he always does. He parks himself at a restaurant and watches everybody who comes in, trying to discover the next Rock Hudson."

Roy told me that after the divorce with Phyllis, he wanted to leave Henry Willson for new management but Willson had threatened him by saying, "If you leave, I'll cut your face." Roy feared Willson would follow through by hiring thugs to do it. He decided that he was no Olivier and that he needed his looks in Hollywood, so he stuck it out with Willson.

Roy wore his fame lightly and was always willing to help another actor, including Michael Wilding. By 1961, Michael had been divorced from Elizabeth Taylor for several years. He was still making a go at it in Hollywood. Although he was never a great actor — in fact, Dirk Bogarde once called him a disgrace to the profession — he was very happy go-lucky. He had more charm than anyone I ever knew in my life. He was funny and quick-witted.

Michael had epilepsy, which made him subject to fits. Elizabeth had shown me once the actual stick that she used if Michael felt a headache coming on to start a fit. She would place this thing between his teeth to keep him from biting his tongue if the fit became serious. He was in agony sometimes.

After the divorce, Michael was doing a movie. I had stayed in touch with him and his father, a wonderful old guy who was almost like a father to me. Pat Fitzgerald from the bridge club had become friendly with Michael too. Pat called one day and said, "Michael's in trouble. He's not feeling well and wants to take time off this afternoon, but the producer is

Rock Hudson was about the nicest, most unassuming star I ever knew in Hollywood.

threatening that if he does, he's going to fire him."

Michael later said that the producer had told him, "Either get back to the set this afternoon, or I'll put out the word that you're epileptic and you'll never get a job in this town again."

Pat said, "We've got to do something. He's got to go back to work."

I called and talked to him, but Michael refused to go back because he felt a fit coming on.

I said to Pat, "Who can we talk to?"

She said, "Let's give Roy a call, or Michael's career will be finished."

I was at home for lunch, so I called Roy at his house to tell him what was happening. He agreed to talk to Michael, so they came over to my house to avoid a scene. I took a walk around the block as Roy somehow

calmed Michael down and talked him into going back to work. He finished the picture, his epilepsy secret was safe, and he continued to work,
all thanks to Roy's way of peacefully talking to him, much like he had
soothed the agitated crowds that evening at LAX.

Roy was even mechanically inclined. One time he was visiting with
friends at my apartment when a fuse blew. Out he went into the alley, not
far from a row of restaurants. Without even thinking that he might have
been recognized, he asked me to hoist him up so he could reach the box
and change the fuse. He was just a helpful, thoughtful man.

I enjoyed my friendship with the world famous Rock Hudson into
1962. In fact, I still have a *Life* magazine that he was going to throw
away. The cover had his picture on it, and below that was a label with his
name and address: "Rock Hudson, Newport Beach." The day that issue
was published, it was just flung over his door like any other piece of mail.

I thought it was so unusual. Most people never know the feeling
of receiving a magazine with their face on the cover. Roy was going
to toss it in the trash but let me have it when I thought it would be a
funny thing to own, a magazine with "Rock Hudson" on the cover and
addressed to him!

CHAPTER NINE

Tales of Terror
to The Outer Limits

Rock Hudson's philosophy on life was something I heard him say many times: "Stay loose as a goose." I always thought, "Sure, if I made $5,000 a week, I could stay loose as a goose, too!"

In many ways, I envied his carefree attitude. My English upbringing had instilled a sort of rigidness in me. In reality, I was a sort of uptight individual. As much fun as it was to be friends with a world famous movie star, his insistence that I become the dummy in his bridge club began to wear on me.

I was really exhausted, and it was telling on me. When we all went back up to Hollywood on a Monday morning, I said to Roy, "I am so tired. I need a change."

"What do you mean?" Roy asked.

"I can't keep up this pace," I told him. "I just don't have the stamina that you three seem to have. Could you find somebody else for the bridge game?"

"Sure," he casually replied.

They must have found another dummy, because I was out of the bridge games. Roy called a few more times to ask if I wanted to come down, but I was trying to concentrate more on my acting career. Patricia Fitzgerald from the bridge club saw me frequently and told me that everyone missed me.

"No," I told her. "I feel better already not knocking back bull shots every weekend."

Another reason for wanting out of bridge club games and rounds of bull shots was the fact that I had one more film to do with American International Pictures following *Master of the World* as part of my two-picture deal for replacing Mark Damon at short notice. I started the movie during those whirlwind weekends of bridge in December 1961.

My third and final picture with Vincent Price came in Roger Corman's *Tales of Terror*. The film was an anthology picture, the fourth of Corman's adaptations of stories by Edgar Allan Poe. Our film was to feature three Poe stories: "Morella," "The Black Cat," and "The Facts in the Case of M. Valdemar." Vincent was to appear in all three because he became a staple in the studio's horror films.

As elated as I was to learn that I would work with Vincent again, the production happily brought me into Basil Rathbone's orbit. He was an actor whom I had admired since I was ten years old, when he had scared the living daylights out of me by mercilessly thrashing poor Freddie Bartholomew in *David Copperfield*. I didn't sleep for a week after I saw that film.

Vincent was to play a wealthy dying man who hires a hypnotist, played by Basil, to put him into a trance. Basil's character leaves Vincent's character, M. Valdemar, in a spiritual trance between life and death as he pursues the dead man's wife, played by Debra Paget. I was to play Valdemar's doctor, protesting the strange proceedings and protecting the wife from Basil's villainy.

Our director, Roger Corman, was terrific, almost shy. The actors enjoyed a day of reading before we started filming. Corman arranged a buffet lunch for Vincent, Basil, Debra, and me. We sat at the table and ran over the script. I took it as a compliment when Corman didn't change anything for the four of us during our run-through.

Debra was a sweet, shy, but accomplished young lady. She had done a number of popular films at Fox in the early 1950s, and had appeared opposite Elvis Presley in his first film, *Love Me, Tender*. When we filmed *Tales of Terror*, I was thirty-five and Basil was seventy, and yet he was challenging me for Debra Paget's hand in marriage! That irony wasn't lost on me during the production. I admired Basil's vitality, his enthusiasm, his discipline, his enduring talent, you name it. He was a marvel — as energetic at seven p.m. as he was on set at seven a.m.

As with Vincent, doing a scene with Basil meant praying that I wouldn't be wiped off the screen. At the same time, I marveled at sharing the screen with one of my idols, Errol Flynn's and Tyrone Power's nemesis! I had seen Basil and his sword fights with Flynn and Power. I just thought he was the best villain ever.

Much to my surprise, Basil rated Power's swordsmanship as vastly superior to Flynn's; he said Flynn didn't take it seriously enough and much preferred to have his stunt double do as many long shots as he could get away with in a scene. I was astonished to learn that while Flynn was good at leaping about and looking athletic, Basil said he didn't know much about the fine points of fencing. When Basil did a job, though, he wanted to tackle it thoroughly. He had been taught well to fence properly, thus, his judgment of Flynn's talent — or lack thereof. "No," he told me, "Old Flynn used to have a double more often than not."

Ironically, I was playing a good guy opposite Basil, back to "Mr. Bland"

Debra Paget and I in Tales of Terror, 1962. (AIP).

in a sense after playing a number of villains or cads, but I didn't mind. The excitement of testing my limited experience against his vast accumulation of acting technique was a challenge.

The next day after our rehearsal, we were doing a master shot for the first scene. We had rehearsed it for camera. I could hear Corman chatting very quietly with the crew. Everything grew quiet and I thought, "Okay, we're doing a run through."

I wasn't giving my scene the full focus. At the end of the scene, all four of us — Vincent, Basil, Debra, and I — heard Roger say, "Cut!"

I thought, "That was a take?" I went immediately to Vincent and said, "I didn't know that was a take!"

Vincent told me, "With Roger, you've always got to be prepared, that's all. It's only a master shot, you know. You just have to get used to what you think might be a camera rehearsal actually being a real take."

Not much of the master shot ended up in the movie, but I can still tell that I didn't realize we were rolling. I can spot myself leaning back casually, not really being into character at all. It was understood that we got the scene right on the first take. Corman was so well-prepared that he would just say, "Action," and we were to do our scene.

Another time, I thought I could do something better, so I asked

Basil Rathbone, Debra Paget, Vincent Price and I worked with breakneck efficiency for director Roger Corman.

Vincent about it instead of going to Corman. He said, "You don't get a second chance on this picture, kid. You've got to give it your all the first time around. Roger doesn't like retakes either."

Corman kept the film within budget by directing like that. He rehearsed scenes very thoroughly to make sure we knew our lines and that the cameramen knew where to move. Provided we were on our toes for the dialogue, we really didn't need more than one take. Nevertheless, Vincent taught me the trick for getting a second take when things were going so well that Corman was otherwise fine with the footage he was getting.

"If a take isn't going well," Vincent told me, "just forget a line. Roger will accept that. He won't get mad if you apologize for not doing your best. If I feel I'm not doing my best, I just deliberately forget a line and Roger gives me a moment to 'get my act together' and do it from that line."

That was wonderful advice. I never used it, because there was an unwritten law in Hollywood that no actor could ever say, "Cut." A director throttled any actor who ever said, "Cut." If we wanted to stop, we just pretended to forget our line and apologized. That prompted the director to say, "Cut," and we got to do the line again.

Part of Corman's one-take philosophy was no doubt influenced by

Working with Basil Rathbone, one of my boyhood idols.

the tight budgets at AIP. We were to film our segment in one week, with every single shot in one take. I think the other segments were also filmed in one week's time, from dawn to dusk. Some scenes that would have taken two or three camera set-ups, Roger did in one to expedite the production.

Toward the end of the film, my character had to walk in a door from a snowstorm, take off his coat, hear a strange noise from Vincent's "dead" body upstairs, race up the stairs along a corridor, break down the door, and walk in to find Basil with Debra in his clutches.

Normally a director filmed that bit by bit, me coming in the door, me taking off my coat, "Cut." Then we would set up the camera, film me running up the stairs, "Cut." Set up the camera, film me running along the corridor, "Cut." Set up the camera for me breaking in the door and looking in on Basil and Debra, and "Cut." That would be four set-ups, but Corman did the whole thing in one!

I thankfully had no dialogue to deliver at the same time, because I had to run up those stairs with a camera rushing in front of me on tracks. I had to break down the door, and it had to be right, because it took about an hour to set up the whole thing technically with the lights in just the right spot. As I moved, the lighting had to move with me so that I was properly lighted all the time.

It was a big challenge for our crew, actually much more for them than me, because they had to pull the camera, and all of the leads attached to the camera, out from under my feet as I ran. Somehow we managed to get that entire scene in one take. I was absolutely amazed. Corman had filming to a fine art, and he rightly earned a wonderful reputation for those four Poe films that he did for AIP. There was such exhilaration in filming correctly for him. Each day everyone had a great sense of pride and accomplishment in meeting Corman's demands and going through all those script pages that we normally wouldn't film that fast on a feature.

The breakneck technical demands aside, I was more nervous about standing next to Basil. He was tall, about the same height as Vincent. When I worked nose to nose with a wonderful actor like that from the 1930s, and there I was in the 1960s, it made me realize that I had to be good. I had to draw upon myself to find the same energy level as Basil.

I was also a little nervous meeting Basil the first time because he had played so many haughty, snobby, unpleasant people — you never know until you meet an actor if that's real or not — but he wasn't like that. He was friendly and enthusiastic. Basil was nearly seventy, but his whole attitude was young.

I had to equal him to be believable. In fact, my character had to be believable in besting him to win Debra's hand. No one ever said, "Why is that old man fighting with that younger fellow for this beautiful heroine?" It didn't enter into anyone's mind because he was so convincing, and that was his secret. Basil worked like a ramrod; I worried about him as the days were long. We were there from seven a.m. until seven p.m. It was only for a week, admittedly, but Basil was nearly seventy, and he never seemed to tire. When we started filming, I was almost losing my wind because I was run down after weekends of late-night bridge games and bull shots at Rock Hudson's beach house, one of the reasons I ended that routine.

The energy level of Basil and Vincent was something to behold. Basil always chatted away enthusiastically at seven in the morning. He was exactly the same at seven p.m. By four p.m., I needed a break or a nap but not Basil.

I saw that he gave so much in a scene. Just being around him was one of the great satisfactions of my life.

Richard Matheson was back from my previous AIP picture, *Master of the World*, to write *Tales of Terror.* He wrote under intense pressure to get the script finished quickly. At one point Basil caught what he thought were a few modernisms slipped into the script. He insisted they be corrected for the time period we were depicting.

Just as he had done on *Return of the Fly* and *Master of the World*, Vincent was still the most jovial person on the set, joking and keeping everything social. We didn't have much time to socialize as we whipped through the script, but Vincent could still slip in a joke on the fly. Halfway through the movie, Vincent growled in my ear that he had worked with Debra in *The Ten Commandments* but "John Derek killed me off!"

At the end of our scene when Vincent returns from the dead, Debra's character faints dead away. I had to pick up her from the floor and escape as Vincent wreaks his revenge on poor Basil. I've learned to live with jokes from friends about how hard it was for me to lift little Debra Paget off the floor! It took take after take, with Vincent chuckling in the background, which didn't help. The last time I saw Vincent, he was still joking about me struggling to lift her up in that scene.

Film poster for Tales of Terror, *1962.*
(AIP)

At the end of production, all of us — the entire cast of the film's three different episodes — assembled on a graveyard set with tombstones and fog. I remember standing there with Vincent Price, Basil Rathbone, and Peter Lorre — talk about a young actor's dreams coming true. Here were people I had loved over the years — Peter from *The Maltese Falcon* and many more — and there I was as their equal, at least for that brief moment. A color still was taken for promotional reasons, but I never saw it because the studio released one with Vincent, Basil, and Peter instead. It was very exciting to pose with those great horror stars.

I was paid $1,500 for *Tales of Terror*, not a lot, considering that amount comes to about $11,000 adjusted for inflation today. AIP movies didn't pay well, but I would have almost worked for free just for the opportunity to meet and work with Basil, not to mention working with Vincent again for the last time. Not counting some later appearances, my true movie career leveled off when I finished *Tales of Terror*. Such was the ebb and tide for jobbing actors. Television, though, was booming for me.

Appearing in high profile films with Rock Hudson and Vincent Price strengthened my credits. By 1962 the exposure led to my work on some of the decade's best television programs. January 1962 saw my appearance on *The Jack Benny Program*. Benny had been one of radio's biggest stars, and like George Burns and Bob Hope, he successfully transitioned to television. He was in his twelfth television season when I appeared with him on an episode called "Jack Gets Passport."

I immensely enjoyed working with Benny. We heard his radio show back in England, so I was in awe of meeting him. Benny was just as I had hoped him to be. The plot depicted Jack trying to get a passport for a trip, and I had to assist him in the process as hilarity ensued. The script called on me to sit at a desk, look up at him and ask, "Age?" to which he replied with his trademark, "Thirty-nine."

At one point, I wasn't delivering my reaction line exactly the way Benny needed to secure a laugh. We went through it a few times until he finally took my head gently in his hands and said, "Watch me," and proceeded to say it just the way he wanted it delivered at the exact moment.

I had first looked up with a kind of "are you kidding me?" reaction to his "age" of thirty-nine. Benny said, "No kid! Hold it!" The director did nothing as Benny took charge completely.

"Look down at the page," he told me. "Now — ask my age."

As I asked him his age, he said, "Don't look up!"

He took my face in his hands and said, "Now look up when I pull." It seemed to me that it took a minute and a half. He was such a master at timing. He said, "Now — look up."

I did, and it worked for him. He said, "See? If you do it too fast, you're going to kill my line, kid."

He knew that it was an unnaturally long pause, but he built his career on that kind of reaction shot. He knew to the second what he was doing. He gave me a valuable master class on timing.

His method worked when we tried it. We got a big laugh when the audience saw it live. I also learned that we had to allow for audience laughter during taping. Benny was such a stickler for timing that he even knew in rehearsal when to allow for a chuckle or an outright roar of laughter from the audience. Benny proved just how easy some of the greatest comics made their work look. From the outside, it seemed so natural. It's

A foray into comedy with Jack Benny and Richard Deacon on The Jack Benny Program, *1962.*

little wonder that so many have tried to find success as comedians, but I saw first-hand that it's harder than it looks.

Richard Deacon, perhaps best known for his role on *The Dick Van Dyke Show*, was the other guest that week on Benny's show. He was a splendid comedy actor who had a big, sad face, but he was very pleasant. I had hoped Mel Blanc would be there, but working with Benny was privilege enough.

From comedy, I returned to intrigue and drama in January 1962, on my second *Alfred Hitchcock Presents*. The episode was called "The Silk Petticoat." Michael Rennie played the lead, a man seemingly haunted by his dead wife. Antoinette Bower was his fiancée who reluctantly marries him, only to discover a silk petticoat belonging to the first wife, who was alive and kept captive in a closet with her tongue cut out!

The plot was classic Hitchcock, and I played a lieutenant in what was the seventh and last season of Hitchcock's thirty-minute shows; that fall, the show went to a one-hour format for another three seasons. I liked Michael Rennie. He was a thoughtful, sensitive man. We both doted on Doris Lloyd, with whom I was working for the fourth or fifth time! John Newland, an actor from the early 1950s, had taken up directing, so we all enjoyed working with a director who could empathize with actors.

Jobbing actors sometimes went from comedy to drama to comedy again, demonstrating the versatility that was expected of us. That same month, I appeared on *The Many Loves of Dobie Gillis*. The show was in its third season and starred two funny men, Dwayne Hickman and Bob Denver, who just a few years later found himself stranded on *Gilligan's Island*.

Another of the characters was Zelda, played by Sheila James Kuehl. Her character was always in love with Dobie, and on my episode, Zelda's in the mood for marriage. Dobie and Maynard go aboard a ship to escape, only to find that Zelda's on board as well. She grabs my character to pose as a romantic rival once she discovers that the others are on board to spy on her. The role was no great shakes on my part, but the show had a big following, and Sheila James Kuehl went on to a career in politics in California.

Later that year, I returned to an anthology series that reminded me of my earliest work in Hollywood. Many actors not known for dramatic work often signed on to introduce a serious dramatic program. Bob Hope, for example, introduced such a series, while Fred Astaire hosted *Alcoa Presents*, a weekly dramatic anthology series.

My episode of *Alcoa Presents* was called "The Contenders," with Suzanne Pleshette as the lead. She reminded me of a younger version of Patricia Neal with her lovely, husky, earthy, warm voice and personality.

We got along very well. Suzanne was such a mature young woman that I just assumed she was my age, but she was actually several years younger. During filming, we took lunch breaks together in the Universal commissary. She had just made a film called *40 Pounds of Trouble*, a sentimental comedy with Tony Curtis. On several occasions, Curtis came over and joined us at lunch. He was always "on" and entertaining. For example,

I would say to Suzanne, 'How's your soup?' And Tony would say, "Ah, that reminds me of a terrific soup story," and then he talked five minutes about soup.

The plot of our *Alcoa Presents* episode took place during the Cannes Film Festival. I played an ambitious fellow whose sister was an actress. My character was trying to persuade her to carry on with half the men at Cannes to advance her career. I was back playing a shifty deviant. When Suzanne's character refused to do as my character asked in order to advance his career, I had to break into tears at a climactic moment.

Suzanne Pleshette.

It was a nice juicy scene, I thought, but it turned out that I couldn't cry when it was time for the tears! For all the times I went crazy or ran amok on camera, I had never been called upon to cry. When I looked through the script to see my scenes, I read those wonderful letters — ECU, for "extreme close-up" — that actors loved to see! Extreme close-ups are an actor's chance to shine, to show thoughts and emotions on screen.

When it came time for the argument with Suzanne's character, I couldn't cry. I felt the emotion, and I thought I was doing a good job, except there were no tears. Our director, David Lowell Rich, said, "Cut! You're not crying!"

"I'm so sorry," I told him. "Let's try again."

Take two came, the cameras rolled, and I heard "Action!" followed by a long pause. "You're not crying," Rich told me again, losing his patience. He paced as the rest of the crew began thinking of a way to get me to cry on camera.

They finally squirted onion juice into my eyes so I would realistically appear to cry. I felt like a phony because I was getting paid to act and cry, but I simply could not shed tears. I think part of it was the tension of being told that I wasn't crying when I was supposed to be. It was humiliating. Rich had the prop man standing just off camera, very close to me. Because it was a big close-up with the camera near my face, the prop man blew onion juice into my eyes to make me cry. I saw disdain on the director's face — "You call yourself an actor and you can't cry." Well, I learned two things from working in Hollywood. I couldn't ride a horse and I couldn't cry.

Others in the cast included Ed Asner, Emile Genest, and Signe Hasso, a fine Swedish actress. She enjoyed a good career playing uptight, intense, neurotic ladies. She was symbolic of the old world in Hollywood. When it was time to film, cast members were driven in limos from the makeup department onto the Universal backlot. When Signe's limo arrived, I happened to be standing near it, so I opened the door for her. She said, "Oh, how kind of you, young man — chivalry is not dead." Then she walked onto the set with a great flourish.

All of us enjoyed a good script on this particular show. I did well, the crying scene aside. Because the plot was about actors and show business, it was a treat to see us looking good in white tie and tails. The show was filmed on the Universal backlot. Nearly every studio had its own French Quarter, Mediterranean area or Spanish Quarter. Universal's was a wonderful old set-up all the way back from the silent days. We filmed around the French village and its apartments and stores, made up to look like a completely authentic French village.

I never forgot that the series was called *Fred Astaire Presents Alcoa*. Astaire introduced each show and the cast, similar to how Boris Karloff introduced the *Thriller* series. When he filmed a little bit introducing each of us by name, I wanted an opportunity to chat with him; after all, he was a living legend. I even wanted to watch how the great dancer walked. Since he only did the intros and wasn't in the rest of the show, he was only there at Universal that one day.

The introduction scene placed the primary actors on a plane supposedly headed for Cannes. Astaire walked down the aisle and said, "Our guests tonight are Suzanne Pleshette, David Frankham, etc.," followed by a close-up of each of us sitting in our plane seat. I was just as thrilled to hear Fred Astaire read my name as I had been with Boris Karloff!

Later in the day we were on a break, so I went to the men's room with only two urinals. In walked Astaire, right next to me. I thought, "Well, this is not an opportune moment to ask him questions about his career," so I didn't say a word. We both stood there, and then I left and he left. That's my little Fred Astaire story. I didn't get to even talk to him, but we did get to pee together!

From Fred Astaire and *Alcoa Presents*, I went to work on another 1960s anthology series called *G.E. True*. The series isn't well remembered today, thanks in part to its similarity to another series, *G.E. Theatre*, and the fact that it was sometimes referred to as *Jack Webb's G.E. True*. Jack Webb did *G.E. True* for just the 1962-1963 season in between his two versions of *Dragnet*. Each show was based on a true story, usually adapted from a magazine called "True." The show aired in the same time slot where *G.E. Theatre* had lived for a decade. The director of my first appearance on the show was Robert Leeds. He had worked with Webb on *Dragnet*.

I don't remember too much about my first episode, called "U.X.B.," other than it taking place during World War II and Michael Evans being in the cast. Evans was working on the movie version of *Bye Bye Birdie* about the time we worked together.

Jack Webb was another example of someone who had worked on both sides of the camera. I was hired to do another episode of his *G.E. True* series, this time a two-parter. Also set during World War II, this episode is memorable for me because James Doohan was in the cast. Doohan had just moved down from Canada. He was nervous about being able to find work and provide for his family. He asked about jobs, and I told him that he would do fine. He had given up a career in Canadian television and hoped to find steady work. Little did he know! Just a few years later, he became one of the stars of *Star Trek*.

Our two-parter together was called "Escape," directed by William Conrad. Conrad had been one of the most prolific stars of radio before transitioning to television. He really knew his stuff from having worked so constantly. I once read that he appeared on more than seven thousand individual radio episodes of various programs!

Ben Wright was also in our cast. Other than Doris Lloyd, I had the pleasure of working with Ben more than just about anybody in Hollywood. He was such a wonderful friend off camera, too, gentle and kind. Like Doris, everyone liked and respected him.

At one point in 1962, I found a beautiful little cottage in West Hollywood, which is nowhere near Hollywood. I paid $90 a month and stayed there for nearly fifteen years. Think of the bargain I had compared to today's real estate prices!

That same year, I quit my weekly acting class. Now the laugh is on me. Two actors were doing a scene for class criticism and needed a younger player. We didn't have one in the group, so they got somebody who had not actually worked professionally. I didn't think he was very good. I was dead set going against our principles of having to be a working actor to belong to the class, so I resigned. The would-be actor was none other than

I played a shell-shocked soldier to Dorothy Provine's nurse in The Gallant Men, *1963.*

Ryan O'Neal! Well, you can't win them all, can you? I was probably lousy, too, when I started, so my apologies to Ryan O'Neal, once and for all.

In 1963, I returned to Warner Bros. for one of my favorite roles, a shell-shocked soldier in *The Gallant Men.* One of several shows that attempted to tell the many stories that came out of World War II, the show aired on ABC. Unfortunately, the series didn't do well in the ratings, and my episode marked the last show in its one-season run.

The bright side was that I worked with Dorothy Provine, a contract player at Warners. The studio used her extensively as a guest star on a number of series and as a star on several programs, including *The Roaring 20s.* She had married English-born director Robert Day. She was very tired from going from show to show, but she really was a good sport. Dorothy really enlivened the show for me.

We had a great scene together as she nursed my character back to health. My character had witnessed some sort of war trauma and stopped speaking. When Dorothy sang to me as I lay in bed, the script called for emotion, and I got to do my obligatory screaming, breakdown-style scene until she sang away my troubles. We even got to kiss, so she cured my temporary insanity in a flash!

DAVID FRANKHAM

Plays The Title Role

In The

"TOMMY" EPISODE

Of

"THE GALLANT MEN"

Tomorrow Night, 8 P.M. — Channel 7

Representation MAURINE OLIVER

An ad in the March 29, 1963, The Hollywood Reporter *promoting my appearance on* The Gallant Men.

She was kind enough to autograph a photograph for my father. He was proud as a peacock to get it and enjoyed the program when the show aired there. Years later, he still recalled the time that Dorothy Provine autographed the photo to him.

In the fall of 1963, I read for *Viva Las Vegas*, a big musical with Elvis Presley and Ann-Margret. George Sidney was to direct the film. I was a great admirer of his because he had done some of the great MGM musicals — *Anchors Away, Show Boat, The Harvey Girls, Annie Get Your Gun, Kiss Me Kate,* and at Columbia, *Pal Joey* and *Bye Bye Birdie*.

The film was written by Sally Benson, who had penned the script on one of my all-time favorite musicals, *Meet Me in St. Louis*. After reading, I was one of two finalists for one of the leads. I was in limbo as the studio decided whether to make the character English or Italian. Unfortunately for me, they opted to go Italian, so the part went to Cesare Danova. Film fans can ponder how the picture would have been different if I had been cast instead.

At one of my readings at MGM, I was leaving the Irving Thalberg Building with Maurine when Roddy McDowall was parking his car.

When he saw Maurine, he came running over to us. "Maurine, how lovely to see you again," he said. She wasn't Hollywood's biggest agent, but she was respected enough that Roddy wanted to see how she was doing. I knew that I was in good hands, even when I didn't get a big MGM musical with Elvis.

Later that year, the world experienced a traumatic event never forgotten by anyone who lived through it. On November 22, 1963, I was at Western Costume, where most actors went to be fitted for clothes. I was about to work on an episode of *The Outer Limits*, when Stephen Boyd walked in to be fitted for a television series. He reported in and was told to wait a few minutes. I rarely gushed to other actors, but I couldn't resist saying, "You were so good in *Ben-Hur* — you should have won an Academy Award."

We were chatting about his career. A radio was on the receptionist's desk across the room. Boyd was talking when he suddenly broke off and said, "Excuse me a moment." He went over and bent his ear to the radio.

Suddenly he began pounding the desk and said, "The bastards, they got him, they got him!" He said to the receptionist, "Cancel my appointment, please. I'll have to come back later." He practically ran out of the building, he was so emotional. That's where I was the day President Kennedy died. The whole world seemed to change after that. I had been fortunate to arrive in America during a peaceful, post-war economic boom time. Life never quite seemed the same.

Somehow fitting that era and the nation's mood, my first episode of *The Outer Limits* was called "Nightmare." A few months before, I had gone to Seattle to film a pilot for the same production company, the Leslie Stevens Company. We were there two weeks with Walter Pidgeon for a show that would have been called *Mr. Kingston*. The pilot had a great part for me as a villain who gets shot in the engine room of a real ocean liner. Pidgeon played the captain of a luxury liner, with Peter Graves as the ship's executive officer.

While we were in Seattle, Elvis Presley was shooting *It Happened at the World's Fair*, so nobody bothered us when we were busy on location at various spots in the city. There was always a crowd following Elvis wherever he went on his film, but nobody pestered us at all.

NBC was going with either our *Mr. Kingston* pilot or a new series called *The Outer Limits*. At a preview, we got to see both the Seattle pilot I filmed and a pilot episode for *The Outer Limits*. The network decided to go with *The Outer Limits*, NBC's answer to *Twilight Zone* over at CBS. Because I had been working with the studio on the other pilot, I was fortunate enough to be cast in two episodes of *The Outer Limits*, both of which are considered to be among the better episodes of the series.

The first episode was called "Nightmare," written by Joseph Stefano, a friend of Alfred Hitchcock's and the writer of the screenplay for *Psycho*. Stefano was also a producer on *The Outer Limits*, and the fact that he could go from writing *Psycho* to working on the *The Outer Limits* suggests

I was part of a terrific ensemble on the "Nightmare" episode of The Outer Limits, *1963.*

that television from that era hasn't received enough credit for being better than many critics admitted.

Stefano effectively captured some of the mindset that went into post World War II, Cold War-era paranoia and mentality. The story follows a group of soldiers taken as prisoners of war after a conflict with another planet. The group is seemingly subjected to torture and mind games by aliens. A shocking plot twist reveals that their own military is experimenting with mind war games to see if they would break under real circumstances.

The director was John Erman, whom I grew to admire. He was a sensitive director. Our show was one of his earliest projects as director. He had moved into directing after a few years as a casting director. In fact, he had earlier cast me in my episode of *Adventures in Paradise*. He's wonderful with actors, so much so that everyone loved giving his best for him. As we geared up for production, John mentioned a young actor coming out from New York. Our episode was one of Martin Sheen's first TV shows. Even then, one could see that he was going places fast, even though I had never heard of him at the time.

Years later, John told me, "When I drove to work in the mornings, I saw

With my friend Ben Wright on the "Nightmare" episode of The Outer Limits, *1963.*

Martin hitchhiking. He didn't have enough money to be able to take a cab or have his own car to work as the rest of us did." The show was one of Sheen's first opportunities in Hollywood. I knew immediately that he was good. He had a wonderful energy in the way he absolutely threw himself into his part without overdoing it or taking it away from the rest of us.

Our characters were a team in the movie, and Sheen somehow knew how to stand out without overpowering the rest of us. To get pumped up for his shots, he ran around the perimeter of the soundstage walls. I didn't realize he would go as far as did, because he wasn't tall. Back in those days, if you wanted to be a series or movie lead, you more or less had to be the standard, average, handsome-looking fellow, and he wasn't that. Sheen was a character star. His energy levels every day on the set were incredible to behold.

My friend Ben Wright was very good in his part as a senior military officer. We had a scene together where his character tries to convince me to reveal some information. The cast also included Whit Bissell and Ed Nelson, who worked frequently with Roger Corman and became one of the leads on the *Peyton Place* television series not too long after working on *The Outer Limits*.

John Anderson, who had appeared in *Psycho* just a few years earlier as a car salesman, was hidden behind a mask as an alien interrogator. He hated putting on the mask because he felt it made him look like Heckle and Jeckle. Bill Gunn, an African-American, was in the cast, demonstrating how the show was groundbreaking by striving for equality early on television. Bill and I talked quite a bit during the show. I liked him and thought he was good. He was going back to do off-Broadway theatre, but he told me that opportunities were few for black actors in the early 1960s.

It was also an honor to work with James Shigeta, another groundbreaker when it came to Asian-Americans gaining acceptance in Hollywood. He had earned notice in the film adaptation of *Flower Drum Song*. During breaks between filming, I raved to Jimmy about how much I liked *Flower Drum Song*, especially Miyoshi Umeki, who had won the Best Supporting Actress Academy Award for her performance.

One day James said, "David, there's a call for you." I went over to the phone on the side of the set, and this little voice said, "David?"

"Yes?" I replied.

"This is Miyoshi." For a second, I thought it was a gag, but I immediately recognized that lovely little voice. I melted talking on the phone to her. I never met her formally, although when I was living in Sherman Oaks in the mid-1980s, I saw her at the supermarket several times but didn't want to bother her by interrupting her shopping.

On "Nightmare," I played an upstanding officer who breaks under the pressure and shoots a man. Watching this episode, I have always been reminded of just how skinny I was during production. All of us were quite good, if I say so myself, and this episode is remembered for its stark depiction of the lengths to which the military can go. Many TV shows had something to say back then, and *The Outer Limits* was no exception.

I was almost forty when I did my second episode, "Don't Open Till Doomsday," playing Miriam Hopkins' young newlywed husband who spends years trapped in a box while his bride ages from a punishment designed by a revengeful scientist using an alien inside the box.

My character was sucked into the box, so for the rest of the story, I remained my age, which was supposed to be twenty-one. That was a big laugh, because I was really thirty-eight! The makeup staff was challenged to keep me young while Miriam's character aged. The makeup artists took an hour to make me younger. Each morning they said, "For God's sake, don't laugh, talk, or eat until we roll film, or the makeup will crack!"

My makeup was like something out of *House of Wax*. It was fun to look in the mirror and see that I appeared much younger. I always had a boyish

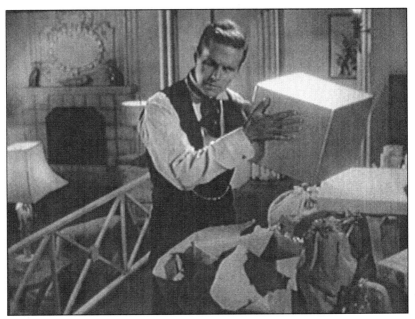

I was made to look twenty-one on the "Don't Open Till Doomsday" episode of The Outer Limits, *1964.*

look; it was my curse when I started in Hollywood at age thirty. I really looked twenty-one back then! Even on *Master of the World* and *Tales of Terror* a few years before, the makeup man used to do all sorts of things to age me a little, much to Vincent Price's amusement. He always used to call me "that damned juvenile," wonderful man that he was.

Miriam Hopkins had memorably worked with Olivia de Havilland in *The Heiress*. I did my scenes in the early part of the week with a girl playing younger Miriam as a bride. Miriam and I actually didn't work together, even though we were playing a husband and wife separated by the time and distance of the alien-inhabited box. Thank goodness we didn't work together, because she proved to be a very difficult lady.

Miriam came onto the set the first day of shooting and said that she wasn't happy with the script, she was going back to her hotel, and she would remain there until her demands for a rewrite were met! "I'm not going to perform with what I've got so far," she said, as she swept out of the studio. She might have been able to do that back in the 1930s under contract at Warner Bros., but it was unfair to do that when a television show was in production.

Joseph Stefano was the writer again for my second *The Outer Limits* episode. I was told that everyone had a very stormy week working with temperamental Miriam. I think her advancing years and vanity may have played a part in it. Somehow it worked out and she acted the scenes she had been given. It always amused me that she still had enough confidence in herself to say, "I don't like this story you're filming; rewrite it for me or I won't do it!" I admired her audacity. Instead of introducing herself on the set, she just marched in and said, "I'll be at my hotel until I get a rewrite!"

My scenes were shot separately from hers, although the editing made it look as though we were both in the same scene. The episode featured my patented mad scene. I was, and still am, a very low-keyed person, slow to anger, if ever. As a character actor, I tried hard to put myself in the mad character's state of mind. Directors would say a few key words to get me going. Afterwards I often heard, "Good take, but give me more" and we worked to build up to my best work in two or three takes.

Gerd Oswald was an excellent director on the episode. As we walked through my breakdown scene for camera moves, Oswald said we couldn't do the scene in more than one take because I had to destroy the set as I went nuts. We walked through the scene to get the staging just right. In television, there's rarely time or money to sit around while sets are rebuilt.

Besides, running amok wasn't really something I could rehearse. I had done enough of those kinds of scenes to know that they were counting on me to be convincingly crazy. Adrenaline is the preparation that an actor really needs for emotional breakdown scenes. I usually took as many sudden deep breaths as possible to hyperventilate. A creative director always said, "Let us know when you feel you're ready and we'll shoot."

So away we went. The cinematographer was Conrad Hall, who became one of Hollywood's best-known cinematographers, earning Oscars for *Butch Cassidy and the Sundance Kid, American Beauty,* and *Road to Perdition*. His cameraman was William Fraker, whose later high profile films included *Bullitt*.

Fraker used a handheld camera strapped to his shoulder. He and I literally broke up the set as I careened around the furniture and screamed my head off. There was a wild sense of release when something over-the-top like that was done. The director yelled, "Cut!" and the dust cleared.

Luckily, the scene went well, so we didn't have to rebuild the set or re-do my makeup to do it over.

The scene was also done MOS, "mit out sound" as the old German directors used to say in the silent days. Since there was no soundtrack of crashing sounds and my screaming was to be recorded later to match to the picture, Oswald shouted directions to me as I staggered about: "Look this way. Now scream. Now look over there. Struggle more," and so on. It was almost like acting by numbers in a way, but I always loved responding to direction like that. I remember that scene with particular satisfaction. Since I had proven to be a pro at dubbing at MGM, I'm proud of my acting and the vocal work that we added to create the final shot.

I was fortunate to work in Hollywood when most series ran to thirty-nine episodes each season. There was so much work for actors that trends and genres really weren't that apparent at the time. The work on the *The Outer Limits* series led to more opportunities to specialize in characters that invariably fell apart before the final reel. Roddy McDowall justifiably had first crack at nearly every sizable role in that category. I often felt that I was contacted only if he was otherwise engaged, but that in itself was flattering. Among the dozen or so of us who dogged Roddy's footsteps, we had to audition, but he got the scripts first. That's how it should have been, given his distinguished career arc.

My peers didn't seem anxious to be typecast as weak-minded characters, yet I reveled in the freedom those roles gave me. By 1963, my paychecks had increased to $1,250 per week, or about $8,500 in today's dollars. The pay wasn't bad at all for a working actor. Truth be told, I almost would have paid that money back for all the opportunities I enjoyed from working in Hollywood.

For all of the hard work, sweat and tears that went into a Hollywood career, it never ceased to amaze me how actors unexpectedly benefited from a scheduling snafu or production delay. I profited a few times from working — or not working — on a few high profile projects.

I think most English actors wanted a part in *My Fair Lady*, Warner Bros.' 1964 extravaganza in which the studio adapted the hit stage musical and famously passed over Julie Andrews in favor of Audrey Hepburn. The studio was sparing no expense in filming it, and the legendary George Cukor was directing. I bombarded Cukor with photos and resumes when he was in pre-production. I had my eye on the Freddy Eynsford-Hill role played by John Michael King on Broadway.

I decided to go for it. I felt that I could be a convincing Freddy Eynsford-Hill. I went to a singing coach for six weeks until I could sing the songs in tune. Determined, I sent resumes, photos and even telegrams to Cukor that read, "PLEASE SEE ME. STOP." Dead silence ensued from Cukor. He completely ignored me. That was crushing. He could have at least talked to me. After all, he had directed my dubbing on *Song Without End* just a few years earlier.

I found out later that Audrey Hepburn had asked for Jeremy Brett because they had done *War and Peace* together. When I saw the film, I thought he was perfect for the part, while Bill Shirley did a fine job dubbing his singing voice. Still, would it have hurt Cukor to at least have a secretary respond to me one way or the other? That's the way it went, sometimes.

My friend Molly Roden was assigned by Warners to be Audrey Hepburn's coach to help her with the Cockney accent required for the Eliza Doolittle part. One day I asked Molly how it was going and she said, "Not well; Audrey doesn't get it." Hepburn was trying, and it was okay for the movie, but even I could tell it wasn't very authentic when the film came out.

I was still destined to work on *My Fair Lady* after all. My dubbing work on several notable films, including one for George Cukor himself, led to me being called to Warner Bros. for post-production dubbing work on the movie. Even though I wouldn't be seen, at last I could work on what was advertised as the most eagerly anticipated film since *Gone with the Wind!*

Cukor sent for me to do post-production at a rate of $1,000 a day. I was signed to a guaranteed "pay or play" contract for five days, meaning that if I finished early, I was still to be paid $5,000 for the week. What an incredible contract that was; in fact, I believe the $1,000 per day rate was the highest daily paycheck I ever received for a cinematic or television project, and all for dubbing! Maurine worked with Eddie Rhine at Warner Bros. to get that rate for me.

When I got the call for *My Fair Lady*, I thought I was destined for another delightful project directed by George Cukor just as we had done together on *Song Without End*. On the first day, four of us actors were there at nine in the morning to dub bits of dialogue for crowds at Covent Garden or other outdoor scenes.

Cukor bustled about in his little white shirt, short sleeves, and spectacles. I stared at him and thought, "You did *Camille* and *A Star Is Born*." People like George Cukor, William Wyler, and Vincente Minnelli oozed talent and power, and it was exciting to be around them.

That morning Cukor chatted away to his assistants. They handed us script pages to line up and match to voices on screen. I looked at mine. While I can't remember what the words were now, the dialogue just didn't strike me as authentic. After filming *David Copperfield*, Cukor prided himself on being an Anglophile and thought he knew all about English customs and the vernacular.

I may have been dismissed by George Cukor on My Fair Lady *(1964), but my friend Gladys Cooper, next to Audrey Hepburn, won great acclaim.* (WARNER BROS.)

Yet the dialogue in front of me struck a false note in my head. I worked well with Cukor before, so I waited until he stopped talking to one of his assistants. I said, "I don't think some of this dialogue is realistic for an English actor to say. May I alter this line, Mr. Cukor?"

"No, you can't," he snapped. "I wrote that, and I want it spoken just as written." With that, he walked away.

"Okay," I thought. "It's early in the morning — maybe he's not in a good mood."

I retired to my chair and waited while some of the other guys recorded their parts. Nobody else asked to change his lines, so my request hadn't meant anything of significance until lunch break was called at noon. By then, I noticed that the other actors had been dubbing away, and I hadn't been called back to the microphone. The line Cukor wanted me to read had yet to show up on the screen.

After lunch was called, I walked out as one of Cukor's assistants came up behind me. He said, "Mr. Cukor doesn't want you to come back."

"Oh," I said. "Then the same time tomorrow?"

He said firmly again, "Mr. Cukor does not want you to come back."

With that, he walked away. It dawned on me that Cukor hadn't made eye contact with me since I had asked to change that line. I stood there thinking, "Have I been fired?" I knew that as a general rule, SAG member actors were simply never fired, so I went over to Warners casting to see Eddie Rhine.

I told him, "I'm through for the day, but Eddie, Cukor says he doesn't want me to come back tomorrow. Does he want me to come back later in the week perhaps?"

Eddie put a call through to Cukor's bungalow and talked to someone who told him that Cukor didn't want me to come back at all because I had been "uncooperative." Eddie reminded them what I and the other actors had done earlier that morning when we walked into the dubbing room — a secretary had appeared with contracts for each of us. I had signed a commitment to be paid for $5,000 for the whole week. None of this seemed to matter to Cukor or his people as they refused to rescind his ultimatum.

Eddie told me, "I guess we're stuck, kid. You can't work for anybody else this week, you know."

"Who cares?" I told him. "It's $5,000 bucks!"

I sat on my patio for the rest of the week. Maurine told me, "Never mind, dear, you got the money." She was happy for an easy commission until somebody from the Warner Bros. legal department tried to null and void the contract because I had been "fired." Maurine had to sign a deposition affirming that I was willing and able to provide my acting services for the week but the director had decided not to use me. Maurine's Irish was up as she went back and forth with the studio. "We're not letting this pass, dear!" she said.

She very rarely lost. When the dust settled, Warner Bros. had to pay me, even though Cukor had fired me. I had to sit at home the rest of that week, unable to work until that week's contract had lapsed, but I was paid for the whole five days. To this day, I still get paid little residual checks that have slowly diminished over the years for dubbing that I never did! I never uttered a single word on *My Fair Lady*, but I was paid well for it.

Being fired by Cukor was the only time I was ever dismissed from a project. I can't feel too bad about it, though, because in my post-production work with Cukor or Minnelli, they were legends of their day. If anything, the episode demonstrates that Cukor was very hands-on in post-production. He and Minnelli felt that if actors dubbed for a character, the actors should become the character. We couldn't just say the lines that were coming out of the actors' mouths on the screen. Those directors wanted us to be fully and emotionally involved. It was challenging to do for men who were task masters. *My Fair Lady* aside, they kept us working repeatedly until they were satisfied with the results. I can't imagine many of today's directors being as hands-on about those small details.

The episode didn't seem to harm my dubbing career. A few years later, I was called back to MGM to dub on *Grand Prix*, John Frankenheimer's opus to racing with James Garner and Eva Marie Saint. With Margaret Booth again supervising the post-production dubbing, Frankenheimer personally directed me as I read page after page of dialogue, most of it for off-camera English announcers on radio or television. He used announcer characters to help with exposition as the race progresses. My voice was heard quite a bit throughout that three-hour film.

The flip side of getting paid not to dub was being paid to sit without working week after week. That happened in the summer of 1964 when I was hired to appear in a virtually silent, yet pivotal role as a POW who cracks under pressure in *King Rat*. Bryan Forbes adapted James Clavell's novel about the atrocities that the Japanese subjected British soldiers to during World War II.

Forbes was a distinguished scriptwriter and director. I was so eager to work for him that I got a copy of the script. As I read about an officer who had a nervous breakdown, I turned the two pages for more, but that was it. There was no dialogue, either. I took the script home and went back the next day. I auditioned a mental and physical breakdown scene for Bryan Forbes without any preparation other than reading the scene once to myself.

Even though the part was brief, it was an integral scene demonstrating the cruelties of a POW prisoner camp. Besides, I liked Bryan Forbes on the spot. He was a generous man and a great director. I was determined to get it, although Maurine and the Columbia casting director told me it was much too brief a role at a time when I was doing guest-star roles on TV.

Because I couldn't truly audition an authentic nervous breakdown, Forbes said, "I really can't read you for this since there's no dialogue. I'll trust you to do it well because I'm told you specialize in doing nervous breakdowns on camera. Do you want to do it?"

I welcomed the opportunity, figuring the part would at least bring a couple of days of work. I was contracted to salary for three weeks on *King Rat* at $1,500 a week. Filming was to begin the following week, but I was told that I would have to be on call, which meant staying on salary until needed.

Getting paid while I waited to film was a fluke. My scene as a POW officer was to be filmed with John Mills, whom I had interviewed once on my radio program. Mills couldn't get to California because he was working on another film in England as the production ran over. I was given a three-week guarantee because Columbia expected him fairly soon. If he didn't arrive by then, my contract was to be extended. The delay was fine with me. A part that would have taken a few days now meant that I would be paid at least three weeks!

God bless John Mills, because his picture went over, week after week. Our poor director had to film everything else that he could while we waited for Mills to arrive. Each day found me sitting in a canvas chair on location out in the San Fernando Valley as I watched the other actors working hard in the sun. Peter Sellers was a friend of Forbes, so he sent out all the British papers to the set each day. Forbes passed them out to those of us waiting for our scene.

I got to know Denholm Elliott fairly well from the cast. Although he had done a couple of terrific movies, he was completely new to Hollywood. One day he said to me, "Do you suppose it would be a good idea to let people know that I'm here?"

I said, "I'm sure everybody knows you're here. You're Denholm Elliott!"

He said, "Well, I've been told that I perhaps should take an ad out in the trade papers to let everyone know I'm here."

"Oh, yes," I said. "That could be very important for your career."

"Well," he said. "I was thinking of doing an ad about three inches by four inches in the papers."

"That's too small," I told him. "You have to take a full page! You're held in great esteem by the community out here, so you can't do less than a full page."

A full page was then $350 for the back page of *Variety* or $250 for the back page of *The Hollywood Reporter*. He followed my advice and took out the ads. Hollywood used him frequently in the coming years, including

I'm behind John Mills and Denholm Elliott on location for King Rat *(1965)*.
(COLUMBIA)

his work with Harrison Ford in a couple of the Indiana Jones movies.

I also got to know George Segal, one of the leads. Both Paul Newman and Steve McQueen had turned down the part before Segal got it. John Mills was playing a part originally offered to Dirk Bogarde, so if Dirk had taken the part, I could have shared the screen with a friend and one of my inspirations to pursue acting.

I talked to Bryan Forbes about his transition from acting to directing. He told me that he felt his greatest strengths never were in acting and that he gradually got into writing and directing. I had promised him that I would look like a POW when we started shooting, so I had lost thirty-five pounds in about eight weeks on a diet of Diet Coke and cottage cheese. (I wouldn't recommend that diet, but it does get results!) Friends saw me in a restaurant one evening and told mutual friends the next day that I looked very ill! But I had a long run on a movie and they didn't. I had to starve myself for eight weeks to get the effect and then keep it going for months on end while I waited for my scene to film!

Three weeks turned into four, and then five, as we waited for John Mills to arrive. The Columbia casting agent, Eddie Rhine, with whom I had worked before when he was at Warner Bros., finally called Maurine and told her that it really wasn't necessary for me to wait week after week on the set. Because I was on call, it would be okay to sit at home instead and wait for a call the day before I was needed to film.

Because I had kept my weight so low for *King Rat*, Maurine got me another part as a POW on a television movie-of-the-week with David Carradine. We didn't tell Eddie Rhine at Columbia that we were doing this, but there had been dead silence from the studio as they went on filming all they could for *King Rat* without John Mills. I went to Universal, met David Carradine and the director, and went through wardrobe. I was about to start filming on the TV movie the following Monday when I finally got the call that John Mills had arrived and was ready to film my scene the next day on *King Rat*.

Maurine had to call Universal and apologize for a "prior commitment" coming up to get me out of the TV work. Had we been able to pull it off, the Universal show would have been double salary. At the same time, it was a close call. If I had started working on the TV film only to be called to *King Rat*, it could have been a disaster.

For his first film, Forbes had directed Mills' daughter, Hayley Mills, in *Whistle Down the Wind*. The entire Mills family seemed very close, and I remember Hayley visiting her father at one point during the shooting of *King Rat*. Forbes had been determined to stick it out in order to get John Mills, so after he arrived and they got to our scene, I thought, "What if I louse this up — it's been weeks since I last ran through it!" That pressure made me all the more nervous, which was just what the scene needed. To get wound up for the part, I stayed by myself, away from the rest of the cast.

Forbes said, "David, just do your own preparation and let us know when you're ready." He told everyone that we would try the scene without a rehearsal. In my scene, the Japanese inform John Mills that they've discovered a forbidden radio in the soldiers' quarters, Hut Sixteen. I'm the guilty party, so I had to sweat and tremble nervously as the search gets closer to discovering my secret. Once discovered, my character had to hoist his bed out of the barracks and off to some terrible punishment.

Forbes was a stickler for authenticity. The bed was heavy, the kind that had actually been used in my time in the army in 1946. Even after the war, we still slept on those damn beds made of ropes. We didn't have mattresses; we had a couple of sheets, one underneath, one on top of us, and a very rough pillow. We slept on rope and scratched a lot. I told Forbes how amazed I was that the studio had constructed a POW camp eerily accurate to the Changi former POW camp I remembered from my Army stint in 1946.

After John Mills and I did our scene, I thought I was through with the picture. My paycheck had lasted from July through October, but all good things must come to an end. Yet several weeks after I said my goodbyes, Maurine called me and said that Forbes wanted me back to film a traveling shot of the officers asleep, a scene he wanted to play under the opening credits. Fortunately for me, the scene couldn't be filmed until December, which meant that I stayed on salary through the whole fall that year. I didn't even have to sit on location the whole time; at one point they let me stay at home to sit by the pool.

I rejoined the group to film the extra scene just before Christmas so Tom Courtney could catch a plane to Spain to film *Doctor Zhivago*. After I had finished my first stint on the picture, the rest of the cast spent two more grueling months recreating life in the POW camp. It was wonderful to see everybody again. When it was done, I had spent about fourteen weeks on the picture at the weekly rate, the best paycheck I ever made for an onscreen part, especially since my role had no real dialogue.

The following year, I was in Beverly Hills to get my hair cut. As I crossed the street, Bryan Forbes came toward me. He greeted me and asked if I was free. He told me that *King Rat* was previewing that evening in Long Beach and that I was welcome to attend.

I took a bus down and arrived at the theatre. Richard Attenborough, who was Forbes' business partner in their filmmaking company, was there, along with Forbes' wife, Nanette Newman. I felt silly being there with those big names, because I think I was the only person in the whole movie who didn't speak. When the credits came on, there was a long list of actors. There lower in the list was "David Frankham." Poor Maurine damn near died. "You've committed professional suicide, that's what you've done," she told me. I went right back into more TV work, so no harm was done, and I was pleased with my movie work no matter how brief. And as my agent, Maurine did very nicely with her fourteen-week commission!

The cast of King Rat *(1965).* (COLUMBIA)

Following the screening in Long Beach, Forbes and Attenborough invited me to ride back to their hotel in their rented limo, a nice consolation for someone who didn't get to speak on camera. Attenborough remembered me from our BBC interview the decade before. I reminded him that he had inscribed a photo to me with words that thanked me for the "best interview ever." He reaffirmed that sentiment ten years later!

I rarely kept my scripts; the pages got loose and I threw them away. For some reason, I kept quite a bit of *King Rat*. I don't know why I held onto it, because I didn't have much to say in the movie. The film wasn't a big hit, although it did earn a couple of Oscar nominations. Today the film is regarded as a fairly accurate depiction of POW life and the psychological torture that so many endured during World War II.

The film shows up every now and then on TCM, so while the subject matter is fairly grim, I recall the time I laughed all the way to the bank that year, earning $1,500 a week for sitting around and waiting for John Mills! Between *My Fair Lady* and *King Rat*, 1964 was a year of creative frustration that nevertheless paid off well in the end.

That same year, I flew home to England to visit my parents. Driving back to the little house where I had grown up, jet lag hit me in the worst way. I hadn't realized how small their house was. I walked in and embraced

Back home in England with my mother, 1964.

my parents. As we started talking, I suddenly got claustrophobia in spades. I had to get out.

I didn't want to offend them. Interrupting my father, I said, "Dad, there's so much I want to see and it'll be dark soon — would you mind if I took a short walk?" They looked at me rather strangely and said, "All right, if that's what you want to do." I shot out of the house and walked for about half an hour until I calmed down. I was so confused over the time change and sitting for eleven hours in the plane. After getting my wits again, I walked happily back in the house a half hour later.

It's funny the things you remember later like that episode of claustrophobia. In spite of my jaunt with jet lag and feeling cramped, we had a good visit that year. By then, I was in my late thirties, well established in Hollywood, so I never had anything to apologize for in terms of my career. It had been nearly a decade since I made my choice to leave for America, and the gamble had paid off. My parents were certainly products of their Victorian generation and perhaps never quite understood my quest for adventure across the ocean. It was hard for them to argue with success, and in those later years, I got the sense that they were a little more proud of me.

CHAPTER TEN

From Hitchcock to Hillbillies to the *USS Enterprise*

My television work continued unabated by the mid-1960s. In 1964, I filmed my last *Alfred Hitchcock Presents* with John Cassavetes and his wife, Gena Rowlands, with whom I had worked in *The Spiral Road*. Gena was just so good, then and now.

For our episode, we portrayed actors playing actors in a fun scene where our characters rehearse a play. Our two characters shared a love scene, so we had to kiss, only to be interrupted by John Cassavetes' character when he nearly strangles my character in a fit of jealous rage that was supposed to be staged as though he was pretending to fight, only to lose control and take the rehearsal too far. Believe it or not, acting like you're acting is never easy. You have to be careful to keep the lines believable and not sound hammy.

The director of the episode turned out to be John Brahm, who had directed my idol, Laird Cregar, in both *The Lodger* and his final film, *Hangover Square*. You can imagine me bending poor John Brahm's ear at every lunch break during that week's shoot, saying "Tell me more." At every chance I haunted him and asked Brahm to share more about Cregar.

He shared a positive opinion of Cregar's talent. Brahm told me that Cregar was scheduled to play the role in *Laura* that was given instead to Clifton Webb. The success of *The Lodger* demanded an immediate follow-up and that left him unavailable for *Laura's* start. So he was stuck in *Hangover Square* while *Laura* was in production. To this day, I watch with but hear Cregar. It put Webb into full orbit as a bona fide star and would have cemented Cregar's above-the-titles position.

Brahm told me that Cregar's acting secret was that he erased himself and became a madman. I thought about how marvelous it was, to float free and lose one's self in a character. I adapted that approach into my acting and thought of Laird's scene whenever I had to run amok. That kind of acting meant that I could not be self-conscious. I had no inhibitions, so I couldn't even think of the crew. All I thought of was going

My mid-1960s headshot.

mad for the moment. I always continued to channel Cregar in later years whenever I had to act crazy for a part. Between John Brahm and Doris Lloyd, I felt I almost knew Laird Cregar personally.

Television offered such a variety in the 1960s that I went from *Alfred Hitchcock Presents* to *Gomer Pyle*. I enjoyed several stints on the show, filming two episodes in 1964 and a third two years later. I enjoyed *Gomer Pyle* because I never got enough comedy to do and the episodes were sort of "out there" in a 1960s way. The work was also high profile, as the series ranked in the top five of the most watched programs all three times I appeared on it.

I sometimes felt like a fraud when I was cast as an American lieutenant, but nobody caught on. In fact, I don't think I ever mentioned the fact that I was really English playing American. I just had to remember to keep speaking in an American accent when we weren't filming. My acting must have pleased Andy Griffith, who had a partnership in the show with Sheldon Leonard, because I auditioned for him the first time.

Jim Nabors was very friendly and lacked the pretension of some of the big stars. A few years before *Gomer Pyle*, friends from the drama class dragged me out to a nightclub in Santa Monica, and I say dragged because I'm not a night person, so I went resentfully. It was called the Horn, a sort of try-out place for new young talent. On came Jim, with his funny, friendly face, and then he suddenly burst into a Pavarotti-type song! I was amazed. I don't think he had done anything much professionally at that time, but shortly after, Andy Griffith discovered him and he was off and running. Later he had a number of best-selling albums and even played Las Vegas.

Most of my acting peers looked down their noses at the *Gomer Pyle* program, but Nabors was a very funny performer and extremely smart in spite of his "Aw, shucks" image. During script read-throughs in the morning, he would kick me on the shin under the table as a friendly greeting and say, "Howdee, how's it going today?" There was no Hollywood side to him at all, just a very pleasant fellow.

One of my episodes, "A Date for the Colonel's Daughter," reunited me with Karl Swenson from *The Spiral Road* a few years earlier. On another one of my three episodes, I had to drive a jeep. I finally had learned to drive, but I didn't yet own a car. I still couldn't drive that well. Truthfully, I was terrified to be driving again on camera, just as I had been on *Return of the Fly* back in 1959.

The script called for me to drive up and get out on camera to talk with Nabors. The poor camera crew didn't know about my unfamiliarity with a stick shift, so I squealed the brakes a little as I came to a halt. With Nabors and the rest of the supporting cast standing there, I thought, "I'm going to mow them all down!" I couldn't tell anybody that I didn't know how to drive well. If I had told them I was a bad driver, I would have lost the part. Miraculously, it seemed to work.

During the mid-1960s, I also stretched my comedic abilities in two episodes of *The Beverly Hillbillies*, which ranked as one of television's most popular comedies. In fact, several of the episodes set Nielsen ratings records as the highest-rated, regular episodes of a TV series. My debut with the Clampett clan also happened to be the first color episode of the series after CBS made the transition to color for the 1965-1966 season. That episode was heavily promoted in previews leading up to the season premiere and even included a snippet of me in the commercials.

The big satisfaction in filming *The Beverly Hillbillies* was working with Buddy Ebsen and Irene Ryan — what troupers! I loved them both. They each brought years of experience to their roles, so an actor could only learn by working with them. They were real masters of their craft and a real joy to work with on every scene. They knew more in their little fingers than I'll know in a hundred years. Buddy and Irene had a sense of timing that can't be taught. I feel they were both greatly underestimated in spite of that show's huge success.

My first episode was called "Admiral Jed Clampett." The plot involved the banker, Milburn Drysdale, wanting to show the Clampetts a yacht for potential purchase. Jethro borrows an admiral's uniform for Uncle Jed, and then the Clampetts end up on a Navy ship by accident. I played an American Naval officer on duty, and we had some great laughs from the reactions of the enlisted men to a surprise visit from an "admiral" and his family.

We drove down on the Los Angeles freeways to Long Beach Harbor for location shooting on the battleship. To save time, Irene Ryan put on her makeup and "Granny" wardrobe before we left the studio. We nearly caused traffic accidents on the way down as drivers in the other lanes took a look and then did double takes whenever Irene waved to people from the back of the limousine! People couldn't believe it was really Granny driving right alongside them! Every time we stopped at a traffic light, people cheered. She was a very dear lady.

My second episode followed a year later. "The Badger's Return" teamed me with the wonderful Leon Ames, who had played Judy Garland's father in *Meet Me in St. Louis*. He had been one of the founding members of the Screen Actors Guild way back in the early 1930s. Also in the cast was a nervous young lady called Gayle Hunnicutt, who later became quite a big star in London theatre and in movies.

We had as much fun on my second episode. Leon Ames and Gayle Hunnicutt played con artists pretending to be long-lost friends of the Clampett family from back in the hills. I played a detective on the crooks' trail. Because situation comedies usually involved mix-ups or misunderstandings, the Leon Ames character managed to convince the Clampetts that I was the real con artist.

Buddy Ebsen had one of his typical, rustic funny lines when he patted my character's coat and discovered the detective's pistol. "Mister, when you come totin' a pistol in my house, you've done muddied up my crick," he said. Donna Douglas, who played Elly Mae, and Max Baer, Jr., who played Jethro, then manhandled me across the set and into the kitchen as they argued over who would guard me.

I never had enough comedy for my taste. We had a lot of fun with both those episodes, and I'll live forever in rerun heaven, thanks to that show. TBS aired episodes repeatedly for years in the early days of cable, and the show remains popular on multiple cable channels and in syndication today.

Another high profile series was markedly more dramatic yet ever so much personal fun for me. Four years after co-starring with Basil Rathbone in *Tales of Terror* for AIP, we reunited to play father and son in a two-part episode arc of *Doctor Kildare*, starring Richard Chamberlain.

Basil was still the same, straining at the leash to get going on the day's shooting. He was staying at the Chateau Marmont Hotel in West Hollywood. Because most of our scenes were together, we had the same call each morning. On our first day of work, we discovered that each of us had taken a separate cab to get to work. Basil decided that we could share a cab since we were both in West Hollywood. He was picked up first, and then he directed the cab to my place on the way to work! We had to report to the set at 7:30, but he liked to get there thirty minutes early at seven, so each morning for two weeks, there was one of the silver screen's all-time great actors sticking his head over my fence and calling that our cab was ready!

Because we got to work early, he gave me a personal tour of the studio each morning! He could still remember and point out the soundstages where he had worked with Norma Shearer or with Greta Garbo in *Anna Karenina*. He still knew where the wardrobe department was. As we walked past those old dressing rooms, he remembered each star who had once been assigned to those same rooms. Basil showed me MGM Lot Two, the street from *Meet Me in St. Louis,* and where Gene Kelly was

Singing in the Rain. It was like a wonderful, first-hand guided Hollywood tour, every morning for ten days!

Our director was Alf Kjellin, which pleased Basil greatly. Alf and Mai Zetterling were two of Sweden's most promising young stars back in the 1940s. They did *Frenzy* together to enormous acclaim. Alf went to Hollywood and became a director. He was very surprised to be working with someone who still raved about *Frenzy*!

For our two-part episodes of *Doctor Kildare*, Basil played a Vladimir Horowitz-type concert pianist at odds with his son, white-bread old me again. We shared some dramatic moments. His character needed surgery to save his life, even though it might rob him of his piano-playing ability. My character selfishly wanted him to postpone the risky operation so he could continue on his concert series as long as possible.

Raymond Massey and Richard Chamberlain were the show's regulars. I liked my dramatic little bit at the beginning of the first episode with Massey. The dialogue allowed me to bark at him in character and resist his assertion that my father's character needed surgery. I was more impressed with how grounded Chamberlain was. He was assured of himself without being brash and boastful. He was also a good actor, fortunate enough to have his talent recognized early in his career.

A lovely actress named Susan Oliver also worked with us. She had such a winsome personality as well as being a good actor. She and I had a scene where we had to dance. I panicked at the idea of dancing socially. I really was never that good at dancing. I thought, "I'm going to embarrass myself; this is going to be terrible." But our dancing turned out fine. Susan said, "We'll fake it," and we somehow did.

Even though Basil and I were always on time at seven a.m., we were still slogging away twelve hours later. Massey, an old war horse of an actor, let it be known that he was sticking strictly to his contract. One day I overheard him as he took Basil aside and said, "My contract says I finish at six, and at six, even if I'm in the middle of a sentence, I walk. You should quit at six p.m. sharp, as I do. Why give them a second more than your contract says?"

Of course, that was said from the security of a long-term contract on the series. I think he might have been a little more cooperative if he had been a freelancer like me. I found him seemingly ungrateful for all the opportunities he was given with the series.

While Basil played my father, the lovely Frances Reid played my mother. On the first day of shooting, another actress was playing that part, but the next morning, I went into makeup and there was Frances

Reid. When he looked at the first scene's rushes, the director thought the original actress had bad teeth and replaced her with full salary. What an awful reason for replacing an actress. I hope she was never told it was because of her dental situation! Not too long afterward, Frances Reid joined NBC's long-running soap opera *Days of Our Lives*, as the show's matriarch.

Becoming unraveled on "The Trap" episode of 12 O'Clock High, *1965.*

Our *Doctor Kildare* episodes were called "Perfect Is Hard to Be," and "Duet for One Hand." Working on *Doctor Kildare* allowed me to team up with Basil Rathbone the second time for two more weeks of acting pleasure. I've never been a big believer in luck, but I must have been lucky to have been teamed with one of the all-time greats twice in the same decade. At the same time, he was touring the country doing *An Evening of Edgar Allen Poe*, and he actually died in harness a few years later on that same tour, just as he would have wished.

About the same time as the *Doctor Kildare* two-parter, I filmed my first of three episodes for *12 O'Clock High*. The series highlighted the adventures of a bombardment group in the U.S. Air Force during World War II. I was cast for my first episode, called "The Trap," because the director, Ralph Senensky, recalled directing me several years earlier in a stage production of Somerset Maugham's *The Circle* at the Pasadena Playhouse. He asked for me not too long after I had finished playing a POW in *King Rat*, so I was still very skinny.

I had gone up to San Bernardino for Christmas. I came down from the snow for wardrobe fittings after I got the script. Because I always flipped through a script to see what kind of part I had won, I remember being pleased to see some really challenging, great scenes.

Ralph came in to say hello and when he saw me so emaciated from my *King Rat* part, he said, "My God, David! If I had known you looked like this, I wouldn't have cast you!" It was always a Friday when these things happened, so in a sense, Ralph was stuck with me for the next Monday morning. "Go home and eat pizza!" he told me, so I went home and stuffed myself all weekend.

Ralph had to contend with other casting drama, too. Gladys Cooper was set to play a socialite. I was thrilled at the prospect of finally working with her. Back in 1942, her riveting performance in *Now, Voyager* made me want to do that kind of work on the big screen. After we became friends in Hollywood, I always dreamed of working with her. We would say, "One day…"

Just when it seemed that we would appear together on the small screen, Warner Bros. made her leave because she was appearing on another show with a rival sponsor, three days before the start of our film date for *12 O'Clock High*. Ralph was quite disappointed, but no one was more disappointed than I. Hermione Baddeley was brought in to replace her. Gladys would have given a classier interpretation in her part as a duchess, as Hermione went for laughs in the role. Hermione was great fun, though. I had known her socially in London, and we had jolly and rather liquid lunches off the lot every day.

Our show's story was a really good one. Robert Lansing was a lead on the series, playing a general. In our episode, he was trapped in a cellar with a group of characters during an air raid. Hermione played a lady of high class, while I played a con man pretending to be a high class doctor, perfect for my specialty of playing characters with hidden moral defects.

John Leyton played a miner. When we did our episode, he was working with Frank Sinatra on *Von Ryan's Express* and had time off from the movie schedule, so 20th Century-Fox put him into *12 O'Clock High* for those ten days. He was very much a lad for the ladies and told me that he met Mia Farrow on the Fox lot for TV's *Peyton Place*. They began seeing each other until one day two gents took Leyton aside and warned him about trying to romance Sinatra's girlfriend.

I had a great scene where my character's high manner status unravels and I start talking in the character's real Cockney accent in response to a line from Hermione. We started rehearsing the scene quietly. It went well, shortly before the lunch break. After we started shooting, my stomach began to rumble. I thought that no one would notice, but then the sound man yelled, "I'm getting a stomach!" Everyone just stared at me. I

With Hermione Baddeley and Robert Lansing on 12 O'Clock High, *1965.*

apologized to Ralph. He said, "Just relax, and take it easy."

It was my favorite scene in the whole script, so I wanted to get it right. We started again and the sound man yelled, "No — still getting the stomach!" I could have killed the sound guy. Ralph looked at his watch and said, "Well, let's take a lunch break, then."

I apologized to him. He said, "It's okay." When we got back, I was full from lunch by then, but there was still a rumble! I calmed down and then the stomach did, too. It was really humiliating to be an actor who can't control his stomach!

The script also called for me to run amok at one point, felled by a knockout punch from Robert Lansing. The amok sequence went well — I could do that in my sleep by then — but our rehearsal of the punch didn't pay off. I failed to duck on cue and Bob's fist landed squarely on my newly capped front teeth. Since he really did knock me out temporarily, it stayed in the final print. "It looked great on the shot!" Ralph said.

Six weeks later, I had to have all my teeth re-capped at my own expense because 20th Century-Fox wouldn't accept responsibility for the damage. Fox insisted the $2,500 worth of cracks in my teeth might have been caused elsewhere. That was an expensive punch. The studio didn't want to recognize it as on-the-job injury and held us actors responsible. I lost money on that episode!

Still, it was a meaty role for me, and I enjoyed working with Ralph again. He made me dig into myself as a common person pretending to be very wealthy. He wouldn't let me just get away with sighing, heaving and almost mugging. Sometimes you can anticipate the pleasure of doing a good scene so much that you tend to overdo it. Ralph just wanted my character's true identity to come out slowly, so he kept scaling me down. He spent almost one hour on me as we prepared to film. "A little less," he told me over and over.

I said, "Ralph, I don't think I can do any better." He said, "Oh, yes you can." Finally, he got me exactly as he needed it. I loved working with directors like that. It was much better than directors who simply said, "Action," and let the scene run before saying, "Cut." With those kinds of directors, I realized that we had no direction at all.

Watching our work more than forty years later, I feel pretty pleased on the whole. In June 2010, when I was visiting with Ralph at his home near Carmel, California, he surprised me by showing me part of the episode and told me that I was very good in it. Sometimes a performance stands the test of time, and a good director should share credit for that work!

At my reunion with Ralph, I also was reminded that things we remember as embarrassing sometimes went unnoticed elsewhere. When I reminded Ralph about my stomach rumbling and how it interrupted shooting, he had forgotten all about it. I, meanwhile, was embarrassed for years by that episode! He also told me that he thought I looked just right for the part when we watched the show all those years later, so my *King Rat* diet hadn't affected my appearance as badly as I remembered. Time changes everything!

My second episode of *12 O'Clock High* was called "The Slaughter Pen." We had a big cast, set at an English hall needed as an operations base by Americans preparing to bomb the Germans. The cast included Michael Rennie and Juliet Mills, the other famous daughter of John Mills. We had a lot of fun together as I told her how I made so much money waiting for her dad to arrive for *King Rat!*

Our director was Robert Douglas. I had seen him in many movies during my youth. He was so genteel in his delivery and excelled at playing both good and bad guys. Ironically, he had appeared in my first episode of *Alfred Hitchcock Presents* a decade earlier and on the last episode of *Thriller*. You could never predict who you would work with again in Hollywood. Only really big stars could influence casting, so it underscored the importance of always doing our best, working to get along and never burning bridges or leaving a bad reputation behind us after a shoot.

We shot the episode at Bronson Canyon, a section of Griffith Park. The weather was unusually rainy, so we made extra money waiting for the rain to stop. Poor Harry Guardino was also in the episode. He needed to leave for New York to appear with Lauren Bacall in a play, and she kept calling him and telling him that he needed to leave for rehearsals. He was relieved when the rain let up and we were able to finish our scenes.

I did one episode each for the first, second, and third seasons of *12 O'Clock High*. My last episode was called "To Seek and Destroy." I played a drunken rocket specialist who has to be pulled from a bar in order to help the Americans retrieve a V-1 rocket that has crashed in Sweden. I had a lot of fun with the episode. Playing a drunk was all part of the qualities I could convincingly convey on screen.

Working so frequently in television those days, I never really thought much about appearing in commercials. In the early 1960s, I befriended Don Garnier when he came over to adopt one of my cat's kittens. He was a brilliant architect who had briefly worked earlier in his career as an artist on Disney's *Saludos Amigos*, a film whose Latin-flavored music I just loved. I had the done the voice of a Disney character, and it turned out that Don was a good friend of Angela Lansbury's husband, Peter Shaw, who had helped get me started when I first arrived in Hollywood.

With so much in common, Don and I struck up a great friendship. I especially liked his mother, Jessie Garnier. She looked like a typically nice, matronly lady, but in reality, she was one of Hollywood's hardest-working commercial actors. She was never really a performer in the traditional sense, but she had just the right older woman look needed to sell detergent or soup. Jessie was represented by Jack Wormser, who owned the top commercial agency in Hollywood.

One day Jess needed to go sign a year's contract. Don asked me to take his mother because he was working. In her sixties at the time, there wasn't that much call for people in commercials from her age bracket, but Jess was very good when given the opportunity. Jack signed her for another year and walked out with her to the reception room. I was sitting there as Jess introduced me to him. Jack asked, "Do you do commercials?"

I said, "No, I'm British."

He said, "First of all, what's that got to do with it, and second of all, you don't look British to me." His comment really threw me because I was making my living by primarily playing British characters.

He said, "No, you look like a typical young American junior executive with a banking firm or a law office."

Jack pointed to his office and said, "You see that on the wall behind my desk? I have a list of the top twenty earners in the agency, people who make the most money for me. You'll be on that top twenty if you'll just sign with me."

I told him, "I don't know anything about acting in commercials."

He said, "You don't have to. No acting is required. You just have to bear in mind that the product is the star, not the performer, and usually you just stand there drinking a cup of coffee or watching your wife do the dishwashing with the new detergent. You don't have to say anything."

I was very reluctant. After all, I had spent a decade as an actor, taking acting classes with my Saturday morning group, working in leading roles in movies and TV. Like many actors, I was snobbish about the whole idea.

Persistent, Jack said, "Try it for a month. You don't have to act. You go in front of several people and if they like your look, you have the job. I'll send you out several times for the next four weeks, and if you get a commercial, then sign with me for a year."

The timing was right, because it was summer and off-season for many of the TV productions. He had spotted my commercial potential. Sure enough, I promptly landed one for Birds Eye Frozen Peas. I suppose I looked like someone who ate Birds Eye Frozen Peas!

After all the worrying I had done about preparing to be an actor, I couldn't believe how simple it was to land a commercial. The process involved nothing more than walking into a room, sitting in a chair, and then being greeted and stared at by three or four ad agency people from Chicago or New York. I couldn't show what a good actor I was; I had to do nothing but sit and stare back at them as they studied my features and decided if I had the right look or not. I would turn to the left and then to the right, just like in a police lineup as they deliberated my commercial fate.

Before long, I had so many commercials going that I couldn't believe it. In the first month, I was put into three commercials. Over and over,

I was told by agencies that I had the right look or that I seemed to fit right into the scene depicted in the commercial. Before long I earned a spot on Jack Wormser's top twenty earners list! I thought, "I should have done this years ago!"

I literally made hundreds of commercials over the course of the next decade. The pay scale on a commercial back in the 1960s and 1970s

LEFT: *From an ad promoting my work in commercials, 1965.* RIGHT: *On location in Lake Arrowhead for a Stroh's Bohemian Beer commercial.*

paid performers very well. Every commercial ran for a minimum of a thirteen-week cycle, several times a day, and the performer got paid every single time. At the end of the third month, my mailbox was stuffed with checks!

I suspect that some of the people I worked with in scripted programs had also done commercials, but there was just that sense that the two shouldn't mix. But as Vincent Price had reminded me during one of our movies, the whole point of being a working actor is to work. Performing in a commercial paid just as well, sometimes better, as acting did on a one-shot, guest-starring spot on a weekly series. I had never hoped to become a Richard Burton or a Laurence Olivier. I wanted to work, and from my pay, I liked to dine or buy the latest LP records. Commercials became a godsend in terms of filling in the gaps between acting jobs.

Amazingly, working on a commercial never prevented me from taking an acting job, nor did an acting job ever get in the way of a commercial. They always dovetailed perfectly with each other. As far as I was concerned, I was living the high life. Some commercials ran two years for paycheck after paycheck. It only took a day's work to do them. Just as Jack had promised, there was little acting to do. If my little "son" came to up me and said, "Hey dad, no cavities," all I had to say was, "Gee, it must be the Crest!" There really was no acting or preparation required.

Because I had to go out several times each day on different calls for commercials, I had to own five suits, a sports jacket, a blazer, five shirts, five ties, and five pairs of shoes to dress for the product being advertised each time I went to audition. To buy the wardrobe, I went to Carroll's in Beverly Hills, an upscale store. I thought, "If this commercial thing works out, I can afford to go there." Wearing the clothes certainly was a confidence booster!

For the next ten years, through the mid-1970s, whenever I wasn't working in television or on a movie, I was signed with Jack Wormser for commercial work, thanks to the mother of a friend and finding myself in the right place at the right time, not to mention being willing to give something a shot right there on the spot. Working in Hollywood may have been unpredictable, but it certainly wasn't unprofitable for me.

In gratitude for doubling my income through commercials, I should note that Jessie Garnier, the lady who inadvertently launched my commercial career, did act on camera for one very major motion picture in a small but well-remembered role.

Jessie had auditioned for Gene Kelly when he was directing 20th Century-Fox's big budget musical adaptation of *Hello, Dolly!* with Barbra Streisand. Gene picked Jessie for a part from all the people he read. Jessie wasn't overly thrilled, because having arrived late to the business, she had no idea of the significance of being directed and selected by Gene Kelly.

I kept saying, "Jess, you don't know how lucky you are to have this opportunity!" She had one little moment in the film as an old lady sitting with groceries on a bench. Michael Crawford sings "It Only a Takes a Moment," and somebody says, "A minute?"

"No."

"A second?"

"No."

And Jess pops up and says, "A moment." And that's her moment. I'm forever grateful to her for giving me a moment that led to my work in commercials.

Just as working at Disney guaranteed that I would be forever heard as a character's voice in one of the studio's animated classics, boldly going where no one had gone before on *Star Trek* in 1968 guaranteed that I would be forever remembered by a whole different set of passionately dedicated fans.

My journey into the world of *Star Trek* came about through director

On Star Trek, *I played Dr. Larry Marvick, a designer of the* Enterprise.

Ralph Senensky. We had worked earlier on *12 O'Clock High* and first met at the Pasadena Playhouse. When Ralph was assigned to direct his *Trek* episode, he said, "I want Diana Muldaur and David Frankham," and it was done. He's one of my favorite television directors ever.

Truthfully, when there was a lot of work going on and I got the call saying, "Report to Paramount on Friday for wardrobe; then report to *Star Trek* on Monday," I wrote down whatever I was doing next after *Star Trek*. Initially it was just a job, but as soon as I got there and walked on that big, familiar set with the inner workings of the starship *Enterprise*, it stopped being just another job.

My episode of the classic NBC series was titled "Is There in Truth No Beauty?" I played Dr. Larry Marvick, an engineer and one of *Enterprise's* designers. When we arrived to work, George Takei walked across the set, hand outstretched and said to Diana Muldaur and me, "Welcome aboard the *Enterprise*." He was quite sincere and wasn't kidding about it. It was a very nice thing to say. He obviously loved being a member of the *Star Trek* team. It made us feel rather special.

Unfortunately, our episode was filmed the week the cast got word that the series wasn't going to be renewed. On the Monday morning that we started, *Star Trek* creator Gene Roddenberry gathered everybody together and said the show was not going to be renewed. Talk about gloom and doom. The cast and crew were stunned.

You never saw such a downhearted group of actors in your life; they were all so depressed and angry. Takei and James Doohan, who played Scotty, seemed to handle it the best and remained fairly calm. Their job security was gone, and these actors, without exception, loved working on the show. It was an awful blow. They were shaking their heads, because they couldn't believe they weren't going to be picked up for renewal. It was almost as if they were working underwater, they were so depressed, but most rose to the occasion and carried on.

We had an eight-day schedule, so on Monday morning, I was told that I would do a few brief scenes after a run-through of a big scene that had Diana and me dining with a group of the show's regulars, including Leonard Nimoy and William Shatner. We started a run-through with Ralph when Nimoy and Shatner simply stopped and said, "We can't shoot this the way it's written."

They both said that the scene promoted some *Star Trek* merchandise by including an insignia pin in the storyline. No doubt they were understandably upset, too, because the show was being cancelled. Because they were in the scene, we couldn't film it without the two leads. They said they were leaving until the script was redone to their satisfaction. If memory serves correctly, Nimoy and Shatner themselves assisted in the re-writing process.

Diana and I had our love scene scheduled for late in the week. In desperation, poor Ralph — stuck with a shooting schedule that plotted out each day's scenes — turned to Diana and me and said, "Well, I guess we'll have to shoot your love scene instead while the writers re-write. Do you know Thursday's scene?" There we were on Monday morning being told that if we could quickly get it together in half an hour, it would be the next thing to be filmed while the bigger scene was rewritten to Nimoy's and Shatner's satisfaction.

Luckily, Diana and I had both learned our lines several days in advance! Diana observed that we weren't really ready, even if we did know our lines.

We had planned to mull it over and think about the little nuances that we were going to do. But there wasn't time for that. Because a production can jump around, the moral of the story is, "Know your lines."

We marched down to another part of the set. The crew started lighting us. Ralph said, "Let's have a run-through." That was it. We had to do it. When I watch the show today, I sometimes think it still looks a little

LEFT: *William Shatner and Leonard Nimoy raised objections to part of our script.* RIGHT: *Diana Muldaur kept her cool as we juggled the shooting schedule.*

under-rehearsed to me. I could have done better if I had a few more days to think about it, because I usually thought about the script's dialogue and the character's motivation. I really hadn't had the time to do that when we shuffled the shooting schedule. With Ralph's direction, though, we did fine. Thankfully, he made what could have been a very depressing week a lot of fun on the *Enterprise* set — nothing ever gets him down.

Diana was a pro. With the love scene being thrown at us off schedule, and working with a depressed cast and crew, working under fire bonded us together. In a way, it was kind of like being on a sinking ship that Monday morning. We were thrown together in the same predicament. I hadn't met Diana before, but I had seen her act on television. She's an extremely intelligent actress, very beautiful, with a wonderful, cool, calm, laid-back presence that came in handy.

Gene Roddenberry hovered about on the set. He was there more often than usual because of the script problems. I believe he was also there to console the cast, all in all, because it was not their happiest episode as they were not to be renewed. He was pleasant in spite of the week's drama.

Everybody eventually rallied and got on with the job of doing the show, even with the frustration and regret of not being renewed. The *Enterprise*

The script called for my character to go literally insane.

set was a beautiful one. In fact, it was the most impressive science fiction set I had ever worked on. Standing on the spot where I was beamed aboard at the start of the show was exciting. I stood on a chalk mark on the floor and then the beaming-in effects were later added. I'm still not sure how they made it look believable.

By 1968, I had nearly patented running amok in Hollywood. Whenever someone had to fall apart or suffer a nervous breakdown on camera, I seemed to get the call. I had come undone on *12 O'Clock High*, so that is probably why Ralph had thought of me. When my character looks at the Medusan Ambassador character, the script called for me to go mad. I had to fall on the floor, foam at the mouth and act deranged. Actors really need a good director then to say, "You're not doing enough, or you overdid it a bit, so let's do it again." Ralph kept me in check. If I had overdone that kind of thing, I could have looked like a blithering idiot on the screen.

The work was physically demanding. I had a few bumps and bruises from the fighting. The cameraman used a handheld camera that fit onto his shoulder. The finished product was sort of a fish-bowl look to suggest the "mad" point of view from which my character saw the *Enterprise*. He just followed me around. No matter what I did, he was there with me.

I played one of those characters about whom Dr. McCoy said, "He's dead, Jim."

When my character had gone completely crazy, I had a fight scene with Shatner. A fight scene was always a little difficult because we had to stage it slowly. It was first choreographed for us by the stunt people. We watched them do the fight in slow motion, saw where the punches were, and then we stepped in to do the less strenuous fighting parts. When we actually filmed it, we concentrated on the close-ups. Shatner and I sweated and glared at each other and then the intense punching and falling was done by the stunt people. I was always nervous, because I didn't want to look stupid, and I didn't want to hurt anyone. Still, it's always fun to pretend to hit someone in the face.

Had we known that *Star Trek* would become an endearing classic to be watched numerous times by Trekkers for the rest of all time, we might have given more thought to the stunts. We could not have foreseen video and a viewer's ability to slow down and watch the action frame by frame.

It's always been amusing for me to slow down my fight scenes and discover how sloppy all my punches really were.

When I did the run-through for my character's climax, I was getting worked up in character to the point that Shatner took me by the shoulders and said, "Calm down — it's only a run-through." I thought, "Damn you — this is my rehearsal, not yours." In spite of him, I went as bonkers as I could!

With James Doohan, my favorite member of the cast.

By the time I started working with them, Shatner and Nimoy evidently had resolved their script differences. Shatner was not jaded or bored by the show as some stars I have worked with have been, having done it so long that there's not much pleasure in it anymore. Nimoy, too, was very bright and keenly concerned with the whole production, not just his part in it. I had to admire them a bit for sticking up for the characters they had embodied on screen.

From working with the cast, I think James Doohan may have been my favorite. He was such a fine actor that I don't think even *Star Trek* gave him enough range. He deserved his success. In my opinion, he was the best actor on the series. We had worked together a few years earlier on an episode of *12 O'Clock High* when he was worried about leaving a good career in Canada. I could empathize with him, because I had left a pretty good career in England. He couldn't have possibly foreseen becoming a vital part of *Star Trek* just a few years later, and his association with the show was still strong through the end of his life decades later.

It was my impression that *Star Trek* truly benefited from a devoted crew, all of them determined that each episode would be the best. The writing also was excellent. *Star Trek* had more than its share of talented writers, and I think that was why the show was more successful than others in making a lasting impression on the public.

One of my two Star Trek *trading cards!*

I didn't have a clue that the show would become a cult classic. The whole experience is sort of bittersweet now. I was a jobbing actor, so that was my job that week — to be on *Star Trek*. While I was happy to be working, the series' regulars were understandably upset about losing guaranteed employment. Ordinarily I would have been more thrilled to be working on a high profile series. I couldn't help but empathize with the rest of them as they wondered what they would do next.

The *Star Trek* actors, though, had the last laugh. The show lived on in reruns and just a decade later, the fan interest was enough to resurrect the series in several hit movies. Diana even returned for appearances on *Star Trek: The Next Generation*. When we worked together, there wasn't the remotest clue that twenty years into the future, she would be back and the show would live on.

I'm always impressed by the power of television. Because I was not a series star constantly in the public eye, I was rarely recognized. In 1988, however, I was eating lunch at a hot dog stand, near Universal on Ventura Boulevard. A young couple was sitting at an outdoor table. The guy came up and said, "Are you an actor?"

I said, "Yes."

He said, "Were you ever on *Star Trek*?"

I said, "Yeah."

He and his friend told me, "We saw you last night — you were terrific!"

I couldn't believe it. I said, "My God, that was years ago!"

He said, "Not to us. That show never ages."

I was amazed at their appreciation of my work. And a few years later, I was also amazed when someone showed me a catalog from a Hollywood auction of props and costumes. The pants I wrote on *Star Trek* sold for $800! In recent years, I contributed to the mania for memorabilia when I autographed several hundred trading cards with my character's likeness. The first card's release was successful enough to warrant a second.

I've kept up with Ralph Senensky in later years. One of television's hardest-working directors, Ralph really loves the business. I went to dinner at his house in 1988 when he had a big gathering of actors. His whole house was lined with movie posters from the 1930s. That's a key to his personality — he loves the entertainment in show business. Ralph also loved working in the theatre. He worked very hard at his success.

In 2009, I discovered that Ralph, a few years older than I, was active as ever. In fact, he blogs about his experience in Hollywood and once kindly recounted the story of our *Star Trek* episode. My actor friend Jonathan Dixon contacted Ralph by email, and the next thing I knew, we made plans to visit during the summer of 2010. In June, Jonathan drove us from New Mexico to Carmel, California, where Ralph and I had a grand reunion.

He still collects movie posters, and I had the privilege of spending a few days with him. We reminisced about *Star Trek* and our work. What a bundle of energy he is! One day we went to lunch, and at several points, Ralph sprinted so far ahead that he had to turn around to see if we were coming along after him. Working with him, especially on *Star Trek*, was one of the happier memories of my time in Hollywood.

In and around the time I worked on *Star Trek*, I began a multi-episode association with *The F.B.I.*, a long-running series that aired from 1965-1974. The show recounted real cases from the files of the F.B.I., and offered working actors and well-known guest stars the chance to appear several times through the years. The practice was commonplace before cable reruns and DVDs; you could play one villain this season, get killed off, and be back the next year as a different guy.

I had become friendly with Dody McClane, a casting agent at Warner Bros. On my first audition for *The F.B.I.*, she met me in the parking lot, told me what the part was about, gave me a script before the other actors even came in to audition, and then gave me thirty minutes ahead of time to study the script. I got the part. It may have been an inside job, but actors and casting agents who could trust each other seemed to work well. That kind of rapport made the business side a little easier.

The show was headed by Efrem Zimbalist, Jr., whom I found always so centered and calm. He was a man of great sensitivity, stability, and humor. Zimbalist was also very tan, and he told me he did it because he could sleep later when working — there was no need for a makeup call with his bronzed skin tone.

When we did a scene at a beach, I could really see the power that went with being the star of the show. We were rehearsing off camera when I saw a seagull not too far from where I was standing. It was moving along, but its wing was dragging. When we stopped the rehearsal, I said to Efrem, "There's something wrong with that bird."

He walked over and crouched down next to the bird. He smoothed its wing and said, "I think it's broken." By then the director was looking at his watch. On location, he was dealing with tight schedules and a lot of money if the production went too long.

Efrem said, "We need to get someone to look after this bird. Can someone call?" A crew member got on the phone to an animal group. The director said, "Shall we resume?"

Efrem said, "No, I want to wait until somebody gets here. This bird's in trouble."

I was impressed. He was no Jack Warner, but Efrem was a big enough star that if he wanted the bird healed, we didn't shoot until the bird was treated. He was full of compassion. He even sent a note to a friend of mine whose husband had died suddenly. I'm a huge admirer of his and proud to have worked with him several times. (In August of 2010, I had a nice note from him recalling our happy work together. Now in his nineties, he remains involved in faith-based work and reads Bible verses on Christian TV programming.)

My first episode of *The F.B.I.* in 1967 was called "The Hostage." I played a man caught up in a hostage crisis, with the hostage victim played by Diana Hyland. She had a love scene with Edward Mulhare, and I remember that she sort of bossed him around as they worked, to the point that I thought she was quite rude to him. He seemed to take it well, though, and handled her calmly.

Her behavior aside, I was most thrilled at the opportunity to meet and appear in the episode with Paul Lukas. What a privilege to spend a week in the company of such a dear man and a wonderful actor. Lukas had won an Oscar back in 1943 for *Watch on the Rhine*. I peppered him with questions about his work. I had the record of *Call Me Madam*, in which he sings charmingly. I asked him how it was to work with Ethel Merman. He smiled gently and said, "Oh, one just remembered to stay out of the way." They must have made quite an onstage contrast.

Watching the episode later, I was disappointed that I hadn't shared as much screen time with Lukas as I remembered. A friend reminded

A villain once more on The F.B.I., *1967.*

me, however, that hundreds of actors would have given their right arm for the privilege of spending time with him, so that certainly reframed my perspective. Whenever I think back on parts that I wanted but didn't get, I'm reminded that the tables were turned whenever I did get a part, big or small; those roles meant that someone felt I was right for the role based upon my abilities and look at that time, and in turn, some other actor looks back and wishes that he had only been given the part! It's all a matter of perspective with acting roles.

Besides working with Paul Lukas, the other thrill of working at Warner Bros. on my first episode of *The F.B.I.* was found in a nearby soundstage where Joshua Logan was directing the big-screen adaptation of Lerner and Lowe's *Camelot* starring Richard Harris and Vanessa Redgrave. The whole studio seemed to be working on *Camelot*, so not much attention was being paid to *The F.B.I.*

I had thought that I was going to be in the movie after I read for Logan himself. He seemed promising enough, telling me, "Yes, you might be right for one of the knights. We'll think about it." It turned out that my acting was okay, but the producers decided that I wasn't tall or broad enough to play a knight, so the film didn't go any further than that for me.

In costume for a flashback scene on The F.B.I., *1970.*

One morning, I found that the big Warners soundstages marked "No admission" were quiet for some reason. I snuck in and saw the big, marvelous hall set constructed for *Camelot*. If I wasn't going to be in the movie, my consolation prize was a clandestine, private tour of the set!

Back on *The F.B.I.*, my next episode for the series came in 1968, and was called "The Flaw." Early in the show, I played a double-crosser who gets shot and killed as the guy rides up the side of a mountain on a ski lift. The ski lift episode almost cost me a very lucrative commercial the following day. I sat at the top of the lift for over half an hour while they set up the shot below. The left side of my face was badly scorched beneath the makeup.

When I got back to Los Angeles, I was peeling badly. The next day I looked like half a rotting tomato. The commercial company considered replacing me but covered my face in makeup and let me go ahead. It was a four-day shoot back up at the ski area 90 miles east of Los Angeles for Stroh's Bohemian Beer. We did four seasons of beer commercials in four days and they ran for two years! What a world — I could juggle acting appearances one day and beer commercials the next.

My January 1970 episode of *The F.B.I.* was called "Deadly Reunion." I had a substantial role as the nephew of a spy. When my character is shot, the F.B.I. agents must convince me to cooperate, even if it means turning in my uncle.

We shot one of our scenes on the New York street sets at Warner Bros. Those streets are still standing and have been used extensively in a number of productions through the years. It was good to see Alf Kjellin again on the shoot. He had directed Basil Rathbone and me a few years earlier on our two-part episodes of *Doctor Kildare*.

Espionage seemed to occupy many of the plotlines on *The F.B.I.*, so in December 1970, I played a big part in "The Target," a story about the F.B.I. protecting the daughter of a Communist official from a spy. Eric Braeden was another guest. He later went on to become one of the stars of *The Young and the Restless*. Also notable was the presence of Karin Dor, who had become the first German "Bond Girl" in *You Only Live Twice*. We all spent a whole day on location at Griffith Park playing "war" as we fired off shots at each other.

My last episode of *The F.B.I.*, "A Game of Chess," was the favorite of the several I filmed for the series. Again, foreign spies and double agents were involved with a great storyline about a blind chess master. George Nader had been working mainly overseas in Europe after being outed by *Confidential* magazine in the 1950s. I was surprised to see his name on a chair. He had returned for what turned out to be one of his last acting appearances in movies or TV. He retired just one or two shows after doing our episode of *The F.B.I.* and became a successful author.

Best of all, though, this episode reunited me with an actor whom I admired and personally liked very much, Patrick O'Neal. We had both appeared in *King Rat* a few years earlier, and we had worked together a year before on a series called *The Young Rebels* at Columbia. I liked working with him; he was very droll and laid back, a method actor who didn't indulge himself. He did his preparation at home, unlike a lot of the method actors who spent all their time being in character.

The Young Rebels was a short-lived program about the Revolutionary War. It was an unhappy shoot for me because the director said I wasn't doing anything he was telling me to do. I played a stiff, upper lip sort of British officer, and I thought I was doing what I felt the script demanded.

The director said, "You're not doing this right. Do it this way." I tried what he suggested, but it felt unnatural to me. He grew irritated and said that I wasn't cooperating. He stopped talking to me and started directing me through the assistant director, saying, "Tell him to move there; tell him to do this."

I wound up not speaking to him over the course of a five-day shoot, so it was a miserable experience, one of few times that I never really enjoyed myself on a TV series shoot. It was a very odd feeling to get up in the morning and think, "Oh God, this man is not going to talk to me at work again today." I'm pretty sure that I had the moral high ground in the dispute. Before long, he turned on an Emmy Award-winning cinematographer and chewed him out, so he clearly just wasn't that nice of a guy. In many ways, I could relate to Tom Tryon being mistreated by Otto Preminger on the set of *The Cardinal*. Preminger famously treated Tryon in a rotten fashion, even firing — and rehiring him — right in front of his visiting parents on the set.

When we finished the shoot on Friday, we were getting out of our costumes. Because I had a full British officer's military uniform, disrobing took me a little longer. It turned out that the director and I were the last to leave. Just our two cars remained in the parking lot — his and mine. We didn't talk to each other even then. Talk about uncomfortable!

There was a downside to show business when I had a bad director, but that sort of thing is true in just about any business. Between appearing in commercials and guest acting on a number of series, I was working so much that I didn't lose much sleep over that one bad experience. My happiness and satisfaction were too important for one bad apple to spoil this jobbing actor's resolve!

CHAPTER ELEVEN

Stanwyck, Hayworth and the 1970s

The late 1960s proved to be a time of transition both for me, personally, as well as the country, the world, and Hollywood. Everything seemed to be in flux and changing. Hollywood became a little grittier. We could just see the town changing. *Midnight Cowboy* and similar films offered more realism.

Even the industry was changing to the point that bad manners almost seemed acceptable. When I was invited to a special showing of *True Grit*, I sat toward the back. After the film had started, I noticed that Natalie Wood entered the theatre. She made her way down the aisle. Not one person — Clint Eastwood, Rock Hudson or several other celebrities — offered her a seat, although to be fair, perhaps they were just so caught up in the movie that they didn't see her, but it seemed to me that they had. Who knows what had happened between them to warrant her getting a snub.

I filmed my episode of *Star Trek* around the time that Dr. Martin Luther King Jr. was assassinated in Memphis. The Vietnam War was escalating, and there were protests, many of them in California. The hair styles and the clothing changed. I had seen America transition from the post-war tranquility and values of the Eisenhower years into a new era.

Not too long afterward, I lost a treasured friend when Doris Lloyd died on May 21, 1968. Leo G. Carroll, in spite of his opinion of me as a stage actor, called me. He said that he was putting together a tribute to Doris, and because he knew how close Doris and I had become, he asked if I would assist him in organizing her memorial. For Doris, I was proud to be asked by someone as revered as Carroll. We put together a fitting tribute for one of the industry's best-loved women.

The service was held at the Wee Kirk O' the Heather Church at Forest Lawn Cemetery in Glendale. Doris was buried not too far from the church. The place was packed with many people who worked with or loved her. Interestingly, Edmund Goulding, one of the big directors in the 1940s, had died years before, but his widow showed up to pay tribute to Doris. She said that Doris was loved by her Eddie, so she was glad to

With Tex Beneke and Paul Tanner from the Glenn Miller Band at the Disneyland Hotel.

represent her late husband and honor Doris.

After a lovely service, the cars began driving away as I stood outside with Carroll. He said in that near-patented droll, Leo G. Carroll style, "Well, my boy, I'd better get home, or you might all be meeting here for me next week!" He hopped into his limousine and away he went.

I was frequently invited to spend Christmas with a group that included a few people I didn't really enjoy seeing, so I had developed a routine where I went out to Forest Lawn to visit Doris each Christmas. For several years I drove up to her little plaque on the hillside and just sat there and had a chat with her. It may sound a little spooky, but I really did enjoy it. Quite honestly, my Christmas mornings always started off well at Forest Lawn. I'd say, "God, I'm hating today, Doris, but I'll get through it somehow." Just visiting her kept me from spending the holidays with people I didn't like.

There were always new friends to be made. A few years earlier, I formed a friendship with Tex Beneke and his wife, Betty. Tex was fronting the Glenn Miller Band by then. Tex had been Glenn's main saxophone man on "Chattanooga Choo Choo" and other hits.

I got to know Tex through Paul Tanner, Glenn Miller's favorite trombone player. He always took Glenn's trombone with him and sat it beside

Tex Beneke took this photo of me and his wife as I proudly held his famous saxophone.

him whenever he played engagements in later years. Glenn's trombone was always there on the stand, so in a way, he was there, too, with the rest of the orchestra. Once in a while, one of the trombone section band members, Jimmy Priddy, let me carry it out to the car after an engagement.

I had listened to a program with Paul on National Public Radio and wrote Paul to tell him how much I enjoyed it. He promptly wrote back and told me that I was such a devoted fan that he was going to put me in touch with Tex Beneke himself. From his house in St. Louis, Tex and I talked for about two hours over the phone. He told me that he would look me up the next time he was playing in Los Angeles.

Tex eventually introduced me to Helen Miller, Glenn's widow, and we became close friends. Helen and I hit it off, because she seemed to sense how much I admired her husband. "Oh, my honey would have loved you," she told me one time. Who would have thought when I was fourteen and idolizing Glenn Miller that his widow would become a great friend! She missed her husband terribly, and the passage of a quarter century had not completely healed the wound in her broken heart.

She felt that her husband had made it across the English Channel, that his plane had crashed somewhere, and that he had survived as an amnesiac. Throughout her remaining years, Helen believed that her husband had been taken in by villagers and that he was still living quietly in a French village. She spent money sending crews of people to check dozens of nearby French villages along the plane's chartered route. They never found an American living there, but she still believed it.

One time she told me about Tuxedo Junction. Just before Glenn Miller left America for England, he brought property outside Pasadena and named it for one of his biggest hit records, *Tuxedo Junction*. There was to be a main ranch house and several guest houses around it on this big tract of land. As the most successful bandleader of his time, he planned for the band to tour forty weeks a year after the war, and then the orchestra members and their families would live in the cottages around the main house where Glenn and Helen would live away from touring.

During my visit, Helen walked me through the area and her southwest hacienda-style ranch house. There was a study there with a day bed for times when Glenn stayed up all night writing and arranging. The bed was still made and ready for his arrival. Helen told me what a tough time her husband had becoming America's number one band. To improve his music, he purged alcoholics from the orchestra and frequently went without money to get from location to location for one-night engagements. He was truly an American hero in every sense of the word.

When Tex brought the orchestra to Disneyland in the late 1960s, I faithfully attended the concerts. One of the highlights of those years came when Tex and the band appeared at the Hollywood Palladium on the twenty-fifth anniversary of Miller's death. Seven thousand fans crammed the ballroom. As I told Betty how I had jived to "Chattanooga Choo Choo," Tex gave the downbeat, and then Betty and I hit the floor. We made such a go at it that people moved back to give us space. I'll remember that pure joy for the rest of my life.

I was even made an honorary member of the "orchestra's wives" club, because I inevitably found myself sitting with the band members' wives at the side of the stage during the shows. I was there every night at the Plaza Gardens at Disneyland, so Paula Kelly, one of the singers in the Modernaires, said, "David, we're making you an honorary orchestra wife."

What happy days those were, listening to the music of my childhood again, played by some of the same musicians!

Most people in Hollywood can tell stories about parts that got away or promising projects that failed to materialize. I had my share, too. In the late 1960s, MGM was considering making a movie called *Big Country, Big Man* starring Rod Taylor. I was up for a part and anticipated a loca-

With Judy Cannon in the short film A Comedy Tale of Fanny Hill, *1964.*

tion trip to Australia, but it never came off. The production got to the pre-planning stages, but it just didn't happen.

There were other interesting projects during the 1960s, including an odd, fifteen-minute adaptation of *Fanny Hill*. The young lady in the film was married to a guy who fancied himself a producer. In reality, I suppose he at least filled the role of a producer, because he was wealthy enough to bankroll this vanity project as a showcase for his wife's "talent" in an effort to get her noticed.

He did everything by the book, so it was a SAG production that paid well enough. I was cast in a part, complete with period piece costume and 1700s-era wig. A number of good English actors were employed, but no one involved seemed to know much about what they were doing. Rather than just be miserable about the whole experience, I rolled my eyes and went along with it and at least got paid well for my effort. It was fun to romp around in costume over two days.

The distributor agreed that the fifteen-minute two-reel short comedy would play one week only in Los Angeles to satisfy its part of the production deal. Was I surprised to hear through a mutual friend that Shirley Booth — an Oscar winner, no less — went to the movies one day with her sister. Shirley sat through this fifteen-minute film and thought it was an extended trailer for an upcoming feature-length production. "That's one movie I'm not going to see," she muttered to her sister. I laughed about that later when I heard that she had seen me in the film.

In 1969, in spite of his insistence that he would never return to Hollywood, my pen pal Dirk Bogarde did come back. He had started a picture, *Justine*, but the director, Joseph Strick, was fired. George Cukor replaced Strick, just as Cukor had come in as a replacement director on Dirk's picture *Song Without End* earlier in the decade.

In spite of telling me that he had hated working on *Song Without End* so much that he was through with Hollywood, Dirk had to return to California for interior scenes on *Justine*. He told me that Cukor apologized for bringing him back to Hollywood one more time. He stayed at the Beverly Hills Hotel, where his co-star, Michael York, also was staying. Dirk thought that Michael and his wife, Pat, were charming, because whenever they weren't working, they got on a tour bus to see Hollywood mansions.

One day Dirk called to tell me that he and his companion, Tony Forwood, were staying in a cottage at the hotel, so I went over to see them. There was no sign of anything to do with *Justine*. All around the walls, though, were enormous blow-ups for *The Damned*, the film he had started making in Italy before the director, Luchino Visconti, ran out of money. He told Dirk that it would take months to get funding to finish the movie so Dirk should work in another film if given the chance.

Justine had come along, but it was turning out to be a disaster, even with George Cukor's help. The script was a mess, Dirk told me. His heart simply was not in *Justine*, evident from his new passion for *The Damned*. He said, "Look at these storyboards and stills." He was big on the film and eager to finish it. He said, "I know we'll get the money to finish this, but in the meantime, I have to put up with this crap, *Justine*." He was on the outs with his co-star, Anouk Aimee, and said she was very temperamental. Things were not going well on the sets over on the Fox lot.

We were talking about *The Damned* one night when Robin Fox came to the door. Fox was the father of James Fox, who had worked with Dirk in *The Servant*. The senior Fox was an agent, and he was there to discuss some sort of crisis. Dirk turned to me and said, "David, I've got to throw you out. I'm sorry, but it's some hyper agent talk that I need to focus on. Goodbye." So he threw me out. I really didn't mind, because I preferred that direct approach to phoniness. That was the last time I saw him during the making of his movie.

Naturally, I went to see *Justine* from curiosity. Just as Dirk predicted, the film was not good. Actors always start with a script, good, bad or indifferent, and that one was bad, I'm afraid. In later years, Michael York appeared in Santa Fe in *Cyrano de Bergerac*, and I wrote to Dirk to tell him that I would probably go see him. Dirk told me that if I went back to say hello to Michael that I would have to also say hello to his wife, whom Dirk had soured on, for some reason.

The late 1960s also brought my old BBC colleague, Hanns Friedrichs, back into my life with an opportunity to combine the best of both worlds — my old BBC reporter's training and my access as a working actor in Hollywood. It all started when I was awakened early on the morning of August 9, 1969. Hanns said, "Hello, Frankham! Have you heard about the Sharon Tate murder? She and several of her friends were found massacred in a house in Beverly Hills."

I told him that I had not yet heard. Hanns told me that he had recommended me to a contact in New York and that a German magazine, *Constanza*, would be calling me any minute to be their man in Hollywood. They needed someone to go up and cover the murder and take photos.

"Absolutely not!" I told him. The whole thing sounded repulsive, and I was just hearing of it early in the morning. I had not even seen the morning's newspapers with details.

"Don't tell me no," Hanns said. "Tell the guy who will be calling you."

Sure enough, the New York rep called, and I had to turn him down. The magazine's rep asked me about my background, so I told him of my radio experience back in England.

"Would you agree to be our man in Hollywood?"

"Doing what?" I groggily asked in the pre-dawn hours.

"Interviewing people, stars, usually."

That was more interesting than covering bloody murders, so we agreed to talk more in a day or two. I went back to bed thinking about how the writing could possibly work and wondering how much I would be paid. I later called Hanns back and asked if I should ask to be paid.

"Of course you should," he told me.

"What should I charge?" I asked.

"I don't know," he said. "How about $1,000 a month?"

That didn't sound too bad, so I decided that would be my asking fee to supplement my income through writing. When the magazine's representative called back, he explained that the publication wanted interviews with stars of interest to German readers. He suggested some American television stars that were well-known in Germany.

"There's a lot of Hollywood history here," I noted. "I would like to talk to some living legends."

"Such as?" he asked.

"Rita Hayworth, Barbara Stanwyck," I suggested. He agreed that I could eventually get to interviewing them.

I was asked to do a weekly column for the magazine, which turned out to be a notable German women's publication along the lines of *Vogue*. The idea was very appealing — I would become a member of the Hollywood Foreign Press and get access to interview some of the biggest stars for pay.

I became an accredited journalist in Hollywood, which meant that I took a letter from the magazine to the Motion Picture Alliance to be approved as a member of the Hollywood Foreign Press. Instantly I began to get telegrams at my house each day inviting me to lunch or dinner at the studios to meet a star or to attend film previews. It turned into a wonderful year. Every night I could see a movie that had yet to be released or go to luncheon at Paramount or MGM.

Remembering how Hanns and I had done a radio show focusing on music, I was also allowed to write a record column about new releases. I was delighted to be getting new discs again in the mail just as I had done back in England. I wrote reviews and sent them off to New York for translation to German before being shipped on to the magazine's corporate offices in Hamburg. One time I went to Capitol Records to interview Al Martino for a story. Ironically, I had interviewed him for the BBC in England.

The magazine always called me at six a.m. because the main U.S. office was in New York. I was told my weekly assignment — "Get Jane Fonda, contact Doris Day" — and I had to be wide awake and on the ball. The editors left me alone to make my own contacts and set up meetings; my responsibility was to make the weekly deadline and finish my stories to send on to New York.

I grew nervous about the possibility of an acting job coming up right in the middle of a writing assignment, but incredibly, that never happened. I was still busy as an actor and continued doing a significant number of commercials. I marveled how the activities worked out without any overlapping. Once I introduced myself to the head of publicity at Warner

Bros., who promptly gave me a tour of the studio! I couldn't tell him that I had worked on the lot many times. Luckily he bypassed the casting department. I would have been mortified if I had encountered someone who knew me as an actor!

One time I was at Warners shooting an opening prologue for *The F.B.I.* with Efrem Zimbalist, Jr. Warners held weekly press screenings in a small theatre directly opposite the New York Street where we were filming. I was sitting in my chair on the street that night as my press colleagues walked by on their way to a screening. They didn't know I was an actor by day, so I was afraid that they would think I was a journalistic phony with no background in the business. I buried my head in my script; the others would have given me a bad time if they knew I was "just" an actor.

I kept my acting/journalist double life a secret, convinced that I would be discovered. The arrangement was touch and go, but I never was discovered. Ironically, I really should not have worried that much about the rest of the Hollywood Foreign Press members, most of whom were part-time waiters. I had little respect for most members I encountered because they really were a lazy bunch, more interested in eating for free than in working hard for their respective publications.

One of them told me in confidence that he didn't make enough money as a correspondent, so he had to work on the side as a waiter. I noticed that whenever we were invited to a studio lunch, foreign press members ignored the guest and stuffed themselves with food. I thought, "God, they must all be starving!" It was a luxury for me to have steady work in TV shows and commercials and to write on the side.

The foreign press's boorish behavior was on display one memorable occasion. It was at Paramount during a luncheon for Jimmy Durante to promote a film for which he sang the title song, "Those Daring Young Men in Their Jaunty Jalopies." He was a funny man, introduced from the head table. At the end of the meal, all the reporters were stuffing themselves with dessert and coffee.

When the head of publicity asked, "Do we have any questions for Mr. Durante?" there was dead silence. I couldn't believe it — they weren't even looking at him. They couldn't promote the film without asking any questions, which was the whole point of our being invited to the studio in the first place.

I put up my hand and asked Durante a few questions, but I honestly liked him, so it wasn't from pity that I stood up to break the silence. I think he felt hurt that I was the only one who spoke, because when our exchange was finished, Durante said, "Thank you, young man. That means a great deal to me."

There was one exception to the sorry lot of the foreign press, a correspondent from my magazine's German competition, a magazine called *Brigitte*. I had a call from an English correspondent from a London paper one day. "David, we have a problem," he said.

A senior member of the foreign press had been writing many years for *Brigitte*. She had just finished a weeklong interview on location with Ingrid Bergman. The poor lady got the feeling that I had been sent out from *Constanza* to take over her job. I asked the English guy, "How do you know all of this?"

He told me that he had lunched with her the day before and that she was practically in tears. She thought I was a threat to her career. I thought it was ridiculous, because I really was an actor who had taken up writing on the side. To put her at ease, though, I called her. She asked me to come see her. She made lunch and told me, "I know I'm getting up in years, but I have just spent a whole week with Ingrid Bergman." She was pleading her case to me!

I almost confessed to her that I was an actor by day and a member of the foreign press on the side, but I didn't blow my cover. I begged her to take my word that I didn't know anyone at *Brigitte* and that I was not out to take her job. She believed me and all was well after that, but it went to show the competition between our two publications.

One of the first stars I interviewed was Barbara Eden, then appearing on TV's *I Dream of Jeannie*. She was pretty and cute. We had lunch in the commissary at Columbia. Another time, I visited the set of *Mission Impossible* to interview Peter Graves. I reminded the magazine that we had discussed talking to some of the old-time Hollywood superstars. With my credentials and the backing of the magazine, I began contacting agents of the stars whom I wanted to interview.

Barbara Stanwyck was at the top of my list of all-time greats to interview. I contacted her publicity agent, Larry Kleno. He told me that she was cautious about talking to the press, because in his words, "She really doesn't need to anymore." He called back thirty minutes later, though, and told me that she had agreed to see me, much to his surprise.

To my great delight, interviewing Barbara Stanwyck led to a beautiful friendship. She was much loved by literally everybody in the industry. "Missy," as she was known to her friends, was the ultimate pro, always on the set thirty minutes before her call. She knew her lines and everybody else's, and would always know each member of the crew by their first names. She also gave gifts to everyone at the end of the show.

I arrived at her house on Sunset Boulevard with a brand new tape recorder that I had purchased just for the occasion. This device even had speakers attached so I could play back what I had just recorded. Stanwyck

Barbara Stanwyck, as she looked when I got to know her in 1969.

opened the front door herself, showed me in, and then suspiciously said, "What's that?" I told her it was a new recorder to help me get everything on the record.

"Oh, well," she replied. "I don't like talking into tapes. If it makes me nervous, out it goes, and you, too!" She loved to kid in that salty way of hers. She was affable, but I was aware that I was dealing with a very strong lady — and not only from her screen image. She was totally professional and very demanding in real life, too. I had only seen her forty feet high on the silver screen, but in person, she was a small lady.

She had marvelous white hair by then. Stanwyck was proud that she chose not to dye her hair. There was no nonsense about her at all. I hadn't seen her series, *The Big Valley*, but that was the whole point of the magazine sending me; her program was a big hit in West Germany.

When she launched into discussing her series, my mind jumped ahead while we talked. That was part of my BBC training when they taught me how to interview; asking a question gives the subject a couple of minutes to answer, and while he or she is answering, I could prepare the next question.

While she talked about *The Big Valley*, I thought about how I would break the news to her that I hadn't seen the show. I thought, "Well, I could try and fake it, but I have a feeling I shouldn't try that with this lady." When she paused for breath, I said, "By the way, I should tell you I haven't had the chance to see any of the show."

There was a long Barbara Stanwyck pause, very *Double Indemnity*, and she said, "Well, don't you think you ought to see a few episodes eventually?" I said, "Yes, of course." Then she laughed, which made me laugh as her good nature broke the ice.

An hour into the interview, her phone rang. It was her press man, Larry Kleno. Stanwyck had told him in advance about my interview, "If I don't like this guy, you call me at three so I can get him the hell out of here." She hung up and told me that we were getting on fine, so we could keep going. We even kept talking after I ran out of tape.

I walked in her house at two p.m. and didn't leave until eight p.m., a little worse for sharing a bottle of white wine with her. She — and I — seldom drank but as she said, "Hell, we're having a great time, aren't we? Let's have a little wine."

When I had finished interviewing her, she interviewed me! I told her all my ups and downs as an actor and solicited advice from her. We spent hours going over her movie career, although she needled me when she found out that I didn't know how to ride a horse. She gave me a photo of her being dragged by a horse at forty miles an hour in *Forty Guns*, directed by Samuel Fuller. She did her own stunt and was so proud of that. Long afterwards, I got notes from her telling me not to waste my money on flowers for her. "Spend it on riding lessons; I've never heard of an actor who can't ride, for heaven's sake!"

When darkness began to fall, we walked out to her pool, and she then proceeded to give me a tour of her entire house. She was one of a kind and kept every award she ever won in glass cases. For a lady who had never won an Academy Award, she had all kinds of other awards on display, including an Emmy.

"No Oscar?" she said. "Well, the hell with them!"

We sat in her big living room, where one wall contained a long counter with a bar. Beneath the countertop sat two levels of leather-bound volumes of books that all looked the same. I asked what they were, so she pulled them out to show me. There were all of her movies' scripts!

She showed me her personal *Double Indemnity* script. On the right-hand side of each page was the script; the left-hand side contained a still photo illustrating that scene from the movie. She pulled out another, *Stella Dallas*. She had all of her scripts bound and illustrated in brown leather.

Oddly enough, I was only in awe of her when I first walked into the house. When I realized that she was just so down to earth and a completely straight in-your-face kind of lady, I relaxed completely. I have always enjoyed straight-talking people. I told her that I lived five minutes away in West Hollywood, or the "wrong side of the tracks" for such a big star.

She lived at the start of Beverly Hills, so when she found out that I lived just five minutes away, she began to call me to come and see her on Wednesdays when she gave her maid the day off from work. Around ten, the phone would ring, and there was Stanwyck on the other end of the line,

I loved how there was no pretense about Barbara Stanwyck.

saying, "Hi, it's me. I'm throwing a steak on the grill in an hour or two, so if you're not busy, stop by."

She always made those invitations casual. I went every time I could when I wasn't working. Over those steaks, she told me many stories. She told me one about her marriage to Robert Taylor that I'm not sure has ever been published. When they first got together, they lived together, an absolute taboo in Hollywood in the 1930s. MGM pressured Taylor to marry her; the studio told him that it was unacceptable for an MGM star to be "living in sin."

Stanwyck, however, was a freelancer, never attached for long to any studio. She liked to work a few times at Paramount, MGM or Fox, but never needed to commit herself because she was such a big star. After they wed, the marriage went on happily until 1953, when Taylor left for Rome to film *Quo Vadis.* The film crew called Stanwyck "Missy," the endearment that she insisted I call her, too. Someone on the crew called Missy to tell her that her husband was fooling around with an actress in the cast.

Missy said she called Taylor about it on the phone. They couldn't resolve the affair, so she flew to Rome to have an in-person chat with him. He confessed that he had pursued a fling, but he apologized and said that there was nothing between him and his fellow cast member. Missy flew back, but about a week later, the same loyal crew member called Missy to say that Taylor was sleeping again with the same actress.

"This time," she told me, "I didn't go to Rome. I went upstairs and packed all of his belongings, the furniture, and put them in the hall and foyer. Then I left the house when it was time for him to return, so Bob came back and found all of his belongings neatly packed away and a note from me saying, 'Get the hell out.' And that was the end of that." Years later, they made another movie together, so they had buried the hatchet. If Barbara Stanwyck liked you, she liked you.

Missy liked to get her exercise by walking along Sunset Boulevard. I asked her one time how she got away without being recognized on such a busy street. "Watch," she said. She went into her closet and came out with a straw hat and glasses. Arm in arm, we walked down Sunset Boulevard. No one gave a second glance as the cars passed us. "See?" she said. "Nobody recognizes me this way." She played a game with not being spotted. I adored my time with her.

In 1969, I was also privileged to interview and befriend my favorite leading lady of all time, Rita Hayworth. I'm very proud that she and I became close friends and remained so until she became ill with Alzheimer's disease and went into her sad decline. I discovered that she was absolutely nothing like the "Love Goddess" of the 1940s and 1950s, one whose emotions probably got her into trouble when she was young and so incredibly lovely.

Hayworth was a reigning beauty of the screen with a tempestuous private life through marriages to Orson Welles and Prince Aly Khan. I came to admire her and care for her very much, and still will sit goggle-eyed at *Gilda* and *The Lady From Shanghai*. I was so lucky to know the real lady behind all the lurid headlines.

Before I interviewed her, I told her publicist, Rupert Allen, that I would bring a photographer with me to her house. Hayworth sent word back that there were numerous current photos of her that her agent could provide, but if I didn't have any, she would agree to the photographer. The magazine's photographer could be a little pushy, so I had a feeling that he might not be the right guy to photograph such a private star.

When we got there, a maid showed us in to meet Hayworth. She wore a brown silk suit with her hair piled up over that marvelous Spanish face, free of artificial embellishments. She was a handsome-looking woman, not the voluptuous sex goddess of the 1940s. She was a little skittish because a few weeks before, Hayworth was interviewed by an L.A. paper over a few beers, and the article had not come across as very complimentary.

Sure enough, Hayworth and the photographer didn't hit it off very well. They went into a different part of the house with two publicists who were there to make sure she didn't repeat her newspaper fiasco. I set up my tape recorder, and Hayworth came back a few minutes later. I said, "Has the photographer finished?"

She said, "Oh yes, I sent him away."

I asked, "Anything wrong?"

"I don't like being pushed around," Hayworth told me.

I thought, "This is going to be a bloody interview, and the blood will be mine."

As we sat down to tape the interview, I worked very hard to have her

trust me. Fortunately, one of the first movies I mentioned was *The Story on Page One*. I said, "You did such a wonderful job in that," and we connected right away. I described scenes that I particularly enjoyed so she would know I wasn't faking it. I even told her that she got me through those obstacle courses during World War II when I learned "Make Way for Tomorrow" from *Cover Girl*. About ten minutes later we were Rita and David, and it went so well.

Hayworth took great pride in her work. She told me that Harry Cohn, the head of Columbia Pictures, was always on the outs with her. He was always asking her to promote herself more than

My favorite actress, Rita Hayworth.

she needed to. "He always knew that if I wanted to, I could walk out of Columbia Pictures and slam the gates behind me and the whole studio would come to a screeching halt," she said. She knew her significance to the studio's success.

She also told me that she despised the "love goddess" name pinned on her by the studio. "I've had to fight that for the rest of my career," she said.

Hayworth's daughter Jasmine was there the day we interviewed. She told me that her other daughter, Rebecca, lived in northern California. Thinking of how Hayworth had famously taken up with Orson Welles as a young woman, I asked her how she would feel if one of her daughters came to her and said that she wanted to live unwed with a man.

"How would you feel about it?" she said in agitation. "No, tell me. How would you feel about it?"

"I don't know," I said, regretting my decision to ask the question.

"Well, there's your answer," she said. "I don't know either. OKAY?"

I was afraid that I was going to lose her, but we got beyond the question, and then Hayworth gave me a tour of the house. "That little painting on the wall there was a present from Aly. See the little signature? It's a Picasso."

She pointed out a guitar that sat on a counter. "I'm taking guitar lessons, because somebody thinks I should make an album," Hayworth said.

Knowing that she was frequently dubbed by Anita Ellis whenever she sang in the movies I said, treading gently, "So you're singing, too?"

She picked up the guitar and hummed a little. I practically foamed at the mouth. She didn't sing, though; she just hummed. I thought of when she seduced Tyrone Power in *Blood and Sand* by strumming the guitar.

"Did you sing "Put the Blame on Mame" in *Gilda*?" I asked.

She said, "Yes, I did. I prerecorded it, but whether they used my voice, I couldn't tell. It was so close to my voice if it wasn't my voice."

Rita told me she despised the "love goddess" label.

Part of her pride was that she had paid for her house. "None of this was paid for by my husbands," she said. I really admired her sense of independence. She had just returned from filming a low budget production in Florida. Love goddesses grow mature, and once they do, they are no longer love goddesses. Almost nobody wanted Hayworth for movies any more.

She spoke, all aglow, about the pleasure of working in the movies again after a dry spell. I remembered back to movies where she was such a fabulous, marvelously sexy dancer who blossomed into a very fine actress. She told me that Harry Cohn always leaned on directors to include a line like "Who me?" in her films because he felt she delivered wonderful reaction shots. He thought that she put her whole heart in reaction shots in answer to on-screen questions.

After our interview, I broke the rules about not letting the subject see or comment on the work in progress. I promised her that she could approve of anything I wrote before I sent it to the editors; she was so special that I was determined that she be happy with the result. She didn't change a word.

Three or four days later, the phone rang. Rita herself told me I was the first writer to ever tell the truth about her. The European editors, though, hacked my story to shreds, and the editor took full credit and never even mentioned my name. I was hopping mad about that, but I had at least showed Rita the first copy before mailing it off to New York and took consolation from that fact.

Another time I was assigned to report on the death of leading man Robert Taylor, a very big star in the 1930s and 1940s. Extremely handsome, he came to fame opposite Greta Garbo in *Camille*. From then on, he was a household name. The magazine wanted me to interview his widow, a well-known, beautiful German actress named Ursula Thiess.

Two days after Robert Taylor died from cancer, the magazine's rep had contacted Thiess, but she refused to talk to anyone about her loss. I mentioned to his ex-wife, Barbara Stanwyck, that my magazine wanted an interview with Taylor's widow.

"You want to talk to Ursula?" Stanwyck asked. "I'll call her up."

Right there, she called Taylor's widow and told her that a friend wanted to talk to her. Thiess listened to my request and said, "Can you promise me that if I talk to you, I won't have to talk to any other interviewers? After all, my husband's just died."

I told her that I really didn't want to press the interview so soon into her grieving, but the magazine was clamoring for an interview with one of Germany's native daughters. She agreed to talk, so I went out to Robert Taylor's ranch just a few days after his death to talk with his widow.

In spite of her grief, Thiess was awfully nice and even had me sit in her husband's black leather chair. She told me how moved she had been when Governor Ronald Reagan came to visit Taylor just two days before her husband's passing. Reagan and Taylor were close friends. Taylor was so ill that he could barely get out of his chair, but when he saw the governor's car drive up to the house, he said to his wife, "Get me up on my feet. I've got to stand up to talk to the governor of California."

Taylor propped himself up and met Governor Reagan. Thiess left the two men to talk. Less than a week after this had transpired in the same room, she was telling me this really good story. I told her I couldn't promise that there wouldn't be other interviewers after me, but she told me that she would just tell them no, that our interview had officially documented her husband's final days.

The article came out and was well-received. Each time I published a story, the magazine sent me a copy. Everything I had written was trans-lated into German, so I couldn't really tell how much of my work had been edited or revised. Sometimes my articles were small pieces on contempo-rary TV stars, but I relished the longer feature stories on the bigger stars. Back in England, I had interviewed stars with my microphone and then went into a recording studio with two editors to shape the final radio show. Working on my printed articles, I had to return home with my notes and tapes to transcribe them by typing with two fingers. I hated the tediously boring work under deadline pressure, but I relished the direct access with Hollywood's royalty.

The writing assignment next led me to interview one of my favorite performers, Doris Day, whom I had interviewed back at the BBC in London when she was in Europe to film *The Man Who Knew Too Much*. Fifteen years later, Doris Day was starring on her own television show, *The Doris Day Show*, and I was invited to the set for our interview. Her son, Terry Melcher, was handling her public relations. He called me and said, "Mom's free tomorrow, so why don't you come out at lunchtime?"

She filmed at the old Republic Studio, where I had filmed *Master of the World* earlier in the decade, so I knew the studio well. In fact, her dressing room had been Vincent Price's dressing room when we worked together on our movie. When I got there, Doris had prepared lunch! Peppy and happy as always, she asked if I would like a drink. The offer threw me, because she was famous for having a bar at her house that served only milk shakes. She asked if I would like a Bloody Mary. It was a shock to just hear her use the word, "bloody." I politely declined, so we sat down and enjoyed a salad lunch.

Doris was now looking forward, not backwards. Once I turned the tape recorder on, I said, "You know, Doris, thirty years ago today was your very first recording with Les Brown."

She replied, "Well, it just seems like yesterday to me, so there!" She laughed as she said it, though, so I steered clear of the past and focused on promoting her television show. She told me that she only ended up in the medium because her husband, Martin Melcher, had committed her to the show without Doris's knowledge, shortly before his death.

During her mourning process, she was told that CBS expected to see her in ten days to start her TV series. Doris said, "What TV series?" She had been committed to the show because her husband had put her in bad movies, got his name on them as producer, and spent her money. When he died suddenly, an accounting showed that her millions had been lost to bad investments. She told me that she was in shock and that the only thing that had saved her was crabgrass. I asked her what she meant.

"Between the house and the pool on the flagstones, a lot of weeds grow up, so I made myself get up each morning to pull out the crabgrass to have something to do."

Publicity photo for The Doris Day Show, *1969.*

In a way, she was glad that she had been committed to television, because the series at least meant she could get busy making money again to replenish her bank account.

She talked about the rumors of "Doris Day lighting" supposedly used to hide wrinkles. Pushing her face close to mine, she said, "I don't have any wrinkles. Look, all I have are freckles, and for some reason, movie people don't like freckles so they always used a special filter to blur out my freckles."

I spent the day with Doris and watched her film on the set of her series. In television, people usually weren't cast too far from themselves, and that was true of Doris. She was chirpy and nice, and we kept in touch for years more through letters. Committed to animals, she was always interested in my pets and signed her letters, "Love to your critters!"

Years later when she received a Lifetime Achievement Golden Globe Award to great acclaim, she looked terrific. I wrote her to tell her how well she had done, but she replied that she had actually been terrified by the whole appearance. In real life, she was very shy. I was reminded of something she told me during our first interview back in London in the 1950s. I had asked her why she didn't perform live at the London Palladium like most of her contemporaries.

"Well, I'll tell you," she said. "If I did that, I'd be standing in the wings, hear the band strike up 'Secret Love,' face the audience, fall over in a dead faint, and pass out into the crowd."

"But what about all of those stints with Les Brown on tour?" I reminded her.

"That was different," she said. "Those audiences came to see the band. They didn't come to see me then. I was just the girl singer. There's a big build-up if you're heading the bill in a vaudeville theatre, and that's just not me. I'm happy with a film set and a crew."

What a sweet and wonderful lady. In later years, I would drive in Beverly Hills and see her on a bicycle with a big basket between the handlebars. I saw her once on Santa Monica Boulevard. People were used to her in Hollywood. She always wore a pink and white checkered shirt and blue jeans. A tour bus went by and the people went bananas when they recognized her. "Hi," she called back to them.

My writing job took me to Las Vegas to interview and cover the opening of Nancy Sinatra's show. I was from a previous generation and found more enjoyment in her father's music. At a reception in his daughter's honor, Frank was cordial, making up for that time he chewed me out for interrupting his dinner to ask for a BBC interview in England. As I was chatting with Nancy, Sinatra walked up to me, put his arm around my shoulder and said, "How they treatin' ya, pal?" So you never knew with ol' Frank.

The party was hosted by Frank's successor on the music scene, Elvis Presley. I was privileged to join Barbara Stanwyck as her dinner guest at the Las Vegas Hilton, where Elvis regularly appeared. I wasn't a big Elvis fan, and no doubt held a little grudge that he had become as popular with the next generation as Frank had been back in the 1940s. I really didn't know what to expect with Elvis. To my surprise, there really was electricity when he entered the room; I think every head turned to look at him. He was a perfect gentleman, working his way around the room and shaking hands with each guest. He introduced himself and asked if I was enjoying myself with Barbara, his co-star in *Roustabout*.

When Elvis left the table, Barbara laughed and said, "You were expecting a real slob, weren't you!" Elvis was elegant that evening. Nearly forty years later, I visited friends in Memphis and they took me to see Graceland. Elvis was the consummate collector, and I couldn't help but think back to that night in Las Vegas as I walked through the man's home and saw trophy cases filled with memorabilia before ending my tour at his gravesite.

After about a year of writing, I told the New York office that I felt I should be given a raise since I was making about $2,500 for a TV appearance and practically only a tenth of that for my weekly scribblings. The magazine kept promising but nothing came of it.

I typically dealt with the New York representative's secretary by phone. One day, she said, "I think I should tell you this, David. He's taking credit for your stories. I don't think it's right. Some of your stories are several pages long, and he's putting his name on your work. I don't think that's fair."

"What can I do about it?" I asked.

"Nothing, I guess," she answered, "but I just wanted you to know about it."

It became a moot point when the magazine suddenly folded. I enjoyed the year when I took up interviewing Hollywood stars again. I learned something from the experience, however, when I contacted Charles Champlin, entertainment editor and columnist at *The Los Angeles Times*. I offered him my stories on Rita Hayworth, Barbara Stanwyck, and Doris Day. Thinking about the possibility of writing for the newspaper, I sent him copies of my articles.

I got a pleasant letter back saying the stories were well written, but that there wasn't much need for them since the newspaper employed other writers; however, if opportunities were to arise, they could consider offering me the going rate for a feature article, $25! I just felt that the time and effort that went into setting up the meetings with the star, and then transcribing the tapes into the written word — (I always insisted upon taping an interview so there could be no arguments afterwards about a misquote) — and arranging it all into an attractive sequence for the reader was worth more than $25.

It was an eye opener for me. Writing can be hard, though very exciting work, but often for little financial rewards. Other than the sheer hard work of typing with two fingers, I enjoyed writing. As the 1970s started, my writing would have to wait forty years until I began sharing these stories again for this book.

By the 1970s, I was more comfortable with being me. The insecure teenager was gone. I could throw myself into acting parts and forget being me. Playing crazy or running amok was a very liberating creative outlet.

Hollywood was changing, too. Most of the studios were in tumult — by the late 1960s, the long-time studio chiefs were dying off or the studios were being sold off to corporate bosses more interested in formulaic, safe profits. The start of the 1960s had seen the likes of pictures along the lines of *Pillow Talk* with Doris Day; the end of the decade brought us *Easy Rider* and *Midnight Cowboy*.

People seemed more open to new ways of thinking. My agent, Maurine Oliver, wasn't very spiritual in the conventional sense, meaning she didn't really go to church, but she did see this strange lady, a psychic. One time I went with her and sat in a group of people talking about world peace. The leader began waving her hands about and then we all had to join hands and sing "He's got the whole world in his hands."

I hated the hand-holding and singing, but Maurine loved it. It was her kind of therapy, except that, without failure, we all sat and listened to talks on world peace, and in about five minutes, Maurine inevitably nodded off without hearing a word about anything that was going on to make the world a better place! Eventually somebody nudged her awake at the end, and she would say, "I just loved the talk today," as though she had heard it all. It was so good for the spirit that it put Maurine to sleep.

One time the lady leading the group very dramatically waved her hands and pointed at me way in the back, even though I did not want any part of it.

"You sir," she said.

"Me?"

"Yes! I see a presence guiding you over your shoulder. I see a shepherd."

That really got my attention, because my grandfather back in Scotland had indeed been a shepherd.

"It is a relative, is it?" she asked, as I nodded in agreement.

"Yes, yes! A grandfather!"

I nodded some more.

"Yes! He is your white angel. He has looked after you all your life and he will as loooooong as you live!"

Skeptical me somehow still couldn't believe it, but Maurine swore that she had never said a word about it to our hostess. I suppose my granddad was being a lot nicer to me in death than he was in life, because he went through my childhood without ever speaking a word to me!

You find meaning in life in so many places. Inspiration can be found in special friends. In 1971 there was a huge fire that jumped the main Pacific Highway and into Malibu, burning down Angela Lansbury's house. My business partner, Don Garnier, was an old friend of Angela's husband, Peter Shaw, the same agent who got me started after Alec Guinness sent me to him.

Don and I joined Angela and Peter one day as we sifted through nothing but ashes left in the rubble. We were looking for Angela's jewels because when the fire broke out, the family had to grab everything and run. Friends in Malibu had loaned them their house and moved out so

Angela and Peter could stay there while they decided what to do next. She had made a big splash on Broadway in *Mame*, and another play was coming up, so Angela needed to be near a phone for negotiations.

I was amazed how well she and Peter just rose above the whole tragedy. As I surveyed the scene, I was devastated. The wreckage looked like the London blitz with so many homes burned in their neighborhood. Angela said, "Well, you just have to take it in stride and move on to the next thing." She was making Irish stew as she said that later in the evening following the search. She never mentioned the fire again that night. She was so down to earth that she owned my heart that day, just the way she had done in the movies during World War II.

Meanwhile, my commercials and television work continued, with an occasional cinematic foray. In late 1971, I filmed a short introduction for a Hammer horror film, *Hands of the Ripper*, after the producers decided that the finished film's plot wasn't making much sense. They had me play a narrator of sorts to set the stage. I understand the film was chopped and diced as much as some of the poor victims in the plot, with various versions being shown on television and in different countries.

Television was moving into grittier material by the early 1970s. Gone were the frothier detective programs from a decade earlier, such as *77 Sunset Strip* or *Surfside Six*. Dramas focused more on human emotions, with more realistic storylines. Early in 1972, I guest starred on an episode of *Medical Center*, starring Chad Everett, James Daly, and Chris Hutson.

Titled "Deadlock," the episode aired on February 16, 1972, my forty-sixth birthday. *Medical Center* was an interesting show. The show was filmed on the MGM lot. When I arrived to work, the hospital setting, the corridor, the elevators, and the reception desk, all looked familiar to me. I had a feeling that *Medical Center* was using the old *Doctor Kildare* set from the mid-1960s, which in turn, might have been the original sets from the B movies that MGM used to make *Doctor Kildare* with Van Johnson and Lionel Barrymore.

The episode involved a young lady targeted by a killer. I played her really possessive and estranged father. The plots of 1970s shows were more complicated, too, with several different storylines running through the episode. The other guest stars were Susan Howard, who later went on to star on *Dallas*, and Peter Brown and Michael Anderson, Jr., both of whom had grown up since romancing Hayley Mills in Disney films during their younger years. Working with Michael Anderson, Jr., I was always amazed at how he could sound so authentically American even though he was British.

The show allowed me to do some satisfying work, and I was pleased when I saw it later. I thought I did an okay job as the jerk I played. The show still has a following, and thanks to a fan in Denmark who taped it off television, I have a copy on DVD today.

The same year took me to another of the newer crop of gritty urban crime dramas, *McCloud*, starring Dennis Weaver. NBC rotated the show

One of my "villain" poses.

with *McMillan and Wife* and *Columbo* as part of its *NBC Mystery Movie* series. Most of the episodes were ninety minutes or two hours long. As part of this line-up, *McCloud* was a popular top ten series in the ratings.

My episode was titled "The Barefoot Stewardess Caper." We shot on the Universal backlot, although to its credit, the studio did a good job using stock footage of Paris, London, and other European locations to intersperse with an international plotline about burglars.

Peter Sellers' ex-wife, the Swedish-born Britt Ekland, was one of the guest stars. Patrick O'Neal, with whom I had just worked on an episode of *The F.B.I.* earlier that year, was also a guest, while I played an English detective on the show.

Best of all was English actor John Williams, who came to fame in Hitchcock's *Dial M for Murder* and *To Catch a Thief* and as Audrey Hepburn's father in *Sabrina*. He and I had a lot of time just sitting around on location at LAX. We became great friends, and he invited me down to have lunch with him and his wife in La Jolla. They had a lovely house looking out on the ocean.

Our director was Harry Falk, who was divorced from Patty Duke just a few years earlier. As we were filming on some of the New York street sets on the Universal backlot, Falk had to stop shooting whenever a tour bus drove through. Universal had started offering tours in an effort to draw tourists and compete with Disneyland. Hollywood was certainly changing in the 1970s!

In 1974, I dubbed on another fairly high profile movie, *Huckleberry Finn*. Starring Jeff East, Paul Winfield, Harvey Korman and David Wayne, the film was a follow-up to *Tom Sawyer*, produced the prior year by *Reader's Digest*. Richard and Robert Sherman, the songwriting duo most famous for the songs in *Mary Poppins* and countless other Disney films and theme park attractions, wrote the screenplay and the film's songs.

Sometimes actors weren't available for post-production work, so I dubbed a few lines for actor Elliott Trimble, who played Uncle Harvey. The film was fairly well received and is remembered still today, thanks in part to the music and authentic production values. The movie marked one of the last times I ever dubbed another actor's voice for an on-screen character.

By the early 1970s, I was so busy with commercials that I sometimes worked less in television or movies, but my accountant didn't seem to mind. Commercials were just so lucrative that the whole process seemed like easy money for those of us who possessed the right look for advertisers.

I did one commercial for United Airlines, sitting in first class in a plane on a tarmac at LAX. All day, I ate steak and sipped champagne while they photographed the joys of flying first class. On another shoot, I went up to San Bernardino, the mountain area east of Los Angeles. There I joined another guy and two pretty girls for a series of Stroh's Bohemian

This look won me parts on McCloud, Cannon, *and other 1970s gritty TV fare.*

Beer commercials. No dialogue was involved the first day as we just rode a boat around Big Bear Lake.

For another Stroh's commercial, the crew had made some phony snow, so down came our group in a sleigh, holding our cans of beer. For some legal reason, we weren't allowed to drink the beer. We could put the product to our lips, but we couldn't drink it as we sang. The next day we went to Pacific Ocean Park and filmed another commercial on a carrousel. We filmed four beer commercials altogether. The networks ran them for two years, because the sponsors liked them so much. The commercials were so well received that I got paid every week for two years for two days' work! Maurine was delighted, but I think I was the most elated.

Before they were banned from television, I even filmed a Tareyton cigarette commercial with the company's motto, "I'd rather fight than switch." Many of the company's commercials depicted somebody with a black eye, presumably a person who chose to fight rather than switch cigarette brands. I had a black eye painted on me for my commercial.

We filmed it off Santa Monica when the tide was out. A back hoe was used to go out into the wet sand and built a little island with a phony palm tree on it. We waited for the tide to come in, and when the water came back, I waded out to the little manmade island. I had to find a pack of Tareyton cigarettes coming in on the tide and put one to my mouth. When there wasn't a match on the island, I ran around frantically looking for matches. That commercial ran a long time.

I even got a corresponding Tareyton billboard on Sunset Boulevard. Now I'm ashamed to say that I was thrilled about that high profile billboard. I had experimented with smoking, but I wasn't good at it. I never really liked to inhale, so I think I was a lousy-looking smoker in reality. I thought I wouldn't be good for Tareyton because I could not puff properly, but it turned out that I was apparently convincing enough that my billboard stayed up in Hollywood for a whole month.

Sometimes I've wondered how many young people saw my commercial or billboard and were enticed to start smoking. I kind of feel responsible for that. Fortunately for my conscience, those were the only cigarette commercials I ever did. There was sort of an unwritten law in the advertising business that once an actor or model had done a commercial for a product, we couldn't do another for the same product for another year or two.

The only other commercial on which I remember speaking was for Mrs. Olson's Coffee. I played a husband coming home from work as a square junior bank executive in a suit and tie. I came home to the pretty housewife who said, "Oh, you're home." She took my briefcase, brought me a cup of coffee and then I said something like, "Gee, honey, this coffee tastes great." The whole premise seemed false to me — how often did that really happen, even back then? That get-up was how the coffee was sold for years.

In 1973, I took a break and flew to England to visit my parents. Regardless of our various disagreements about my acting ambitions in the past, I wound up caring very deeply for them. While they never really understood the film-making process or an actor's challenges, they did their best toward the end of their lives. By then my success was demonstrable and something they could point to with pride when discussing it with relatives and friends. I was the one in the family over in America appearing on television and in the occasional movie.

Because of the expense of making trans-Atlantic phone calls of any length, my father recorded cassette tapes to me. My mother never would, though, because she said she sounded funny when she heard herself played back. Mother passed away at the end of 1974, and I flew back for her service. It was a sad occasion, but I did enjoy a rare visit with friends and cousins afterwards.

That same year, 1974, I found an uptick in a number of appearances on some of the top-rated urban crime dramas of the decade. I appeared on an episode of *Cannon*, starring William Conrad. He had previously directed me and James Doohan a decade earlier on a two-part episode of *G.E. True*. I really admired and respected him because of his working knowledge and sensitivity to performers that he had as a former actor. Quinn Martin Productions, the same production company responsible for *The F.B.I.* series, produced the show. I had a pretty big part in our episode, called "Triangle of Terror," filmed on location on Catalina Island. I was still waiting for those exotic location shoots in Australia or Hong Kong, but Catalina was about as good as I could get!

The same year, I guest starred on an episode of *The Magician*, starring Bill Bixby. Angela Lansbury's younger brother, Bruce Lansbury, produced the episode, called "The Illusion of the Cat's Eye." I can't remember much about the plot, but when I got the script, a key scene called for a leopard to kill my character up on a landing.

As I read the script, I thought, "Oh, they'll do this with process photography." I got to the set and there was the landing with some stairs. Up at the top was a cage with a real black leopard inside! I thought the scene would be done in two shots, one of me reacting, and one of the leopard jumping without me in the actual shot.

The director, Paul Stanley, said "No, we need you on camera as the leopard leaps toward you." I was very apprehensive about the idea, so the big cat's trainer led me upstairs and put my hand into the cage. "He's very tame," the trainer told me.

Ye gods, but I was nervous as the leopard paced up and down. He seemed to be tame enough. "He's trained to do this," the trainer explained. "You'll be on camera, and I'll be off camera to the left. At a sign, I make a move, and the leopard will just leap toward yet over you."

The shot had to be done in one take for realism and for the leopard's sake since he was trained to do it right from the start. If I botched my role, the mistake would impact the leopard's work. The trainer clicked his fingers. I looked startled as that huge animal leapt right over my head into the arms of the trainer. He was like a big pussycat. It looked very real on camera. Even though I was absolutely petrified, the shot worked beautifully just as the trainer said it would.

The end result at home for the viewers was that I was depicted sitting in a room. My character heard a sound, started upstairs, and then a giant leopard leaped on me from the darkness and clawed me to death. Fortunately we didn't have to do that part!

In between commercials and guest appearances on crime dramas, I appeared on a Bob Hope TV special in 1974. We worked together in a sketch about three astronauts, British, Russian, and American — you can figure which one I played. Three of us actors rehearsed for an afternoon with a stand-in reading Bob's lines. Minutes before taping, he arrived at NBC in Burbank by way of helicopter from Palm Springs. He walked in, shook hands, said, "Let's make it, fellas!" and did the whole thing from cue cards!

Moments later, Hope was out the door and up in his whirlybird once more. Unlike the time I worked with Jack Benny, I thought working with Hope was a disaster. He didn't even make eye contact with us actors. Hope wasn't exactly rude, but he didn't have much time for us. Still, we were working together, so I watched the show with great anticipation, because he had been another one of my heroes back in the 1940s in his pictures with Bing Crosby. Imagine my disappointment when the sketch was cut out completely! The producers trimmed it out altogether for time, but it showed intact in Japan when the special aired there.

From Bob Hope, I went to work with another entertainment icon, Andy Griffith. By the 1970s, he had proven that he could do more than the comedy that had made him so famous. After working on *The Beverly*

Hillbillies, Buddy Ebsen had joined TV's crime-fighting crusaders as *Barnaby Jones*, so a TV movie was developed for Andy Griffith in a similar vein. This telefilm was intended to launch a series for him, but not for me, because I got a shotgun blast in the face halfway through.

The film was called *Winter Kill*, and it was actually a lot of fun to do. I played a priest who counseled a mixed-up teenager. The villain, a serial killer in a Colorado resort town, did away with me because I knew too much.

We filmed it out at MGM as the only company shooting on that vast lot. It was sad to see all thirty soundstages closed except for ours. Even the commissary was closed, so we ate at trestle tables between the soundstages. Griffith provided a catered lunch for the company each day at a huge personal expense to him. I found him to be a warm, generous man.

One day we were all enjoying his hospitality when James Stewart sauntered up from nowhere and sat and chatted with us. He had started at MGM in 1936 or thereabouts and kept shaking his head at what had happened to the old place. He was there working on *That's Entertainment*, MGM's opus to the studio's great musical numbers. Even the makeup man on *Winter Kill* went back as far as 1939 and had worked on *The Wizard of Oz*. He gave me some rare photos of Judy Garland testing in various blonde wigs.

When it came time to shoot my murder scene by shotgun blast, they cleared the crew back behind plastic sheets and protected the camera, located about four feet from me. The thought crossed my mind just before the take, "Who's protecting dumb old Frankham, sitting here like a lamb for the slaughter?"

I never backed away from anything I was asked to do because I always felt that a double would take away from the conviction of the scene. Nevertheless, I was a bit nervous about the shotgun blast. I rehearsed moving my face a split second before the trigger was pulled and just prayed that the prop man and I had our act together. It was a blank shell, but in a small place like that — a priest's study, of course — it could do, and did do, total damage. Everything was shattered to shreds behind me. I slumped on the desk a second before the prop gun fired, so I was ok. Then they covered my head in raspberry topping, and I looked totally demolished in the close-up!

Those days were before strict SAG regulations were enacted after actors' deaths on the John Landis picture *The Twilight Zone*. A couple of actors also died in the 1980s and 1990s on sets from blanks in prop guns, so in hindsight, we were probably pretty foolish to shoot that shotgun live as we did. I can't say the actor's life is a dull one!

The next year, 1975, took me to an episode of *The Six Million Dollar Man*, titled "Outrage in Balinderry." We filmed on the backlot at Universal, where I seemed to work quite a bit in the 1970s. The other guests included the glamorous Martine Beswick and Alan Caillou. Our director was the

I almost lost my face shooting Andy Griffith's Winter Kill *TV-movie in 1974.*

prolific Earl Bellamy, who literally directed nearly two thousand episodes of television series. He was a dynamo and went from scene to scene like clockwork. He really had the art of directing television episodes down to a well-oiled machine.

I must confess that in spite of its popularity and its star, Lee Majors, *The Six Million Dollar Man* didn't leave much of an impression on me. Truthfully, by the 1970s, most of the action or crime-based series followed the same formulas: a mystery or a murder, the set-up, the investigation, the action sequence, and the resolution. I'm sure our episode was a good one, or the show wouldn't have been so popular, but by the middle of the 1970s, the scripts were almost forgettable.

As I neared fifty, I transitioned from playing those fun, unstable characters running amok into roles for sedate bureaucrats or diplomats. There wasn't much challenge to memorizing dialogue that contained pleasantries or explanations of why an ambassador needed a mystery solved and so on. The parts seemed less fun and more like work each time I was cast.

My friend Don Garnier was a notable architect in Los Angeles. His talents were always in demand, so much so that at one point, he needed help with project management so he could attend to architectural renderings and blueprints. There was much work to be done just arranging schedules and checking out details. When I found myself not working on a commercial or TV show, I went into business with him and began to help out on some of Don's construction projects.

A decade earlier, he had designed a house and got the plans approved. The foundations were poured. He worked on the house on the weekends in a methodical process. Don asked if I wanted to learn how to do floors to help him finish his house. I went up to his house with clothes in case an audition came up and placed them near sawdust and planks in a makeshift closet. I loved working with my hands on the construction site. It completely removed me from acting and grounded me. Many times I cleaned up, changed and went on an audition and then came back up and worked more on floors.

One time Don was working on a house where the roofing was ready to be done. He asked if I wanted to help as I had done with the flooring several years earlier. After all, I had started adulthood as an architectural student. I hadn't thought any more about architecture, but the whole process was suddenly fascinating to me.

I worked on the two-story house on Coldwater Canyon. Given the equivalent drop of the canyon, going to the roof was like being five stories off the ground! The chimney stacks were in, so the roofing tiles needed fitting together by nailing. Long lines were drawn across the roof's wood so we could tell where the tiles should go. Don and I tied ropes about ourselves, hung them around the chimney stacks, and dangled five stories above Coldwater Canyon as we completed the entire roof by ourselves. If the rope had given way, that would have been the end of us.

The whole business of homebuilding seemed to correspond well with show business. Many leading entertainers — Bob Hope, Lawrence Welk, even Rock Hudson — wisely re-invested their earnings in real estate development and holdings. Building homes or rental properties was a lucrative business in Southern California, where real estate prices always seemed to come at an ever increasing premium.

I learned that I could still network and meet fascinating people in show business as I supervised home construction. We were building a home in Beverly Hills across the street from a friend of Robert Osborne, and that's how I was introduced to Bob. Trained as a journalist, he worked with Lucille Ball's acting group and wisely combined both of his loves to become one of Hollywood's leading historians.

In the days before home video, he always seemed to have access to 16mm prints of movies that were rarely screened on television, so seeing a long-lost classic back then was a real treat. Every Saturday on the dry wall in this house that we were building, Bob brought movies over to show via projector.

One evening we all went over to Bob's apartment to watch *Earthquake*. He turned it up so loud that the floor and the walls actually shook in his apartment when the earthquake happened on film. He loved movies and could talk about a film's background or the biographies of a film's performers.

In his bathroom, he had about a dozen stills from various television shows he had appeared in as an actor. I went out afterwards and said, "I didn't know you had done so much as an actor." He was very modest. By then, he had begun to be recognized as a fine historian and interviewer. He was with *The Hollywood Reporter* and had become great friends with Bette Davis and several other people who appreciated his knowledge, as is evident each time he talks to someone on Turner Classic Movies. He's done remarkably well for himself and deserves all his success.

As I got into real estate, I learned about what later became a very popular trend. By "flipping" a house, one could buy a property, improve it, increase the value, and then sell it for a handsome **profit**. Once the house was suitable for habitation, I had a place to live while adding the finer touches or special lighting, book shelves or any other number of enhanced improvements to add value before selling for a profit. Homebuilding proved to be an excellent investment. I stopped renting in 1976 and built and lived in my own homes until just a few years ago.

In 1976, Don and I were building on a quiet country lane in Beverly Hills. One Sunday afternoon, I drove up to the site to check on the workers' progress because I had been filming during the week. As I was getting into my car to drive back home, three people, obviously out for a Sunday stroll, walked down the road toward me. There were two men in their sixties and a slightly familiar-looking lady about the same age, wearing a Chinese coolie-style hat and a black shirt and slacks, no sunglasses.

When the three were about ten feet from me, I realized that the lady was Greta Garbo. I couldn't even start the engine. I just sat there. I'm sure my mouth was wide open. I found myself grinning like an idiot and waving. She waved back and laughed! My first instinct was to say to myself, "I've no one to share this with. Nobody's going to believe me." But then I realized that *I* knew it was happening.

The lane was a dead end. I was headed back up to the highway but I told myself I would never see her again, so I backed the car into a neighbor's driveway and started following them down the lane to a dead end where they were looking at the scenery of the San Fernando Valley. Garbo turned when she heard the car about twenty feet from her and laughed again. I guess she was used to people following her. When they reached the end, I came to my senses and reversed and drove away. She waved one more time! I'll never forget my actual Garbo sighting.

In Hollywood, I always bumped into people I had worked with in my career. I ran into Vincent Price at the West Hollywood Post Office in the late 1970s. Vincent was suing American International Pictures because the studio wasn't paying him his royalties on all those movies that he had made. He always took a nominal up-front fee, usually $5,000, and then a percentage of the profits. He said those profits were immense, only he would never know it by the meager checks the studio sent him. "They have very imaginative book-keeping," he said.

I once ran into Shelley Winters at the supermarket. She had been one of my favorite guests back at the BBC. During our interview, she wore a mink coat that kept falling onto the floor. This time, she had traded her mink for a tent-like, Hawaiian-style caftan. She was peering through her Ben Franklin spectacles, cursing the small print on a soup can. I volunteered to help her read, and then I reminded her of our lunch interview two decades earlier in England. Peering over her glasses, she said, "I don't remember that, but did we have fun? That's all that counts!"

In 1977, I worked on an episode of *The Waltons*, but I never appeared on screen. Combining my early radio experience, voiceover, and acting abilities, I portrayed Neville Chamberlain on a radio broadcast that the Walton family hears in the buildup to World War II.

The producers had a copy of Chamberlain's actual "Peace in our time" announcement over the BBC, the wireless, as we called it back in September 1939. I actually read what he said that day. The real day was heart-stopping when I was thirteen, sitting by the wireless and waiting for this announcement. It was a really extraordinary moment when he said, "As of this moment, (pause), this country, (pause), is at war, (pause) with Germany." I think the whole country was worried that bombs would start dropping that night, but for the first six months, nothing happened before the London Blitz.

It was a heart-stopping day to record that part, too, because Maurine, having a memory lapse, occasionally sent a client to the wrong studio, and she sent me out to MGM that day. I sat there quite passively by myself in a small dubbing studio until somebody stuck his head in the door and figured out that I was at the wrong studio! By then my time for showing up to do the Neville Chamberlain reading had passed. Breaking all the speed laws, I drove straight across town from MGM to Warner Bros. out in the San Fernando Valley. When I breathlessly arrived, the producers were fine and told me to relax. The show is still well loved by audiences today.

For more than a decade, I did so well with commercials through the Jack Wormser Agency that he automatically renewed my representation. I had done so well, however, that it was the reason I left commercials around 1976. Being in demand for commercial work meant that I had to go out five days a week, several times a day, to see if I had the right look for advertisers. That practice went non-stop. I was growing tired of the breakneck routine, and I found my enthusiasm waning.

I had grown so accustomed to the money and seeing myself on commercials that for most of a decade, I felt very good about working for advertisers. It was only toward the end that I began to tire of it. I sometimes worried that acting peers would snootily look down on me if they spotted me in commercials, but it never seemed to happen. To my knowledge, nobody on the acting side ever caught on to my moonlighting, even though once or twice as an actor, I tuned in to see a show that I had filmed and spotted myself in a commercial during the same program! Whenever that happened, I just knew that I would never work in Hollywood again, but it seemed to work out fine.

I thought of commercial work as a day job. The whole process began to make me a little cynical. On one commercial, I was cast as a husband. The sponsors were going to cast someone as the wife. They said, "Dave, sit in on this because we've got to choose the wife and it might be good to have a rapport between the two of you."

Each of the girls was so pretty. I would have cast any one of them. After the first one or two came in, I was shocked to hear what the casting directors said: "Her boobs were too flat," or just the most God-awful raunchy takes on these otherwise beautiful women.

Eventually, it began to wear me down. It meant that every day I wasn't working as an actor, I was out for commercials. Exhausted, I often drove home from auditions and then the agency called to tell me I was needed out in the Valley in thirty minutes for a look-see on a commercial.

Sadly, I started lying to get out of doing commercials. I went home after three p.m. one day and had a call to go back out that evening at 7:30, after dinner. I just didn't go. Working in commercials meant that performers had to sign in at the shooting site. I got a call the next day from the agency asking where I had been, so I fibbed and said that I had experienced car problems. I felt awful because the agency was so nice.

Being tired will show up in an actor's life. I thought, "That's not good, Frankham, there's no need to lie," so I decided that I would walk away from commercials altogether. My zeal really took a hit when Jack Wormser retired and sold his agency to someone that I hated on sight. I chose not to renew. I had enjoyed a very good commercial career, more than a ten-year run, when I quit cold turkey.

I was so burned out from commercials that I gave away a lot of things, gave up my apartment while my house was being built, and then went on a two-day train trip to stay with friends in Jackson, Wyoming. There was a sleeper car, and I got a sitting room with a very comfortable bed and my own bathroom. What a wonderful treat it was to leave Hollywood behind and gaze out on the western vistas. I ended up staying in Wyoming for a whole year, doing nothing but relaxing, reading, enjoying the scenery, and celebrating a life that had prospered me well enough to take a break at age fifty.

Priorities change as you get older, and I found that I preferred working to live than living to work. I still liked acting, but as the parts changed, I changed, too. Twenty years earlier, I had been so eager to act, and my youthful energy had landed me leading parts on television. Ironically, after playing bland best friends to heroes, I had developed a niche for playing cads or unstable villains. In a way, I had done so many of those parts that it was inevitable to lose a little interest as I began playing boring bureaucrats or investigators.

After twenty years of good, steady work in a profession I really loved, I left Hollywood in 1976 to get away from commercials. I decided to go back from time to time over the next several years, all at a time and place of my choosing for a part that interested me. Sometimes I was requested to audition by casting agents or production companies I had worked with earlier in my career. When I was up for an episode of *Hawaii Five-O*, the casting agent looked over my credits — all the way back to 1956 — and said, "David, you were in the golden age of television!"

He was right. I had arrived in America just as television really took off in popularity. For twenty years, I had worked with everyone from Shirley Temple to Basil Rathbone to Andy Griffith, from dramas to comedies, and from a more innocent time in the 1950s to shifting trends and tastes of the late 1970s. For someone who really didn't believe in luck, how remarkably fortunate I had been!

CHAPTER TWELVE

Losing, and Finding, My Voice

By the late 1970s, I had done well enough — and for long enough — to ease up and concentrate on other interests, including building and selling homes. I enjoyed the luxury of choosing acting projects that interested me. In 1978, I appeared in NBC's television movie *Little Mo*. The film starred Glynnis O'Connor as real-life tennis star Maureen Connolly, the first woman to win all Grand Slam titles in a year.

I had interviewed Connolly back at the BBC one time between sets, so her biopic naturally interested me. I played a doctor who examined her when she's concerned about her health. The film's stars included Michael Learned, Anne Baxter, Mark Harmon, and Leslie Nielsen. The film was an enjoyable experience, one of the few projects I pursued in the time when I began to take a break from working.

I went back to my Hollywood life from time to time, but life there was getting so smoggy and congested that I decided to move to Santa Fe, New Mexico in December, 1978. Before leaving, I went to work December 14th on *The Great Santini*, a big-screen adaptation of Pat Conroy's novel with realistic depictions of American military and family life. I took a part as a military captain for the pleasure and challenge of working with Robert Duvall, whom I greatly admire.

I thoroughly enjoyed the production. My first day of shooting was at the Goldwyn Studios, and the second day was at a Santa Monica restaurant. It was a small role, but one I savored because I had a one-on-one scene with Duvall himself. At an officer's club, Duvall's character gets drunk, makes a big scene, and talks rudely to my character, a higher-ranking officer. Duvall's character's tirade only escalates as he grabs my character's wife from the dining table to dance with him and then pretends to vomit in front of me.

445

Unfortunately, I had dental surgery the day before we shot. My mouth was so sore that I could hardly speak. I was full of painkillers because my new porcelain caps weren't finished. What a mess. But I loved every minute of working with Duvall. He was a great improviser, and I'm not, so I really had to have my wits about me.

At one point, to get a fresh reaction from the extras working in the res-

Dressing down Robert Duvall in The Great Santini *(1979).* (ORION)

taurant scene — Hollywood extras can be a jaded lot — Duvall dropped his pants and mooned them! The extras were astonished, which was just the reaction the director, Lewis John Carlino, needed. It was the last scene, on the last day of filming. They had been shooting in the Carolinas all summer and fall and only went back to Hollywood for my scenes.

Sharp-eared viewers can catch a minor goof in the film. The actress playing my wife did call me "David" by mistake instead of using my character's name, although I suppose there's nothing in the script that would have prohibited "Captain Weber" from having the same first name as the actor who played him.

While *The Great Santini* underwhelmed at the box office, the film scored well with critics. Robert Duvall received an Academy Award nomination for Best Actor, and it was satisfying to know that I had wisely picked a good feature film for the right reasons. Working with such an

accomplished and talented pro as Duvall provided just the kind of touch
I needed to motivate me to act from time to time.

Life back in Santa Fe, meanwhile, was simply wonderful. California
had grown so smoggy and congested that New Mexico was a welcome
change of scenery. Santa Fe's opera company was, and is, one of high
quality. Restaurants, art, culture — there was so much to enjoy. An occasional star visited in a theatrical production, and I enjoyed going to shows
and movies. The winters, too, brought snow and ice, quite a change from
Hollywood's year-round smog.

For the next five years, I lived in Santa Fe, only going back to Hollywood
from time to time when my friend, the director John Erman, made me a
few offers that I couldn't refuse. The work was for TV movies at Warner
Bros. that inevitably left some of my performances on the cutting room
floor and a couple of generous checks in my bank account.

It was hard to say no to John. He had directed my famous "Nightmare"
episode of *The Outer Limits*, one of his first directing jobs in Hollywood.
After going on to prolific directing work on a number of series, John had
directed the world's most acclaimed mini-series, *Roots*. He established
himself as one of the premier television directors, so his projects were
high status enough to guarantee a quality experience. I liked him very
much, too, so it means a lot if a director is liked by his actors and vice
versa.

When John directed a 1981 remake of Somerset Maugham's *The Letter*,
with Lee Remick in the famous Bette Davis movie role, I was up for
a week of filming as an attorney. Remick's husband was the executive
producer, so even though John wanted me for the role of an attorney
who believes in his client's innocence, I would have to pass muster with
Remick's husband.

I wanted to read first for John, even though he said I didn't have to,
just to see how the experience would go. He told me that my reading was
just right. I first had an inkling that Hollywood had changed when I then
went upstairs to see Remick's husband. He said, "And what can we see
you in currently?" meaning local theatre or television.

That really shook me because I was living in Santa Fe and didn't think
I would have to prove myself at that stage of my career. As it turned out,
I didn't have to because John had asked for me, so it was a fait accompli,
but the experience was a bit unsettling just the same.

To make it more complicated, my voice came across as a little gravelly
at the reading. John covered for me, saying that I had a slight cold. John
read the scene with me, but Remick's husband decided against me for

the attorney's role. He didn't say why, but he brought in a younger British actor, Christopher Cazenove.

John felt bad and said, "You've come all the way from Santa Fe, and I feel terrible. How about staying for another part?" So, I got the smaller role of a prosecuting attorney. That was fine by me, because it still meant I would have a big courtroom scene with Lee Remick. I also had a terrific scene with Wilfrid Hyde-White playing a judge. I didn't have a lot to do, but I enjoyed the work.

After we finished and I had gone back home to Santa Fe, I heard from John. He said, "We're having a screening at the Director's Guild, and of course you're welcome, but I have to tell you that because the film is running too long, there's nothing left of your courtroom scene except for one long shot of you and Wilfrid Hyde-White."

I didn't attend, naturally, but I watched the movie when it finally aired on television in 1982. As an actor, I couldn't help but be a little disappointed to see my work reduced to a long shot. At that stage in my career, it didn't really seem to bother me as much as it would have had I been a young actor starting out in the business.

John asked me back again in 1982 for *Eleanor, First Lady of the World*, a biopic about First Lady Eleanor Roosevelt's post-White House life as a humanitarian. Jean Stapleton from *All in the Family* was cast as Mrs. Roosevelt. I had interviewed the real Mrs. Roosevelt thirty years earlier on my BBC radio show, so the subject matter was definitely interesting. I was eager to see how Stapleton would bring the character to life.

I was up for the part of the Australian Secretary-General of the United Nations. John told me that if I could convincingly master an Australian accent, the role was mine. I rented the 1979 Australian film, *My Brilliant Career*, with Judy Davis and kept playing the video enough to get the accent right. I practiced sounding Australian with my tape recorder and then sent off the tape for John to hear. My work was believable enough that the part was mine, so I took a week away from Santa Fe and had a very enjoyable time back in Hollywood.

After learning all my lines and going through makeup, I climbed up into the set representing the UN dais on the first day of shooting. Our star climbed up a ladder and said to me, "Hi, I'm Jean Stapleton; welcome to the show!" I thought that was a sweet thing to do.

The assistant director came up to me and said, "Well, you got the blue pages?" meaning the revisions, but they hadn't sent them to me! Everything that I had learned was no longer in the script! Fortunately, I had to sit behind a lectern, so I spread out all the blue pages and tried to keep my eye on the camera as I performed a cold reading. There was no time to explain to John that I had not received my revised lines, and that would only have meant getting someone in trouble.

I managed to do the scene somehow, even though my voice sounded a little scratchy for some unknown reason. John noticed my gravel throat and said, "You've still got a cold," which is what he had said earlier when

By the early 1980s, I transitioned from playing villains to portraying lawyers and diplomats.

we worked on his remake of *The Letter*. It was something that I needed to check out if the gravelly sound continued.

Back in Santa Fe, a theatrical movie part found me, a welcome treat since it meant that I could stay in New Mexico to work. I had never considered working locally in Santa Fe because I'm not really a stage actor, although the city has a number of excellent professional theatres.

In 1982, a local agent in Albuquerque contacted me about a film Richard Brooks was directing there, called *Wrong Is Right*, with Sean Connery as the star. I greatly admired Brooks' work, so I agreed to a meeting. We chatted amiably enough about why an Englishman was living in New Mexico. I told him that I would very much like to be in his film, so we shook hands on the deal. I was to work the following day with Connery and Henry Silva, two actors for whom I hold much respect.

I had made it clear to the local agent that my minimum fee per day was $1,000. That sounds like a lot for 1982, but it wasn't really once I deducted taxes and ten percent for the agent's commission, and it's what I was getting per day back in Hollywood. The agent said she understood, and I agreed to do the film, albeit with some developing grave misgivings because Brooks had the reputation of never letting the actors see the script until a few moments before the scene was rehearsed. He said it kept them on their toes, but I'd say it was more like them having a nervous breakdown!

Sure enough, no script was sent to my house in Santa Fe, and SAG rules said that we had to have a script at least twenty-four hours before shooting. Brooks ignored that, the only director to do so that I'm aware of. I got up before dawn for the sixty-mile drive to Albuquerque, where I got into my clothes, had makeup done, chatted with Connery and Silva — and still no script. Connery told me that he had one when the film began, but Brooks took it away from him once the scenes got underway.

At eight a.m., Brooks promptly arrived, started screaming and yelling at the extras, smiled at Connery and completely ignored me. Half an hour later, he grabbed me by the arm and stood me on an escalator. He said, "Here's Henry Silva, he's a sheik, you're a reporter, go ahead and interview him. Roll 'em!" and we were off and running, up and down, up and down, half a dozen times. Luckily I had once been a radio interviewer, or I would have been even less believable!

"Cut!" yelled Brooks. "Next scene!" and that was that. I was thinking, "Well, those twenty-five years of hard work are down the drain when THIS comes out — I'll look like an extra!" The worst was to come. While we filmed, the agent who negotiated the deal (at least I was getting my standard fee, so it wasn't to be a total loss) watched the escalator going up and down with an expression of absolute bliss on her face. She kept talking about how exciting the process was, in spite of my mounting fury at being trapped in the whole thing.

After my escalator scene was all done to Brooks' satisfaction, the agent took me to the production office to sign my contract. It was for $500. I had never worked for that little. I said to her, "What's this? Where's the other $500?"

"Oh," she said. "They wouldn't pay any more than that." I was beginning to turn purple at that point.

"Then why on earth didn't you call and tell me — that what's agents DO, for heaven's sake. Do you realize that you could have ruined my entire career?" I dashed to my car and fled back to Santa Fe, called my real agent, Maurine Oliver, in Hollywood to tell her how dumb I'd been, and she said, "Don't worry, nobody will ever see it."

The Albuquerque agent called about a month later, no apologies, mentioning nothing about the experience, to tell me that there was another local role she wanted to discuss with me, and for the first and last time in my life, I shouted into the phone, "Don't EVER call this number again!" and hung up on her.

Not one of my finest hours, I'm afraid, and my parents would have turned red in shame at such bad manners on my part. As an actor, the moral of the story is that even though your agent is supposed to look out for you, always look out for your own reputation and best interests, because there is no guarantee that anyone else is obligated to do so. Besides my tiny part as a soldier to get a Screen Actors Guild card in Disney's *Johnny Tremain* back in 1957, *Wrong Is Right* is the one other film role that depressed me, but I see the funny side of it now. I've almost recovered from it.

For all the lack of professionalism associated with some of those working on *Wrong Is Right*, I was fortunate to know one of the entertainment industry's consummate pros not too far from me. Greer Garson lived near Santa Fe, so I was able to build a friendship with the great actress. We reminisced about the time I interviewed her for my BBC program. She had become a great pen pal, and for years she sent encouraging notes. Now we were living not far from each other in New Mexico, and it was a pleasure to get to know her better.

When my father was dying in 1982, Greer wrote that she wished she could send him a dozen "Mrs. Miniver" roses to cheer him up. I sent her letter on to him, and he actually did live on for several months on the strength of her encouragement. Toward the end of his life, I flew home to England to visit my father. He had been a widower for more than six years. One night he decided that he wanted to reunite with her, so he just went to sleep and never woke up.

After he died, I discovered that he had kept stills and photos from my movies with notations on the back as to which film was which. It turned out that he had silently been more proud of me than he let on, so it was some consolation for those early years when my parents weren't supportive of my decision to become an actor.

I had time on my return back to stop in London to see *The Little Foxes*, which Elizabeth Taylor had the great courage to do live on stage. She was quite good, and I was very impressed. I sent a note back and asked if I could stop by the dressing room and say hello. I hadn't seen her since 1956, when Michael Todd swept her off her feet following my spring and summer spent with her and her soon-to-be divorced husband, Michael Wilding.

Elizabeth very sweetly agreed to see me. We had champagne and talked about the time when her two sons were little boys back in 1956. It was good to see how unpretentious she still was. We talked about how that had been a very happy summer, as I was just about to start my first NBC live shows and went almost every day to swim at Elizabeth and Michael's house. They had almost adopted me that year.

We said goodbye as I left for Santa Fe. I enjoyed life there, but those early 1980s trips back to Hollywood for TV movies made me miss acting. I was nearing sixty, so I thought there might be different kinds of parts to play at that stage in my life. Variety is always interesting to an actor, especially if it means the opportunity to play a new kind of role.

I honestly enjoyed auditioning. It was very challenging when I went in for my appointment and saw about six other fellows up for the same part. I always found it exciting to try to be the best or at least the one chosen. Sometimes I was selected, and sometimes not, but it was always stimulating and competitive. Over the years it became less so, as the casting directors became less personally interested in one's career, less supportive, and more impersonal. They were affiliated with large corporations rather than the cozy studio set-ups of the 1950s and 1960s.

Around 1983, I moved back to Hollywood and bought a nice little house. Back at work as an actor, I was pretty disgusted to find myself twice on an audition for a Michael Keaton movie — the same role — because they were too disorganized to have remembered that I had already been seen. I started saying to myself, "Frankham, I think it's time you got out of this rat race." The early times had been so wonderful with friendly faces at Fox, Disney, MGM, and Warners, and always so encouraging.

Being in the business as long as I had, I learned professionally that you must always put yourself first. More than once in the 1970s, Universal shoved me into something at the last minute because another actor canceled, saying, "You're really helping us out, David; we won't forget it." Months later, I would be eager for a crack at another role yet couldn't get a foot in their door. It happens all the time as life in the professional wars, and it's not a bitter experience. The winners are the ones who don't let it get them down and who don't believe every literal word they hear!

By the 1980s, Hollywood had changed so much that it grew tough for actors to even get representation. When I arrived back in Hollywood, Maurine cut short a social lunch because she had to return to the office to videotape prospective clients. She hated it, but it had become the only way, she said. The list of young people anxious for a meeting was several pages long. She disliked the process because it took up valuable time which would otherwise be devoted to finding work for her regular clients. I was quite taken aback from those changes. I had taken a lot for granted in my early days in Hollywood, but then I think we all did, because it had been so pleasant and so easy.

The awful disease AIDS was growing in public awareness, so John Erman set out to make what was the first big dramatic look at its impact. *An Early Frost* was to be a groundbreaking television movie with Aidan Quinn as an AIDS patient. John told me that there would be a part for me as a lawyer.

As it often happens in Hollywood, though, the part was written out of the script, so there was nothing for me to do. The film went on to great critical acclaim and is still remembered for helping raise awareness and compassion for sufferers in those early years when there was so much fear surrounding the disease.

Undaunted by acting parts that didn't materialize, I knew that I had left behind a very successful commercial career, and it turned out that I still had the right look and sound for commercials. I promptly landed a high-paying British Airways commercial doing voiceover work. The job was very easy with a great fee, so the commercial was a good way to start up again after being away for several years.

When I went to record on a Friday, the sound engineers told me that my voice sounded husky. They asked me to come back on Monday to record it again, thinking that I might have a slight vocal irritation. When I tried recording again on Monday, however, my voice was still raspy sounding, and I had to be replaced.

I went to a highly touted voice specialist on Rodeo Drive in Beverly Hills. As I sat in the waiting room, out came Martin Sheen, with whom I had worked on the "Nightmare" episode of *Outer Limits*. "You'll love

I don't know how I was ever talked into this cowhand-with-a-rope publicity shot in the mid-1980s.

this guy," Martin told me. "He's the best throat doctor in town. He gets me going whenever there's something wrong with my voice."

The doctor promptly diagnosed me as having myasthenia gravis, a very serious disease which affects vocal cords and other muscles to the point of atrophy. He told me that there was nothing to do but wait for nature to take its course. In the meantime, he sent me to a voice therapist for six months to try to get my voice as reasonably good as possible so I could try to keep working.

Without a great pressing financial need to work — after all, I had decided to pursue work again just because I wanted to — I had little reason to question his diagnosis. When I went back for a follow-up, the singer Tom Jones was coming out of the office and looked very happy. I thought, "Well, I've seen Martin Sheen and Tom Jones here, so this guy must be good."

It seems incredible now that I didn't get a second opinion. I accepted the sentence that I had a disease and worked with a therapist who did the best she could, but my voice just was not coming back. In a very short time, I was unable to speak beyond a whisper. One day I thought, "Okay, my career is over."

Imagine the shock to a former BBC radio host and announcer, no less, someone who had used his voice to make a living. Without my voice, I would have been unable to speak in Disney's *101 Dalmatians* or to dub on *Ben-Hur*, not to mention appearing on camera. I gradually accepted the diagnosis and for the next several years, I sat by the pool, reading book after book, waiting for the disease to progress. Usually I communicated with friends by writing on note pads because the voice had almost completely disappeared.

My agent was ever faithful as a friend. We saw each other every Sunday. "It's all right, dear," Maurine would say. "I'll do all the talking." She was a bubbly Irish lady who did most of the talking during those years.

For an old film buff, I couldn't have lost my voice at a better time. Home video was making great strides as studios released tons of classic films, many of them unseen since their initial release. I was always interested in the newest entertainment equipment, especially the cutting-edge pieces from Japan.

I soon discovered laserdiscs and threw myself into collecting them. There was a wonderful store in the San Fernando Valley called Dave's Laser. The moment a new release came out, I rented it there, and I soon learned that Roddy McDowall was hooked on them, too. We ran into each other, with Roddy carrying out stacks that he had bought or rented.

He could well afford them, because I don't think he ever had a slow time as an actor!

A nice guy named Bill worked as a clerk at Dave's Lasers. He had previously worked at Tower Records, another one of my haunts. We talked about music as I shopped. He always looked kind of sad to me, so I asked him one day if he was in show business, because a lot of actors between jobs worked in retail. No, he told me — he was writing music and working there to help pay the bills.

One particular day, Ted Donaldson from *A Tree Grows in Brooklyn* walked into Dave's Lasers, all grown up. Bill said, "David's an actor, and I thought you two would like to meet." I didn't recognize Ted, but when he shared that he had been in *A Tree Grows in Brooklyn*, I told him that the film was one of my favorites and that I watched it all the time, thanks to Dave's Lasers. That was nice of Bill to introduce to me to an actor from one of my favorite films.

Trying to be encouraging, I asked Bill one time if he had composed any music that I could hear. "No," he told me. "I'm getting into conducting."

I knew that could be difficult work, so I thought it might be the end of the story. Bill, however, turned out to be William Stromberg, who now has dozens of soundtrack or recreation scores to his credit. He's extremely successful on the Marco Polo Classic Film Label series and even started his own label of tribute classic soundtracks. Even in the 1980s, those Hollywood success stories could still happen!

In 1985, I tuned in to see my old friend Rock Hudson on television. He had gone up to Carmel to appear on Doris Day's new TV series about animals. In a clever publicity move to boost interest in the new show, her first guest was to be her old friend and co-star, Rock Hudson, from *Pillow Talk*, *Lover Come Back*, and *Send Me No Flowers*.

Even Doris seemed shocked by how gaunt and awful Rock looked. The media started asking what was wrong with Rock Hudson. Could he have AIDS? The disease had rapidly emerged into the public consciousness, so the big word was that Rock might have the disease.

Everyone in Hollywood followed what happened next with great interest, and given my friendship with him back in the 1960s, I, too, was concerned about him. With only himself and some medics on board, he chartered a big plane to fly to the American Hospital in Paris, where it was confirmed that he had AIDS. Rock was in denial about the whole thing, thinking that he had contracted a tropical disease. He flew back and took a helicopter from LAX to the hospital at UCLA, where the doctors sent him home to die.

I was then living in a nice little house in the San Fernando Valley. The property had trees, was peaceful and secluded, and I had a small swimming pool. For old times' sake, I remembered how Rock had been so kind to me. I wrote and told him that I was living in a very peaceful place away from the media glare and spotlight. I remembered the word he had used twenty years earlier — "runcible," meaning pleasant, in his mind — so I wrote, "You could just sit here and have a very runcible afternoon." I thought mentioning his old favorite word might cue him in and jog his memory, but I never heard back from him. I suppose he was just too ill or the letter never reached him. Not too long afterward, he died. He was a good guy, and I'll never forget him.

After a few years of mutely watching movies or reading books around my pool, in desperation, friends insisted that I seek a second opinion at UCLA about my vocal condition. I'm eternally grateful that I did as they suggested. It turned out that I didn't have myasthenia gravis at all, and in fact, I had been wrongly diagnosed by a Beverly Hills specialist who should have known better.

The second doctor said I had a much less serious hiatal hernia; in fact, millions of people have it. Caused by acid reflux, it affects the voice and can be controlled through diet and medication. Foolishly, I spent nearly four years with a wrong diagnosis, no doubt a part of my British upbringing that conditioned me to just settle for whatever comes along in life.

Once I started a regimen of antacids, my voice came back very quickly. Imagine that — had I simply taken Maalox, my voice would have returned four years sooner, and I could have gone right on working. Four years of poolside reading, watching movies, and listening to records meant that I was more than ready to pick up my acting career.

Soon after my sentence of silence was lifted, Maurine urged me to get over to CBS for a new daytime soap opera called *The Bold and the Beautiful*. The casting director had been one of the good guys from my earlier years. When he saw me, he said, "David, the part's yours!"

Truthfully, I took the job just to prove to myself that I could still do it. At age sixty-two, I was far and away the oldest member of the cast; I think the median age was twenty-five! All the actors were very pleasant, good-looking young people, but I couldn't help feeling a little like a dinosaur. They were very nice kids, but I was just an old guy to them.

Other than working on the radio soap opera *One Man's Family* thirty years earlier, I knew nothing about soap operas, or at least how sexually oriented television soap operas had become by the 1980s. My part was so dull and boring as a kindly old minister. I somehow had thought that my character would have more to do. I had waited four years to work, and there I was, playing a mundane, dreary man of the cloth.

All of the good-looking young people on the show played bed-hoppers, while my character would say, "There, there, my child — mend your ways and cease from sin." My role didn't even require me to run amok or go crazy, that patented brand of acting that I had become known for in the 1960s and 1970s.

I had seen 1982's *Tootsie* with its plot about soap opera actors. Dustin Hoffman's character had a teleprompter, or an "idiot's sheet," as actors sometime called them. I had always learned my lines before I went on the job, but because of *Tootsie*, I just assumed we would be using teleprompters on *The Bold and the Beautiful*. Before I reported to work the first time, I just quickly scanned my script.

We rehearsed from ten until noon before going upstairs to tape. It didn't occur to me that I was the only person reading my script during rehearsal! Nobody seemed to be bothered by that. The younger actors probably thought, "The old guy needs the security of a script during rehearsal."

During the lunch break, I looked around the set, the first time I had set foot on one in four years. I didn't see a teleprompter anywhere! I thought, "Oh my God — there isn't one!" Thank goodness I was a quick study. I managed to pack all the lines into my head over lunch. I actually had a lot of lines for a wedding ceremony involving two of the main characters, Ridge Forrester and Caroline Spencer, played by Ronn Moss and Joanna Johnson.

As it turned out, my near disaster at not memorizing the script was just about the most exciting time I spent on the show. I was soon very bored, stuck reading books between set-ups and waiting for my scenes. Soap opera work can be very long and tedious. One day the director came up to me. "I like what you're doing with the part," she said. What I was doing was trying to memorize the lines each day! That was my entire motivation. I had no sense of characterization or anything else, so I felt, very defensively, that there was little I could do with it. At least she seemed to like my work.

I must confess that I didn't enjoy my return to acting very much. For thirteen weeks, I was stuck playing a minister and not having a good time. In fact, I hated it. It was the most boring role I had ever played. The money was good, though. Soap opera characters are typically running parts, meaning a character can disappear but then pop back into the plot a few months later. At the end of my thirteen-week stint, the producer told me that the show wanted me to return in the following fall.

CBS has a long hallway out to the stage door at Television City. I remember walking down the hall thinking, "I don't want to do this anymore. I don't want to come back." It was a relief to think that I didn't have to return in the fall.

I was sixty-two and had spent more than thirty years — minus those four lost voiceless years — working as an actor. I had accomplished what I set out to do. I had become a working actor, made a decent living, and there was no need to go on in a profession that was changing too much for my taste.

I worried about how I would break the news of my retirement to my long-time agent. Maurine had been so happy that I had returned to acting. Nervously I took her to lunch and asked would she mind if I retired. We had been together for most of those thirty-plus years, so I was quite anxious about her reaction to my decision.

I began by telling her that the soap opera work had proven too mundane.

"I know what you mean, dear," Maurine said. "The magic's gone out of it. I feel the same way. It's just not the same way of doing business anymore."

"So you wouldn't mind if I retired?" I asked.

"Mind?" she said. "I'm going to retire next year myself!" So, that settled it. I was through with acting. After four years of silence, I had proven that I still had what it took to get back into acting. I had nothing else to prove to anyone, so I could go out forever on my own terms. I declined to return to *The Bold and the Beautiful*. (Ironically, by the 1990s, the show became such a hit that many notable actors, including Charlton Heston, often paid guest star visits to be on the program!)

As we talked about my decision to retire permanently, Maurine told me how the business was changing for her as an agent. When she had started in the 1940s, she met all of her clients individually and helped decide if they were right for her to represent. "Now we just videotape and watch them," she said. "They have to come in with another actor and play a scene for us to decide if we want to sign them on with the agency. There's no excitement in the business anymore."

Show business is a young people's business, and I was lucky to be a young person in it as long as I was. As actors go along in years, the parts are fewer and far between. If you look at most shows now, you won't see that many senior citizens. As funny as it seems, especially considering how hard I had worked to get to Hollywood and establish myself as an actor, I had no regrets about leaving for good. I was relieved that my time had come to an end. It was also more satisfying to say, "Well, I'll stop while I'm ahead," than to be sitting and thinking, "Why doesn't the phone ring?" or "I hate this part I'm doing this week because there's really nothing interesting in it."

I retired with no regrets, just a lot of wonderful memories of my years in Hollywood. Acting was what I had wanted to do since I sat in the dark watching Laird Cregar back in 1944. I don't like the word "luck," but if "luck" has a definition, it is being in the right place at the right time as well as being suitably prepared for when opportunity knocks. I have to give heartfelt thanks that I was indeed in the right place for thirty years of the right time.

Following my retirement, I lived several years in the 1990s in Santa Barbara, about ninety miles north of Los Angeles. It's right on the ocean, which I still miss now in my current living in the high desert of the southwest. A really beautiful coastal city in the traditional Spanish style, Santa Barbara offered a superb climate. I was only two hours of driving from Los Angeles if I wanted to visit the big city, usually to see friends or buy CDs at Tower Records.

Even in Santa Barbara, I still encountered other actors; in fact, I frequently lunched at a deli and often sat two tables away from one of my favorite actors, Richard Widmark. I grew not to miss Hollywood, because the traffic defied description with gridlock at almost every big intersection. I was lucky to have had so many wonderful years living there when Beverly Hills was like a lovely old Spanish-style village and not the glitzy place it is today.

In retirement I had more time to devote to living life and cherishing good times with friends. I traveled back to Santa Fe to visit several times, where I enjoyed my ongoing friendship with Greer Garson. In her later years, she lived near Santa Fe on her Forked Lightning Ranch. I was very impressed with how she seemed to keep the ravages of time at bay. She always gave me a hug whenever we parted, and that was a real close-up; she remained so beautiful into her golden years, both inside and out.

Greer wasn't that interested in her distinguished career any more. She told me during a conversation that she thought her films were too slow by contemporary standards. She had grown more interested in building a theatre in Dallas and a $3 million grant she gave the College of Santa Fe, which already had a Greer Garson Theatre, for a Communications

Center. She became very much alive when we talked about those projects. The newly retired President and Mrs. Reagan attended the inauguration of the Communication Center's grand opening, though Greer was too ill to attend the dedication herself.

After I saw *Reversal of Fortune* with Glenn Close in 1990, I wrote Greer to say that it looked as though a trend was emerging for better roles for women. She had just lost her Oscar statuette for *Mrs. Miniver* when her Los Angeles apartment was destroyed by fire and was very proud to receive a replacement Oscar from Karl Malden.

Once I told her that Ted Turner was showing at least a couple of her films each month on TCM, and she just smiled and said, "Well, that's very nice of him, isn't it?" For her birthday one September, I gave her a book about Madame Curie, whom she had played in 1943, and she was genuinely pleased and interested. But for her, the door to the past was firmly closed. She could have written a fascinating book about her fifteen years at MGM if she had been so inclined, but she wasn't.

In later years, friends from my acting and social circle began to slip away. In 1989, one of my dearest friends, actress Irene Tedrow, suffered a massive stroke. She was attending an AFTRA meeting and simply fell over while she spoke. Her son flew over from his job in Germany to play the cello to her, and her daughter read Walt Whitman to her. I sat with her and reminisced about some of the shows we did together many years ago. We hoped that the continuous flow of positive sounds made her content.

Irene worked in countless movies and TV shows, and was quite a name in radio in the 1930s and 1940s. She was the kind of all-around pro that I admired very deeply, apart from my affection for her as a human being. As late as age eighty-three, she was on so many committees and active in show business organizations and church events — what a shining example of somebody who refused to let the calendar slow her down, something I emulated as I grew older.

I went to see her every day. She had done *Driving Miss Daisy* to great success in a San Diego theatre. I asked her if she would like to watch a video of the movie with Jessica Tandy. She nodded, so we watched the movie several times. She couldn't speak, but she could still laugh silently.

I asked my pastor and spiritual advisor, Robert Bitzer, to come with us one day at lunch. After all, Irene had introduced me to him back in the 1950s, and his encouragement had meant so much to the both of us, spiritually, and career-wise. He came to visit and talk with her. She was at peace, so happy that he was there, and that the three of us were there together one last time before her passing.

Dirk Bogarde, too, began to communicate less after he suffered a mild stroke. After his second stroke, he said that he could not wait months for a doctor to see him through the National Health Service, so he had to pay a great deal of money, privately, to be constantly monitored.

In 1990, I was back in the spotlight when I was interviewed for a feature story in *Starlog* magazine. The writer, Jim Hollifield, had written me a few years earlier about my Disney work, and we had struck up a pen pal writing friendship. I had great fun sending copies to friends. My science fiction and fantasy film and TV work was naturally spotlighted, so I shared the article with Ralph Senensky and others.

In 1990, I was invited to the Los Angeles Hilton for a salute to Vincent Price on his seventy-ninth birthday organized by the Starlog Magazine Group. Roger Corman was there, so we all enjoyed a fine reunion reminiscing about *Tales of Terror*. We hadn't seen each other for almost thirty years, so it was quite an emotional get-together.

Vincent was frail and walked with the help of a cane by then. Backstage before an evening of film clips and discussion, I was initially shocked that he was so feeble. He had a great deal of trouble with his feet and had taken to wearing slippers all the time. He tripped a little before we started and I almost stuck out my hand but stopped, realizing that Vincent would hate the appearance of having to be helped. He apologized for stumbling and explained that he had recently tripped over an object d'art at his home, but I suspected that he was just being gallant, not admitting to physical limitations as a disciplined man.

Vincent's mind, however, was razor sharp as always, and he had the audience laughing from start to finish, two hours later. Tim Burton moderated the panel; he had just directed Vincent in *Edward Scissorhands*, Vincent's last movie. Vincent's wit was sharp and savage. I couldn't help but be reminded how I owed him so much, as he was always so encouraging and generous. He autographed one of his books to me: "Master of the World — and don't you forget it!"

I remember asking Vincent where his wife was, and he said she had been feeling poorly, but I had no idea that she was dying from cancer. They were inseparable. Coral Browne died about a year later. I ran into her in a pharmacy in Beverly Hills around 1985 and went up to her to tell her how much I admired her work and said she should be working all the time. She was never one to overlook an opportunity to speak like a truck driver when the occasion allowed. Without batting an eye, right there in a crowded pharmacy, she said, "Too f@%*ing old, my darling." I almost dropped dead. That was Coral Browne, one of a kind.

At one point during Vincent's tribute evening, the audience saw clips from *Tales of Terror*, including a scene where I had to lift Debra Paget off the ground. Vincent got a big laugh when he turned to me and said, "I'll bet you couldn't do that now!" In turn, I think I embarrassed him a little by telling him publicly just how much it meant to me to have made three films with him: *Return of the Fly, Master of the World,* and *Tales of Terror.*

Enjoying my retirement in the 1990s.

At the end of the evening commemorating Vincent's birthday and marvelous career, two people assisted Vincent off the stage. He spoke the last words I ever heard him say to me. "Old age stinks!" he said as he left the hotel that night. I still get emotional thinking about our farewell that evening.

Following my 1990 visit to Vincent's birthday party and after tiring of driving back and forth between Santa Barbara and the Los Angeles area, I settled only a mile or so from a home where I had previously lived in Sherman Oaks. The property had a huge peach tree and tangerines and figs, as well as a big old elm that sheltered the back garden from the midday sun.

Being back in Los Angeles, there was always something to do. The County Museum started a retrospective of Vincente Minnelli's films with a reception and outdoor dinner, followed by a newly restored *Meet Me in St. Louis.* Liza Minnelli and Michael Feinstein performed a live concert that ended at two a.m. It was great to start the next stage in my life with such a wonderful social event.

My business partner, Don Garnier, and I worked on renovating and expanding a house as a full-time job. It seemed that I always had electricians crawling around, putting up ceiling fans, changing light switches or re-wiring a room.

In the summer of 1990, I was planning to make a big trip back to Britain to visit my old DDC colleagues and a few remaining relatives, but while I was having an annual physical, a couple of tumors were discovered.

The doctors advised me to postpone the trip while they checked out the biopsies. Happily, the tumors were benign, and the doctors decided to leave them where they were and monitor me every six months to be on the safe side. I was very relieved that there was nothing life-threatening involved.

After several years in Los Angeles, the Rodney King riots and a sour economy led me to sell the property in Studio City and move ninety miles north to Montecito, California in the summer of 1993. The new house was beautiful, on 1.75 acres, surrounded by its own running stream and sycamores. It was very private and a welcome change from the urban violence; a singer who lived across the street from me in Studio City was beaten up and had her car stolen. I had been fortunate that I had enjoyed so many good and happy years there, but it was time for a change in scenery.

That fall, Vincent Price died. Roddy McDowall had toured with Vincent in some plays in the 1980s and maintained a close friendship with him. Roddy visited and stayed with him frequently. He really cared about people at the end of their lives. He and Elizabeth Taylor had done that for Donald Crisp, too. Roddy was always concerned that someone he cared about and respected was not in the best of health. He spent time with people he admired when they had tough times.

After a few years, the home in Montecito turned out to be a damp one; on two occasions, I had to replace the private road after being washed out by spring rains. It was back to Santa Fe, where I purchased land above the city, looking over two mountain ranges with a ski area above the property. The lot was covered with pine trees, and yet the city was only ten minutes down the hill. By then, Santa Fe had become a very hip city with Hollywood people living there, including Shirley MacLaine, Carol Burnett, Val Kilmer, Brian Dennehy, and many others. Many actors go to New Mexico on a picture and fall in love with the scenery, and even if they don't stay more than a few years — it can move a little more slowly than Hollywood — they more than get their investment back because land is at a premium.

By the time I was seventy, my BBC colleagues back in England had retired and didn't get around much, apart from the obligatory two weeks in Venice or Switzerland. Many of them thought I was mad to be moving and building as much as I did for a long period of time.

Up on the construction site and supervising the work, I moved around the property and climbed over foundations; mostly I consulted with the contractor. Don was the real brainchild of all the construction projects. As architect, he monitored on-site construction to make sure that the work was how he had envisioned it according to the blueprints.

In 1996, more than forty years after I first met and interviewed Greer Garson on the BBC, never knowing that I would someday be fortunate enough to call her a friend, she died after a period of declining health. The last couple of years were very trying for her; she couldn't write or phone friends any longer after a series of strokes, although she was awake and aware. She was an extraordinarily vital woman, and I do feel privileged to have crossed paths with her in Britain and America.

Visiting the Greer Garson Theatre Center in 1996.

The local college in Santa Fe did her proud with a Sunday morning of celebration. The place was packed, and the general atmosphere was very upbeat, which is how she no doubt would have wanted it. The students at the college were her "children" and several of them spoke warmly of her inspiration, even though none had ever met her. Several well-chosen clips from her movies were shown. They ended with the final scene from *Madame Curie*, with an "aged" Curie's last speech to great applause. Most appropriate. In a way, I felt as though Greer was still there. My real estate broker and her husband bought half of Greer's ranch a year before her passing, and I was frequently out there, thirty miles from Santa Fe, to visit on weekends and enjoy Greer's river and cottonwood trees.

When I wasn't building, selling, and moving to start the process all over again, I relished spending so many hours enjoying videos and movies from films from the 1930s and 1940s unseen since childhood. At one point when I moved in 1997, I discovered twenty-seven boxes of videos and then vowed to stop taping every movie I saw on cable. Having watched movies since the 1930s, I was fascinated to bear witness to changing film trends and styles through the decades. By the 1990s, movies such as *Fargo* and *L.A. Confidential* were so inventively clever that I couldn't help but stay current with the latest Hollywood productions.

In 1997, my friend Jim Hollifield mailed me *Variety's* obituary announcing the death of my longtime agent, Maurine Oliver. She and I had lost touch over the few previous years with my moves from Los Angeles to Santa Barbara and then to New Mexico. When I was back in Los Angeles in 1990, I had driven over to see Maurine, but her house was being completely renovated with just a shell remaining. The contractor had no idea where she was, or who she was, for that matter, since he was working for new out-of-town owners. Since I rarely socialized with other actors on her books, I had nobody to call for information and lost touch with her.

She was such a vital part of my life from 1956 to 1988. In later years, she got a little flustered and disorganized, and sometimes I found myself sitting for an hour or two at MGM when I should have been at Warners, but it was impossible to get mad at Maurine. "Oh, well darlin'," she would say, "at least you got to where you were supposed to be eventually, so it worked out nicely!" Then I laughed and hugged her.

In front of an entire crew of sixty-five people, Vincent Price used to kid me about Maurine and joke that she and I were more than friends. "No wonder the kid's doing okay — he's sleeping with his agent!" Picture me mortified; I turned crimson from head to toe, but Maurine loved it.

By the late 1990s, many of my long-time Hollywood friends had retired or passed away. I still maintained contact with Dick and Bobbie Bull. Dick had two series, *Voyage to the Bottom of the Sea* and *Little House on the Prairie*. Bobbie, too, was truly an excellent actress.

Roddy McDowall died in the fall of 1998. Angela Lansbury wrote and said that when he learned he was dying, Roddy sent out invitations to his close circle of friends. She and her husband, Peter Shaw, attended. He was chatty and charming as always and concerned that his guests were having the best time. He had said, "No mourning, let's have a nice dinner." Not a word was said about his illness, nor did he wish anybody goodbye or dwell on the fact that he would not see them again. He died a few days later. Although I didn't know him well, I owed him quite a bit; I had made my television debut after he gave up a role to go to Broadway.

On July 2, 1998, I finally got my U.S. citizenship in Albuquerque. It had taken so long, from being on a waiting list, to memorizing the Constitution, but it was very exciting. At the ceremony, there was pomp and circumstance, and there were flags and speeches by U.S. Senator Pete Domenici and Congresswoman Heather Wilson. Flowers lined the stage as family members hugged all of us new citizens. I was quite moved by it all.

In May of 1999, my friend Dirk Bogarde died. We had corresponded for decades and kept our friendship going through the mail. Dirk was a famous letter writer, and I must say that I always enjoyed writing letters as well. In later years, sad things happened to Dirk. Earlier in his career, he had walked away from the Rank Organisation and moved to France. He began freelancing in films, and with his name, there were plenty of jobs going around. In the 1960s, he had found a wonderful old house above Cannes shown to him by Simone Signoret. He loved this old farm house and got down and scrubbed off the dirt from the tiles and worked very hard on improving it. He lived there a very long time, surrounded by some olive trees that gave him great pride.

In later years, his manager and companion, Tony Forwood, began to be unwell. Tony went over to London for an MRI and discovered that he had a brain tumor. Tony had first spotted Dirk in Repertory Theatre and represented him; that's how their lives began together. In the late 1980s, Dirk had written a letter to me, telling me how they had to stay in a hotel in Paris before they could find a flat in London. Dirk said he was writing on an upturned suitcase to tell me that they were on route for Tony's care. He signed the letter, "As ever, Dirk."

When they got back to England, things did not go well. Dirk wrote a sad letter that said, "Tony died last night with just the nurse and me by his bedside. It's been a good long run, so life goes on. As ever, Dirk." I'm sure I'm not the only person he wrote to that day, but it was touching that he was reaching out to friends to share his sense of loss.

By the 1990s, things had started to go wrong for Dirk. He smoked incessantly and could not stop. "I'm not going to fight it," he would write. He had a stroke and only knew it when he lost control of his bodily functions. His letter describing it later was just like him, no drama or concern that his life could have ended.

Dirk semi-recovered and hired a minder, or a personal assistant, who was always with him. He wrote to effect, "For some reason, I have this enormous affection from the British public, so when I finish a book, they have me appear at various events." A prolific writer, he would walk onstage to a lectern, open his book and start reading, and everyone would cheer and shout for him. He couldn't understand the fuss.

His minder got him in his limo to take him around England for book tours. In his last years, he really enjoyed that attention, and the loyalty of the British public touched him deeply, because he always mentioned that in his letters. He was astonished that he got standing ovations before even getting to the "bloody lectern," as he put it.

Then he had a more serious stroke. I heard from him through a few letters after that, telling me, "What a bloody nuisance this stroke is." He had to be taken around everywhere, but he was still defiant. Lauren Bacall went to see him, sitting quietly and leaving, and as she left, he died. Given this enormous devotion that the British public held for him, his last recorded comment sadly was, "I want to be forgotten." He had suffered a serious stroke, so maybe that explains his bitter, cynical comment.

I was so pleased to be on the receiving end of decades' worth of letters, a number of which were later published in a well-received book, *Ever, Dirk: The Bogarde Letters*, edited by John Coldstream, who also authored Dirk's biography. I wasn't sure at first that I wanted to share our personal letters in the book, but I couldn't help but think about Dirk's dying comment that he wanted to be forgotten. He was such a gifted actor and a marvelous friend, that if he ever had one ungranted wish, I wanted to see that memories of him continued. He was one of the greatest film actors ever. I miss those letters. He will never be forgotten.

As the 1990s came to an end, I began to notice a disturbing change in my vision. During the winter of 1999, I went to see Matt Damon in *The Talented Mr. Ripley*. When the lights went down, I couldn't see the film very well and just thought that the light bulbs in the projector needed changing. That was my first clue about macular degeneration, a vision-robbing condition in which blood vessels leak into the back of the eye.

My sight in my right eye began to deteriorate at an alarming rate, followed by a seemingly never-ending series of surgeries to stem the damage. By 2001, I began to experience difficulty with my other eye. New injection treatments seemed to arrest the condition's development. Macular degeneration spares peripheral vision, so with the aid of a big screen TV, I could sit close and still enjoy my favorite movies without cell phones or chewing gum on the theatre floor.

One of my hobbies has been listening to music, so my vision hasn't really affected this pastime. I still love classical music, big band and jazz from the 1940s and 1950s. So much of my generation's music was reissued that I have always enjoyed completing my collection, an almost daily hobby. On a number of occasions, I've enjoyed the opera in Santa Fe, and even attended the grand opening of the city's new opera house a few years ago. The sides of the opera house are open, so when the sun goes down at nine, the opera starts, staged by these brilliant sunsets.

In 2002, Rosemary Clooney died. When *White Christmas* aired that Christmas, I thought of her, the first holiday in many years without a

Clooney Christmas Card to look forward to seeing in the mail. What a dear friend she was to get me started in radio. She was literally the only soul I knew in Hollywood when I arrived in 1955.

The following year, that last house in a long series of construction projects sold, and I began to downsize a little by leasing and letting some other owner worry about the upkeep and responsibility of home ownership. I didn't downsize my DVD collection, however, as I added favorites from the golden age of Hollywood. The Criterion Collection has long been managed so well, and who could have ever dreamed of owning DVD releases containing multiple hours of bonus features, including original theatrical trailers and behind-the-scenes documentaries. DVDs have brought me a long way since the days of renting classic 16mm films to watch projected on a makeshift bed sheet screen!

By the dawn of the new millennium, I was renting or buying DVDs every Tuesday when the new releases hit the shelves. From the newer generation, Tobey McGuire became one of my favorite actors; I particularly enjoyed seeing him make a big splash in *Cider House Rules* and *Wonder Boys*. As a member of the Screen Actors Guild, I looked forward each winter to receiving screener copies for consideration when submitting votes for the Screen Actors Guild Awards. I welcomed residual checks to fund my hobby of buying CDs and DVDs. For work done after 1960, actors still get residual checks, although they shrink with repeated screenings and releases. I can't help but chuckle when I get one for a few dollars or just a few pennies are left after taxes!

As some of my friends have reminded me, it's important for older people to remain in touch with contemporary culture and not dismiss everything just because it's new. I discovered Jamie Foxx in *Collateral* and rooted for him at the Oscars and was pleased when he won for *Ray*. I think he has potential to be the equal of the formidable Morgan Freeman, another of my favorite actors. I also admire the work of Guy Pearce, an Australian actor. I've followed his career with great interest since *L.A. Confidential*. He and Cate Blanchett are my favorite performers from today's younger generation. They're both chameleons, capable of changing into remarkably convincing characters.

Yet I still enjoy vintage films and love watching movies fondly remembered from my youth. I've developed a number of traditions. Each Christmas season, I enjoy a number of traditional pre-Christmas videos, including Loretta Young and Celeste Holm in *Come to the Stable* and *The Bishop's Wife*, Albert Finney in *Scrooge*, with its fine score by Leslie Bricusse; the *Nutcracker*, performed by the New York City Ballet, Judy

Garland's famous 1963 Christmas show, Garland again in *Meet Me in St. Louis*, and then the Crosby-Clooney *White Christmas*. Such happy memories!

On Valentine's Day 2006, two days before my eightieth birthday, I had some rather serious blood vessel leakage behind the macula in one eye. I rushed to get that stabilized the next day with laser treatment in Albuquerque. It was a chore getting to and from Albuquerque for eye surgery when I couldn't see to drive. I caught a cab from my house to a shuttle bus that then drove sixty-seven miles south, only to take another cab from the shuttle into the clinic where I had my procedure.

People are kind; a young lady led me by the hand to a bench where I could sit comfortably until the shuttle back to Santa Fe was due. I decided to use the restroom and wandered into the ladies' room by accident! I couldn't see well from my procedure, so as I headed to what I thought was a stall, a lady shouted, "HEY! This is for ladies! Didn't you see the sign?!?" I replied that I had poor vision. "Oh, SURE!" she said. I was certain that I would be leaving the premises in handcuffs. Well, it does me good to have a fling occasionally, and keeping a sense of humor intact helps through such ordeals.

Needless to say, my eightieth birthday was not fun; I slept with shades drawn until late afternoon. The mailman awakened me with a birthday package that contained a DVD of one of my TV appearances found on eBay by some friends who brightened my spirits considerably.

Later that spring, my eyesight continued to fail in my right eye to the point that it was beyond help. My doctors worked hard to stabilize the vision in my left eye. In May that year, I had a direct injection with additional follow-up treatments throughout the summer. My central vision faded to the point that I began to have difficulty writing or reading script without the aid of a primer, a monitor hooked up to a TV screen for reading. I could still read books and magazines, but news print became too difficult to read without the help of a magnifier that I plugged into a television screen. The text is enlarged in giant print. It makes for slow reading, but it does give me the ability to enjoy reading. In the summer of 2010, I was introduced to several pairs of special glasses and lenses that enabled me to see a little better for reading. We live on hopes, I like to say.

I miss being able to drive from time to time, but I never feel bored. There's always so much to do that's interesting. Through the years, I've kept in contact with many of the people from my life. For example, before my military service in World War II, I met my friend Jimmy in architecture school. We hit it off when we both learned that we both were born at the same hour and minute, on the same day, February 16, 1926! Although we have not seen each other in person since the 1950s, we've stayed in touch by writing letters, telephone calls and recording audio cassette tapes for each other. Jimmy met and married a wonderful lady, Mary, and just through telling our stories in tapes or letters, I feel as though I know their children and extended family.

After I turned eighty, I made a New Year's resolution to rejoin the human race and not just fade into the background. I never think about being my age. One time my friend, the director Ralph Senensky, and I were riding together in a car and he asked me, "David, how old do you feel?" I said, "About thirty-five." He agreed that he felt — inside — about the same age. Perhaps that's the age any of us feels when we age. It's a good age; you're at your peak, still physically and mentally fit. The thirty-five-year-old inside me gets up in the morning and says, "Well, what are we going to do today?" and then I try to do too much, like shoveling snow and burning the broccoli.

Several years ago, I met a spirited Irishwoman at one of my favorite restaurants in Santa Fe. Marcy became such a good friend and confidant, helping with chores by taking me to the market or post office. Marcy has a great saying that I've picked up and like to repeat: "In life, nothing is ever wasted. Everything will be helpful." That's true of great friends, particularly!

Other good friends of later years in New Mexico have included Patrick and Erica Mehaffy, very talented filmmakers. They're such creative, talented people. Patrick had been a carpenter years ago on the first house in Santa Fe. Patrick showed great imagination on the moldings. He became a very successful sculptor. He had always been a writer just for his own entertainment and gradually began to turn them into screenplays.

He did a short film a few years ago and then another that won a Best Short Subject award at a film festival in Oregon. Erica produces their films. They were invited to take part in the Santa Fe film festival. Their thirty-four-minute film was submitted to thirty-nine festivals before being accepted in California. I admired their perseverance!

Early in 2008, Erica told me about a production of the acclaimed play *Doubt* in Santa Fe. There was a young actor in the cast who was nervous about opening his first scene in a monologue. I told Erica to tell him about the time I had to do the same thing in front of twenty-five million people during my live television debut on NBC's *Matinee Theater*. She passed on my story, and then when this terrific actor, Jonathan Dixon, opened to sensational reviews, I wanted to see the show, even though I had stopped attending shows because of my vision. That night friends led me on stage early to see how the stage was set up to help me picture it later when I couldn't see as much with the lights down.

I was greatly impressed by Jonathan's acting. He is a real pro on stage, and as it turned out, he is a big Disney fan, so much so that he knew Sgt. Tibs the cat, the character I had voiced for *101 Dalmatians*. We enjoyed dinner, talking about movies and acting. I was fascinated to learn more about stage acting, because it had been years since I had done two plays in the late 1950s, and I never really considered myself a stage actor at all.

Jonathan and I became good friends. When my vision became less sharp, he became my eyes. In fact, with his help, I decided to start traveling again for the first time in years. That July, we flew to Memphis to visit my friends, Jim

With my friend Jonathan Dixon at Disneyland Paris. (JONATHAN DIXON)

Hollifield and Todd Sawvelle. Jim was the writer who had profiled me for *Starlog* back in 1990, and we had enjoyed a Dirk Bogarde-style pen pal friendship since 1988!

We visited in July, with humid, muggy temperatures near one hundred degrees, yet we had a lot of fun staying at the city's historic Peabody Hotel and seeing the Mississippi River. I even enjoyed a trip to Graceland, where I marveled at just how many costumes and scripts Elvis had kept from his film career.

Jonathan and I next traveled to Disneyland in Anaheim, where I was treated like Disney royalty with a trip on the Lilly Belle train car around the park. Being the voice of a Disney cartoon character has its perks! I also enjoyed seeing Hollywood again after being away nearly a decade.

With a newfound interest for getting out and about, I took inspiration from my friend Angela Lansbury, who returned to Broadway with great triumph in her eighties. When her husband, Peter Shaw, died a few years earlier, I wrote Angela to tell her just how kind he had been to get me an agent when I started as an actor. I also told her how much I admired her gumption as well as her talent. What an extraordinary woman she is.

With my friend Jim Hollifield. (TODD SAWVELLE)

With Jonathan's help, I traveled to New York City for the first time since I arrived in America back in the fall of 1955. We enjoyed seeing a number of sights, but the highlight was getting tickets to see Angela in a revival of *Blithe Spirit.* Before we left, I contacted Angela to let her know that we were coming, and she graciously sent word that she wanted us to meet her backstage. After the show, we enjoyed our visit with her. Her stamina and talent had earned her a standing ovation, and in short time, she received a Tony Award for her performance.

Inspired by Angela, I agreed to appear in a short film made in May 2009 by my friends, Patrick and Erica Mehaffey. A *film noir* tribute, *Heat Lightning* is a fifteen-minute short set in New Mexico. I enjoyed my first film work in more than twenty years as a mysterious doctor who orders a mafia-style hit. Working on the film lasted from dawn to dusk, but I was proud to keep pace with the cast and crew.

David Olson, a fine stage director, suggested that Jonathan and I could play a father and a son in Moliere's play, *The Imaginary Invalid*. I thought it would be wonderful to play an old codger. We had a big laugh about that, so we set out to do the show with rehearsals starting in May 2009.

Jonathan and I read our parts across the dining room table and that seemed to go well. On a Monday, I started learning my lines, but I found that I couldn't memorize my part. Panicked, I thought I would try again the next day. On Tuesday, I looked at a page, closed the script, and not one word stayed in my head. The thought occurred to me that I was eighty-three and maybe I couldn't retain a script as I had twenty years earlier.

I began to feel upset about it. I was so nervous by Thursday that I passed out. I began to worry that something was physically wrong with me, and then I fainted again. Dejected, I called our director to tell him that I wouldn't be much help at the reading because I was having trouble memorizing my lines.

Visiting Saarburg, Germany in 2009.
(JONATHAN DIXON)

David said, "Well, at least come to the reading, and we'll figure out something."

When Jonathan arrived to take me to the reading, he found me sweating and in bed. He said, "You are not going to the reading — you're going to the hospital!"

I spent a couple of days under observation in the hospital. After a series of tests, nothing came up definitively. I had fizzled out as a stage actor. I'm glad really, because I think I would be a liability to any theatrical company. Since then, I've tried looking at a magazine page just for fun, and I just can't memorize any more, even though memorization once came to me easily. Where the spirit is willing, the flesh is sometimes weak, I suppose.

In the fall of 2009, another great adventure awaited. Jonathan has friends who live in Germany. I grew up with my country being at war with

Hitler's army. A modern, changed Germany had always been on my list of places to visit, so it was off to Germany for several weeks of sightseeing.

We visited some of the great cities and enjoyed seeing architecture and the local culture. I must have caught a bug at some point on the plane, because I woke up violently ill one night. I was rushed to a German hospital, where I'm happy to report, I was treated with the utmost care and professionalism. After a day or so of recuperation, I was back on my feet for more sightseeing and smooth sailing after that. We even made it to France and toured Disneyland Paris!

The Internet has done much to keep interest alive in the careers of actors from the past. Friends have shown my credits to me on the Internet Movie Database site, *IMDb.com*, as it's more commonly known. Although fascinating, the site lists a few erroneous credits from someone with the same name who was working in the 1990s after I retired. It also leaves out a great deal of early programming, especially live broadcasts, because the documentation from that era is so spotty, but all in all, it's fun to scroll down and read a lifetime of work all contained on a single webpage.

Websites are the twenty-first century equivalent of the old fan magazines with articles and photos about actors, but unlike publications that were tossed out or used in the birdcage, the Internet stays there forever, waiting for someone to watch an old actor in a show and then go online to learn more about him or her. The whole thing amazes me.

In fact, through the Internet, I was able to reconnect with Ralph Senensky, one of my favorite directors. Ralph is a marvel. He's so tech savvy that he took up blogging. The Internet also reconnected me with my other favorite director, John Erman.

In the spring of 2010, it was back to New York City again to see Angela Lansbury, this time in the revival of Stephen Sondheim's *A Little Night Music*. Angela was paired with Oscar winner Catherine Zeta-Jones, and the show was another big hit. Afterwards, we visited with Angela, who invited us to visit her in California following her exit from the musical.

On our way back, we enjoyed a stopover in Chicago. I was reunited for the first time in many years with Richard Bull and his wife, Barbara Collentine. Our friendship began more than half a century ago as members of the same acting group. Richard became a member of the *Little House on the Prairie* cast, and now he and Barbara live in Illinois. Like me, they were a little older, but still full of life and appreciation for good friends and wonderful memories together.

In June of 2010, it was off for a road trip to California. Jonathan and I visited Disneyland again, proving you're never too old to be young at heart. While we were there, we attended a retrospective cast reunion for *My Three Sons*, the 1960s sitcom. When I saw Tina Cole, one of the show's cast members, I was reminded that we once worked together, but thanks to one of those "missing credits" on the Internet Movie Database, and one

of my "missing" memories, I still can't place which show or production we did, and I didn't want to risk embarrassing either of us by mentioning it to her!

From Anaheim, we drove up to Carmel at the invitation of Ralph Senensky. What a grand reunion Ralph and I enjoyed! I had last seen him in the late 1980s or early 1990s, once after running into each other at a mall, and then at a fabulous party at his house. I remembered that his walls were covered with movie posters, and I was delighted to see that his new house was similarly decorated with vintage posters from Hollywood's golden era.

Ralph treated us to clips from some of our work together, and we enjoyed trips through the pictur-

Visiting the Empire State Building.
(JONATHAN DIXON)

esque scenery along northern California's coast. He's just a few years away from ninety, yet he outpaced us every time we went anywhere, turning around to see how far I had fallen behind! He was a delight in every way, and I treasured the opportunity to revisit our work together from more than fifty years ago at the Pasadena Playhouse and then on television in the 1960s.

Next it was up to beautiful San Francisco, where Jonathan and I were joined by our friends Mike Vaughn, Jim Hollifield, and Todd Sawvelle. Together we visited the new Walt Disney Family Museum at the Presidio. This fantastic tribute to Walt Disney the man was lovingly put together by his family as a tribute to the personal genius and contributions of one of Hollywood's greatest visionaries.

As we looked at displays of his awards, photos from his early life and vintage video clips, I thought back at how proud I was to be cast as a voice in his *101 Dalmatians*. Even though Disney's live-action film, *Ten Who Dared*, isn't regarded as one of the studio's best films, that was the movie that allowed me to meet the man who had brought *Snow White* and *Fantasia* to life for me as an adolescent back in England. I sat and marveled at the museum's *Fantasia* display, with a giant TV screen big enough for me to see clips from this masterpiece.

Visiting the Walt Disney Family Museum. (TODD SAWVELLE)

At the end of our visit, I was introduced to the museum's director, Richard Benefield, and Don Hahn, the Disney artist and producer of *Beauty and the Beast* and *The Lion King*. He told me how much he enjoyed meeting someone who had worked with Walt and that *101 Dalmatians* was one of his favorite films. Our group so enjoyed the museum that we returned again the next day to tour its thoroughly comprehensive examination of Walt's life in its entirety. I cannot recommend it enough to fans of Walt and his work.

A few days later, Jonathan and I visited Pixar Animation Studios in Emeryville. It turns out that the new school animators are highly appreciative of traditional animation. After all, most of them grew up on Walt's hand-animated classics. As we toured the Pixar campus, we saw artists hunched over computers and working on the next big animated film. Gone were the days of the hand-sketched storyboards that Woolie Reitherman showed me at Disney in the early 1960s. The technology simply was amazing, and we enjoyed meeting a number of artists, including production designer Harley Jessup, who asked to be called from a meeting to meet me. He told me that *101 Dalmatians* had inspired much of his design work on the film, *Ratatouille*. The sight of computer animators whizzing about on scooters as a mode of transportation was especially delightful.

Meeting Oscar-winning songwriter Richard Sherman. (TODD SAWVELLE)

Our two-week trip to California concluded with a visit to Angela Lansbury's house. By the time we arrived, the San Francisco air had not gone well for me, so I was nearly voiceless when we visited Angela. She hurried about making tea and lemon for my throat! Nevertheless, we enjoyed reminiscing about her husband, Peter Shaw. I told her about meeting her producer on *Beauty and the Beast*, Don Hahn. The two of us each voiced Disney animated characters, so Angela and I are both Disney fans. In fact, she's a Disney legend!

More than that, Angela is a legend in the truest sense of the word. My mind went back to how I had seen her more than sixty-five years ago in *Gaslight*. Her contributions to film, theatre, and television history have endeared her to new generations of fans. She told us that Hollywood has really changed, so much so that it is now a town where the business side of show business gets emphasized more than artistry. Theatre still seems to bring appreciation for the craft more than the business side, and she had praise for Broadway and the theatre world from her recent successes there.

As we said our good-byes and headed back for our homes in New Mexico, I began to feel really rotten. By the time we returned home, I was feverish and coughing. It turned out that I had developed pneumonia, but a trip to the doctor soon had me on the road to recovery. I think the moral of the story is to not ride in an open air bus across the Golden Gate Bridge in San Francisco! Still, I enjoyed the adventures back in California.

Visiting the Grand Canyon.
(JONATHAN DIXON)

December 2010 brought a visit from director John Erman during the holidays. We reminisced about working together on *The Outer Limits* and some of our other projects together. I've always said that John and Ralph Senensky were my two favorite directors, so what a treat it was to visit with them both again in 2010.

In recent years, I also reconnected with old friends from my BBC past, including Gillian Renton and Rita Arnold Stimpson, the secretaries from my days in Birmingham. Ironically, Gillian ended up living in Hollywood and worked for a producer on the *Perry Mason* show before retiring back to Brighton, England. Rita also came to America and now lives in Maine. My Army friend, Graham Fairley, is active on the Internet and sends emails. A few years ago, I was feeling really "retired," but thanks to my friends, I'm enjoying a new lease on life by getting out and about on a regular basis and staying in touch with acquaintances from years past.

Epilogue

As July 2010 came to a close, I spent time finalizing the text you're reading in this book. One day I was working on the book, and the next day I was acting in a movie, simple as that, which just goes to show that once an actor, always an actor.

I had a call from my friend, Erica Mehaffey, about a movie being filmed in New Mexico tentatively called *Ink*. The film stars Wes Studi, who appeared in *Avatar* and *Dances with Wolves*, among others. The production needed to film a scene of a father and son walking down the road, and Erica had recommended me and Jonathan.

Filming was to start the next day, breaking my fifty-year-old record of being hired to appear in *Master of the World* on a Friday and then filming the following Monday. Jonathan and I were game to work, so the next day, we found ourselves on location along a dusty road in Santa Fe. In spite of temperatures in the nineties, we were fitted for our period piece costumes. We filmed a scene with a few lines as we walked down the country lane with two Great Danes. The dogs were a handful, but after several takes, we shot our scenes and filled out my paperwork for the Screen Actors Guild.

Somewhere, my late agent, Maurine Oliver, must be smiling. Fifty-five years after arriving in Hollywood, and nearly thirty years since my last feature, it was fun to rush into a production with just a moment's notice. Acting is rarely predictable, and that aspect of the craft has kept me interested in film and television work.

Thinking about my life as an actor, I enjoyed acting so much because it gave me the opportunity to be somebody besides myself. It might surprise you to learn that it's not uncommon for actors to deal with insecurities just like other people, but actors can lose themselves in characters and parts totally unlike themselves. I was never destined to be an astronaut, or a sailor, or worse, a criminal, but I had great fun pretending to be those characters in the movies or on television.

In England, I had never really felt secure, in spite of the fact that I had been taught how to write and produce radio programs and to interview people. If I may say so, I had a flair for radio work, but I had very little confidence in myself. I got no encouragement from my mother, who was a passive Scot. "Oh, it's his life," she would say. It was okay with her if I was a success or a failure.

My father, his inhibitions related to growing up when he did in England, thought of me as a sissy because I was no good at games. He once came to see me play a game of rugby. I was doing a wonderful pass with the ball, but I was playing against my own team. The word "macho" didn't exist then, but that finished me in my father's eyes. He dismissed me until he took great pride in my BBC accomplishments. That pride quickly evaporated, though, when I left the BBC for Hollywood. "You're giving up your pension — do you know what you're doing?" he asked. It was right back to Square One with my father, which reflected on my own lack of confidence. He was the authority in the house that I could turn to, and he had dismissed me as a sissy.

Later in Hollywood, my agent Maurine gave me professional confidence, but I still did not possess great confidence in myself. When I attended the Actor's Church in Hollywood, I found inspiration in the teaching of Ernest Holmes and counsel of Dr. Robert Bitzer. I saw him in his office twice a week for several years as he built up confidence in me. He taught me a number of phrases that I still use to this day. I suppose it's slightly religious, but I don't think of it as such; rather, these thoughts reflect a daily building up of my own confidence.

I believe there is a universal intelligence, the reason for everything. It's Spirit, not in the sense of an individual on a golden throne, but this universal Spirit is alive and within me. Cognizant of this fact, each morning I quietly sit in my room and say aloud to myself:

> *This universal intelligence is always guiding me. I recognize it and act on it. Perfect, right action is the result. It guides me from error. Perfect, right action is permanently established in every area of my life — spiritually, emotionally, physically, financially, and creatively. Perfect, right action has already taken over so that my ongoing good is always going on as long as I don't interrupt it.*

That positive thinking sustained my career as an actor and became my philosophy of life. If I had a problem, guidance came to me in some way or another. Sometimes there are days that this positive thinking doesn't work, but if it doesn't take effect, it's because I haven't held to this mindset or sustained it. If I'm off track, it's simply because I'm not maintaining the words I said aloud.

I think that whatever's done to me is done because of my thinking. If I don't heed these positive thoughts, I can feel unguarded, but those beliefs really represent the essence of *me*. They have seen me through good times and bad as an actor, and as a person. When an audition came up and I was waiting to hear if I got the role, I knew that perfect, right action was established for me with that part or its equivalent. There wasn't a loss if I

Visiting the grave of my hero Laird Cregar (TODD CAMWBLLE)

didn't get the role; that meant that the part simply wasn't right for me. I always felt that the right action would bring the next job to me. It always did. If I lost a part, another one inevitably came along a few days later.

To clarify, this belief system doesn't mean that we can control things to the extent of saying, "I've decided to win this role." But if you decide that you're up for the challenge in every way, then you've done your best, and right, perfect action will be the result in some way. If you believe there's some sort of universal intelligence that set forth a perfect order, it helps to believe that this perfect order would include the best possible outcome happening for you if you will allow it.

In many ways, I can look back at my life and see this philosophy tied into all sorts of unusual coincidences or interconnections that have run throughout my years. There has to be a reason why I'm here, being me and being what I was supposed to be. I wasn't supposed to be good at rugby, even though it disappointed my father. Being able to express yourself fully applies to everybody. I felt that as a broadcaster. The very first day I sat behind a microphone in a radio station, I almost said aloud to myself, "I'm home. I feel comfortable. I don't have to play rugby or care what my father thinks about me. I have a flair for this and I like doing this."

I did okay at the BBC, and it was a promising career, but the work still wasn't what I wanted. I finally came to believe that I WOULD be an actor, and I became one. I embraced the power of decision. I decided to go to Hollywood because it was a gut feeling. That was my gut feeling from the time I saw Laird Cregar and Gladys Cooper acting in the movies when I was a teenager. I don't mean it to sound phony, but I believed I was meant to be in Hollywood practicing my craft. The power that backs up a decision is really exhilarating. It's a great force that urges you to go with the flow of the universe.

As a boy, I passed many happy hours by listening to music on the radio or on my records. Radio was a way to escape the horrors of World War II, and I loved music as well as movies. When I was drafted into the Army, I chose not to be an officer and was punished by being sent to Calcutta, where I found a way to play records for my Army buddies over the public address system.

One of the radio programs I loved as a kid was called *Desert Island Discs*, where a celebrity picked his eight favorite songs. I had practiced doing that as a kid, and when I later saw an Army contest advertised on the mess hall bulletin board, I entered and won. The prize allowed me to give my reasons behind my favorite records live on Radio Malaya, where I was then asked if I wanted to work there full-time. Working there for free prepared me for going into the BBC, because I would not have been there prior to my military service.

All that musical preparation — and inspiration from the movies — also had prepared me when I began interviewing celebrities on my own BBC radio program. A long line of Hollywood stars talked to me and my microphone. I was building up preparation for the precise moment when the right opportunity would present itself. It wasn't luck; mine was preparation by experience and going after an opportunity. I had talked with Doris Day, Howard Keel, all the American singers, and I was just looking for an opportunity to say to one of them, "Do you think I could make a go of it on radio in America?"

Yet I had no one to say it to, especially since I knew the real reason I wanted to go was because Hollywood was where I could finally discover if I could be an actor. On my show, I would get the guest talking and then withdraw into myself as they talked, thinking, "Should I ask him? No..." as my gut feeling told me, "Not yet."

Like a railroad track leading somewhere, my life presented me to Rosemary Clooney, who agreed to help me in Hollywood. She had been scheduled to appear on my show a year before, but when she became ill, I was stuck with José Ferrer filling in for his wife. It took waiting a year to interview her again, and who knows? The year may have given me the final preparation and determination to follow my dream, because she was certainly the right person to ask about my chances in California. She and I laughed for thirty minutes and had such a wonderful time together that at the end, I instinctively knew that SHE was the one to ask, "Do you think I might have a chance?" With that, the connection fell into place. My ongoing good was to go on without interruption for years.

Without knowing another soul, I moved to America to pursue my dream of acting. Another person who passed my way, Dirk Bogarde, gave me the phone number for Elizabeth Taylor, and how else but universal intelligence would have prompted her to ask me to wait for her assistant at the Beverly Hills Hotel. I would have not been there that day in the hotel's lobby to bump into another one of my former BBC guests, Alec Guinness, who sent me to agent Peter Shaw, who in turn helped me find my lifetime agent, Maurine Oliver.

And had Roddy McDowall not gone back to Broadway, I might not have been offered my live television acting debut, still a marvel when I think that I had never formally acted. On my *Matinee Theater* debut at NBC, I got over the initial excitement by becoming afraid that the other "real" actors would discover that I was a fraud. As my first morning of rehearsals passed, I knew that I could act, something my instincts had always told me since childhood, and I knew that I could make a career of it.

I will always believe that good happens because it is done to me as I believe. This belief ties into all the unusual interconnections about my life — connecting to Dirk Bogarde, who gave me Elizabeth Taylor's number, which led to a hotel where I ran into Alec Guinness, who sent me to my agent — even to ending up with my childhood inspiration Gladys Cooper, who then taught me how to drive in Hollywood!

If I have learned any wisdom in my eighty-plus years, it's that you should believe in yourself. Sometimes you get there through trial and error. I was no good at rugby, so I could not believe in myself as a rugby player. I came to believe in myself as a radio communicator. Without being able to back up my conviction in any way, I believed that I would feel fulfilled as an actor. That decision wasn't to get away from myself, although in a way it was. When I was another character, if I was fully into it through rehearsal and preparation, I wasn't me. I funneled or channeled some of myself into the character, but I went home and left the character behind at the end of the day.

For those precious hours on the set or on location, I was somebody else. I loved that feeling. That doesn't mean that I shuddered at the thought of being me. Even when I did my most recent movie in July 2010, I felt that wonderful feeling of getting away from it all and just having a wonderful life without a care in the world. I wasn't an actor worried about the problems of close friends or my inability to see well of late; instead, I was an old-time farmer from a few hundred years ago, walking down a dusty road.

I still think back to one of the first times that I didn't feel like "me," standing there in 1956, realizing that I was talking to one of the most beautiful women in the world, Elizabeth Taylor. It was Elizabeth Taylor, of all people, who gave me one of my earliest acting lessons when I asked her, "Can you tell me about film acting?"

One of the world's greatest performers patiently explained to me about long shots, medium shots and close-ups. "You save your best work for the close-up," she said, "because if you're really into character, then there's truth in your eyes when you're doing a close-up.

"Save it for those close-ups," she continued, "because for all those long shots, you could be thinking about what you'll have for dinner and the camera will never know from that far away."

From her, I learned acting. At her invitation, I accompanied her early the next morning as she filmed her death scene in the mud for *Raintree*

County. There she lay, under the Raintree, a regular tree sprayed gold. "I'm not doing any acting at all, really," she said, "because my dying thoughts aren't going to show up on this long shot. I save it all for the close-up!"

Throughout the rest of my acting career, I thought of that advice. I loved the idea of a film's close-ups. Now I look back at my work and see myself really concentrating. I believe the camera can read thoughts, so

LEFT: *Rediscovering how fun life can be in your eighties.* (JONATHAN DIXON)
RIGHT: *Awaiting life's next adventure.* (TODD SAWVELLE)

you absolutely have to be in character as you mentally block out a camera a few feet away from you. As you become another person, you make eye contact with another actor pretending to be someone else.

It's ironic, really, that I had to become other people through acting in order to find the real me. Whoever the real "you" may be, find him or her. I don't believe it's ever too late. Even though I knew who I felt destined to be in terms of my professional identity — an actor — I was twenty-nine years old before I finally listened to my heart as the right moment intersected the perfect opportunity.

In my later years, I've found the new me, someone whose life story seems to interest younger people who hear it. As a jobbing or working actor, I'm remarkably fortunate to have performed in films or television shows that continue to resonate with new fans, be it *Star Trek* or *101 Dalmatians*. As long as there are new mediums to release movies or reruns on television, an actor can be rediscovered over and over again as though it was the first time.

"Which one was David?" my father asked my mother when they saw my first performance.

I'm an actor.

David Frankham
Santa Fe, New Mexico
July 2012

(JONATHAN DIXON)

Credits

RADIO

Radio Malaya, *My Kind of Music*, 1947

BBC European Service, London, news reader, 1948-1951

BBC Home Service, Birmingham, producer/writer/interviewer, *What Goes On*, 1951-55

BBC Home Service, Birmingham, producer/writer/interviewer, *The Bright Lights*, 1954-55

CBS, *CBS Radio Workshop*, "The Noh Plays of Japan," April 7, 1957

NBC, *One Man's Family*, (as Skipper Barbour), 1958-1959

FEATURE FILMS

1957: *Johnny Tremain* (uncredited role as British officer); DISNEY

1959: *Return of the Fly* (Ronald Holmes, alias Alan Hinds); 20TH CENTURY-FOX

1959: *Ben-Hur* (uncredited dubbing for Roman Centurion, lepers, slaves); MGM

1960: *Song Without End* (uncredited dubbing for Prince Felix Lichnowsky); COLUMBIA

1960: *Ten Who Dared* (Frank Goodman); DISNEY

1961: *One Hundred and One Dalmatians* (voice of Sgt. Tibs, Skye Terrier); DISNEY

1961: *King of Kings* (uncredited dubbing for various characters); MGM

1961: *Master of the World* (Phillip Evans); AMERICAN INTERNATIONAL PICTURES

1962: *Tales of Terror* (Dr. James); AMERICAN INTERNATIONAL PICTURES

1962: *4 Horsemen of the Apocalypse* (uncredited dubbing for various characters); MGM

1962: *The Spiral Road* (Drager's replacement); UNIVERSAL

1965: *King Rat* (Cox in Hut 16); COLUMBIA

1966: *Grand Prix* (uncredited dubbing as radio, TV and race announcers); MGM

1972: *Hands of the Ripper* (uncredited American introduction); HAMMER FILM

1974: *Huckleberry Finn* (uncredited dubbing for various characters); UNITED ARTISTS

1979: *The Great Santini* (Captain Weber); ORION

1982: *Wrong is Right* (British Reporter); COLUMBIA

2011: *Ink: A Tale of Captivity* (Country Gentleman); INKWELL PRODUCTIONS

SHORT FILMS

A Comedy Tale of Fanny Hill, 1964; PEBBLE PRODUCTIONS
Heat Lightning, 2010; PIEBOY FILMS

FEATURE FILMS
(THE ONES THAT GOT AWAY)

Lafayette Escadrille, 1957: cast, but called back to NBC for a role
Never So Few, 1959: cast but production started sooner than planned
Homicidal, 1961: considered for a role
Viva Las Vegas, 1964: English part was turned into an Italian one
My Fair Lady, 1964: cast for dubbing but dismissed by George Cukor
Camelot, 1968: considered for one of the Knights
Big Country, Big Man: MGM film with Rod Taylor, never made
Robin Hood, 1973: considered for title voice role that went to Brian Bedford in Disney animated film
An Early Frost, 1985: part as a lawyer was written out of the TV-movie script

TELEVISION

August 31, 1956: *Matinee Theater* ("September Tide"); NBC
September 1956: *Matinee Theater* ("Smilin' Through"); NBC
October 1, 1956: *Matinee Theater* ("Pride and Prejudice"); NBC
November 15, 1956: *Matinee Theater* ("Savrola"); NBC
December, 1956: *Matinee Theater* ("The Flashing Stream"); NBC
January 25, 1957: *Matinee Theater* ("Mr. Pim Passes By"); NBC

c. 1957: *The Silent Service*; SYNDICATED

October 23, 1957: *Navy Log* ("P.T. 109"); ABC

January 19, 1958: *Studio 567*, aka *Heinz Playhouse* ("A Source of Irritation"); SYNDICATED

March 15, 1958: *The Gale Storm Show*, aka *Oh, Susanna!* ("Ghosts Aboard"); CBS

April 11, 1958: *The Thin Man* ("The Tennis Champ"); NBC

June 22, 1958: *Alfred Hitchcock Presents* ("The Impromptu Murder"); CBS

October 9, 1958: *Death Valley Days* ("Ship of No Return"); SYNDICATED

November 16, 1958: *Northwest Passage* ("The Assassin"); NBC

January 16, 1959: *77 Sunset Strip* ("The Secret of Adam Cain"); ABC

September 20, 1959: *Maverick* ("Royal Four Flush"); ABC

c. 1959: *Border Patrol*; SYNDICATED

c. 1959: Ernie Kovacs show with André Previn and Louis Jordan, unknown

1959: *The Further Adventures of Ellery Queen*; NBC

August 31, 1960: *Men Into Space* ("The Sun Never Sets"); CBS

October 16, 1960: *Walt Disney Presents* ("Rapids Ahead" segment promoting Disney's *Ten Who Dared* feature film); ABC

January 10, 1961: *Thriller* ("The Poisoner"); NBC

January 29, 1961: *The Shirley Temple Show*, aka *Shirley Temple Theatre* ("The Terrible Clockman"); NBC

February 20, 1961: *Surfside 6* ("Black Orange Blossoms"); ABC

March 4, 1961: *The Best of the Post* ("Brief Enchantment"); SYNDICATED

April 3, 1961: *Tales of Wells Fargo* ("The Remittance Man"); NBC

April 24, 1961: *Adventures in Paradise* ("A Penny a Day"); ABC

May 23, 1961: *Thriller* ("The Prisoner in the Mirror"); NBC

November 27, 1961: *Thriller* ("The Closed Cabinet"); NBC

January 2, 1962: *Alfred Hitchcock Presents* ("The Silk Petticoat"); NBC

January 21, 1962: *The Jack Benny Program* ("Jack Gets Passport"); CBS

January 30, 1962: *The Many Loves of Dobie Gillis* ("For Whom the Wedding Bell Tolls"); CBS

April 30, 1962: *Thriller* ("The Specialists"); NBC

December 6, 1962: *Alcoa Premiere* ("The Contenders"); ABC

December 9, 1962: *G.E. True* ("U.X.B."); CBS

1962: *The Exchange*; CBS

February 10, 1963: *G.E. True* ("Escape, Part 1"); CBS

February 17, 1963: *G.E. True* ("Escape, Part 2"); CBS

March 30, 1963: *The Gallant Men* ("Tommy"); ABC

December 2, 1963: *The Outer Limits* ("Nightmare"); ABC

c. 1963: *Mr. Kingston* (unsold pilot with Peter Graves and Walter Pidgeon)

January 20, 1964: *The Outer Limits* ("Don't Open Till Doomsday"); ABC

March 6, 1964: *Alfred Hitchcock Hour* ("Murder Case"); CBS

November 13, 1964: *Gomer Pyle* ("Gomer and the Dragon Lady"); CBS

November 27, 1964: *Gomer Pyle* ("A Date for the Colonel's Daughter"); CBS

March 5, 1965: *12 O'Clock High* ("The Trap"); ABC

September 15, 1965: *The Beverly Hillbillies* ("Admiral Jed Clampett"); CBS

December 27, 1965: *Doctor Kildare* ("Perfect Is Too Hard to Be"); NBC

December 28, 1965: *Doctor Kildare* ("Duet for One Hand"); NBC

January 10, 1966: *12 O'Clock High* ("The Slaughter Pen"); ABC

April 8, 1966: *Gomer Pyle* ("A Desk Job for Sergeant Carter"); CBS

October 12, 1966: *The Beverly Hillbillies* ("The Badgers Return"); CBS

November 18, 1966: *12 O'Clock High* ("To Seek and Destroy"); ABC

February 19, 1967: *The F.B.I.* ("The Hostage"); ABC

April 14, 1968: *Walt Disney's Wonderful World of Color* ("Ten Who Dared" abridged 60-minute version of the theatrical film); NBC

October 18, 1968: *Star Trek* ("Is There in Truth No Beauty"); NBC

December 15, 1968: *The F.B.I.* ("The Flaw"); ABC

January 25, 1970: *The F.B.I.* ("Deadly Reunion"); ABC

November 8, 1970: *The Young Rebels* ("The Hostages"); ABC

December 6, 1970: *The F.B.I.* ("The Target"); ABC

February 16, 1972: *Medical Center* ("Deadlock"); CBS

November 5, 1972: *The F.B.I.* ("A Game of Chess"); ABC

December 3, 1972: *McCloud* ("The Barefoot Stewardess Caper"); NBC

March 13, 1974: *Cannon* ("Triangle of Terror"); CBS

March 25, 1974: *The Magician* ("The Illusion of the Cat's Eye"); CBS

April 15, 1974: *Winter Kill*, ABC-TV movie

April 8, 1975: Bob Hope Special, (segment cut in U.S., aired in Japan); NBC

April 19, 1975: *The Six Million Dollar Man* ("Outrage in Balinderry"); ABC

September 15, 1977: *The Waltons*, voiceover as Neville Chamberlain on radio ("The Hawk"); CBS

September 5, 1978: *Little Mo*, NBC-TV movie
May 3, 1982: *The Letter*, ABC-TV movie
May 12, 1982: *Eleanor, First Lady of the World*, CBS-TV movie
December 19, 1985: *Shadow Chasers* ("The Many Lives of Jonathan");
    ABC
1987-1988: *The Bold and the Beautiful*, CBS

COMMERCIALS

1964-1976: Appeared in hundreds of commercials for the Jack
    Wormser Agency

PLAYS

Separate Tables, Steve Allen Theatre (Los Angeles), 1958
The Circle, Pasadena Playhouse, 1959
Lewis Carroll's La Guida Di Bragia, Theaterwork (Santa Fe, NM), 2009

Index

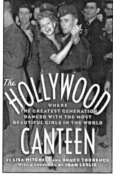

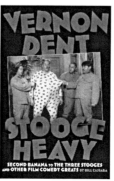
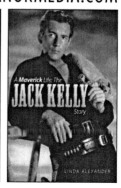

CPSIA information can be obtained at www.ICGtesting.com
Printed in the USA
BVOW011343100213

312788BV00008B/89/P

9 781593 93